THE BOTTOM LINE
BARGAIN
BOOK

How to Get the Best Deals on Anything and Everything

**Bottom Line
Books**

Written and designed by
Lightbulb Press, New York, NY

Editorial Director: Virginia Morris
Editor: Renée Ryerson
Editorial Assistant: Ann Fisher

Writers: Jeff Bushell, Sophie Forrester
Jennifer Jett, A. J. Meier
Lenore Person, Jane van Dyke
Proofreader and Indexer: Cynthia Gibson

Design Director: Dave Wilder
Design: Leslie Daley
Production Artist: Thomas F. Trojan

Copyright © 2000 by Boardroom® Inc.

10 9 8 7 6 5 4 3 2

Bottom Line® Books publishes the advice of expert authorities in
many fields. The use of a book is not a substitute for legal,
accounting or other professional services. Consult a competent
professional for answers to your specific questions.

Library of Congress Cataloging in Publication Data
Main entry under title:

The Bottom Line Bargain Book

    1. Life skills—United States.   I. Bottom line personal
ISBN 0-88723-199-3

Bottom Line® Books is a registered trademark of
Boardroom® Inc.
55 Railroad Avenue, Greenwich, CT 06830

Printed in the United States of America

W atch the pennies and the dollars will take care of themselves.
—Anna Garber

Contents

**Thinking like
A Bargain Hunter**

**Free and
Almost Free Stuff**

Great Deals on Recreation

**"Remember: A penny
saved is a penny earned."**

Chapter 4

**Savvy Shopping
Secrets**

Chapter 5

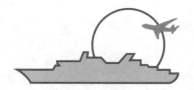

**Cutting Back
Travel Costs**

**Get the Best Deals in
Real Estate**

Chapter 6

Chapter 7

Household Bargains

Chapter 8

Staying Healthy For Less

Cheap Eats

Chapter 9

Automotive Discounts

Chapter 10

Chapter 11

Cutting Your Personal Finance Costs

Chapter 12

Cutting Education Costs

Thinking like a Bargain Hunter

Get to know the bargain-lover's basics, including how to be a smart consumer, shop for high-quality goods at low prices, get the service you want, avoid cunning scams and access the most important bargain aid of all: information.

Consumer Know-How

Becoming an educated consumer is the surest way to get the best value for your dollar. You're far more likely to get a good deal if you do a little research before spending your money. Three ways to ensure that you're shopping smart and getting the most for your money are comparing prices, asking advice, and knowing that if a deal sounds too good to be true, it probably is.

Before you rush to make your next purchase, consider some tips on how to extend the life of your budget.

Make a Checklist

A great way to make the most of the money you have is to shop with a checklist. When you make a checklist of what you need, it's easier to suppress the desire to impulse shop and spend too much money. Decide what you need and how much you want to spend before you enter a store—and then try to get all the items on your list for the best price.

BARGAIN FINDER

Shop Sales

Good sales can save you a considerable amount of money. Most sales occur at the end of a season. For example, beach chairs and towels are the least expensive after Labor Day, and furs cost less in the spring and early summer.

Since there's a better chance of impulse shopping when prices are really low, know what you're looking for and what you actually need.

Always ask questions about return policies and warranties on sale merchandise. Then consider price and value to make sure that the purchase is a smart one.

Auctions are great places to hunt for deals on antiques, art, furniture and rare books.

Shop Around

Shop around for the best deal you can find before you rush to make a purchase. Consider comparing the cost of the same item at more than two stores. One store may sell the refrigerator that you want for $100 less than another, and a third store may even sell it for $150 less.

Also, many times stores will sell you an item at a competitor's lower price if you bring in a competitor's advertisement showing the lower cost. Leveraging competing stores against each other when you're shopping for value can get you a great price. But if you don't shop around, you'll have nothing to tip the scales with.

Buy Quality

Buy quality the first time and save yourself the expense of repeat purchases. Many people think that a cheaper price is better than the higher cost of a quality purchase. But if you have to replace an item (such as a dishwasher or television) every year or two, you can wind up spending twice what you would have for a quality item that would last for much longer.

The same applies for clothing and other products. If you buy a shirt that falls apart after the second wash, or juice glasses that melt or crack in the dishwasher, you have to repeat your purchase. It's smarter to spend a little more for quality than to spend less three or four times over.

Auctions and Estate Sales

Auctions and estate sales are great places to find antiques and heirlooms. Many times these items are more expensive than most people can afford, but sometimes you can find fabulous items (such as jewelry, paintings and furs) for much less than they'd cost in a store.

And, if you're a collector, going to an auction or estate sale is a great way to add priceless pieces to your collection. Call local auction houses or estate sales agents to find out about any sales occurring near you. Or check your local newspaper for upcoming events.

Try the Other Side of Retail

You can find great bargains when you shop outside the traditional retail store. If you want to save money but hate malls and department stores (especially during sale time), try outlet, off-price, garage- and yard-sale shopping.

Outlets

There are many different types of outlet stores. From clothing and housewares outlets (such as J. Crew and Pottery Barn) to food and hardware superstores (such as Costco and Home Depot) you can get what you need for less.

Off-price Stores

Off-price stores are a great alternative to retail clothes shopping. They often offer current designer styles at a quarter of the cost, and help extend your budget (so that you can make that one impulsive purchase you really want). The return policies at off-price stores are usually similar to those at regular retail stores, but always ask to be sure.

Garage and Yard Sales

Garage and yard sales are great ways to furnish a college student's apartment, buy your grandchild a classic Barbie, or find that Sinatra album you lost last time you moved.

Not only will you spend a fraction of the money you would in a retail store, but garage sales and yard sales can be a free, fun activity to enjoy with your whole family. Most sales have items that are in great condition. So, the next time you're driving by a garage sale, stop and take a look. You never know what treasures and bargains you may find.

Secondhand Stores

Secondhand stores often sell clothing, toys, furniture, bicycles and household items at very low prices. Many secondhand stores, such as thrift stores and antique stores, sell items that are in very good condition. Some stores will even repair any damaged items and still sell them at very reasonable prices.

If you like vintage furniture and clothing, you should check out the secondhand and antique stores in your neighborhood before you pay a high price for a reproduction. You might get the real thing for less.

DID YOU KNOW

Be a Frugal Consumer

If you want to read about how to save the most money when you shop, there are a few books that reveal bargain hunters' tricks of the trade. You can find help on everything from living frugally to shopping smart.

Here are a few books you may want to check out:

- *The Best of the Cheapskate Monthly: Simple Tips for Living Lean in the '90s* by Mary Hunt (St. Martins Press, $4.50). This book gives advice on how to live frugally within a budget that's right for your family.

- *Buying Retail Is Stupid! USA: The National Discount Guide to Buying Everything at up to 80% off Retail* by Trisha King and Deborah Newmark (NTC/Contemporary Publishing, $16.95). Learn how to save money in the stores and while shopping from your home.

- *The Consumer Bible: 1001 Ways to Shop Smart* by Mark J. Green (Workman Publishing, $15.95). This book teaches you how to be a savvy shopper. It's a great guide for saving money, time and aggravation.

- *The Frugal Almanac* by Melodie Moore (NAL/Dutton Books, $5.99). Find your money-saving strategies for every area of your life. It's like having your own financial advisor.

- *The Tightwad Gazette III: Promoting Thrift as a Viable Alternative Lifestyle* by Amy Dacyczyn (Villard Books, $12.99). This collection of past newsletters guides you on how to compare your food bills, save on college and find the best bargains in stores.

Shopping by Phone

Consider taking the following precautions to protect yourself from telephone sales fraud:

❏ Don't ever give your credit card number or checking account number for any reason other than making a purchase.

❏ Know the company you're dealing with. If you have questions or doubts about a company, check with your state or local consumer protection office, or the Better Business Bureau where the company is located before you make a purchase.

❏ Keep a record of your transactions, including the name, address, and telephone number of the company, and the purchase cost and date.

❏ Always ask if there are additional fees for shipping, handling, sales tax or insurance.

❏ Ask about refund and exchange policies.

❏ Know the total cost of the merchandise before you buy.

❏ Don't be pressured to act on impulse. Take time to understand an offer and talk it over with someone you trust. Reliable offers don't expire at "midnight tonight."

Questions and Complaints

Two of the best ways to safeguard your wallet are asking questions before you make final decisions about a purchase or investment, and making complaints if you have any problems with a purchase or service you received.

Inquire about Future Sales

Before you make a significant purchase at full price, ask if the item is going on sale anytime soon. If so, find out when, and consider waiting until then to make your purchase. Ask if the salesperson thinks the item will still be available by sale time. If you are unsure about the salesperson's response, ask someone else.

When you enter a store, it's always a good idea to question managers or salespeople about sale items. Many stores have permanent areas devoted to sale merchandise. If you don't ask where these areas are, you may lose out.

Keep in mind that all types of stores have seasonal sales. If a store can't tell you when the next sale is, think about when the season ends and consider waiting to do your shopping then. Fall and winter sales are in December and January, spring sales are usually at the beginning of the summer, and summer sales usually start in July. Also, don't forget the many holiday sales scattered throughout the year (such as Presidents' Day and Father's Day sales).

Take Advantage of Customer Service

If you have any problems with or questions about a purchase or services you received, call customer service. That's what it's for.

You can ease your dissatisfaction by asking customer service to help you receive a refund, locate a product you can't find, or solve a service problem with a store. If you've been wronged by a store or salesperson, customer service should help you get what you paid for.

Many chain stores have toll-free customer service numbers. You can find a store's number by calling toll-free information (800-555-1212) or by calling a local store and requesting the number.

If you can't find a customer service number, or the store is not helpful, consider asking the company's corporate office to help you or guide you to assistance.

Request a Refund If you aren't satisfied with a product or service and feel you deserve a refund, it's important to make a formal complaint. Customer satisfaction is a top priority to most reputable companies.

Many times, contacting a store's customer service department or corporate office will get you more than a refund. Some places may give you a refund plus a discount coupon on future purchases or services, a free gift, or a brand new replacement product or free repeat service.

If you want to make sure that you get your money's worth, it's important to voice your dissatisfaction when it occurs, and keep a record of your complaints.

- What's the store's return policy: full refund, credit, how many days, do you need the receipt and original packaging?
- What happens if you are not satisfied with the service you receive? Do you get a repeat service free of charge or do you get nothing?
- Is there a warranty or insurance included? Does it have an extra fee attached?
- Does the store have a repair policy? Are there any contracts to sign? (Make sure you read the small print.)
- Is there another brand that would cost you less?
- Did you compare prices at a few different stores?
- Did the salesperson seem knowledgeable about your questions?
- Are you comfortable with the price and quality of the item?
- Is this purchase a necessary buy or an impulse buy?
- Can you wait to buy this item until it goes on sale?
- Is this service something you can do for yourself or is it really essential to hire some help?

Ask Questions

Before you sign on the dotted line or give away your dollars, know the answers to the above questions.

DID YOU KNOW

Say Thanks for a Job Well Done

Consider the perks of voicing your satisfaction with a product or service. Many times, companies reward compliments with discount coupons, samples of a new product or service, or free gifts. So, if you're really satisfied with something you bought, consider telling the customer service department or corporate office, either by letter or telephone. You never know what you might get in return.

IT PAYS TO ASK

Ask for Free Samples

Many different types of companies provide free samples to consumers. You can receive free samples of food and personal beauty products as well as information and advice from financial, real estate, health and travel companies.

Many times there will be free samples of products in a store or supermarket, or advertised in a newspaper, magazine or on television. Sometimes seeking out free samples of a new product line, or free estimates for a particular service, is as easy as calling a company's toll-free customer service number.

Take advantage of the possibility of getting something for nothing, and ask if you can sample the product or service before you invest your time and money. The worst answer you'll receive is no.

Avoid Costly Frauds and Save Yourself Money

Being aware of common consumer scams and knowing how to avoid them can save you a fortune. If an offer sounds too good to be true, your educated-consumer warning bells should start to ring.

Telemarketing swindles are the most prevalent scams, and cost consumers millions of dollars every year. When you hear words like these, chances are the person on the other end of the line is trying to scam you:

- You must act now or the offer won't be good.
- You've won a free gift or prize—but you must pay a small fee.
- You must send money, give your credit card or bank account number, or have a check picked up by a courier immediately.
- You don't need to check out our company with anyone like the Better Business Bureau—we're legitimate.
- You don't need any written information or referrals about our company.
- You can't afford to miss out on this offer.

How to Complain Effectively

If you're having trouble returning a defective product, feel that you've been the victim of a scam or believe that the services you received from a company were less than satisfactory, contact your local Better Business Bureau, your state attorney general's office or your local consumer protection agency. You can obtain a free listing of local, state and federal agencies and Better Business Bureaus from the U.S. Office of Consumer Affairs. Write to Consumer's Resource Handbook, Consumer Information Center, Pueblo, CO 81009.

Put It on Paper

Often, the best way to complain is to write a letter. Here are some tips on the best ways to write a complaint letter that will get results:

- Find out whom you should be writing to. Start with the store manager, and consider sending a duplicate to the owner. If you're dealing with a larger company, send letters to the director of consumer affairs or the chief executive officer.
- Describe your problem calmly and carefully. Be polite but firm, and don't include obscene language or wild accusations.
- Get the correct names of everyone involved. Give times, dates and locations of any conversations, and include serial or model numbers of products.
- Include copies of any receipts, invoices and warranties involved, including those for any repairs you had to pay for on your own. Keep the originals for your files.
- Mention anything you tried to do to remedy the situation yourself.
- Consider sending the letter return receipt requested so that you have proof that it was received and the name of the person who signed for it.
- Keep copies of any letters you send. Also get the name of anyone you speak with on the phone or in person, and jot down the dates, times and details of your conversations.
- If you fail to get a satisfactory response, contact your local Better Business Bureau, state attorney general's office, or department of consumer protection. Send one of these agencies a brief explanation of the problem and your attempts to resolve it, plus copies of any letters you sent to the company. Send a duplicate of this explanation to the offending company and you may receive results before the public agency even gets a chance to respond. Most companies would rather settle without government intervention.

- Comment on how you would like the problem to be corrected. If you were a victim of fraud, you may be interested in regaining the money you lost. If you bought a defective product and can't get the company to repair or replace it, you may want your money back, or may be satisfied with a store credit.

Remember, if you complain when you've been a victim of fraud or negligence, you may help prevent someone else from being victimized.

Stop Telephone and Mail Solicitations

If you've ever ordered from a catalog, donated to a charity, used a credit card or subscribed to a magazine, your name has been put on a variety of mailing and phone lists. These lists are sold to direct marketers who hope to sell you their products. Such offers are rarely good bargains. If you're tired of junk mail and telephone solicitations, you can do something about it. Here's how.

No More Calls During Dinner To be placed on a do-not-call list for telephone solicitors, send your name, home address and home telephone number (including area code) to the Telephone Preference Service, Direct Marketing Association, P.O. Box 9014, Farmingdale, NY 11735-9014. Telephone solicitations should decrease about two months after your name has been entered into the file. The Direct Marketing Association does not guarantee that calls will stop completely.

No More Junk Mail If you want to decrease the amount of commercial and non-profit mail you receive, send your name and address, and a request to be placed on the removal file, to the Mail Preference Service, Direct Marketing Association, P.O. Box 9008, Farmingdale, NY 11735-9008. You should see a decrease in the amount of unsolicited mail you receive within three months after your name is entered into the file.

The Direct Marketing Association takes only postal requests, so you can't call in your request. If you move, remember to send in a new request.

Use an Agency to Find the Best Value

Many agencies, such as travel agencies, non-profit consumer agencies and resource groups, can help you to find the best value for the product, service, or investment you're considering. Here are a few particularly useful agencies:

- Call the **People's Medical Society** (610-770-1670) for guidance in getting the best medical care for the best value.

- Call the **National Committee for Quality Assurance** (202-955-3500) for information on managed care organizations, so that the health insurance you purchase is an educated investment.

- Contact the **Certified Financial Planner Board of Standards** (888-237-6275) for free brochures, information materials and services that will help you choose a reputable certified financial planner and make wise investment purchases.

BUYER BEWARE

Florist Scam

If you love to send flowers, you should be aware that there are unscrupulous telemarketing firms that pose as local florists, charge you high fees for your order, and take business away from the legitimate florists in your town.

How It Works

Here's how the scam works: The telemarketer takes out a fake listing in the white pages of your telephone book using a local town name to make consumers believe it's a neighborhood store. When you call the number, you're unknowingly forwarded to an out-of-town telemarketing operation. Your order and credit card information are taken, and the information is forwarded to an area florist. The telemarketer pockets a processing fee and usually a percentage of the sale. But the real scam occurs when you receive your credit card bill with higher than expected charges from an out-of-town company. You may also learn that the flowers weren't delivered as ordered or were never delivered at all.

Better Safe than Sorry

To safeguard yourself from florist scams, ask neighbors, family, friends and co-workers for florist recommendations. Deal only with shops that list a street address with their phone number. If you get a number from directory assistance, ask for the street address too. If there's not one listed, consider doing business with a different florist. Also, if you're unsure about a florist, check with the local **Better Business Bureau** and consumer protection officials in your area, or of the area in which the shop is located. Ask if there are any consumer complaints on file and verify the street address.

And finally, ask for an itemized bill from the florist. You may be charged an unusually high delivery fee or too much tax for an order. Know exactly what you're paying for.

Scams Galore

In order to safeguard your money, and consequently the stability of your financial future, here are some of the most common scams to watch out for.

Scholarship Scams

College is one of the biggest expenses a family can have. Unfortunately, many students and parents fall victim to scholarship scams when they're trying to find money to help pay for school.

It is not really necessary to use a scholarship service to find ways to cut your college costs. Most scholarships can be researched in the library and on the Internet for free. But many people use a scholarship service to cut down on the work they'll need to do on their own. The only problem with using a scholarship service is figuring out which ones are legitimate and which ones you need to avoid.

One of the first, key signs that a scholarship offer could be a scam is if the service says it can guarantee you'll get a scholarship or grant. Scholarships can never be guaranteed. And paying an advance fee will not secure you a financial award. Most likely, if you do pay a fee for a scholarship, even under a money-back guarantee, you won't receive either the scholarship or your refund.

Here are some other precautions to take:

- Don't believe a company that tells you that you can't get the same information anywhere else. Before you consider paying for lists of sources, do some research on your own.
- Beware of companies that tell you that you need to give them your credit card or bank account number so they can hold a scholarship or grant for you. A legitimate scholarship will never require this.
- Avoid companies that tell you they'll do all the work for you, because this is impossible. You will always have to fill out any legitimate scholarship paperwork yourself, such as personal essays or personal history information.
- Watch out for companies that tell you the scholarship will cost you money. Scholarships and grants are created to save you money and should never have a fee attached.
- Never believe an organization that calls you to tell you that you've been selected as a finalist in a contest you never entered. Legitimate scholarship and grant organizations do not solicit you. You must go to them.
- If you want more information on scholarship fraud, contact the Federal Trade Commission (202-326-2222, www.ftc.gov).

Travel Scams

Bargain travel packages may be more than you bargained for. The most common travel fraud is a mail or telephone offer: You're presented with an unbelievably good travel opportunity that changes in price as soon as you give your credit card number.

Usually, telephone scam artists offer you a deal that they couldn't possibly deliver. They will ask for your immediate decision, and tell you if you don't act now you'll lose out. Also, they'll skirt any questions or concerns you present to them. And you won't know you've been scammed until you receive the confirmation of your deal. The confirmation rarely bears any resemblance to the offer you thought you accepted. Once you see the deal in writing, you'll notice lots of hidden fees, terms and costs that were not disclosed over the phone.

The best way to avoid these scams is to always check out a company before you accept a deal. Find out if any complaints have been made with the National Fraud Information Center or the Federal Trade Commission. But be aware that fraudulent businesses frequently change their names. If you are in doubt about the legitimacy of a company, turn down the offer and hang up the phone.

Counterfeit Goods

If you want high-quality products that won't fall apart a week after you buy them, watch out for counterfeit goods.

Counterfeit goods almost always have a price that's too good to be true. If you're looking for the real thing, such as a Rolex watch or Gucci handbag, know whether what you're buying is worth the money you're spending.

Counterfeit goods are sold by street vendors or small, questionable-looking stores. Quality products are sold by established merchants at fixed locations. A product without a manufacturer's label, wrapped in flimsy packaging, and lacking a warranty is most often a fake.

Unfortunately, once you buy a counterfeit product there's not much you can do. A manufacturer of the genuine article won't be able to help you. The only way to get your money back is to find and confront the original seller, which is usually next to impossible.

BUYER BEWARE

Magazine Subscription Scams

Magazine subscriptions are frequently sold by phone. Unfortunately, there are fraudulent telemarketers who will sell you a subscription that's much more expensive than the regular rate.

- Never accept a subscription to a magazine without fully understanding the total cost. If a seller won't divulge this information, hang up the phone. Also, be careful of sales pitches that tell you the subscription amount only in dollars per week. Some deals sound great until you add up the yearly cost. You can wind up paying more than twice the regular subscription rate.

- Make sure that you have cancellation rights before you accept a deal. Some states mandate that you are legally required to pay for a subscription once you verbally accept the deal.

- To safeguard yourself from scams, ask for a written copy of the contract before you agree to make a deal. Read the contract very carefully and figure out the cost of the entire package.

- And finally, be very careful who you give your credit card or bank account number to, because it may be used to debit your account without your permission.

Shoddy construction, flimsy packaging and misspellings are red flags of counterfeit merchandise.

Amy Dacyczyn on How to Become a Conscientious Consumer

Amy Dacyczyn, an expert on frugal living, is the author of *The Tightwad Gazette* book series.

Why is being a smart shopper important?

Getting more for your money ultimately gives you more freedom and choices. Living frugally prevents you from being weighed down by debt, and consequently lets you choose what you spend your money on.

What are some basic skills that a conscientious shopper can use to save money?

Researching your purchases is very important. I break shopping down into two basic groups: short-term purchases and long-term purchases.

Short-term purchases (food, clothing) I try to make as cheaply as I can.

Long-term purchases (a car, a home, furniture) I spend more time on.

I look around for the best deal, but it won't necessarily be the cheapest option. It will be the choice that most suits me.

I learned early on that no one store has the cheapest price on everything. Shopping at different stores allows you to get the cheapest price on more things. For example, if you shop at a different store each week and buy a month's supply of its least-expensive items, you will save both time and money.

Patience is an important skill. If you look for the best price before you make a purchase, you will definitely save yourself money. Try to anticipate your needs as far ahead as you can so that you are not rushed into spending more money than you would like.

Another strategy is to buy new merchandise only when you absolutely have to. There are many opportunities to find what you need, whether it's clothing or cars, second-hand.

Also, consider starting at the bottom in price and working your way up. If you're looking for clothing, start at a yard-sale. If you don't find what you need there, move up to a thrift shop, and then to discount stores such as TJ Maxx or Marshalls. Along the way you'll find what you need, and you won't be paying more than you have to.

Does frugal shopping have to be all-encompassing?

How frugal anyone wants to be has to do with a lot of very individual factors. It's important to cut corners only where you feel the most comfortable. Ideally, you shouldn't have to buy cheaply if it makes you feel uncomfortable.

What are five steps you can take to shop smarter?

1. Do your homework. Research and compare prices.
2. Determine the lowest quality level that will satisfy you.
3. Realistically determine what your needs are. Compare the cost of what you buy with the use factor: Ask yourself if you'll use the item enough to justify the purchase.
4. Give yourself the largest window of time in which to make a purchase.
5. Negotiate for the best price. You can negotiate at any yard sale, many retail stores and especially when buying a car.

Are there any pitfalls in shopping for price as your first objective?

You have to determine if the quality you're buying satisfies your needs. It's not always price first. With some goods you really get what you pay for. For example, you should never cut corners on dental care, medical care or safety issues such as buying a child's bicycle helmet.

Prize Scams

The most important thing to know about prize scams is that if you have to give any money to receive your prize, it's not a prize. If you receive a letter or phone call telling you that you've won a prize, be skeptical. Here are some ways to make sure that a prize is really a prize:

- Don't be lured by official or urgent-looking letters.
- Always read the letter carefully, especially the small print. Look for fees or special requirements involved in receiving the prize.
- Find out the odds of winning the prize before you enter a contest. Winning a prize usually has very slim odds.
- Be cautious of 800-numbers that direct you to call a 900-number. Charges for 900 telephone calls are usually very expensive.
- Never give your credit card or bank account number to a company you're unfamiliar with.
- Check out the agency awarding the prize with the Better Business Bureau or your local consumer protection office.
- Read all contracts or agreements very closely before you sign anything, because once you sign your name you're obligated.

Investment Scams

Investment frauds have very particular sales pitches. Be careful when you hear the following lines:

- You'll receive a better return on this investment than any other you're involved in.
- You'll make a really big profit in no time at all.
- No risk is involved.
- You have to act now.

Always invest in opportunities that you know something about. It's unlikely that you'll make money in a business deal you can't understand. Be skeptical about a seller's opinion of an investment's value. Attempt to thoroughly understand and verify a business deal before you invest any money. And be wary of unsolicited investment phone calls (especially those from out-of-state salespeople or companies you've never heard of). Once you commit your money, it will be hard to get it back.

Always do a full check on a company before you invest any money. Ask a financial advisor or close friend to help you check the seller's materials.

Beware of phony referrals and references. Many fraudulent companies hire people to lie and give testimonials of sudden wealth.

Before you invest, ask tough questions and get information from a variety of sources. And finally, if you have any doubts about the company or investment, say no.

HERE'S HOW

Don't Become a Victim of Phone Scams

The most common reason people become victims of phone scams is that it is very difficult to tell if a sales call is legitimate. Con artists have fine-tuned their skills to sound believable when they're telling lies.

Older people tend to get scammed more than others because the con artists prey on people they think may be feeling lonely. They frequently call every day until the recipients of the calls feel as if the con artist is a friend, not a stranger trying to sell them something.

Con artists have an answer for everything, and will not easily be deterred. They may promise you free gifts, prizes or vacations as incentives for buying their scam. Usually what they are offering sounds too good to be true.

Here are the best ways to avoid being scammed:

- Don't purchase something over the phone from an unfamiliar company.
- If you are interested in a telephone sales pitch, ask for written information or brochures. And then ask a trusted friend to review them with you.
- Always check out unfamiliar companies with the **Better Business Bureau**, your local consumer protection agency, **State Attorney General** or the **National Fraud Information Center.**
- Take your time when making a decision. Legitimate companies won't rush you into a decision.
- Never respond to an offer you don't thoroughly understand.

Check Out a Charity before You Give

If you are unsure of the legitimacy of a charity, call one of the following organizations for help:

- **Philanthropic Advisory Service**, Council of Better Business Bureaus (703-276-0100)
- **National Charities Information Bureau** (212-929-6300)
- **The American Institute of Philanthropy** (301-913-5200)

Stop Fraud From Spreading

If you want information about spotting or stopping fraud, or you want to report a scam, contact the **National Fraud Information Center** (800-876-7060, www.fraud.org).

The National Fraud Information Center tries to fight telemarketing fraud by improving prevention and enforcement. It will give you advice about telephone solicitations and report your experiences with possible fraud to the law enforcement agencies. Counselors will help you identify the danger signs of possible fraud and direct you to the right resources for more information, if necessary. The National Fraud Information Center counseling and consumer reporting services are free of charge.

Charitable Scams

If you donate money to charities, it's important to be sure that your money is actually going to benefit the people and organizations you want to help. Unfortunately, there are fraudulent solicitors for charitable contributions that you need to be aware of. The best way to ensure that you are supporting an actual charity is to follow these guidelines recommended by the Federal Trade Commission:

- Before you give to a charity, ask for written information, including the charity's name, address and telephone number. Legitimate charities will be able to send you information on their goals and how they use donations, and proof that your donation is tax-deductible.
- Call the charity to make sure that the solicitation was authorized, and that the solicitor you spoke with wasn't a fraud.
- Watch out for charities that have similar-sounding names to ones that are highly respected and legitimate. This may be a sign that the solicitation is a fraud.
- Look out for professional fund-raisers. Some charities find it more efficient to pay professional fund-raisers (rather than use staff or volunteers) to handle large-scale mailings, telephone drives and other solicitations. Professional fund-raisers, however, keep a portion of the money they collect. If you're solicited for a donation, ask if the caller is a paid fund-raiser and what percentage of your donation the fund-raiser will keep. If you're not comfortable with the amount, you may want to consider other options for donating (such as contacting the charity directly).

- Make sure the money you're donating goes toward activities which makes it legally tax-deductible. Donations to a wing that runs politically-motivated advertisements might not be deductible, while donations to other wings of the same charity are.
- Be wary of organizations that use meaningless terms, such as "tax-exempt charity."
- Don't rely on an invoice that tells you to "Keep this receipt for your records." It doesn't mean your donation is tax-deductible.
- Be on alert for calls and invoices thanking you for a pledge that you don't remember making. Keep records of your donations so that you're not falsely convinced that you've donated to a charity when you haven't.
- Specify how you want the money you donate to be used.

Free Resources for Consumer Education

Federal and state organizations (such as the Department of Education, the USDA Forest Service, state park associations, the Federal Trade Commission, and the Food and Drug Administration) supply consumers with advice, information materials and guidance on how to lead healthy, cost-effective lives.

If you need information on the health and safety of food and drugs, how to finance your child's college education, or how to find a great, low-cost camping area in your state, there are government agencies and independent agencies that will help you for free.

Here are some government and non-government agencies you may want to contact:

Federal Trade Commission (FTC) (877-FTCHELP, www.ftc.gov). Provides free consumer education publications (such as an energy guide on how to cool and heat your home and a brochure on how to make sure that a scanned price is correct). Or, for free consumer brochures on scams (how scams work, and tips for recognizing and avoiding them), call the FTC's Public Reference Branch (202-326-2222).

US Department of Education (800-872-5327, www.ed.gov). Offers free guidance and information on college financial aid. Visit their website to research scholarship and loan programs or fill out federal financial aid applications.

USDA Forest Service (202-205-1706, www.fs.fed.us/recreation). Supplies free information on forest activities and opportunities nationwide.

Food and Drug Administration (800-INFO FDA or 888 463-6332, www.fda.gov). Provides free information on food and drug benefits and hazards.

National Fraud Information Center (800-876-7060, www.fraud.org). Operates a consumer hotline to provide service and assistance with filing complaints against fraudulent businesses.

Council of Better Business Bureaus (703-276-0100, www.bbb.org). Gives consumers free information on how to spend their money wisely and safeguard against scams, and provides reliability reports on businesses.

FOR YOUR INFORMATION

Consumer Information Center

You can contact the **Consumer Information Center** (888-878-3256) to request free or extremely low-cost booklets (approximately 50¢–$4.50) on a broad range of topics:

- Cars (buying used cars and airbag safety).
- Children (how to make adoption an affordable option).
- Employment (health benefits under **COBRA**).
- Federal programs (**Social Security** number privacy and a guide to **Medicare** benefits).
- Financial planning (what you should know about financial planning).
- Food and nutrition (guide for eating healthy).
- Home maintenance (cooling your home naturally).

The publications are sponsored by numerous government agencies, such as the **Center for Disease Control**, the **Department of Transportation**, the **Federal Trade Commission**, the **Internal Revenue Service** and the **National Cancer Institute**. Call the Consumer Information Center for a free catalog of the most up-to-date booklets.

State Consumer Affairs Offices

When you've tried everything you can think of to settle a dispute with a company, and your complaints and protests of unfair treatment are still being ignored, it's time to take advantage of the consumer affairs department in your state.

If you're a victim of fraud or have been mistreated by a business, you can call your state's consumer protection division to help you correct the matter for free. The consumer protection division will file a complaint against the business and attempt to remedy the situation through mediation (obtaining resolutions that satisfy the consumer's interests). If enough complaints are filed against the business, the matter goes to the attorney general and further action is taken.

Here's a listing of the consumer affairs departments, by state:

Alaska
Better Business Bureau
Anchorage, 907-562-0704

Arizona
Office of the Attorney General
Consumer Protection Division
Phoenix, 602-542-5763
(800-352-8431 in Arizona)

Arkansas
Office of the Attorney General
Consumer Protection Division
Little Rock, 501-682-2341
(800-482-8982 in Arkansas)

California
California Department of Consumer Affairs
Sacramento, 916-445-1254
(800-344-9940 in California)

Colorado
Office of the Attorney General
Consumer Protection Unit
Denver, 303-866-5189

Connecticut
Department of Consumer Protection
Hartford, 860-713-6050
(800-842-2649 in Connecticut)

District of Columbia
Department of Consumer and Regulatory Affairs
Washington, 202-442-4400

Florida
Department of Agriculture and Consumer Services
Division of Consumer Services
Tallahassee, 850-488-2221
(800-435-7352 in Florida)

Georgia
Governor's Office of Consumer Affairs
Atlanta, 404-651-8600 or
404-656-3790 (800-869-1123 in Georgia)

Hawaii
Department of Commerce and Consumer Affairs
Office of Consumer Protection
Honolulu, 808-586-2636

Idaho
Office of the Attorney General
Consumer Protection Unit
Boise, 208-334-2424
(800-432-3545 in Idaho)

Illinois
Office of the Attorney General
Consumer Protection Division
Chicago, 312-814-3000

Indiana
Office of the Attorney General
Consumer Protection Division
Indianapolis, 317-232-6330
(800-382-5516 in Indiana)

Iowa
Office of the Attorney General
Consumer Protection Division
Des Moines, 515-281-5926

Kansas
Office of the Attorney General
Consumer Protection Division
Topeka, 785-296-3751
(800-432-2310 in Kansas)

Kentucky
Office of the Attorney General
Consumer Protection Division
Frankfort, 502-696-5389
(888-432-9257 in Kentucky)

Louisiana
Office of the Attorney General
Consumer Protection Section
Baton Rouge, 225-342-9638

Maine
Office of the Attorney General
Consumer and Antitrust Division
Augusta, 207-626-8849

Maryland
Office of the Attorney General
Consumer Protection Division
Baltimore, 410-528-8662

Massachusetts
Department of the Attorney General
Consumer Protection Division
Boston, 617-727-8400

Michigan
Office of the Attorney General
Consumer Protection Division
Lansing, 517-373-1140

Minnesota
Office of the Attorney General
Consumer Services Division
St. Paul, 651-296-3353

Missouri
Office of the Attorney General
Division of Consumer Protection
Jefferson City, 573-751-3321
(800-392-8222 in Missouri)

Montana
Consumer Affairs Unit
Department of Commerce
Helena, 406-444-3553

Nebraska
Consumer Protection Division
Department of Justice
Lincoln, 402-471-2682

Nevada
Commissioner of Consumer Affairs
Department of Commerce
Las Vegas, 800-326-5202
(800-992-0900 in Nevada)

New Hampshire
Office of the Attorney General
Consumer Protection and
Antitrust Bureau
Concord, 603-271-3641

New Jersey
Division of Consumer Affairs
Newark, 973-504-6200

New Mexico
Office of the Attorney General
Consumer Protection Division
Santa Fe, 505-827-6060
(800-678-1508 in New Mexico)

New York
Office of the Attorney General
Bureau of Consumer Frauds
and Protection
Albany, 518-474-5481

Ohio
Office of the Attorney General
Consumer Frauds and Crime Section
Columbus, 614-466-8831
(800-282-0515 in Ohio)

Oklahoma
Office of the Attorney General
Consumer Protection Division
Oklahoma City, 405-521-4274

Oregon
Financial Fraud Section
Department of Justice
Salem, 503-378-4732

Pennsylvania
Office of the Attorney General
Bureau of Consumer Protection
Harrisburg, 717-787-9707
(800-441-2555 in Pennsylvania)

Rhode Island
Office of the Attorney General
Consumer Protection Division
Providence, 401-274-4400
(800-852-7776 in Rhode Island)

South Carolina
Department of Consumer Affairs
Consumer Fraud and Antitrust Section
Columbia, 803-734-4200

South Dakota
Office of the Attorney General
Division of Consumer Affairs
Pierre, 605-773-4400

Tennessee
Office of the Attorney General
Division of Consumer Affairs
Nashville, 615-741-4737

Texas
Office of the Attorney General
Consumer Protection Division
Austin, 512-463-2070

Vermont
Office of Attorney General
Public Protection Division
Montpelier, 802-828-3171

Virginia
Office of Attorney General
Antitrust and Consumer
Litigation Section
Richmond, 804-786-2116

West Virginia
Office of the Attorney General
Consumer Protection Division
Charleston, 304-558-8986
(800-368-8808 in West Virginia)

Wyoming
Office of the Attorney General
Cheyenne, 307-777-7874

Free Consumer Resources on the Internet

You can get great advice and information for free on the Internet. Most government agencies and many independent organizations include vital information on their websites, promoting consumer education and awareness. You can protect yourself from fraud, illness, and spending your money unwisely by simply knowing what to avoid.

If you have Internet access, check out the following websites and increase your consumer savvy.

- **Department of Health and Human Services** (www.hhs.gov). Gives free information on health, medicine and health products.
- **Federal Trade Commission** (www.ftc.gov). Provides consumer publications online.
- **Privacy Rights Clearinghouse** (www.privacyrights.org). Supplies information on how to control and secure your personal information, such as your Social Security number and medical records.
- **The Better Business Bureau** (www.bbb.org). Helps you locate your local Better Business Bureau and provides fraudulent business alerts and reports.

Toll-Free May Not Always Be Free

You may be surprised to learn that there are some exceptions to 800- and 888-number telephone calls being free. Many companies that provide entertainment or information services charge you for calls to 800-, 888- and other toll-free numbers. They're supposed to follow the Federal Trade Commission's (FTC's) 900-number rule, which requires companies to inform consumers of their service charge and method of billing before they provide the service (called a presubscription arrangement). But sometimes this law is broken.

Here's what the FTC suggests you do to minimize the risk of unauthorized charges on your next telephone bill:

- Remember that dialing a number that begins with 888 is just like dialing an 800-number. Both are often toll-free, but not always. Companies are prohibited from charging you for calls to these numbers unless they set up a valid presubscription agreement with you first.
- Recognize that not all numbers beginning with 8 are toll-free. For example, the area code 809 serves the Dominican Republic. If you dial this area code, you'll be charged international long distance rates.
- Make sure any 800- or 888-number you call for entertainment or information that costs money provides security devices—including PINs—before you enter into a presubscription agreement.
- Check your phone bill for 800, 888 or unfamiliar charges. Calls to 800- and 888-numbers should be identified. Some may be mislabeled as "long distance" or "calling card" calls and are easy to overlook.
- Dispute charges on your phone bill for an 800- or 888-number if you don't have a presubscription arrangement. Follow the instructions on your billing statement.
- Know that if the telephone company removes a charge for an 800- or 888-number call, the entertainment or information service provider may try to pursue you through a collection agency. If this happens, you may have additional rights under the Fair Debt Collection Practices Act.

Free and Almost Free Stuff

From free information to free recipes, free dog food to free beauty supplies, there are quite a few things in life you can get without spending a cent.

How to Find Free Stuff

Getting free stuff starts with knowing where to look. Before you whip past the advertisements in your favorite magazine or newspaper, throw away a mailer, or switch off a TV commercial, you may want to consider paying attention to the small print.

Advertisements

Most freebies are publicized through advertisements. Many corporations and organizations offer consumers the opportunity to read about or sample products before making a purchase or other commitment. For example, you can call 888-GO-RVing for a free informational video if you want to buy a Recreational Vehicle. Or ask for it at RV dealers. Learning as much as you can about a product (for free) before making a purchase can save you lots of money in the long run.

With so many product lines available to consumers, most companies know that a free sample or discount coupon can attract new customers and encourage the loyalty of current ones.

Stock up on Perfume Samples

Perfume samples from department stores are great to use while traveling. Tell the salesperson that you are interested in purchasing a new scent, but want to try it for a few days. Request a sample-size vial. Frequently, the salesperson will hand you more than one sample, each of which is good for at least three applications (or more if you use it sparingly).

Choose the salesperson you speak with carefully. Don't ask someone who seems to be having a bad day. Before you ask about a free sample, you may want to ask a few questions about different perfumes. When you have warmed up the salesperson, it's time to ask for a freebie.

Size Matters

When you order free samples, keep in mind that they can vary greatly in size. Some free samples are quite generous while others are only good for one use (and sometimes not even that). It's possible to receive a hand lotion sample as small as a packet of sugar, or one that will last you a month. Sometimes you may get only a 50¢ coupon and other times you may get over $5 worth.

Brand Names

Sometimes brand-name companies will offer perks (such as free recipes, rebate coupons or how-to brochures) to consumers who buy their product lines. You can find these offers in the small print of an advertisement (usually in the classified section of newspapers and magazines) or on TV commercials (either as the main focus of the commercial or in small print at the bottom of the screen).

For example, Reynolds Wrap offers free recipes and cooking tips if you call their toll-free number, 800-745-4000, or visit their website at www.rmc.com/wrap.

800-Numbers

Quite often there's a customer service or customer comment 800-number on a product label, coupon or advertisement.

Even if they don't advertise a special freebie or gift, you can call this number to find out about any unadvertised perks the company may offer.

If you call, many companies will send you free samples of new or existing products, free recipes featuring their products or free information booklets on their product line.

Tylenol is a perfect example. Call 800-962-5357 to receive coupons, samples and pain-relief information on new and standard Tylenol products.

Coupons and Labels

Companies often publicize new products by sending out coupons, rebates and free samples. When a popular brand-name comes out with a new product, companies frequently advertise it on the label of their most popular item (or on a coupon attached to the item). Sometimes there's even a free sample of the new product attached to the existing item.

You may also receive coupons and free samples in the mail, or delivered with your newspaper. Sometimes you have to fill out a form and send it back to the company to receive the free item.

Labels sometimes also offer rebates, which usually require you to mail in a receipt and proofs of purchase in return for money back. Companies usually offer more money back on a rebate than on a coupon, because they assume most people won't get around to sending it in. If you do, you could save a lot of money. Just make sure the offer is worth your time and the cost of a 33¢ stamp.

Junk Mail Isn't Always Junk

Don't automatically throw out the product mailers that crowd your mailbox, because many mailers include ways to receive free samples and information.

Companies use mass-marketing mailers as a way to inform consumers of new product lines and services. You might find discount, rebate and buy-one-get-one-free coupons, as well as offers of free how-to brochures and free home-maintenance upgrades (such as new window treatments or water-quality tests).

Books on Freebies

There are a few noteworthy books on freebies that can help you locate a bundle of free and almost free (usually a postage-and-handling charge under $5) stuff. You can often find these books in the reference section of your library, but you might want to make a small investment (under $20) so you can keep the book at home.

Here are some freebie books to look into:

- *Free Stuff For Kids,* (Simon & Schuster Children's, $5).
- *Free Stuff for Seniors* by Matthew Lesko and Mary Ann Martello (Information USA, $19.95). This book tells you how to get a wide variety of free information and some free stuff, and lists important phone numbers and addresses for aging adults.
- *The Official Freebies for Families: Something for Nothing or Next to Nothing* by the editors of *Freebies* magazine (Lowell House, $8.95). If you have problems finding the publication you can contact *Freebies* Magazine at 805-566-1225.
- *The Official Freebies for Kids: Something for Nothing or Next to Nothing* by the editors of *Freebies* magazine (Contemporary Books, $5.95). If you have problems finding the publication you can contact *Freebies* magazine at 805-566-1225.
- *The Official Freebies for Teachers: Something for Nothing or Next to Nothing* by the editors of *Freebies* magazine (Lowell House, $6.95). If you have problems finding the publication you can contact Freebies Magazine at 805-566-1225.

Free Gift with Purchase

If you shop at department store cosmetic or fragrance counters, you know that different brands frequently offer free-gift-with-purchase deals. These gifts are usually worth at least $30, and may even include items you were already planning to buy.

You usually have to spend a certain amount of money (around $20) to get a gift. By buying a container of eye-makeup remover and a blush, you may get a lipstick, mascara, eye pencil and cute carrying bag for free. Or, if you buy an eight ounce bottle of perfume, some labels will give you a gift set that includes body lotion, powder and toilet water in the same scent.

It's a good idea to pay attention to advertisements for free gifts, because you can wind up only having to pay for half of the items that you would have purchased during a non-gift period. Also, unless you're undeniably committed to a certain label, you may want to shop around at the counters and take advantage of the free gifts other designers may offer.

The best way to make the most of the freebies that are out there is not to buy perfume or makeup until a gift is being offered (you won't have to wait much more than a month).

Act Fast for Freebies

When you find a freebie you want, order it immediately, because most offers expire quickly. Whether it be a coupon, rebate, brand-name sample, free publication or trial issue of a magazine, if you don't call or write for the sample immediately you may miss out on the deal.

If a freebie expires before you find out about it, ask the customer service representative if there are any offers still in progress. You may well wind up getting a freebie you never expected. Save the telephone number, address or website address on an expired offer so that you can check for new offers at a later date. Frequently, companies who offer a special once will offer special deals or gifts again in the future.

Free trial offers almost always have an expiration date, so if you want to try a product that advertises a free sample, you'd better act fast.

A Complaint or Compliment May Get You Something for Free

By voicing your opinion, either positively or negatively, you may receive a free sample, rebate or discount coupon for your next purchase of a product.

Check the Small Print

If you read the small print on the packaging of products you buy, you'll see there's frequently a manufacturer's phone number or address included. Consider taking advantage of this contact information to let a company know what you think.

If a toll-free number is not available, a letter to a company's customer service supervisor can get the same response. In your letter, explain your disenchantment or satisfaction with a product. Include the label, date and store where you purchased the product, and let the company know exactly why you are writing the letter. Companies will do a lot to keep their customers satisfied, and to let satisfied customers know that they appreciate their business and loyalty.

Get Satisfaction

Many times a customer's dissatisfaction with a product warrants a rebate or replacement of a damaged product bought in a store. And many companies will reward a customer's satisfaction and

IT PAYS TO ASK

Know Whom You're Calling

Many companies offer free samples through marketing agencies, which don't know what other offers the company is making. When this happens, ask for the company's own customer-service phone number. Then call the company directly to find out if you can get any other perks, such as free coupons, recipes or information brochures. Many times they'll also tell you when the next free sample is going to be available, and what it will be.

loyalty to a product line with a coupon toward their next purchase or a sample of a new item in the product line.

Alka-Seltzer offers not only a question-and-comment number (800-800-4793) but a way to get a free sample from their website (www.alka-seltzer.com). If you don't have access to the World Wide Web, think about calling the toll-free number and asking for a sample or information on their product line.

Ask for a Sample

If there's a new item you'd like to try, but you don't want to buy an entire box or jar (only to find you don't like it), call the comment line and ask the customer service department if a sample is available. You won't know what you can get for free until you try.

Fly for Less

If your flight with an airline isn't up to par, your complaint may get you money off of your next trip. Many airlines provide disgruntled customers with coupon vouchers (sometimes for as much as $50) for future flights. Contact the customer service department by letter, on the phone or in person, and explain your frustration and disappointment in the service you had. A freebie can ease the stress of a bad trip.

Order Free Information

Many organizations offer free information booklets that can help you to be a better-educated consumer. There are booklets available on every topic imaginable.

Free through the Mail

If you want to learn about low-cost funeral options or how your pet's hair may be making your child sick, there are organizations that will help you for free.

Here are a few companies that publish free information booklets for consumers. Just send a self-addressed, stamped envelope and a request letter to get information that will help you make educated choices for your life.

American Academy of Allergy, Asthma & Immunology 611 E. Wells St., Milwaukee, WI 53202, 414-272-6071. Write for free information on allergies to animals. The pamphlet includes information on what causes these reactions and how to treat them.

American Academy of Dermatology Attn: Communications Dept., 930 N. Meacham Rd., Schaumburg, IL 60173, 847-330-0230. Write for a free guide on warts, what causes them, different types and the available treatments.

BUYER BEWARE

Get Ready to Wait

When you call or send away for free stuff, remember that immediate delivery is not guaranteed. Sometimes you'll receive an information brochure, video or even a free sample in less than a week, but it often takes up to two months to receive the item you requested. Although many companies and corporations offer freebies, it is not their top priority, so don't be surprised if you have to wait.

TRY SOMETHING DIFFERENT

Freebies by Subscription

If you don't want to spend your time searching for freebies, consider subscribing to **Freebies** magazine (1135 Eugenia Pl., P.O. Box 310, Carpinteria, CA 93014-5025, 805-566-1225). For $7.95 a year (five issues) or $16.95 for three years (15 issues), you'll find out about free offers such as food recipes, finger puppets, sports stickers and house-care brochures sent directly to your home.

Consumer Information Center Dept.

551-E, Pueblo, CO 81009, 719-948-3334 (www.pueblo.gsa.gov). You can get free and low-cost federal government publications, such as the free booklet called **Non-prescription Medicines: What's Right for You?** This literature talks about dangerous drug interactions, and the importance of reading labels and checking your medicine cabinet for expired items. Also, consider requesting a free catalog that includes the other publications they offer, such as:

- **Being an Executor**
- **Fixing Up Your Home and How to Finance It**
- **66 Ways to Save Money**
- **Prostate Cancer**
- **The Sun, UV and You**

American Academy of Pediatrics (847-228-5005) provides many Public Education Brochures on its Web site, *www.aap.org*. Topics include Toy Safety, Choking Prevention and First Aid for Infants and Children, Discipline and Your Child, Ear Infections and Children, Teen Driver, and Know the Facts About HIV and AIDS.

Funeral and Memorial Societies of America (FAMSA) P.O. Box 10, Hinesburg, VT 05461, 802-482-3437. Write for information on how to beat the high cost of funerals. You'll receive information from the FAMSA chapter in your state. Also, consider checking out their website (www.funerals.org/famsa) for more free information.

Parks Corporation 1 West St., Fall River, MA 02720, 508-679-5938. Write for a free brochure called *Using Solvents and Sundry Chemicals*. This guide tells you about the proper use of paint thinner, turpentine, acetone, kerosene and other related chemicals.

Free by Phone

These organizations send out pamphlets to help you make the best choices for a balanced and healthy lifestyle, or provide information on how to enhance your life and make educated purchases.

American Institute for Cancer Research, 800-843-8114. Call for free information on healthy ingredient substitutes for cheese, chocolate, cream, nuts and oils. You can also request a unique guide to Asian ingredients.

American Lung Association, 800-586-4872. Call for free information on what to do to eliminate biological pollutants in your home.

Environmental Health Center of the National Safety Council, 800-424-5323. You can call for a free information booklet on the dangers of lead in the home and how to protect your family.

Metlife Consumer Education Center, 800-638-5433. Call for a booklet on how to keep your home safe. You'll get information on preventing fires in your home, what to do if a fire breaks out, how to prevent theft in your home and how to insure your home against loss. Included with this information is a checklist and other useful resources.

T. Rowe Price, 800-638-5660. Get free information on many aspects of financial planning, such as a *Guide to International Investing, Investing for College*, and *Retirement Planning*. Information packages include worksheets that will help you organize your portfolio.

U.S. Small Business Association, 800-827-5722. This organization provides free information on how to start your own small business.

Freebies from the World Wide Web

I f you're looking for free samples, recipes, information, coupons and chances to win prizes, the World Wide Web may be your best resource.

The World Wide Web offers a vast amount of information on freebies all in one place. You can gather information from multiple resources without leaving your seat. Not only will you find listings of books devoted to finding freebies (on sites such as barnesand noble.com and amazon.com), but you can locate brand-name free samples, sweepstakes and giveaways from companies' own websites or sites dedicated to gathering freebie information.

Most freebie sites combine totally free and almost-free offers. Sites that highlight free stuff and freebies, such as www. angelfire.com, list brand-name toll-free offers that range from coupons for razors and Christmas card samples, to instant coffee and bandage samples.

How to Find Free Stuff Online

The best (and probably easiest) way to find free sites when you go online is to use a search engine such as Yahoo, Excite or Web-Crawler. Simply type in "freebies", "free stuff" or "free samples," and you'll get tons of listings. You may want to print the query page the search engine brings up, or consider bookmarking a few site links so that you don't have to do a search each time you want to visit a new freebie site.

Not every site is going to be fabulous, so you may want to pay attention to any ratings that the search engines give to the popularity of a site.

Think about using a few different search engines for your quest, because some may have links that others don't include.

General Web Freebies

Certain general Internet advantages, such as free e-mail and free information (such as how-to brochures, access to library catalogs and archives, and printable recipes) provide online consumers free access to knowledge through their fingertips.

Free Information If you're looking for guidance on health, education or financial concerns, consider using your computer before you buy a how-to book. In a search engine such as Excite or Lycos, enter words related to the topic you want to research and use the query results to find databases that can help you. You'll probably find more information on the World Wide Web than you could gather in a day at your local library.

FOR YOUR INFORMATION

Free E-mail Update Of Fabulous Freebies

Using the Internet for freebies can have a lot of advantages, such as a free e-mail update of the best and most current freebies on the Web. Check out **Free Stuff** (www.ppi-free.com), to get a free e-mail newsletter that includes both website and toll-free free stuff you can order. You can sign up for the e-mail update and pass it around to all of your friends. It's great way to find free stuff (such as body cream samples, shopping guides, food recipes and freebie links) without having to do the work.

BARGAIN FINDER

Free Can of Wood Stain

Cabot Stains (800-877-8246) offers customers a way to sample the wood stain they want to use before making a final decision. If you call, you'll get a free four-ounce can of stain, applicator brush and product selection guide. Also, the toll-free number is manned by wood-care experts who can give you advice or information on any of Cabot's products. (They may even let you sample a few different stains.)

Links to the Best Freebies on The Web

You may be too overwhelmed by the volume of free things on the Web to search through every site. This is where freebie resource websites come in handy. These sites are devoted to providing Internet users with links to the best freebies on the Web. They can help you wade through the garbage you may come across so you can find the real freebie treasures.

Also, because offers do expire, freebie resource websites try to update their information more frequently than other sites. This helps you spend less time calling or filling out forms for free stuff that is no longer available.

Some of the freebie resource links advertise ways to get free stuff in addition to providing links to free-stuff pages. If you can't find anything you want on their pages, you're sure to find it through their links.

Here are some freebie resource sites to check out:

- **#1 Free Stuff** (www.1freestuff.com)

- **123 Freebies** (www.cappyscove.com/ 123freebies)

- **Free-Items.com** (www.free-items.com)

- **The Free Site** (www.thefreesite.com)

- **Freebie Frenzy** (www.geocities.com/ RainForest/7678/free.html)

- **Free-n-Cool** (www.free-n-cool.com)

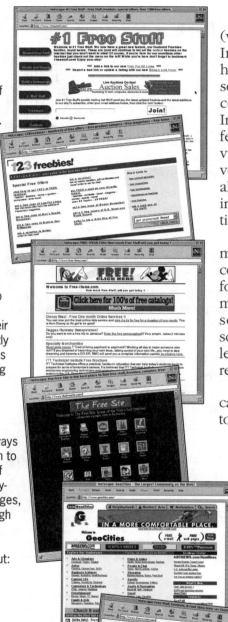

The U.S. Department of Agriculture (www.nal.usda.gov/fnic) and the Consumer Information Center (www.pueblo.gsa.gov) have online databases where you can research information on health, parenting and consumer-related concerns. The Consumer Information Center has hundreds of the best federal consumer publications that you can view for free online, or order for free (or at very little cost—usually under $2). You can also get free college financial aid advice and information from the Department of Education online (www.ed.gov).

Many magazines, federal and state government agencies, and private institutions or companies now have websites filled with information that once cost consumers time and money to find. If you or your child are researching colleges, you can locate most schools on the Web, take virtual tours, and learn about campus activities and academic requirements without ever leaving your home.

If you want to visit a foreign country, you can obtain information on where to go, what to see and how to get there right from home.

Freebie Websites

There are a great number of sites devoted to finding free stuff. Some of the sites are divided into categories, including home, food, kids, games, free samples, sweepstakes, free catalogs, coupons and toll-free freebies.

Many times the same freebies will be listed in multiple sites, but other times you can find treasures in one site that another won't have.

Here's a listing of some of the top freebie websites and what they have to offer. Take your time when you visit them and remember two very important things: Bookmark the webpage because freebies are updated daily, weekly or monthly (and every offer expires at some point), and don't give up if you don't have great luck the first time.

All About Freebies (www.all-about-mall.com). Free offers are broken up into categories: animals, apparel, beauty, books, calendars, catalogs, CD-ROMs, food, games, health and house. Look for free magazines and instant freebies such as your horoscope, sport news, stock news and world news. Also, play a trivia game and possibly win $25.

Smart Shopper Super Site, Catalog Request Center (www.smartshop1.com). If you are looking for free catalogs, this is the site to visit. There are over 300 catalogs listed by category, catalog name, product or brand. There is no charge for the visit, but you can only select up to 12 catalogs per visit and you must make your selections within 30 minutes. If you're looking for certain products, this is an easy way to get some catalogs sent to your home so you can compare prices and shop from the comfort of your living room.

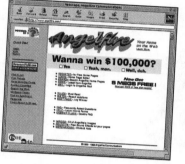

The Dollar Stretcher (www.stretcher.com). The Dollar Stretcher's slogan is "Living Better…for Less." And you'll find over 400 free articles explaining how to care for your car, balance your budget or make an inexpensive gourmet dinner quickly. There are tips about parenting, opening your own business and low-cost gift buying. You can also subscribe to a free weekly e-mail newsletter that features money-saving ideas and tips.

About.com (freebies.about.com/index.htm). About.com is a general interest website that happens to devote a portion of its content to freebies. You may find that many sites will do this. But the great thing is its lists of travel freebies. You can find out how to get free travel brochures, time zone charts, AT&T in-flight phone cards, subway navigators and hotel directories. There's also a way to sign up for the weekly *Freebies Features Newsletter*.

Free2b's Fantastic Freebies (www.free2bs.com). Free2b's lists and updates its freebies daily. You can find ways to get free postcards, recipes and graphics, as well as ways to enter contests and win awards. Like on many freebie sites, you can also find a list of other freebie links you may want to check out.

Treasure Island (members.xoom.com/tisle/index.htm). Treasure Island is a great site for finding offers of free stuff by phone. Get toll-free numbers to call for recipe cards, trial versions of software or a halogen lamp bulb safety kit. This is also a great site for finding links to other freebie sites. You can join a free-stuff chat room, or browse and place your own free personal advertisement. As its name suggests, this site is a treasure chest filled with all sorts of free wonderful stuff.

Free Stuff And Freebies

Angelfire (www.angelfire.com) is a great site if you're looking for brand-name freebies, sweepstakes and contests, toll-free offers and great links to other free-stuff sites. You can find products that range from free fonts to a free **Pepcid AC** sample, a free sample of **Wisk** to a free **Duraflame** log. Maybe you want to enter a contest to win a free **Perry Ellis** giant golf umbrella, or $1,000 in online time from **Reader's Digest**. You can not only find great free stuff, but many times you'll be linked to the company site, which is another great way to locate lots of freebies.

BARGAIN FINDER

Free E-mail

Many sites, and even some search engines (such as **Yahoo** and **AltaVista**), provide **World Wide Web** users with free Web-based e-mail addresses. They can afford to do this because they put ads on your e-mail page. Most of the time, you can access your free Web-based e-mail account from any computer, which is appealing for people who have an account they can only access from one station.

Some services you may want to look into are:

- **MollyMail** (www.mollymail.com)
- **Yahoo** (www.yahoo.com)
- **DWP, Daily Web Planner** (www.dwp.net)
- **Hotmail** (www.hotmail.com)

Linda Bowman on How to Find Great Freebies and Get a Lot for Nothing

Linda Bowman is the author of the *More for Your Money Guides*, including *Freebies and More for Folks over Fifty, Free Food...And More, How to Fly for Free* and *Freebies for Kids and Parents Too.*

In your opinion, what are the best resources for finding free information, products and services?

Great resources can be found everywhere you go, and in nearly everything you read. This may seem awfully general, but it's true. You can begin by looking through your daily newspaper, in consumer and specialty magazines, in markets, drugstores, banks, coffee houses, movie theaters, restaurants—literally everywhere you go. The point is to be aware and keep an eye out for free offers in all kinds of advertising and promotional literature.

How much money do you think seeking out freebies can save you in a year?

That depends on how much effort you put into your savings campaign. You can decide you only want to save money at the grocery store, and simply cut coupons (making sure you take advantage of double and triple coupons). This can add up to hundreds of dollars for a year's worth of family groceries. Or you can go all the way, and look for bargains when you travel and take vacations, at restaurants and theaters, on your pet supplies, at the bank (savings clubs, senior accounts) and everywhere you spend money on retail goods.

What kind of freebies are the most worth spending your time and energy looking for?

That depends on your tastes and the areas in which you want to make a conscious effort to save money. For example, If you are a pet lover and have several pets, you may be spending more money on food, treats and other supplies than you like. Read some of the several magazines that are specifically for pet owners, check the coupons in your Sunday newspaper, and cruise the aisles of your pet supply store for free samples, coupons and specials. Also, a great source of pet freebies are dog, cat and pet shows and fairs, at which manufacturers give away loads of free samples and savings coupons. Your veterinarian may also be a source of free samples.

Are some freebies a waste of time?

Simply put, if the effort isn't worth the reward, don't do it. Spending a lot of time mailing away for small items that you can live without, even if they're free, is a waste of time. Saving on useful, necessary products and services is fun and productive. My general rule of thumb is, "If you would buy and use the product or service anyway, why not make the effort to save money or obtain it for free?" If you have no use for a freebie, forget about it.

What's your opinion of so-called freebies that have a shipping and handling fee?

I have no problem with paying for postage and handling to get a free item that has value and that I will definitely use. My ceiling on postage and handling depends on the value of the freebie. Generally I won't go over $10, and that has to be for an item that I perceive to be worth $50 or more.

Free Trial Issues Of Magazines

You'll find the most offers for free, no-risk magazine trial issues on the World Wide Web, but keep your eye out for magazine inserts and direct-mail advertisements as well.

Magazines offer free trial issues so that consumers can see if the publication is something that they'd like to receive regularly. If you can't find an advertisement for a free trial issue of a magazine you're interested in, consider calling the publication to see if they will send you an issue before you make an annual investment.

Before you request a trial issue, however, consider the drawbacks: You will have to cancel within an allotted time period if you don't want to pay for the full subscription, and there's a chance you'll be mistakenly billed for an annual subscription even if you cancel your order.

Also, if you aren't seriously interested in possibly subscribing, consider leaving this free offer for people who are.

Locating Free Trial Offers

To locate magazines with free trial offers, you may want to check out the #1 Free Stuff website at www.1freestuff.com or the Electronic Newsstand at www.enews.com. Or go directly to the website of the magazine you're interested in to find out about special deals.

Another free way to locate trial issue advertisements is by checking out inserts in magazines at the library. Most libraries keep current issues on hand.

Remember, it is your responsibility to cancel your subscription if you aren't interested after receiving the first issue. Make sure you cancel before the prescribed deadline.

Free Magazine Subscriptions

Very rarely, but once in a while, you may find a magazine that offers free subscriptions. Sometimes these offers are limited to a certain age category, or are for a limited amount of time (such as one year).

Usually, this type of special magazine is produced by an agency that offers the publication as an added perk to attract a consumer's business. Some new magazines make special offers so that people will learn of their existence.

A couple of companies that offer free subscriptions or complimentary issues are Saga Holidays (*Modern Maturity Travelers Magazine*, 800-343-0273). And check out *Yotta* (www.yotta.com) for details on free online magazine subscriptions.

Freebies at Your Fingertips

Many magazines contain classified sections that put freebies at your fingertips. Publications, such as **Food & Wine** magazine, list their contributors and special offers they may have in the last pages of the magazine's issue. You can find website and toll-free number listings that offer free recipes, such as the **American Dairy Association** (www.ilovecheese.com) They also list ways to receive free brochures and catalogs.

If you read home-related magazines, such as **Good Housekeeping** or **Woman's Day**, keep an eye out for offers to get free craft-project instructions. For example, **Rit Dyes** has offered free directions on how to make sock critters, an easy, at-home activity that's great for children.

Read the fine print and small ads before you throw away any magazine. Otherwise you may be passing up free offers every month.

Entrepreneurial Freebies

Starting your own business or creating an invention doesn't have to cost you a fortune. You'll be happy to know there are agencies that help entrepreneurs for free.

Inventors Only

If you're an inventor, you can contact American Invention Associates (AIA) in Troy, Michigan (800-214-2044) for free information on how to create, license and promote a new product. The AIA will also help you patent your idea so you can receive the credit you deserve.

Create Your Own Cookbook

If cooking is your passion and you have some great dishes that deserve public notice, you can call Cookbook Publishers, Inc. in Leneza, Kansas (800-227-7282 or 913-492-5900) for help publishing your own cookbook. You'll receive a sample book and a mass of information on how to design and market your book. Once you have gathered the recipes you want to use, this company will actually help you produce the cookbook you've always wanted to create.

You can visit their website, www.cookbookpublishers.com, for more information.

Health and Food Freebies

Many companies offer health and food freebies. From cancer and nutrition information to free pet food and pain relief samples, you can find free things to reduce your monthly expenses.

For Your Health

If you have recently come down with an illness, or you have noticed a new product advertised that may help relieve one of your ailments, it may be in your best interest to pick up the phone and contact the company or organization you're interested in for free information.

Companies and organizations frequently offer free information, and sometimes free samples, that can help you choose the best treatment. And many alternative health-care companies offer free samples and information to help market their wares.

Many of these institutions advertise their freebies in health magazines, such as *Prevention* and *Health*. Others publicize their free information on television or in the newspaper. If there's an organization you would like information from, call toll-free information (800-555-1212) for its phone number, and ask the customer service department what the organization can do for you.

Here are some health-related companies and organizations that offer freebies to the public:

Alliance for Lung Cancer Advocacy, Support and Education (800-298-2436). Provides free information on lung cancer and guidance for those affected by the disease. You'll also get a free support pin.

American Cancer Society (800-ACS-2345). Sends out free breast self-examination instruction cards that you can hang on your shower head.

Excedrin (800-580-4455). Will send you two samples, a $1 coupon, an informative pain-relief newsletter.

Nu-Salt (800-206-9454). Offers four free sample packets of Nu-Salt salt substitute. You also get a 35¢ off coupon for Butter Buds.

Maharishi Ayur-Ved (800-255-8332). Offers a free total health catalog.

Salada (800-645-1190). Sends out a free green tea newsletter.

Tylenol (800-962-5357). Will send you a $1 coupon toward your next Tylenol purchase.

Many pet-care companies offer free trial samples of new and existing pet food lines to promote their products to consumers.

HERE'S HOW

Food for Your Pets

Many pet-care companies offer free trial samples of new and existing pet food lines to promote their products to consumers. Along with free samples, many companies will also send you free coupons and nutrition information. For example, **Pedigree** (800-292-2111) sends out a free newsletter and a chance to win dog food for life.

Here are some pet food companies that offer free samples, coupons and information for the care of your pet:

Advanced Nutrition Formula (800-489-2770). Offers generous four-ounce trial-size packages of both dog and cat food.

Lafeber Company, Avi Cakes (800-842-6445, ext. 850). Sends out free trial-size gourmet bird treats good for parakeets, cockatiels, lovebirds and conures.

Purina (www.purina.com). Order a free Pet Safety Kit on the Purina Web site. Kit includes a pet safety booklet, emergency care magnet and pet rescue sticker.

Sunshine Pet Nutrition Center (800-705-2111). Sends out two eight-ounce samples of Nurture lamb and rice dog food, and over $3 worth of money-saving coupons, plus brochures on ingredients and nutrition.

Don't Turn up Your Nose at Coupons

Don't turn up your nose too quickly at cutting coupons. Frequently there are free offers advertised on or near the coupons themselves. For example, **Cesar** dog food company offers two coupons (one for $2 off and another for buy-two-get-one-free) and a chance to win a $5,000 shopping spree down Rodeo Drive (in Beverly Hills, CA), all in the same advertisement. To enter the contest you simply return the postage-paid postcard and try your luck.

But remember that entering a sweepstakes can get you put on a wide variety of mailing lists. You may soon be getting a lot of junk-mail from other companies who bought your name from the sweepstakes' mailing list.

Val-pak is Full Of Value

If you love great savings, stop throwing away the **Val-pak** mailers you regard as junk-mail. Val-pak mailers can have terrific savings—from half-off on a new health club membership or a free night's stay at a hotel, to a free month's rent at a mini-storage facility or $2 movie rental. With more than 20 coupons included, you're likely to find savings on something for you or your family.

Food for You

Many food companies produce free information materials. If you are interested, call the 800-number of a brand you use and request free information. Some companies also provide free recipes and coupons—if you ask.

Here is the contact information for some popular name-brand companies that provide free food and nutrition publication materials.

Arm and Hammer, 469 N. Harrison St., Princeton, NJ 08543, 800-524-1328 or 800-624-2889. www.armhammer.com

Beech Nut, P.O. Box 618, St. Louis, MO 63188, 800-523-6633. www.beech-nut.com

Butterball Turkey Company, 2001 Butterfield Rd., Downer's Grove, Illinois 60515, 800-Butterball. www.butterball.com

Campbell Soup Company, Corporate Communications Center, Campbell Pl., Camden, NJ 08103, 800-257-8443. www.campbell soup.com

Dannon Company, 120 White Plains Rd., Tarrytown, NY 10591, 800-321-2174. www.dannon.com

Del Monte, Consumers Affairs Dept., P.O. Box 193575, San Francisco, CA 94119, 800-335-6668. www.delmonte.com

Gerber Products, 445 State St., Freemont, MI 49413, 800-443-7237. www.gerber.com

Hershey Foods Corporation, Consumer Relations Dept., P.O. Box 815, 100 Crystal A Dr., Hershey, PA 17033, 800-468-1714. www. hersheys.com

Kellogg Company, Consumer Affairs Dept. P.O. Box CAMB, Battle Creek, MI 49016, 800-962-1413. www.kelloggs.com

Kraft General Foods, Consumer Response and Information Center, 1 Kraft Court, Glenview, IL 60025, 800-432-6333. www.kraftfoods.com

McCormick, Consumer Affairs Dept., 211 Schilling Circle, Hunt Valley, MD 21031, 800-632-5847. www.mccormick.com

Nabisco Brands, Inc., P.O. Box 1911, East Hanover, NJ 07936, 800-622-4726. www.nabiscorecipes.com

Nestle Food Company, Nestle Consumer Affairs, 800 N. Brand Blvd., Glendale, CA 91203, 800-637-8537. www.nestleusa.com

Ocean Spray Cranberries, Inc., One Spray Dr., Lakeville-Middleboro, MA 02349, 800-662-3263. www.oceanspray.com

Pepsi-Cola Company, Consumer Relations, One Pepsi Way, Somers, NY 10589, 800-433-COLA. www.pepsi.com

Quaker Oats Company, P.O. Box 049003, Chicago, IL 60604, 800-234-6281. www.quakeroats.com

Free Stuff for Personal Care

Personal care companies tend to offer the best freebies because they are in fierce competition to get the most customers. Companies that sell soap, body lotion and toothpaste offer free samples in hopes of attracting new customers and keeping their old ones loyal.

So if you notice that a new scent, flavor or strength of a product is being advertised, call the company and ask whether you can receive a free sample or a coupon for the new item. Tell the operator what comparable product you are currently using, and that you may be interested in switching brands. Because there is a lot of competition in this area, most companies will jump at the chance of taking a consumer away from a competitor.

Take advantage of a new product promotion by calling for a free sample.

Here are some companies and their recent free offers:

Alka-Seltzer (800-800-4793). Free two-tablet package and a $1 coupon for any Alka-Seltzer product.

CAMOCARE Gold (800-226-6227). Gold alpha hydroxy face-care samples, a $2 coupon and product information, lists and order form.

DHC (800-342-2273). Free catalog of skin-care items including a free mild soap bar, packet of balancing lotion and packet of light moisturizer.

Nature's Plus (800-937-0500). Brochure of tea tree oil products and a $1 coupon for Nature's Plus tea tree products.

TRY SOMETHING DIFFERENT

Free Professional Makeovers

If you have a favorite cosmetic brand or you want to try a new product, stop by your local department store and find out if you can receive a free makeover. Many times the designers send special consultants out to the stores to give free makeovers as a way to attract new clients. You can arrange an appointment and get a great new look. You may want to plan this service around a special event in your life: If you know you're going out to a romantic dinner, try to make the appointment then.

Free Film for Everyone

Free film is available to everyone from **Seattle Filmworks**. You can call 800-345-6967 for a free deluxe film package that includes two rolls of 35mm color film and information on Seattle Filmworks processing center, which will process your film as slides, prints or pictures on disks, and use **Kodak** paper. (Sample price: Two sets of 4" x 6" prints for 36 exposures costs $16.25 plus $1.45 per roll shipping.)

They can also process Kodak, **Fuji**, **Konica** and **Agfa** brands of film. If you're looking for a quality film processor that cares enough to give you a great freebie, why not try out Seattle Filmworks?

Playtex (800-240-2036). Free trial size box of Playtex Slimfits or Playtex Gentle Glide odor-absorbing tampons and a $1 coupon.

Rembrandt (800-548-3663). Free quarter-ounce sample packet of Rembrandt whitening toothpaste with fluoride mint flavor and coupons.

Free Recipes for the Chef In Your House

Do you love to cook but hate spending money on expensive cookbooks? Many food companies, such as Del Monte and Jello, offer ways for consumers to get free recipes. It's as easy as calling the customer service 800-number.

Check out www.whymilk.com to find great recipe secrets. Milk's marketing department has developed an entire series of recipes, which they list on the World Wide Web to promote the use of milk products. You can also find this unique promotional advertisement as an insert in many magazines.

If you have a favorite product that you use and find that you have very little time in the day to make the great meals that you'd like to create, check out the 800-number on the product's label. You can get great, free recipes for dishes that take only minutes to prepare.

Toll-free Phone Offers
- Del Monte fruit and vegetable recipes (800-335-6668; www.delmonte.com)
- Jello Sugar-Free recipes (800-431-1001; www.jello.com)
- McCormick Spice Company recipes (800-632-5847; www.mccormick.com)
- Meyenberg Goat Milk recipes (800-891-4628; www.meyenberg.com)
- Milk Super Stars milk recipes (800-949-6455; www.whymilk.com)
- Ocean Spray offers recipes using their products (508-946-1000; www.oceanspray.com)

World Wide Web Offers

- Betty Crocker recipes (www.bettycrocker.com)
- *Bon Appetit* and *Gourmet Magazine* recipes (www.epicurious.com)
- Hershey dessert and pasta recipes (www.hersheys.com) and (www.nwpasta.com)
- Kellogg's Rice Krispies recipes (www.treatsrecipes.com)
- Kraft Foods recipes (www.kraftfoods.com)
- Nabisco snack food recipes (www.nabisco.com)

Free Catalogs

Have you ever considered the amount of money you could save if you took the time to compare different companies' prices?

Many brands carry similar products under different labels. For example, shirts made from the same quality material and in the same color may sell for three separate prices under three different brand names.

The convenience of shopping from home is another perk catalogs offer. Ordering free catalogs can save you the time it takes to visit many stores when you want to shop for the best price.

Where to Find Free Catalogs

There's more than one way to get free catalogs. Sometimes you can pick up the most recent catalog in a store's retail location.

Many freebie websites, such as the Smart Shopper Super Site (www.smartshop1.com), Catalog Link (cataloglink.com) and Catalogs Across America (www.catalogsusa.com) allow you to order free catalogs online. Or you can always call toll-free information (800-555-1212) for the customer service number of a manufacturer, and order a catalog directly.

Catalogs also provide you with access to products that may be hard to find in the stores. And sometimes stores won't carry all of the lines their own catalog may offer. Calling for free catalogs can expand the number of choices you have as a consumer.

Once you are on a mailing list, however, you will probably start receiving catalogs from places you have never heard of. For smart shoppers, this can be a blessing. But if your mail box is small, you can get quite overwhelmed. If you only want to receive particular catalogs, make sure that you inform a company's customer service department that you don't want your name released to other manufacturers. This should help keep you from being put on mailing lists.

Catalogs Can Cost You

Catalogs can cost you, but they don't have to. Some companies, (such as **Victoria's Secret**), charge you for catalogs if you want to pick one up at the store. Instead, ask for the company's 800-number. Often, you can order the same catalog for free over the phone.

Home Remodeling Ideas

Are you getting ready to build or remodel a home? If so, two booklets—the "Insider's Look at Building Your Home" and the "Insider's Look at Remodeling Your Home" from **Andersen Windows**—are essential items. Your creative juices will begin to flow as you thumb through these beautifully-illustrated idea books. The answer books will provide help in solving your remodeling problems, whether you are adding a room or simply changing a window. Call 800-426-4261, ext. 2837. Or visit the Web site at www.andersenwindows.com

Free for Parents

Parents will be happy to know that many companies and organizations offer free information to help them with child rearing. Many companies also provide freebies, such as coupons and samples, that can help new or expecting mothers lessen their expenses. If you're a parent or grandparent, or you're going to be one soon, the following information may help you get some great things for your baby.

Allstate Insurance Company Call a local agent for a great new fire-safety package that includes a 16-minute video, refrigerator magnet, phone sticker, coloring book and information booklet to help you teach your children what to do in case of a fire. You'll also receive a blank map to draw an escape route for your household members and a great certificate to give to your children when they have learned the rules of fire safety.

Babies Online (www.babiesonline.com). Go online for free baby announcements. If you have a lot of friends who use the Internet, this may be the best way to let them know of the new addition in your family (without the hefty cost of paper birth announcements). This website will also lead you to other great links, buys and freebies for parents.

Baby Catalog of America (800-752-9736; www.babycatalog.com). Get a free catalog of great baby products at the lowest prices you can find.

Department of Health and Human Services (800-505-CRIB). Request a video on helping to reduce the risk of Sudden Infant Death Syndrome.

Crayola Products (800-CRAYOLA; www.crayola.com). You can call for a 50+ page, stain-removal suggestion booklet that will help you safely remove most arts-and-crafts materials from your children's clothes. Full stain-removal procedures are enclosed.

Fisher Price (800-432-5437; www.fisherprice.com). Call for a catalog, brochures and coupons.

Gerber Baby Food (800-443-7237; www.gerber.com). Get a quarterly magazine and coupons for each stage of your baby's life.

Toys R Us (800-TOYS-R-US; www.toysrus.com). Get a seasonal catalog filled with coupons at any store.

Great Deals On Recreation

Great deals on recreation aren't as hard to find as you may think. Whether you want to enjoy yourself inside a museum or out in the sun, you don't have to spend a lot of money to have a great time.

Where the Recreation Deals Are

You can get real deals on recreation for anything from camping and outdoor sporting events to enjoying the nearest natural history museum, attending free bookstore lectures and participating in free festivals and parades. The best way to get the most for your money is by knowing what's going on around town.

Finding Entertainment in Your Neighborhood

You don't have to live in the big city or on top of a state park to get quality low-cost or free entertainment for you and your family right in your own backyard.

One of the best ways to learn about the great recreation events in your town or city is to contact your local tourist information center. You may be surprised to find out that most major cities,

BARGAIN FINDER

Parenting Publications

Regional parenting publications are free monthly publications that provide parents with low-cost children's recreation and entertainment ideas in their local towns and cities. The papers frequently have **Parent, Parenting, Family** or **Kids** in their titles along with the name of the city, town or county (area), such as the **Rhode Island Parents' Paper** or the **Fort Worth Child** (Texas).

Parenting publications can be found in forty states across the country. Some states have only one publication, while other states, like California (14) and Ohio (9), have many.

Most of the publications include a calendar of events which highlights daily activities in the areas they cover. You can find out about inexpensive classes, workshops, fairs and cultural events in these monthly listings.

The activities listed in these publications are not only for kids. For example, a New York area paper lists such events as the **New York International Orchid Show**. So it may be worthwhile to check one out even if you don't have small children.

If you can't remember to pick up a free copy at the beginning of the month, you can usually get home delivery of local parenting publications for as little as $3 a month, approximately $30 a year. Prices vary according to location.

To find a parenting publication in your area, check in your local bookstore or grocery store. Or call **Parenting Publications of America** (323-937-5514) and ask about the free parenting publication in your area.

and many smaller ones, have tourist centers that catalog current happenings in the area. You can call tourist information centers (see tourist information center listings at the end of this chapter), state or city chambers of commerce, and sometimes town or city halls for listings of local events.

Calendars of Events

Local calendars of events frequently list new museum collections, festivals and fairs, sporting events, and educational programs and workshops open to the public. The calendars are free, and are produced for tourists who are traveling to the area for the first time. But if you want to take advantage of the recreational events in your own neighborhood, getting a hold of a calendar of events is a great place to start.

Most calendars of events are annual, but some areas may issue only monthly calendars. You may have to call at the beginning of each month for a new set of listings.

Local Postings

Another great way to find out about local events and entertainment is through postings.

Most libraries, coffee shops, college campuses, town halls, local hang-outs and community centers have some sort of community bulletin board where you can look for news about public events. Frequently merchants, corporations, public groups, state and not-for-profit organizations, and traveling theaters or performance groups post advertisements on these bulletin boards because it is a low-cost way of attracting an audience.

So the next time you are in a public building, such as the library, don't forget to look for a community bulletin board. And if you can't find one, don't be afraid to ask where it is.

Local Papers and Radio Stations

Local newspapers advertise events all the time. If you don't have a subscription to your local paper, consider picking one up at the newsstand, or local grocery or drug store. Check out the classified section or the entertainment and weekend section of the paper (often in the Thursday or Friday edition) for local happenings. Chances are you'll find some appealing events that you never knew existed.

Also, consider listening to your local radio station, especially on Fridays. Many local stations highlight weekend events and tell you about worthwhile day and evening activities.

Taking Full Advantage of Your Public Parks

Taking your family to a public park may be one of the least expensive recreation options around. When's the last time you took a stroll through the woods, or had a picnic with your family in the park? And if you live in the city, public parks offer a rare opportunity to enjoy the outdoors. It may be the most worthwhile money you spend this year.

You may be living just a few miles away from one of the most scenic and historic sites in the country. If you haven't been to your local state or national park recently, now is the time to go. State and national park systems not only have beautiful scenery, but many offer camping and sports facilities, or activities such as guided nature walks and jazz concerts.

Low Fees

There is usually only a small entrance or parking fee to the park, often less than $5 per person.

Sometimes parks and forests only charge fees during the summer or on weekends, so they're completely free to the public the rest of the time.

Most events held in public parks are free, or cost less than the price of a movie ticket. But activities such as camping, water sports and tours generally have a small additional fee that is set by each park facility.

A Variety of Activities

Depending on the park and the time of year, you may find activities that focus on living history, environmental education, nature programs or seasonal festivals. Parks that permit boating or horseback riding may rent equipment or horses. (If that's what you're planning, make sure they rent equipment before you go.) Some parks also allow hunting and fishing.

If you like to go camping, you will usually need a reservation to camp in a park's designated camping area. Camping at a park's designated site has a small fee attached. Prices vary depending on how modernized or rustic a site you choose. Many parks allow you to camp in non-designated areas for free. Usually, these areas are a specified distance from the official camping sites and don't offer any amenities.

Most state and national recreation areas have a visitor center or information station where you can find out about the park and its activities.

Golden Park Program

The **New York State Parks System** provides a special senior citizen discount as part of what they call the **Golden Park Program** (518-474-0456).

This program offers New York State residents 62 or older free weekday admissions to state parks (except on holidays). The pass provides access to state parks and arboretums, discounts at state historic sites and state-operated swimming, golf, tennis and boat rentals. To obtain a pass, you need a current, valid New York State driver's license or non-driver's identification card (which can be obtained at your local **Motor Vehicle** office).

What's Happening at Your State Park?

State parks are state-recognized areas of historical significance or natural beauty. They provide inexpensive (sometimes free) recreation areas for local inhabitants as well as out-of-state visitors. Here are a few examples of notable state parks and the kinds of activities they offer.

Amicalola Falls State Park and Lodge

Amicalola Falls State Park and Lodge is located in Dawsonville, Georgia (706-265-8888). The park is open 7 a.m. to 10 p.m. year round. This beautiful park has 729-foot waterfalls, which are the highest in Georgia. An eight-mile approach trail leads from Amicalola Falls to Springer Mountain, the southern end of the Appalachian Trail, which runs from Georgia to Maine.

Besides many hiking trails, this park features annual events that highlight subjects like spring wildflowers, the pioneer trading days and Christmas.

Park Fees All of Georgia's state parks can be accessed with a ParkPass that costs $2 daily or $25 per year. The passes are valid from April 1 through March 31 of the following year. The Parks System offers a 50% discount on the pass for senior citizens and a 25% discount for disabled veterans.

Every Wednesday at Georgia state parks is a free day.

Lake Bemidji State Park

Lake Bemidji State Park is located in Bemidji, Minnesota (218-755-3843). This park is open from 8 a.m. to 10 p.m. all year. It offers its visitors swimming, boating, fishing, bird-watching, hiking, camping, biking, picnicking, snowmobiling, cross-country skiing, year-round nature walks and nature lovers' activities.

Bird-watching is a favorite activity in this park. Hobbyists spot red-eyed and warbling vireos, loons, eagles, herons and osprey.

Hikers frequently come across deer, porcupine and an occasional black bear.

Park Fees A vehicle permit is required for entry to any Minnesota state park. You can purchase the permit at the park or by calling the Department of Natural Resources Information Center. An annual permit costs $20. A daily permit costs $4. Camping fees are an additional $12 for a site with showers, $8 for a site with no showers.

Half-priced camping is available to Minnesota senior citizens 65 or older Sunday through Thursday.

Harriman State Park

Harriman State Park is located in Rockland and Orange counties, New York (845-786-2701). This park holds 31 lakes and reservoirs, three beaches, two camping areas and 200 miles of hiking trails. You can fish, hike, ice skate or just lie on the beach.

This park's facilities include Lakes Welch, Sebago, Tiorati and Silvermine.

Park Fees Entrance to New York state parks costs approximately $5 a car. But you can obtain an Empire Passport for $49 which provides unlimited entry to most of New York's state parks and recreational facilities.

The Empire Passport is an annual pass that is valid from April 1 through March 31 of the following year. It pays for itself in just eight visits.

You can also purchase a second passport at a discounted rate of $40 if you purchase it at the same time as the first passport. This second passport must be purchased for a second vehicle in the same household, and would be useful to those with a motorcycle, boat or second passenger vehicle.

Raven Rock State Park

Raven Rock State Park is located in Lillington, North Carolina (910-893-4888). This park is open year round, and there is no entrance fee. If you go to Raven Rock, you can find hiking trails, bridle trails, picnic areas, camping grounds and fishing spots. There are also educational programs such as the Natural History program, which arranges a special exploration of Raven Rock for a group or class.

Raven Rock State Park lies along the Cape Fear River, and there are six campsites along the trail that offer accommodations for canoeists. The canoe camping area sites must be reserved at the park office.

Park Fees Entrance to this park is free. But there are minimal fees for camping (approximately $8 a day) as well as rowboat and canoe rentals.

DID YOU KNOW

State Park Information Online

You can get all the information you want on park destinations from **State Parks Online** (www.mindspring.com/~wxrnot/parks.html). If you have Internet access, you may want to consider looking into the fees, activities and calendar of events at the state park near your home. This site is easy to maneuver and can help you plan your weekends and free time from home.

State park visitors can look forward to low-cost water activities such as canoeing, boating, fishing and swimming.

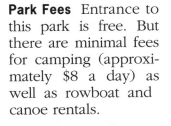

Low-Cost Fun at U.S. National Parks And Forests

U.S. National Parks and Forests are federally protected historical, natural and recreational areas of national importance. Located across the country, National Parks contain a wide variety of offerings. For example, some of the parks in the National Park System contain biosphere reserves, which are ecosystems protecting the diversity of life. And other parks are examples of natural wonders or illustrate outstanding human achievement.

Here are a few favorite U.S. National Parks around the country.

U. S. National Parks

California The Golden Gate National Recreation Area is located in the San Francisco, Marin and San Mateo counties of California (Western Information Center at Fort Mason, 415-556-0560, or Fort Funston Visitor Center, 415-239-2366). This park is the largest urban national park in the world. It is more than twice the size of San Francisco.

Most of this park's recreation areas are accessible all year, but hours of operation vary according to the individual facilities. Within its boundaries you'll find Fort Point National Historic Site, Muir Woods National Monument, Alcatraz Island and the Presidio of San Francisco.

Golden Gate also offers golf, picnicking, swimming, guided tours, scenic walks, hiking, biking, cultural programs and museums.

There is a $2 entrance fee for the Muir Woods and a $1 daily use fee for Alcatraz plus ferry transportation to Alcatraz Island ($7.75 round-trip, $6 for seniors, $4.50 for children ages 5 to 11).

West Virginia Harpers Ferry National Historical Park covers 2,300 acres in the states of West Virginia, Maryland and Virginia (304-535-6298). This park is open in the summer from 8 a.m. to 6 p.m., and in the winter from 8 a.m. to 5 p.m. Besides hiking, fishing and camping facilities, this park offers ranger-guided tours and Elderhostel programs. You can also visit the Industry Museum, Restoration Museum, Wetlands Exhibit, John Brown Museum and Civil War Museum.

Harpers Ferry holds special events (304-535-6029) throughout the year, such as a Black History Month Program and Exhibit in February, and a 19th Century Celebration of the Fourth of July.

A three-day family pass is available for $5 per vehicle or $3 per person (cyclists and walk-ins). The Golden Age Passport is honored at this park.

Camping and hiking are two great ways to stay fit—and stay within your budget.

Wyoming Yellowstone National Park is located primarily in the northwestern corner of Wyoming, with portions extending into southwestern Montana and southeastern Idaho (307-344-7381). The summer season runs from mid-April to late October. The winter season runs from mid-December to mid-March. There are many activities that you can do here, including backpacking, bicycling, boating, cross country skiing, fishing and horseback riding.

Yellowstone's most popular attraction is its vast collection of natural geysers and hot springs. It also has one of this country's largest and most varied large mammal populations.

The entrance fee to the park for a non-commercial vehicle is $20, $15 for each snowmobile or motorcycle, and $10 for each visitor over 16 years of age entering by foot, bike or on skis. This fee provides a visitor with a seven-day entrance permit for both Yellowstone and Grand Teton National Parks. You must keep your admission receipt in order to re-enter the parks.

You can also purchase an annual pass for $40, which gives you entrance to both Yellowstone and Grand Teton National Parks. The pass is valid for one year from the date of purchase and can provide you with considerable savings if you visit several times during the year.

The Golden Age Passport is honored at this national park area.

National Forests

Like national parks, national forests are federally operated, financed and protected natural regions of importance. The Forest System provides safe, clean and inexpensive fun for everyone.

The Inside Scoop The U.S. Forest Service (202-205-1706) and the U.S. Fish and Wildlife Service sponsor nature watches highlighting flora and wildlife abundant in the forests across the country. Contact the service to find out what to look for when you go to a particular recreation area.

From April through August, you can call the Wildflower Hotline (800-354-4595), which features weekly updates on wildflower viewing sites and wildflower events across the country.

Missouri The Mark Twain National Forest is located in Roll, Missouri (573-364-4621). This forest lies mostly within the Ozark Plateau, which is marked with hills from the United States' oldest mountains, the Ozarks. A wide population of wildlife attracts many visitors to this forest, especially those on the lookout for wild turkey and white-tailed deer.

Along with the many streams, rivers and valleys, this forest provides visitors with floating and canoeing opportunities, hiking and horseback riding, and campground facilities. You can also hunt, fish and study the many aspects of nature in less-developed areas of the forest.

FOR YOUR INFORMATION

National Parks: A-I

Here's a listing of our nation's designated national park areas. Call for a copy of their calendars of events and information on the great, low-cost activities you and your family can take advantage of:

- Acadia National Park (Maine, 207-288-3338)
- Arches National Park (Utah, 435-259-8161)
- Badlands National Park (South Dakota, 605-433-5361)
- Big Bend National Park (Texas, 915-477-2251)
- Boston National Historical Park (Massachusetts, 617-242-5642)
- Bryce Canyon National Park (Utah, 435-834-5322)
- Carlsbad Caverns National Park (New Mexico, 505-785-2232)
- Crater Lake National Park (Oregon, 541-594-2211)
- Everglades National Park (Florida, 305-242-7700)
- Gettysburg National Military Park (Pennsylvania, 717-334-1124)
- Glacier National Park (Montana, 800-338-5072)
- Grand Canyon National Park (Arizona, 520-638-7888)
- Grand Teton National Park (Wyoming, 307-739-3300)
- Great Smoky Mountains National Park (Tennessee, 865-436-1200)
- Haleakala National Park (Hawaii, 808-572-9306)
- Harpers Ferry National Historical Park (West Virginia, 304-535-6371)
- Hawaii Volcanoes National Park (Hawaii, 808-985-6000)
- Hot Springs National Park (Arizona, 501-624-3383)
- Isle Royale National Park (Michigan, 906-482-0984)

National Parks: K-Z

- Klondike Gold Rush National Historical Park
  (Alaska, 907-983-2921)
- Kobuk Valley National Park
  (Alaska, 907-442-8300)
- Lowell National Historical Park
  (Massachusetts, 978-970-5000)
- Mammoth Cave National Park
  (Kentucky, 270-758-2328)
- Mesa Verde National Park
  (Colorado, 970-529-4465)
- Morristown National Historical Park
  (New Jersey, 973-539-2085)
- Mount Rainier National Park
  (Washington, 360-569-2211)
- North Cascades National Park
  (Washington, 360–856-5700)
- Olympic National Park
  (Washington, 360-452-4501)
- Petrified Forest National Park
  (Arizona, 520-524-6228)
- Redwood National Park
  (California, 707-464-6101)
- Saratoga National Historical Park
  (New York, 518-664-9821)
- Shenandoah National Park
  (Virginia, 540-999-3500)
- Shiloh National Military Park
  (Tennessee, 901-689-5696)
- Valley Forge National Historical Park
  (Pennsylvania, 610-783-1077)
- Vicksburg National Military Park
  (Mississippi, 601-636-0583)
- Voyagers National Park
  (Minnesota, 218-283-9821)
- White Sands National Monument
  (New Mexico, 505-479-6124)
- Yellowstone National Park
  (Wyoming, 307-344-7381)
- Yosemite National Park
  (California, 209-372-0200)
- Zion National Park
  (Utah, 435-772-3264)

A recreational fee of $2 is charged for daily parking at this area. You can buy a seasonal pass for $20, which is good from May 1 to October 15.

Camping in designated campgrounds has an additional charge of approximately $8 for a single-family site and $16 for a double/multiple-family site. Generally it is free to camp outside of the designated camping areas. To reserve a picnic shelter equipped with concrete ground and electricity for family reunions and weddings costs $25. The Golden Age Passport provides a 50% discount for all recreational facilities.

New Hampshire The White Mountain National Forest is located in Laconia, New Hampshire (603-528-8721). This forest holds the highest mountains in the Northeast, including the Presidential Range and Mount Washington. White Mountain is noted for its world-famous ski resorts. It is one of the nation's most heavily used forest areas.

Hiking is also a big activity at this area because the Appalachian Trail (which draws hikers all year) runs along the White Mountain range.

A recreation opportunity guide providing detailed accessibility information for each campground in the White Mountain National Forest is available from the District Ranger Office or the Forest Supervisor's Office.

A recreation fee of $5 provides you with a seven-day access pass to the forest area. You can purchase an annual pass for $20, which is good from May 30 to April 30. The Golden Age Passport gives you an additional 50% discount on the park's daily and annual pass prices.

Wisconsin The Chequamegon National Forest is located in Park Falls, Wisconsin (715-762-2461). This national forest holds 800 lakes and many campground and hiking possibilities. Trails for mountain biking, skiing, snowmobiling and horseback riding are also available.

This forest offers some of Wisconsin's best hunting for black bear, ruffed grouse and white-tailed deer. There is no additional fee for hunting, but you are required to have a Wisconsin State Hunting License (which has a fee when issued). Contact the Department of Natural Resources to find out how to obtain a license.

A recreational fee of $3 per day is charged for parking at a hiking trail or picnic area. You can obtain a seasonal pass for $10, which is good from April 1 to March 31 of the following year. The Golden Age Passport gives you an additional 50% discount on the daily and annual pass prices.

An additional fee is charged for camping, and the amount varies among the campgrounds depending on the services provided and the site's proximity to the lakes.

Festivals for the Whole Family

Most people don't take full advantage of the hundreds of free festivals going on all the time in their home states.

Festivals are great, inexpensive ways to entertain yourself and your family. You can choose from among the many themed festivals that go on each year: food, music, theater and specialty festivals such as seasonal carnivals and cultural or ethnic, craft or holiday festivals. Some festivals last for a day or two, or occur over two consecutive weekends. Others may go on for as long as four days, or even for a week or more.

Every local area has its niche. Many events celebrate local harvests or promote local foods. Some merchants and organizations have fairs and festivals to link cultures and share cuisine, and others use festivals to raise money for local or state charities and other projects.

Sometimes you'll find festivals that are organized just to provide inexpensive family entertainment and fun.

What You'll Find

Besides food and entertainment, many festivals have games, sporting events, instructional booths (such as on how maple syrup is made or how a certain historical event came about), kiddy parades, contests, and clothing or craft bazaars. Festivals are a great time for merchants and entertainers to introduce themselves to their communities.

Although admission to many festivals and fairs is free, you will have to pay for food, drink, merchandise and rides. And if you are traveling by car, you should expect to pay a small parking fee ($2 or more, depending on location). This means, if you're not careful, that a day at a free local festival could end up costing you a bundle.

Money for Charity

Many different types of fairs are held to raise money for charities. Local food festivals, craft fairs and specialty fairs that highlight more expensive items, such as wine, sometimes donate their proceeds to organizations that benefit cancer victims, children in need, or foundations concerned with the preservation of a local natural area. Therefore a small worthwhile admission fee is attached.

DID YOU KNOW

Seasonal or Holiday Festivals And Fairs

Many festivals revolve around a season or historical person or event. You may find celebrations based on famous heroes, such as Dr. Martin Luther King Jr., or on holidays such as the Chinese New Year.

Some areas have winter festivals with sleigh rides and skiing events. Others hold summer festivals with outdoor water activities and game booths.

43

TRY SOMETHING DIFFERENT

Anniversary Celebrations

Many government entities and other organizations have milestone anniversary celebrations. Usually they have free events (such as concerts and fireworks) to draw a large number of people. If you notice an anniversary celebration advertised in your local town or city paper, this may be an inexpensive extravaganza you don't want to miss.

Most local festivals and fairs want to attract people, however, not scare them away with hefty prices. Since these fairs are usually organized for the enjoyment of their community members, prices of activities, food and merchandise may be much less than you'd expect.

Food Festivals

Food festivals can center on a celebration of the coming harvest, like Kansas' Wheat Festival (Wellington, 316-326-7466), held in July. This festival, which is close to celebrating its 100th year, has baking contests, arts and crafts exhibits, a parade and carnival rides and games.

Often, food celebrations are based on the love of a local product, like Maine's annual Lobster Festival (Rockland, 207-596-0376) held in July and August. You can find thousands of pounds of Maine lobster at this festival, see exhibits and crafts, and enjoy boat rides and children's events that are great for the whole family.

State Fairs and County Celebrations

Many states, counties and towns have their own fairs, festivals and parades. Usually the events take place at the beginning or end of a season in celebration of a particular time of year.

State and County Fairs and Festivals   State and county fairs are a great way to build an area's revenue. Because the organizers

If you've never been to a county fair, you have to go at least once (especially if you have kids). Low-cost, all-day entertainment is there for you to enjoy. From pie-eating contests and tractor pulls to square dancing and pony rides, you'll find activities for everyone.

want to draw as many people as possible, the fees for state and town cele-brations are usually heavily discounted and there are sometimes days when the admission is free. To find out about upcoming events, check with the county Chamber of Commerce or the state Tourist Information Center. Your local calendar of events generally lists state and county events as well as local town activities.

Parades Parades are another popular type of local function. And one of the best things about parades is that they are free. Entertain your kids by taking them to see the displays, costumes and entertainment at a parade. You might even consider going early to watch marchers set up at the beginning of their parade route.

Craft and Specialty Festivals

Specialty festivals allow local artists to sell their art or local merchants to introduce and sell their goods. The Jonquil Festival held in Arkansas during March (Washington, 870-983-2684), showcases over 100 crafters and antique dealers. The festival is held in Old Washington Historic State Park, so you can look forward to Civil War reenactors, blacksmith demonstrations, trail riders and antique cars, and plenty of entertainment. Also, the jonquils are in bloom so there's beauty abounding.

Another type of specialty festival benefits charity. Nevada's Winter, Wine & All that Jazz, is held in January (Carson City, 775-883-7477), and proceeds go to the Carson advocates for Cancer Victims. At this festival, vineyards display their wares alongside a buffet, and there are a number of wine tastings and live jazz bands. Because these types of festivals are often charitable functions, expect an admission fee.

Music Festivals

Music festivals are a significant part of North American culture. Over 1,000 music festivals take place across the country each year. Many require an admission fee, but most offer low-cost prices for seats or viewing from their lawn areas (usually called general admissions areas or lawn seats). At these events it is the extras like food and souvenirs that are expensive. But if you can resist $6 slices of pizza and $8 beers, and concentrate on enjoying the music, you can have a great time for not much money.

These music festivals offer a lot of music for a little price.

Arcady Music Festival The Arcady Music Festival (Bar Harbor, ME, 207-288-3151, Tourist Information Center 207-288-5103) is a diverse music affair with classical, eclectic and jazz performers, which occurs from the end of July to the beginning of August. Prices range from $15 for each concert to $40 for a winter season pass and $72 for a summer season pass.

BUYER BEWARE

Non-Food Festivals May Have Fancy Food Prices

At the festivals where themes are not food-related, you will usually find that the prices for food and drink are unusually high. This is how many festivals earn money, especially the ones that have free admission.

Consider bringing your own food and drink to craft, theater and music festivals. Unfortunately, many times you won't be allowed to bring food into the event area, so you may have to eat before you go (or have a picnic in the parking lot). If you aren't sure if you can enter the festival with your picnic basket, call the information center ahead of time and ask them what's permitted.

FOR YOUR INFORMATION

Food Festival Resource Website

Abundance Across America (www.foodfestivals.com) is a terrific website for locating food festivals in your area. You can surf through listings of food and food-related events, as well as check out great food event recipes. This site lists the names of the events, days and times they're occurring, and who you can call with questions and for more information.

Also, if you're running a food festival of your own, you can make use of this site to publicize your event and let everyone in your area know it's going on.

Grand Canyon Music Festival The Grand Canyon Music Festival (Grand Canyon, AZ, 800-997-8285, Tourist Information Center 800-842-7293; www.grandcanyonmusicfest.org) presents some of the nation's finest chamber musicians in concert each September (the weekend after Labor Day). A per-car fee of $20 is charged for entrance to the park and is valid for seven days.

The Colorado Mid-winter Bluegrass Festival The Colorado Mid-winter Bluegrass Festival (Denver, 970-482-0863) takes place in February. You'll find programs in addition to bluegrass, like Celtic and folk performers. Specialty events are scattered around this festival, including an underwater banjo contest and arts-and-crafts booths.

A three-day admission pass bought in advance costs $45, and an advance Saturday and Sunday pass costs $38. A pass for Friday costs $15, and a pass for Saturday costs $22 and a pass for Sunday costs $20 in advance.

OK Mozart International Festival The OK Mozart International Festival (Bartlesville, OK, 918-336-9900, Tourist Information Center 918-336-8708) presents world-class artists and has extras like equestrian competitions and craft workshops during June. Ticket prices for evening concerts range from $28 to $50.

Musical Festival Resources

If you have **World Wide Web** access, a great place to research music festivals is **Festival Finder** (www.festivalfinder.com). This website provides a listing of festivals which includes dates, times and a description of what you'll find when you get there.

You can also go to your local bookstore or library and check out *Music Festivals from Bach to Blues* by Tom Clynes (Visible Ink, $17.95). In this book, Mr. Clynes tells readers when, where and how to join in musical feasts. He includes every genre of music, has located even the most remote festivals in the country, and lists events by their location, dates and festival names.

The New Orleans Jazz and Heritage Festival The New Orleans Jazz and Heritage Festival (504-522-4786), which takes place from April to May, is one of the most famous music festivals.

This two-weekend event not only highlights jazz, but also includes traditional Caribbean, R&B and Gospel music.

Tickets cost $15 for advance-purchase general admission, or $20 at the door. If you live in the area, you can purchase advance tickets at the City Super Dome Ticket Office or the Municipal Auditorium Ticket Office. Don't forget that if you order from Ticketmaster you pay an additional $3.50 surcharge per ticket.

The Saratoga Springs Performing Arts Center The Saratoga Springs Performing Arts Center (Saratoga Springs, NY, 518-587-3330; www.spac.org), has an annual summer season full of events, including performances by the New York City Ballet and The Philadelphia Orchestra.

For $100 (in 2000) you can get a full-season lawn pass which provides admission to most of the New York City Ballet performances and all of The Philadelphia Orchestra performances. There are also special rates for matinee and twilight performances, but if you live in the Saratoga area, consider the season pass for the best deal. Regular tickets to see these kinds of performers in their home theaters could easily run you $100 or more per person.

Best Deals on The Performing Arts

If you enjoy the theater and performing arts, you'll be happy to know that there are bargain theater festivals all around the country.

Chautauqua Institution

From the end of June to the end of August, Chautauqua, New York holds the Chautauqua Theater Festival (800-836-2787, 716-357-6250 for tickets; www.ciweb.org).

If you go to the festival, expect many morning, afternoon and evening seminars, recitals and performances of every sort.

This is an extremely popular festival, so reserve your tickets by mid-spring at the latest.

Kentucky Shakespeare Festival

The Kentucky Shakespeare Festival (Louisville, 502-583-8738; www.kyshakes.org) generally runs from the end of June until the beginning of July. There is generally one main-stage production and one intern production per season. Admission is free.

Oregon Shakespeare Festival

The Oregon Shakespeare Festival (Ashland, 541-482-4331) runs in the spring, summer and fall. See Shakespearean plays, receive backstage tours, go to music and dance concerts, and view the exhibit center. Plus, attend free informal talks with company members in the park, and check out low-cost lectures and play readings.

Admission for adults in the summer is around $29 to $42, and slightly less in the spring and fall. If you become a member by providing a $35 or higher donation to the festival, you'll receive a 20% discount on all tickets. Students ages 5 to 17 receive a 20% discount as well. Also, you may want to consider attending a special matinee performance in March, April, May or October, when you can save 50% off regular ticket prices.

Concerts cost $7 for adults, $6 for members, and $5.25 for children 5 to 17. Lectures are $6 for adults, $5 for members, and $4.50 for children 6 to 17. Play readings cost $5 for adults and $3.75 for children 6 to 17. For details, check the Festival web site: www.osfashland.org.

TRY SOMETHING DIFFERENT

Save Money And Watch The Rehearsals

Organizations such as the **New York Philharmonic** have free rehearsals of specific performances throughout the year. All you have to do is show up (and keep quiet). Most performers expect you to stay through the entire rehearsal. Check with the orchestra, ballet or other performance groups in your home state and see what you can see for free.

Sometimes open rehearsals are restricted to contributors, but if you give $50 (which is tax-deductible) and see three or four rehearsals, you're ahead of the game.

BARGAIN FINDER

Plays in the Park

Middlesex County Department of Parks and Recreation (Piscataway, NJ, 732-745-3900) sponsors a summer season (June through August) of theatrical entertainment called **Plays-in-the-Park**. This event takes place at **Roosevelt Park Theater** (Piscataway, NJ, 732-548-2885). Generally there are four plays per season, and each play has about ten performances.

For $3 per person, you can see great classic shows like **My Fair Lady, She Loves Me** and **Tommy**. Children under 12 are admitted for free.

Shows start at 8:30 p.m. Seats cannot be reserved in advance, but there are two box offices located in the park. The box offices open at 5:30 p.m.

Broadway Shows At Bargain Prices

You may be surprised to hear that even the most popular Broadway shows can be seen at bargain prices.

Two organizations in New York City, **TDF** (212-221-0013) and the **Hit Show Club** (212-581-4211), offer ways to pay less for the best shows around.

TDF, through their **TKTS Ticket Booths**, sells tickets for Broadway and Off-Broadway theater shows at 25% to 50% below box office prices. There is a $2.50 service charge per ticket when you purchase your tickets at one of these booths. There are two TKTS ticket booth locations in Manhattan. One is located at Broadway and 47th Street, and the other is located in lower Manhattan at #2 World Trade Center. You can buy tickets on the day of performances only, for evening shows and Wednesday, Saturday and Sunday matinees. You need to pay for the tickets in cash.

With a Hit Show Club coupon, you can save 40% on Friday evening tickets or 2 p.m. Wednesday matinees of hit shows. Sometimes there are other special performance times when the coupons are also valid. You cannot request specific coupons from the Hit Show Club. You must leave your name and address on their machine and coupons will be sent to you in the mail.

Affordable Theater for Children and Adults

Going to the theater does not have to mean spending a fortune. You can find low-cost theater options all over the country. From your local community theater to your neighboring city's theater hall, finding inexpensive ticket prices depends on knowing where to look.

Community Theater

Most areas have a community theater. If you enjoy seeing plays, dance recitals and shows, but don't want to spend a fortune, this may be your best theater bargain. Check with your local community center to find out about plays or shows scheduled throughout the year. Request a calendar of events.

School-run Theater

Another option for inexpensive theater is to look into the performance schedules or calendar of events at your local high school or college. Most schools charge under $10 per ticket.

Many secondary schools and colleges hold plays, shows, dance and music recitals during the entire academic year. You can save money and support the developing talent at your local high school or college.

Religious Organization Performances

Also, many religious organizations sponsor low-cost entertainment and theater performances. So, if you don't have a community theater, check with your local church or synagogue to see if they have performances and to request a calendar of events.

Matinees May Save You Money

Matinees usually cost less than evening theater performances. If you want to save money but still want to enjoy a play or dance performance, consider going to a matinee.

Many theater organizations and performance centers offer discounted rates for matinees. All you have to do is ask.

Membership Discounts

By becoming a member of a theater or performance organization you can sometimes receive a discount of 20% to 50% on all ticket prices.

You can become a member, usually, by donating a certain amount to the organization. Donation amounts depend upon the organization and area, but usually you don't have to spend more than $50 a year.

If you enjoy the theater in your area, ask about its membership options and other ways to save.

Seasonal and Subscriber Packages

If you know you'll want to see at least two performances offered by a particular theater company or auditorium this year, look into buying a seasonal or subscriber package. With a seasonal or subscriber package you can save at least 20% on individual ticket prices. Most companies and performance centers offer packages that have a range of performances and prices. Next time you go to a theater, be sure to get information on its ticket packages.

Children's Theater

Children's theater can be fabulously sophisticated and remarkably inexpensive—and you don't have to be a kid to enjoy it. As with regular theater companies, subscriber packages are available for multiple performances.

Here are a few children's theaters to look into.

Seattle Children's Theater The Seattle Children's Theater (Seattle, WA, 206-441-3322) has a six-play season which runs from September through June.

Individual ticket prices are $21 for adults and $14.50 for seniors, full-time students with ID, and children 12 and under. There are four subscription packages available. The most expensive is a six-play package for approximately $126 per adult or $84 per child.

The Children's Theater Company The Children's Theater Company (Minneapolis, MN, 612-874-0400; www.childrenstheatre.org) has six main-stage productions per season, which run from August through June.

Individual ticket prices are approximately $17 to $26 for adults and $11 to $20 for children 17 and under, college students with ID, and seniors 62 and older.

Subscriber packages are available and cost from $25 to $100. There are two types of packages: one for three plays and one for five. The least expensive package is for three plays at $25 (children's ticket pricing), and the most expensive, $100, represents the cost of five adult-priced tickets.

Puppet shows range from free community-based theater to low-cost professional events. Children are always welcome, no matter what age.

49

Free and Low-Cost Factory Tours

Free or low-cost factory tours can be loads of fun. Factory tours are both educational and entertaining. You can see how a television station is actually run, learn how candles or chocolates are made, or taste the finished product at a local brewery.

Some tours must be booked in advance while others have walk-in hours at specific tour times. It is always best to call the factory before you go to find out if they charge an admission fee or if you need to reserve a space for a tour.

Here are some factories around the country that you may want to consider checking out.

Los Angeles Times (Los Angeles, CA, 213-237-5757)

Two tours are available. One is of the original editorial plant, and the other is of the printing press. Reservations must be made to tour the printing facility. The tours are free. No children under 10 allowed. Call for details and to reserve one week in advance.

Wild Turkey Distillery (Lawrenceburg, KY, 502-839-4544)

Find out how bourbon is made during this free tour of the Wild Turkey Distillery. Tours are available Monday through Friday at 9:00 a.m., 10:30 a.m., 12:30 p.m. and 2:30 p.m.

Hershey's Chocolate World (Hershey, PA, 717-534-4900)

Since 1973, the Hershey plant has been closed to the public, but chocolate lovers can get a free tour of Hershey's Chocolate World simulated factory. And after the tour you can look forward to a free sample.

Hill & Valley Cheese (Cashton, WI, 608-654-5411)

Located in the heart of Wisconsin's Amish community, this factory preserves the tradition of Amish cheese production and you'll learn about Amish culture and traditions. An outlet store is located on the facility where you can buy Amish crafts, candy, maple syrup and even cheese.

Kids under 12 are free

Ben & Jerry's Ice Cream

(Waterbury, VT, 802-244-5641)

You can take tours of the **Ben & Jerry's** factory for $2 per adult. Children under 12 can go for free. This tour includes a history of the factory, a view of the production room, and (of course) a free sample at the end of the tour. This facility is wheelchair-accessible.

Wild Savings at Zoos And Aquariums

Zoos and aquariums are great choices for low-cost entertainment and family fun. If you're an animal lover, it's about time you started taking advantage of the animal world around you.

Saving on Admission

Many zoos offer you the opportunity to become a member, which can let you pay less or nothing for daily admission. The average cost of attending a zoo is approximately $7 to $10 for adults, and $2.50 to $5 for seniors and children under 13. Children under a certain age (often 2) are admitted free of charge. Most of the time, the cost of visiting an aquarium is a little higher.

Animals around America

Here are some zoos and aquariums across the country you may want to consider visiting:

- Birmingham Zoo (205-879-0409). Admission is $5 for adults and $2 for children 2 to 12 and seniors 65 and over. Children under 2 are admitted for free.
- Brandywine Zoo (Wilmington, 302-571-7788). Admission is $3 for adults and $1.50 for children 3 to 11 and seniors 62 and older. Children under 3 are admitted for free.
- Denver Zoological Gardens (303-376-4803). Admission is $6 for adults and $3 for children 4 to 12. For seniors 62 and older the price is $5. Children under 3 are admitted for free.
- The Florida Aquarium (Tampa, 813-273-4020). Admission is $12.95 for adults and persons over 13, $11.95 for seniors 50 and older and $7.95 for children 3 to 12. Children under 2 are admitted for free.
- Henson Robinson Zoo (Springfield, IL, 217-753-6217). Admission is $2.50 for adults, $1.25 for seniors 62 and older, and $1.00 for children 3 to 12. Children under 3 are admitted for free.
- Los Angeles Zoo (323-644-6400). Admission is $8.25 for adults, $3.25 for children 2 to 12, and $5.25 for seniors 65 and older. Children under 2 are admitted for free.
- Miami Metrozoo (305-251-0400). Admission is $8 for adults and seniors, and $4 for children 3 to 12. Children under 3 are admitted for free.
- Monterey Bay Aquarium (831-648-4800). Admission is $15.95 for adults, $7.95 for children 3 to 12, and $12.95 for students 13 to 17 or college ID and seniors 65 and over. Children under 3 are free.
- National Zoological Park (Washington, D.C., 202-673-4821). Admission is free for everyone.
- Phoenix Zoo (602-273-1341). Admission is $8.50 for 13- to 59-year-olds, $7.50 for those 60 and older, and $4.25 for children ages 3 to 12. Children under 2 are admitted for free.
- National Aquarium (Baltimore, 410-576-3800). Admission is $14 for adults, $10.50 for seniors 60 and older, and $7.50 for children 3 to 11. Children under 3 are admitted for free.
- John Ball Zoological Garden (Grand Rapids, 616-336-4301). Admission is $3.50 for adults 14 to 62 years old, $2 for seniors 63 and older and children 5 to 13. Children 4 and under are admitted for free.

- North Carolina Aquarium (Roanoke Island, 252-473-3493). Admission is $4 for adults, $3 for seniors and active military personnel, and $2 for children 6 to 17. Children 5 and under and members of the North Carolina aquarium society are admitted for free.
- Wildlife Safari (Winston, 541-679-6761). Admission is $13 for adults, $11 for seniors 65 and older, and $8 for children 4 to 12. Children under 4 are admitted for free.

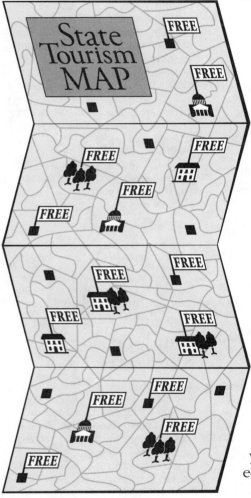

Next time you are going to have out-of-town guests, call ahead of time for a free map from your state's tourism department. Take your friends and relatives to the great, free historic and cultural attractions in your area.

Getting to Know Your Home State's History

If you thought everything had a cost, think again. Many cultural and historical attractions are free for everyone. You can tour your state's capitol, locate a historical figure's burial site, pay homage to a war memorial, or enjoy the beauty of a local botanical or sculpture garden without paying a cent.

How to Find Free City and Town Attractions

If you want to find out about your town's attractions, just locate the local tourism office and ask for a brochure listing of the free things to do in your area. Or if there's a major city right next door to where you live, call the state's tourism office for the same information and make it a day trip.

You can look at the art, history and the foundations of your state (such as the first candy store or shoe repair shop) while making the most of and learning about where you live.

Free Cultural and Historic Sites

If you don't know the history of where you live, touring your own state's cultural and historic sites may be the best education, as well as recreation, bargain you will ever find.

If you are traveling by car, expect to pay a fee for parking. Parking fees vary depending upon the size and population of an area. Here are a few free sites worth visiting:

Illinois
- Chicago Botanic Garden (847-835-5440)

This is a 385-acre living museum with 23 different gardens. Admission is free. Parking costs approximately $7.

Indiana

- State Capitol Tour (Indianapolis, 317-233-5293)

You can tour the Indiana State House for Architectural and Political Education at no cost.

- Indianapolis Museum of Art (Indianapolis, 317-923-1331)

This museum is situated on a 152-acre estate which houses a sculpture garden, botanical gardens, greenhouses and a wild-life refuge.

Kentucky

- State Capitol (Frankfort, 800-960-7200)

You'll find statues of prominent Kentuckians and a dome patterned after Napoleon's tomb in Paris. Free tours are available.

- Governor's Mansion (800-960-7200)

This mansion rests high above the Kentucky River, and was designed after Marie Antoinette's summer villa. Twenty-two governors have lived there. Free tours are available.

Museums Are For Everyone

Museums provide low-cost (or no-cost), high-quality entertainment for everyone. If you haven't been to a museum in a while, you may be surprised to discover how much entertainment you can find, and the wealth of knowledge you can walk away with. You can visit a museum to experience another time and place while building your understanding of how culture and history have evolved.

Most state museums and public historical museums are free. But sometimes you must pay a fee, usually under $10 per person, to enter the museum for the day. Museums that charge fees frequently designate certain times during which you can enter for free (such as Thursdays from 6 p.m. to 9 p.m.).

Other museums may ask you to make a small contribution/donation, of your choice, instead of paying a regulated fee. This means you can pay less than the suggested donation if it's out of your price range—you just have to be tough and shameless.

What You'll Find at Museums

Museums cover every area of interest and focus on every aspect of life. From painting and crafts to methods of transportation and natural history, there are museums built to exhibit and preserve the histories and cultural affairs/records of every state and region of the country.

DID YOU KNOW

Fair-Weather Street Fairs Are Free

You can enjoy art for free at fair-weather street fairs. Many cities set up sidewalk art fairs during the spring and summer. Attending local street fairs is a great way to support your local artists and artisans. This is a great time to buy art at prices that are lower than at galleries or indoor exhibits, because you are dealing directly with the artist. You can find art that ranges from oil paintings and sculptures to woven baskets and jewelry.

But you don't have to buy anything. You can just enjoy the art as you'd do in a museum. Check the entertainment section in your local papers for a listing of outdoor art events in your neighborhood.

National Museums, Galleries and Monuments Are Free

Did you know that all of the national museums, galleries, monuments and most federal buildings in **Washington, D.C.** are open to the public for free? If you live near D.C. or know that you're traveling there soon, don't miss out on the many free recreation bargains you pay for with your tax money.

You can visit the **Air and Space Museum**, the **Natural History Museum**, the **National Zoo** or the **National Gallery**. You can go to the **Lincoln Memorial** or the **Washington Monument**, go on a **Capitol tour** or see the inside of the **FBI**. You can even watch money being made in the interior of the **Bureau of Printing and Engraving**. It's all free. Washington, D.C. may have the best deals on cultural entertainment around.

Although each museum designs its own program determining what extra activities it offers to the public, some special events you may want to look out for are film and video programs (on a wide range of topics), special lectures (gallery talks) and educational workshops. Sometimes museums have musical entertainment in their cafes or dining areas free of charge.

Often, the costs of these extra activities are included in the admissions to the museum, but sometimes they are not. It is important to check with the museum information desk or their brochure to find out what is offered and how much, or how little, it will cost you.

Specialty Museums

Museums are not always about art. For the same low cost as visiting art museums and sometimes for even less, you can visit museums that focus on natural history, watercraft, or a certain type of craft, such as quilting.

Here are some specialty museums that may pique your interest.

Smithsonian Institution's National Air and Space Museum (Washington, DC, 202-357-1400; www.nasm.si.edu/nasm)

The National Air and Space Museum (NASM) maintains the largest collection of historic aircraft and spacecraft in the world. It is also a vital center for research into the history, science, and technology of aviation and space flight. Located on the National Mall in Washington, D.C., the Museum has hundreds of artifacts on display including the original Wright 1903 Flyer, the "Spirit of St. Louis," Apollo 11 command module, and a Lunar rock sample that visitors can touch.

The museum is open from 9:30 a.m. to 5:30 p.m. every day except December 25. General admission is free.

National Bottle Museum (Ballston Spa, NY, 518-885-7589)

This museum highlights the history of our nation's first major

industry, glass-bottle manufacturing. The museum exhibits, researches and preserves historical bottles and related artifacts. You can view exhibits of early bottle-making tools and watch short videos.

There is a suggested donation of $2 per person.

Virginia Quilt Museum (Harrisonburg, VA, 540-433-3818)

The Virginia Quilt Museum is a center for the study of the role of quilts and quilting in the cultural life of peoples from around the world. This museum preserves quilts and related artifacts. It exhibits quilts of all cultures and countries, and frequently has exhibits that highlight a certain country or quilter.

Admission is $4 for adults, $3 for seniors and students, and $2 for children 6 to 12. Children under 6 are admitted for free. Membership is available for this museum.

Museum Memberships

For the same cost as a month or two of cable TV, you can become a member of a museum for a whole year. Museums offer individual and family membership plans that entitle you to free entrance for a year. Many times the membership also guarantees free admission to special museum events, like films or concerts, as well as gallery openings and members-only lectures.

Some membership programs also include monthly members' calendars that inform you of new exhibits and special programs at the museum.

Many museums are quite large, so one trip may not be enough to cover all the rooms and displays the museum has to offer. With a membership, you save yourself from having to pay each time you enter the museum, and you allow yourself the luxury of taking your time to absorb all there is to see. Getting an annual membership to a museum provides you and your family with high-quality entertainment that can truly enrich your life.

DID YOU KNOW

Small-Scale Art Museums

Many smaller art museums call themselves galleries. These galleries may house many types of artwork by many different artists. Usually, the exhibits are by artists who have lifetime accumulations of work and have been recognized in the art world.

Often this type of gallery offers free entertainment on a regular basis.

Exhibits in specialty museums range from odd-ball and unexpected to fascinating, educational or just plain fun.

Free Maps and State Travel Information

Most states have toll-free phone numbers you can call to order free tourism information. The type and amount of information you will receive varies from state to state, but items often include free maps, calendars of events, travel guides and brochures containing information about accommodations, campgrounds, restaurants and seasonal recreational activities.

Ordering a tourism packet from your state will give you great ideas for weekend excursions and daytrips near your home.

Alabama
Bureau of Tourism and Travel
P.O. Box 4927
Montgomery, AL 36103-4309
800-ALABAMA or 334-242-4169

Alaska
Division of Tourism
P.O. Box 110801
Juneau, AK 99811-0801
907-929-2200

Arizona
Office of Tourism
2702 N. 3rd St., Suite 4015
Phoenix, AZ 85004
800-842-8257
www.arizonaguide.com

Arkansas
Department of Parks and Tourism
One Capitol Mall, Dept. 7701
Little Rock, AR 72201
800-NATURAL or 501-682-7777

California
Division of Tourism
P.O. Box 1499
Sacramento, CA 95812-1499
800-TO-CALIF or 916-322-2881

Colorado
Tourism Board
800-265-6723 or 303-296-3384
www.colorado.com

Connecticut
Department of Economic Development, Tourism Division
505 Hudson St.
Hartford, CT 06106
800-CT-BOUND or 860-270-8081

Delaware
Tourism Office
99 Kings Hwy.
Dover, DE 19901
800-441-8846 or 302-739-4271

Florida
Tourist Bureau, Inc.
P.O. Box 1100
Tallahassee, FL 32302
888-735-2872
407-931-1119

Georgia
Department of Industry, Trade & Tourism
P.O. Box 1776
Atlanta, GA 30301-1776
800-847-4842
404-656-3590

Hawaii
Visitors & Convention Bureau
2270 Kala Kaua Ave.
Honolulu, HI 96815
808-586-2423

Idaho
Division of Tourism Development
700 W. State St., Dept. C
Boise, ID 83720
800-635-7820
208-334-2470

Illinois
Bureau of Tourism
100 W. Randolph St., Suite 3-400
Chicago, IL 60611
800-226-6632

Indiana
Department of Commerce/Tourism
One North Capitol, Suite 700
Indianapolis, IN 46204-2288
800-ENJOY-IN

Iowa
Division of Tourism
200 East Grand
Des Moines, IA 50309
800-345-IOWA (tourism guides only)
800-528-5265 (events calendar)
www.state.ia.us

Kansas
Travel & Tourism Division
700 SW Harrison St., Suite 1300
Topeka, KS 66603-3712
800-2KANSAS or 913-296-2009

Kentucky
Department of Travel Development
500 Mero St., 22nd Fl., Dept. DA
Frankfort, KY 40601
800-225-TRIP or 502-564-4930

Louisiana
Office of Tourism
Attn: Inquiry Department
P.O. Box 94291
Baton Rouge, LA 70804-9291
800-33-GUMBO (tourism guides only),
800-261-9144 or 504-342-8119

Maine
Office of Tourism
P.O. Box 2300, 325 B Waters St.
Hallowell, ME 04347-2300Z
800-533-9595 (tourism guides only)
800-932-3419 or 207-623-0363

Maryland
Office of Tourism Development
217 Redwood St., 9th F.
Baltimore, MD 21202
800-MDISFUN

Massachusetts
Office of Travel and Tourism
100 Cambridge St., 13th Fl.
Boston, MA 02202
800-447-6277 or 800-227-6277
617-727-3201

Michigan
Travel Bureau
P.O. Box 30226
Lansing, MI 48909
888-784-7328

Minnesota
Office of Tourism
121 Seventh Place E.
100 Metro Square
St. Paul, MN 55101
800-657-3700 or 651-296-5029

Mississippi
Division of Tourism
P.O. Box 1705
Ocean Springs, MS 39566-1705
800-WARMEST or 228-875-0705

Missouri
Division of Tourism
P.O. Box 1055
Jefferson City, MO 65102
800-877-1234 or 573-751-4133

Montana Travel
1424 Ninth Ave., P.O. Box 200533
Helena, MT 59620-0533
800-VISIT-MT or 406-444-2654

Nebraska
Division of Travel and Tourism
P.O. Box 98913
Lincoln, NE 68509
800-228-4307 or 402-471-3796

Nevada
Commission on Tourism
Capitol Complex
Carson City, NV 89701
800-NEVADA-8 or 702-687-4322

New Hampshire
Office of Travel and Tourism
Development
P.O. Box 1856, Concord, NH 03302
800-386-4664 or 603-271-2666

New Jersey
Division of Travel and Tourism
P.O. Box 820
Trenton, NJ 08625
800-JERSEY-7 or 609-292-2470

New Mexico
Department of Tourism
491 Old Santa Fe Trail
Santa Fe, NM 87503
800-733-6396 (tourism guides only)
800-545-2070 or 505-827-7400

New York State Division of Tourism,
State of Economic Development,
P.O. Box 2603, Albany,
NY 12220-0603
800-CALL-NYS or 518-474-4116

North Carolina
Division of Travel and Tourism
301 N. Wilmington St.
Raleigh, NC 27626-2825
800-VISIT-NC or 919-733-4171

North Dakota
Department of Tourism
604 East Blvd.
Bismarck, ND 58505
800-435-5663 or 701-328-2525

Ohio
Division of Travel and Tourism
P.O. Box 1001
Columbus, OH 43266-0101
800-BUCKEYE or 614-466-8844

Oklahoma Tourism
15 North Robinson, Suite 801
P.O. Box 52002
Oklahoma City, OK 73152
800-652-6552

Oregon Tourism Commission
775 Summer St., N.E.
Salem, OR 97310
800-547-7842
503-986-0013

Pennsylvania
Office of Travel Marketing
Room 404, Forum Bldg.
Harrisburg, PA 17120
800-VISIT-PA or 717-787-5453

Rhode Island
Tourism Division
One W. Exchange St.
Providence, RI 02903
800-556-2484

South Carolina
Division of Tourism
P.O. Box 71
Columbia, SC 29202
800-346-3634 or 803-734-0122

South Dakota
Department of Tourism
711 E. Wells Ave.
Pierre, SD 57501-3369
800-732-5682

Tennessee
Department of Tourist Development
320 Sixth Ave. N., 5th Fl.
Rachel Jackson Bldg.
Nashville, TN 37243
800-462-8366 or 615-741-8299

Texas
Department of Commerce
Tourism Division
P.O. Box 12728
Austin, TX 78711-2728
800-888-8839 or 512-462-9191

Utah
Travel Council
Council Hall/Capitol Hill
Salt Lake City, UT 84114
800-200-1160
800-233-8824 (southwest Utah only)
801-538-1030

Vermont Department of
Tourism & Marketing
6 Baldwin St.
Montpelier, VT 05602
800-VERMONT

Virginia
Division of Tourism
901 East Byrd St.
Richmond, VA 23219
800-VISIT-VA

Washington
State Tourism
Development Division
P.O. Box 42500
Olympia, WA 98504-2500
800-544-1800

West Virginia
Division of Tourism
2101 Washington St. E.
Charleston, WV 25305
800-225-5982 or 304-348-2286

Wisconsin
Department of Tourism
P.O. Box 7606
Madison, WI 53707
800-432-TRIP (out-of-state)
800-372-2737 (in-state)
608-266-2161

Wyoming
Division of Tourism
I-25 at College Dr.
Cheyenne, WY 82002
800-225-5996 or 307-777-7777

Galleries

Art galleries come in two varieties. One is a small art shop that sells moderate to high-cost, quality art. You can find art galleries in most towns or cities. The other type of gallery is a small-scale museum. This type of gallery is often found on college campuses, or as an addition to a larger museum.

Art Gallery Shops

Art gallery browsing is free. Some people may feel that if they enter an art gallery they are expected to buy a piece of art, but this is certainly not the case. Many cities have certain areas with a large number of art galleries. Galleries are located in close proximity to one another to allow customers as well as browsers easy maneuvering from shop to shop.

Some art galleries specialize in displaying and promoting local artists. Others focus on a certain type of art, such as sculpture or painting. Many galleries are responsible for the discovery of famous artists, because the artists first displayed their work in small gallery shops. Most often, because the galleries are the size of a small boutique or restaurant, they only display one artist or a small group of comparable artists at a time.

Even though the salespeople in some galleries may make you feel awkward for not wanting to buy, it's your right to browse for free. Most art gallery customers purchase a piece of art only after they have looked at many types and pieces of art in more than one gallery. You're not expected to be a customer the first time you enter a gallery or experience a certain artist. Besides, who has to know whether you're a buyer or not?

University Galleries

University galleries often feature new artists or student artists. Admission to this type of gallery is usually free.

Universities tend to display students' and professors' work for a portion of the year, and contemporary, established artists during the summer or non-school seasons. Visiting this type of gallery is a great way to support your local college or university and find out about new artists at the same time.

University galleries don't always offer the displays for sale to the public.

Free Wine and Cheese

One of the best things about public gallery openings is the free wine and cheese you're provided with while you browse. Gallery openings are generally held on Thursday or Friday evenings at 6 p.m. or on weekend afternoons. An opening is the celebration of the beginning of a new display at a gallery. Openings are generally held to give buyers a sneak preview of the artist's work. But the free wine and cheese is for everyone who comes.

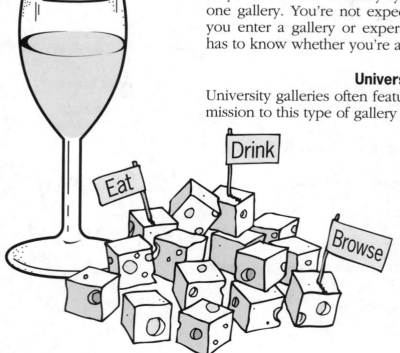

Halls of Fame
Don't Cost a Fortune

Halls of fame can be fun for the whole family, with themes ranging from sports to television. Most charge a fee, but it's usually less than $10.

A hall of fame is like a museum, but it focuses on highlighting famous and established people or topics. Halls of fame are located all around the country and are most commonly dedicated to a certain sport and the heroes of that sport who have become regionally and nationally recognized.

And better yet, some regionally-based halls of fame, such as the Delaware County Athletes Hall of Fame (Woodlyn, PA, 610-586-8074), have free admission.

All about Sporting Museums

If you're a sports buff or you have a sports buff in your family, take advantage of the free or low-cost sports museums in your area.

Almost every sport has a hall of fame, and many teams have halls of fame set up in their home town. You can find halls of fame highlighting professional football, the Rose Bowl, golf legend Jack Nicklaus, and even some that cover many types of sports in one museum. Sporting museums frequently have interactive displays where you can experience the team action or the sport for yourself—a great way to entertain kids.

Find out if one of the following halls of fame is near you.

National Baseball Hall of Fame & Museum (Cooperstown, NY, 607-547-7200; www.baseballhalloffame.org)

This is one of the best-known sports halls in the world. It focuses on the historical development of baseball and its impact on our culture, and honors the outstanding players of the game.

Admission is $9.50 for visitors 13 and older, $4 for children 7 to 12, and free for kids 6 and under.

Legends of the Game Baseball Museum (Arlington, TX, 817-273-5059). The center has interactive exhibits about geography, science, math and history, but all have a baseball spin. Admission for the children's center is $6 for adults, $5 for seniors 62 and older, $5 for students with ID, and $4 for children 6 to 13 years old.

International Tennis Hall of Fame (Newport, RI, 401-849-3990)

This tennis hall of fame is housed in the Newport Casino and is the world's largest tennis museum. You can view videos and see

Sports Halls of Fame

If you want to know if there are any sports halls of fame in your area, call your state tourist information center (check in the blue pages of your phone book) and ask them about your options. You can also contact the **International Association of Sports Museums and Halls of Fame** (337-407-2980) to find out about the sports museums and halls of fame nearest you. If you have World Wide Web access, you can check out their website at www.sportshalls.com.

The National Cowboy Hall of Fame and Western Heritage Center

(Oklahoma City, OK, 405-478-2250) This hall of fame portrays the history of western life and the life of a cowboy. It holds special events and exhibits year-round that focus on everything from Native Americans to chuck-wagons to a chili cook-off.

Admission is $8.50 for adults, $7 for seniors, and $4 for children 6 to 12. Children under 6 are admitted for free.

popular memorabilia from historic champions and the tennis superstars of today.

Admission is $8 for adults, $6 for seniors and those active in the military, and $4 for children under 16. You can also buy a family pass for $20, which is good for 2 adults and all children.

Mississippi Sports Hall of Fame (Jackson, MS, 601-982-8264)

This is a large sports museum. You can learn about the history of sports and all of Mississippi's sports heroes. They have interactive technology where you can play championship golf courses or take kicks against a tough soccer goalie. You can even try your hand at being a sports announcer.

Admission is $5 for adults and $3.50 for seniors and children 6 to 17.

Green Bay Packers Hall of Fame (Green Bay, WI, 920-499-4281)

If you go to this hall of fame you'll find the Packers' history highlighted by art exhibits, video theaters and multimedia shows. You'll get to see the great plays and historic moments of the Packers team and even get to join in the action with interactive football displays.

Admission is $7.50 for visitors 12 and older, $6 for seniors 62 and older, and $5 for children 6 to 11.

The National Soccer Hall of Fame and National Soccer Museum (Oneonta, NY, 607-432-3351)

This museum houses an extensive archive (covering almost 20 years) of memorabilia associated with soccer. 216 members have been elected to this hall of fame for their outstanding contributions to American soccer.

Admission is $7.50 for adults and $4.50 for children under 12.

Halls of Other Kinds of Fame

You may be able to find more halls of fame than you'd ever imagine. Sometimes you'll find museums dedicated to television and broadcasting, like the ones in New York City and Beverly Hills. You can also find museums and halls that highlight other types of characters from our culture's history. Here's one example:

The Clown Hall of Fame (Milwaukee, WI, 414-319-0848)

The Clown Hall of Fame celebrates the world of clowning. You can find out about the history of clowns and even see one of the weekend clown shows.

Admission to the museum without a tour is $2 per person, and children 5 and under are admitted free. If you want a guided group tour, admission rates are $8 per adult, $7 for seniors, and

$5 for children. The admission to the weekend clown shows is $5 for adults and $3 for children and $4 for seniors. Children 3 and under are admitted for free.

Bargains on Books
(And Bookstore Bargains)

Books and bookstores have been reborn as a means for individual and family entertainment. Avid readers, and those who want to make reading one of their new hobbies, may be happy to know that many bookstores now offer more than one way to entertain yourself frugally.

Book Catalogs and Discount Bookstores

If you are going through books faster than you can buy them, or if you have a family with a variety of reading interests, book clubs may be an option to consider. When comparing prices, remember that there is an additional shipping charge for any books sent through the mail.

Daedalus Catalog   The Daedalus Catalog (800-395-2665, www. daedalus-books.com) offers many different categories of books at sale prices. You can find adult and children's fiction, self-help titles, nonfiction and how-to publications. Listed in the catalog is the price of the book, bibliographical information, and a synopsis of the plot or subject matter. Daedalus publishes seasonal catalogs that you can receive once you're on the mailing list.

WordsWorth Books   WordsWorth Books (800-899-2202, www. wordsworthbooks.com) is an independent bookstore located in Harvard Square, Cambridge, MA since 1976. They discount a large number of books—most paperbacks are discounted at 10% off list price and most hardcovers are discounted 15%. *New York Times* bestseller list hardcovers are discounted 30%, and every week they choose a select number of books that are discounted 40%. And for Web customers, WordsWorth runs a weekly contest for a free book. Identify the mystery first or last line of a book correctly and you're entered.

The Strand Bookstore and Catalog   The Strand Bookstore (212-473-1452 for a catalog, 800-366-3664 to order), New York City's largest independent bookstore, has a catalog available for people across the country who want a discount on the books they buy.

The Strand acquires new and used copies of books that cover topics ranging from bestsellers to art books, children's books, travel books, and even books on health and religion. With this 70-plus paged catalog you're sure to find what you're looking for.

INSIDE INFORMATION

Antiquarian Bookstores

Many used bookstores are referred to as antiquarian because they specialize in locating and selling rare, first edition publications. The older and more famous authors, like Charlotte Bronte or Herman Melville, are likely to carry a hefty price. But if you have a favorite contemporary author, or just like the feel and look of an aged book, it is possible to find some real treasures at very reasonable prices in this type of store.

TRY SOMETHING DIFFERENT

Yard Sale Bargain Books

A great way to find low-cost, current best-selling novels is at yard sales. You can find great books at prices as low as 25¢. Many times you'll be able to fill a box for as little as $5. The types of books you can find range from fiction and children's books to cooking books and biographies.

And, if you love old books, you may want to keep your eyes open because you can sometimes find rare books, such as first editions or special illustrated copies. Look carefully through the piles or boxes, since many treasures lay hidden at the bottom.

And, if you are a collector, you can contact their rare books department (212-473-1452, ext. 28).

Also, if you live in New York or will be traveling there soon, don't forget to check out either of the Strand's two bookstore locations at 828 Broadway (at 12th Street) or 95 Fulton Street (212-732-6070).

Used Books are a Great Buy

A great way to get the most for your money when buying books is to shop at used bookstores. Second-hand bookstores exist in almost every city and town across the nation.

For less than half the normal retail cost, you can find almost any book you want in a used bookstore. Like traditional bookstores, second-hand stores sell children's and adult fiction, non-fiction and how-to publications. Sometimes there are small stains or tears in the books, so it is important to flip through the pages and make sure you approve of how the book has been handled before making a purchase.

Many book store chains have lunch-time lectures on a wide range of topics. You might hear a talk by a financial advisor or health care expert. Book store lectures are a great way to learn something new for free. And most of the time you can get an autographed first edition of the author's book at the regular price.

Free Bookstore Events

Bookstores offer events for people of all ages. If you haven't visited a bookstore chain lately, such as Barnes & Noble or Borders books, you're in for a surprise. Not only are many chain stores equipped with cafes where you can browse through a magazine or book while enjoying a cup of coffee, they now hold free events to draw in their local customers (often as many as 25 to 35 events per month).

Many bookstores hold lectures and author signings. You can go to your favorite bookstore on a weekday or weekend evening and hear authors read passages from their newest novels. You may even get a chance to meet the authors in person and ask them to autograph your copy of their book.

Children's Programs Readings from favorite children's storybooks are a common event for both local and national bookstore chains. The readings by storytellers are free. This is a great activity for small children and a great way to find out about and introduce your child to new books. Many times the readings include costume character appearances, craft activities and musical performances. Ask what's available at your local bookstore.

Musical Attractions Some bookstores, such as Borders Books and Music, hold free live musical performances. This is a great way to support local musicians. And you may learn of a performer or new type of music you never knew you liked.

Also, if you're a musician yourself, you may want to check with a bookstore's events coordinator to find out if you can perform at the store. This is a great way to receive local recognition and it costs you nothing. You'll never know unless you ask.

Local Book Nooks At many smaller state chains or one-location bookstores such as Denver's Tattered Cover Book Store (303-322-1965) and Washington D.C.'s Politics and Prose (202-364-1919), you can find free events for adults and families. Some of the smaller bookstores started the trend of attaching a coffee shop to their store and extending their hours, making bookstores a social meeting place and entertainment option.

These local bookstores, like the larger chains, hold readings for children and adults, as well as seminars and musical performances. Ask your favorite local bookstore if it has an events schedule or calendar. Chances are it does.

To stay competitive with national chain stores, some local stores offer frequent shoppers membership cards. With membership to a local store you can take part in special discount days, weeks or months, and sometimes receive a monthly newsletter informing you of upcoming special events and book signings.

INSIDE INFORMATION

Get a Tax Break By Donating Your Old Books

Give your old books to a non-profit organization, such as Goodwill or the Salvation Army, and you can get a tax deduction for your charitable contribution. The charitable deduction you can claim for your donation may be more than you would receive selling your old books at a garage or yard sale.

Books usually sell for 25¢ apiece at a yard sale. When you donate them to a charity, their value is closer to the original retail price, especially if the books are in excellent condition. Get a receipt for your donation.

Read All about It For Less

Discount magazine clubs can save you 20% to 90% off a magazine's cover price for a yearly subscription. If you read magazines frequently, or would like to try a new publication you've never received before, discount magazine clubs may be your most cost-effective choice. Frequently, the clubs provide discounts for new as well as renewal subscriptions.

Buyers should be wary of any magazine club that does not sell magazines at a publisher's authorized price. If you aren't sure, ask before you make an order. Most clubs have a toll-free customer service number.

With some mail order clubs, you receive continuous advertisements as well as renewal notices. Be aware before you subscribe.

Here are a couple of discount magazine clubs you might want to try. To get the best deal, compare prices before you buy from any one company.

Below Wholesale Magazines

Below Wholesale Magazines (BWM), located in Reno, NV (800-800-0062), advertises a possible 70% savings when you subscribe to a magazine through its service. They provide subscriptions to everything from *Smithsonian* magazine to *Martha Stewart Living, Sports Illustrated* or the *Economist*. BWM also offers trade rates (for which you must supply your business card), which are as much as 90% below cover prices. This club offers discounts for both new and renewal subscriptions.

Publisher's Clearinghouse

Publisher's Clearinghouse offers up to 70% savings on magazine subscriptions. You can find magazines you won't find at the newsstand, such as *Sesame Street Magazine* and *Jack and Jill*. You'll also find standards like *McCall's, Runner's World* and *People* magazine. Also, Publisher's Clearinghouse has a policy that it will match any lower, publisher-authorized new subscriber deal. (And there's always the chance that you might win their sweepstakes.)

Browse Before You Buy

Both of these discount music suppliers have websites that you can browse through before you buy. If you can't wait for the catalog and want to see what's available and at what price, you may want to consider checking out their websites:

- **Daedalus**
  (www.daedalus-books.com)

- **Columbia House**
  (www.columbiahouse.com)

Get the Best Music For Less

If you're a music buff, discount music catalogs and clubs can save you lots of money. Most discount music catalogs and clubs offer a 25% to 60% discount on retail prices. You can find a variety of music genres, hard-to-find music collections and limited-edition imports at sale prices. As with other mail-order offers, however, don't forget to add in shipping and handling costs when estimating your final price.

Required Listening

Music catalogs don't require you to purchase a certain amount of music, and offer savings of around 25%.

Most music clubs, on the other hand, require you to purchase a certain number of CDs or cassette tapes in order to join. Sometimes you may only receive a discount on the first five or so items you buy, and are then required to purchase more items at full cost. Be sure that the club offers enough choices that interest you before you invest your time and money.

Daedalus Music Catalog

Daedalus (800-395-2665), also a book catalog, has a discount music selection. It sends out seasonal catalogs with recordings that its editors like and want to recommend. Most of the items are available only on CD. In the catalog you can find classical, opera, vocal, jazz, world music, blues and children's music. Daedalus offers individual selections and collections at approximately 25% off regular retail prices.

Unlike music clubs, you can buy individual pieces without being required to purchase anything else later on.

Columbia House Music Club

Columbia House (812-460-7000) frequently changes its membership offers. It attracts customers with deals like "12 CDs for $1.99" and then requires you to buy more CDs at its "regular prices" to get the amazing offer. These kind of music clubs can be a good deal if they offer a large selection of music you want to buy (most selections are at least a year old).

But don't even think about joining unless you're organized enough to send back the return postcard each month saying you don't want to buy the monthly selection. Otherwise you'll end up with a collection of expensive CDs you never wanted. Also, be sure to cancel your subscription after you fulfill your membership obligations if there are no more selections that appeal to you. If you're trying to build your collection of classic rock, however, you might want to take advantage of the low, low prices that are available on certain selections after you have purchased your required number of full-price CDs.

Columbia House offers a variety of music from rock and country to compilations, singer-songwriters and classic hits. Columbia also offers music in CDs or cassette tapes (sorry, no 8-tracks).

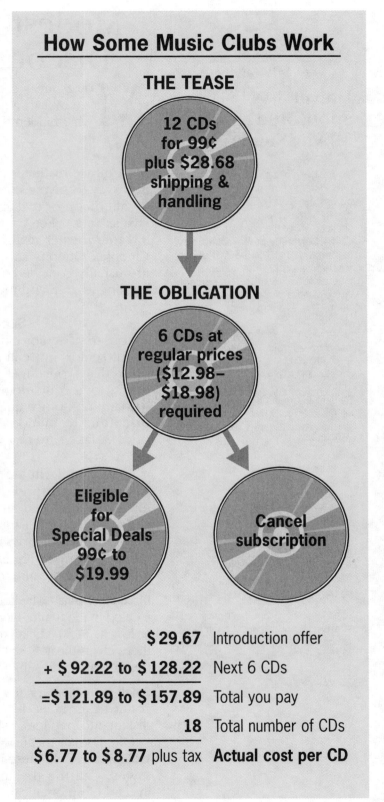

How Some Music Clubs Work

THE TEASE

12 CDs for 99¢ plus $28.68 shipping & handling

THE OBLIGATION

6 CDs at regular prices ($12.98–$18.98) required

Eligible for Special Deals 99¢ to $19.99

Cancel subscription

$29.67	Introduction offer
+ $92.22 to $128.22	Next 6 CDs
=$121.89 to $157.89	Total you pay
18	Total number of CDs
$6.77 to $8.77 plus tax	**Actual cost per CD**

University-Sponsored Movie Nights

Many universities and colleges offer low-cost or no-cost movies to everyone. These not-for-students-only movies are usually currently running theater movies, or movies that have not yet reached the video store.

The University of Massachusetts in Amherst (413-545-3600) offers free movies on Friday nights. The movies are shown in the student union, campus center or other auditorium. The evening begins with a comedic act at 8 p.m. and then the movie begins at 9:30 p.m. The University shows movies that have not yet reached the video store and welcomes non-students to attend.

Call the Dean of Students or the Student Information Center at your neighboring college or university to see what type of movie bargains they may offer.

Discount Days

Some theaters charge lower prices on a certain day of the week, often Monday or Tuesday. Check with individual theaters to see what they offer, and then plan to make that night your weekly movie event.

Modest Movie Prices and Discount Movie Rentals

Movie prices seem to increase daily, but it's still possible to see movies at yesterday's prices. Your first step is to find out what hidden discounts are available at theaters near you.

Bargain Matinees

Most movie matinees are less expensive than evening shows. The best way to save a couple dollars on your movie ticket is to go to an afternoon or twilight show. Matinee shows can be as inexpensive as $4 a ticket.

Large theater chains like Loews Theaters, Sony Theaters and Cineplex Odeons all have bargain ticket times. Bargain matinees are usually considered all shows before 6 p.m. But this varies according to area and theater chain.

Senior and Child Discounts

If you are a senior citizen or have small children, be sure to ask about senior and child discounts. Don't expect a discount to be offered to you. Most theaters sell senior and children's movie tickets for a couple dollars less than the price of an adult ticket.

Many box office attendants shy away from offering age-related discounts to avoid offending anyone (and so you'll pay full price). Make sure that you ask for the appropriate discount.

Discount Theater Chains and Lesser-known Theaters

You may be surprised to find out that there are many discount chain theaters and small-town theaters across the country that show movies for a fraction of the price of regular chain tickets. Frequently the movies shown at these movie houses are no longer playing in regular theaters, or have been on the market for a month or more already.

Discount Chains Theater chains like O'Neil and Rio Entertainment, located in the South, have extraordinarily low ticket prices (sometimes as low as $1.50 a ticket for all shows or shows before 6 p.m.). Some of these chain theaters sell adult tickets for $3 and frequently offer matinee bargains and senior, student and child discounts as well.

Small-town Theaters If you know of a theater that specializes in discount ticket rates, it may be worth your while to travel a small distance to pay less, especially for a large group.

Often small theaters have special rates for their ticket prices as well. Sometimes these theaters are located in small, less populated towns. Call the theaters in advance and compare ticket prices instead of automatically choosing the closest theater.

Great Deals on Your Favorite Hobbies

Hobbies are a great way to provide low-cost, at-home entertainment for yourself and your family. Hobbies include everything from stamp or coin collecting to bird watching, calligraphy writing, antique and craft collecting, or even being a spectator at the racetrack.

And you can get started with some hobbies, such as stamp and coin collecting, without spending a dime.

Stamp Collecting

The best thing about collecting stamps is that it's amazingly affordable. You can buy a stamp that is over 100 years old for as little as 75¢. Also, you can get your hobby on its way for free by simply removing the stamps on the mail you receive.

Stamp collecting is a very personal and individual venture that allows you to collect any type of stamp you want. You can collect stamps from the U.S., Russia or other country. You may even want to focus on collecting stamps of famous people, or a certain time period or style. Or you may just want to collect every stamp that's out there.

Mystic's Guide to Stamp Collecting Get a free beginner's guide to stamp collecting from the *Mystic Stamp Company* (800-433-7811). This guide tells you how to begin collecting stamps, how to identify stamps, how to locate them, how to preserve them and how to tell if a stamp is valuable.

Also ask for Mystic's *Catalog of U.S. Stamps* (800-433-7811), a 112-page, full-color free catalog of United States stamps which is published every year. With over 3,000 stamps, this catalog helps you get your stamp collecting hobby on its way.

Stamps Etc. and ***Introduction to Stamp Collecting*** These two free books on stamp collecting are available at your local post office or the U.S. Postal Service Philatelic Sales Division (202-268-6338) in Washington, D.C.

These guides instruct you in the different types of stamps, such as booklet format or peel-and-stick, and give guidance on how to remove stamps from envelopes, how to organize your collection, and stamp-collecting groups you may want to join.

In the back of the beginner's guide is also a listing of free nationwide museums, libraries and displays that focus on stamps and stamp collecting.

FOR YOUR INFORMATION

Free Hobby Booklets

You can get tons of free publications from hobbyists' organizations and private companies. Also, consider checking out the **Encyclopedia of Associations** in your local library to locate groups for your hobby or interest.

- *Guide to Attracting Birds* (800-446-5489)
- *Guide to Making Bead Jewelry* (800-446-5489)
- *Information on Calligraphy* (800-898-7224)
- *Tips for Better Picture Taking and Picture Taking in Five Minutes* (800-242-2424)
- *Your Introduction to Model Railroading* (800-446-5489)

Once you start stamp collecting, tell your friends, relatives and co-workers. You'll be surprised by the number of free stamps people will start sending you in the mail.

Breakfast at a Racetrack

You can often get a very inexpensive cup of coffee, and sometimes a full breakfast, during the horses' exercise hours at a racetrack. You don't have to pay an admission fee and you may even get a free barn tour. Contact a racing group, such as the **New York Racing Association**, to find out what you can do for free at stables like those at Saratoga.

And you may want to consider staying for the day because general admission at race tracks is usually very inexpensive, especially if you can resist making bets and simply enjoy the thrill of the races instead.

Coin Collecting

Coin collecting is another great hobby. You can collect a variety of coins at a variety of prices. If you collect old pennies, dimes and quarters, you won't have to spend much money at all, but other types of coins can run anywhere from $10 to over $100. (Coin collecting refers to paper as well as metal currency.)

One of the best ways to start coin collecting is to start reading magazines about the subject. There are magazines such as *Coins World* (800-253-4555) and *Coins* (715-445-2214) which can tell you how to start your collection and where to find worthwhile currencies to collect.

Bird Watching

Bird watching is not only a great hobby, it's one of the least expensive recreation options available. It's also flexible, educational and relaxing.

There are no admission fees for bird watching. You can sit outside in your backyard or take a stroll in the park. Either way you just have to pay attention to the birds.

Bird watching associations and community groups have turned bird watching into a global pastime. There are nationwide birding festivals which can provide you with an active birding education. The National Fish and Wildlife Foundation (202-857-0166) organizes a Directory of Birding Festivals, and if you have World Wide Web access you can get birding information from the U.S. Fish and Wildlife Service's website, www.fws.gov.

Birding festivals are a great way to see new birds and habitats while being guided by local birding experts. Many festivals offer guided field trips that take you to local hot spots. Some provide transportation and self-guided tours.

You can also learn about bird watching by reading or subscribing to birding publications like *Birder's World* (800-446-5489.

For bird watching, the most you need to purchase is a pair of binoculars and a guide book.

A Bird Lover's Best Bargain

The National Audubon Society (212-979-3188 or 800-542-2748; www.audubon.org) is birding's best bargain. You can join the National Audubon Society for as little as $20 a year, or $15 if you're a student or senior. And for $30 you can join for two years.

With a membership to the National Audubon Society you'll receive six issues of *Audubon* magazine, membership in your local chapter and many member benefits, including free or low-cost admittance to all National Audubon activities and events. You'll also receive a monthly newsletter and be invited to a once-a-month program for the entire chapter. The monthly programs are also open to the general public free of charge.

The society offers a wide variety of bird-watching field trips every month, which range in cost from $2 for members to $4 for non-members. Some field trips are even free.

Great Deals on Your Favorite Sports

I t's not hard to find good deals on playing (or watching) your favorite sport. If you like tennis, swimming or baseball, here's how to enjoy them for less.

Playing a Sport for Less

Most towns and communities have sporting programs and facilities with very low usage fees. Through the Department of Parks and Recreation, you can play on municipal tennis or golf courts for free or at a very low cost.

Also, you may want to consider checking out the policies at your local high school's or college's swimming facilities. Sometimes you can swim at a local high school or college pool for free or at the discounted student cost.

Golf Courses Town or county golf courses usually charge residents of the area much lower greens fees than non-residents. And residents usually get priority on booking tee times. Many times you can also rent golf equipment so that you can save money on expensive clubs and golf bags. Sometimes there are additional fees for renting a cart or having a caddie carry your bags. Call your state's department of recreation to locate municipal and public courses in your area and ask about pricing.

Playing at a municipal course saves you the money required in joining an expensive golf club.

Tennis Courts Frequently, you can play tennis at a municipal, high school or college campus tennis court for free or at a low cost. You will most likely need to sign up for a court ahead of time. You usually need to have your own tennis racket and balls. Locate the recreation departments of your town or local school, and ask about the policies of playing tennis at their courts. If you play at

---

DID YOU KNOW

The Big Days

If you're a bird lover, there are two **National Audubon Society** events you won't want to miss. One is an annual spring event called **The Big Day**, which is a bird-watching event at the peak of migration. And the second event is **The Christmas Day Bird Count**.

The Christmas Day Bird Count is an annual hemispheric early-winter bird census. National Audubon volunteers join forces to count every individual bird and bird species over the course of one calendar day. Representatives from each counting group meet at the end of the day to compile a master list which is then used by the government as the official bird census.

National Audubon members not only experience the fun and relaxation of birding, but contribute to the welfare of our environment.

BARGAIN FINDER

Discount Mail-Order Golf Supplies

With **Ralph Maltby's GolfWorks** catalog (800-848-8358) you can get golf supplies for less. From clubs to balls to bags, shopping through this catalog may save you enough money to pay the extra caddie fees. Save 50% by purchasing unassembled golf clubs (They're easy to put together). You'll also find informative golf booklets which may help you to improve your game at 15% lower prices than retail.

Spring Games And Pre-Season Training

A great way to save money on sporting events is to watch pre-season training workouts and games. Since training times are not as intense as the regular season, you may even get a chance to meet (or shake hands with) your favorite players. Call the stadium where your favorite team plays and ask where you can get information on practice sessions and pre-season games.

For about half the price of a regular season ticket, you can be a spectator at most spring training baseball camps. Call your favorite team and ask for its between-season schedule. Also ask how and where you can watch the players train, or when you can purchase tickets for pre-season games.

For baseball spring training camps and session information in Florida, you can call the **Florida Sports Foundation** (850-488-8347) to receive a guide of spring training information and contact numbers. Tickets are usually under $15 for box seats and approximately $8 for general admission seats. The highly ranked teams may charge higher fees, even for spring training games.

public courts like these instead of joining a private tennis club, you can save a considerable amount of money.

Recreational Leagues for Children and Adults Many towns and cities have recreational softball, basketball, tennis, football and soccer leagues for children and adults. Some of these leagues charge a higher fee than others, but most of the time you pay less than $50 for a season.

Joining a recreational team is a great way to stay active and meet new people. The teams usually consist of players of all ages. Children's teams are usually separated into age-appropriate groups.

Contact your town or city's recreation department to find out if there are any local recreational sporting leagues.

Sporting Associations that Cater to 50+ Adults

All around the nation, there are a variety of sporting associations and clubs that cater to members 50 and up. You can find associations that sponsor sporting activities and those that keep you informed about sporting events in your local area. If you are interested in getting involved with a particular association but aren't sure how to do it, consider looking in large sporting publications like *Runner's World* or contacting national associations like the United States Field Hockey Association.

Here are some sporting associations that run events and activities for the 50 and up crowd. Consider calling them for more information.

Aerobic and Fitness Association of America (818-905-0040)

Aerobic training instruction is a program associated with this organization that trains senior fitness instructors to conduct and develop exercise programs for the 50+ participant.

International Swimming Hall of Fame (954-462-6536)

The International Swimming Hall of Fame sponsors and promotes swimming activities including diving, water polo and water aerobics to encourage swimming as a physical activity to help older Americans keep fit. They support numerous over-55 swimming competitions and events each year.

National Recreation and Parks Association (703-858-0784)

The National Recreation and Parks Association represents over 4,000 parks and recreation facilities that offer programs in recreation and physical activity. They have a special leisure and aging division catering to the interests of older adults.

North American Senior Circuit Softball (804-231-4254 or 810-791-2632)

This group sponsors a fall tournament for senior softball players. There are 16 regional tournaments where older adults compete in five-year age divisions. The event is endorsed by the American Softball Association.

Road Runner's Club of America (703-836-0558)

The Road Runner's Club is a not-for-profit running club dedicated to promoting long-distance running as both a competitive sport and recreational exercise, and 35% of their members of are over age 50. They have over 600 clubs throughout the U.S., and hold an annual convention.

Bargain Sports Events

Finding a bargain at a sporting event may be just a matter of rooting for the second-best team. If you love sports and don't need to watch top players, there are tons of ways to see an event for less than $20.

Major League Ticket Pricing Professional sports admissions tickets can range from very expensive (and impossible to get) to relatively reasonable ($15 or so). Be warned, however. Less expensive tickets may mean that your seat is far, far away from the playing field.

Most baseball, football and basketball events have an upper tier general admission ticket price of approximately $15. It is almost impossible to see a team like the New York Giants or the Chicago Bulls, however, for less than $40 a ticket.

Minor League Teams You can be a spectator at a minor league game for approximately $14 for the best seats. If you are willing to sit further from the action you can purchase a ticket for around $5 to $7 a game.

Call the local stadiums that hold sporting events and ask for a calendar of events and ticket pricing list. Or call your state's second-tier teams for a schedule of their home games, and watch sports up close at a price you can handle.

College and High School Sporting Events Another alternative to expensive professional sporting events is being a spectator at college or high school games. Some schools offer free admission to their games. Contact a school and ask for an event schedule and pricing policy sheet.

Keep in mind that, like top professional teams, top college teams may be sold out for most games as soon as the season begins. For great bargains in sports it is important to think ahead and make your plans before the start of the season. Also, some schools may give priority ticketing to their students and alumni, so if you know someone who goes (or went) to the school, you may want to consider asking them to get you tickets for a game or a season ticket package.

BARGAIN FINDER

Best Bargains for Senior Skiers

Ski for Free!
The **70-Plus Ski Club** was founded by 90-something avid skier Lloyd Lambert. For a lifetime membership fee of $5, you receive Lambert's newsletter listing over 220 ski resorts that allow skiers ages 70 and up to ski for free.
   More Information: 70-Plus Ski Club, Ballston Lake, NY 12019, 518-399-5458.

Over the Hill, It Keeps Getting Better
The **Over-the-Hill Gang** has more than 6,500 members across the United States, all skiers ages 50 and up. The annual membership fee is $40 per person or $65 per couple ($285 to $485 for a lifetime membership), and members participate in highly discounted group ski trips (both downhill and cross country) to ski resorts around the United States and overseas. Members also receive lodging and transportation discounts when they ski on their own.

   The Gang takes advantage of group, seasonal and age-related discounts to bring you high-quality skiing at the lowest possible prices. Packages include lodging, lift tickets and social activities, plus airfare on overseas trips. And, no doubt, you'll meet some of the country's top mature bargain hunters on your trip.
   More Information: Over the Hill Gang, 3310 Cedar Heights Dr., Colorado Springs, CO 80904, 719-389-0022; www.skiersover50.com.

Dennis Beasley on Finding the Best Recreation Values For 50+ Adults

Dennis Beasley and his wife, Sherrie, are the executive officers who run the Over the Hill Gang, International®, an organization devoted to skiers 50 and up. In addition to their administrative duties, the Beasleys also personally host many of the Gang's group trips to ski resorts all over the world.

What kind of outdoor activities for people over 50 does the Over the Hill Gang facilitate?

The Over the Hill Gang developed as a way for those 50 and up to ski with compatible people their own age. Four years ago, the Over the Hill Gang also began offering non-skiing adventure-type activities such as hiking, biking and white water rafting. It's important for people, as they get older, to know that there is a place for them out there if they want to stay active.

Do companies and resorts give the Over the Hill Gang discounts and special benefits?

Absolutely. Companies recognize that those over 50 are skiing more and can afford to frequent the resorts more often than younger skiers, so an investment in members' benefits is really a reciprocal relationship. Seniors tend to spend more money than young folks by bringing their families and eating at the area's food spots.

Do you have any advice on how to buy low-cost, good-quality skiing equipment?

Ski areas and ski shop chains offer a variety of discounts that can help you cut costs throughout the year. It's a good idea to try out new equipment by renting it from the ski shop or lodge before you decide to buy. The store may then offer you a good deal on the purchasing price, or at least give you a discount for what you've already paid in rental fees. Buying later in the season may also get you a better price.

The problem with renting equipment on a regular basis (instead of buying) is that there's a chance the equipment won't be as easily accessible and dependable as you would like.

Besides the Over the Hill Gang, what would you recommend to adults 50 and up who are looking for good deals on outdoor recreational activities?

There's lots of information out there. Try the Internet, local papers or your library. There are a number of books that focus on adventure activities that are good for seniors. One is Joan Heilman's *Unbelievably Good Deals and Great Adventures that You Absolutely Can't Get Unless You're over 50.*

You could also look into The National Senior Sports Association (703-549-6711) or the American Senior Golfers Association (561-863-4600), which focuses on creating nationwide golf tournaments for its senior members.

What's one secret that people 50 and up should know about finding recreational values?

There are clubs and associations that cater to people your own age: A lot of ski areas are beginning to focus on seniors. They're starting to provide special deals, such as free hot chocolate in the morning, reserved seating for lunch and special senior gathering days.

Elderhostel (617-426-8056) also offers great opportunities for seniors. It's a great program for people who want to continue to learn things and get a chance to experience different places around the world.

Big Bargains in Your Community

Community-sponsored recreation activities and programs are big bargains. If you like to take craft, exercise or dance classes you may want to consider looking into programs at your local church, YMCA/YWCA or YMHA/YWHA (JCC), or municipal community center.

Religious Organizations

Many churches and synagogues sponsor free or low-cost activities such as book fairs, sewing classes or educational programs about religious history. Most of the time, you don't have to be a member of the organization to join in their activities. Call your local religious organizations and ask if they offer events, classes or workshops that are open to the public.

Try the Y

Christian and Jewish Y organizations are located across the country and offer local residents (adults and children) a variety of activity choices at a fraction of the price charged by private recreation facilities. You can join arts-and-crafts, self-help, fitness and educational classes that enhance your life without emptying your wallet.

Exercise Facilities You can join a Y for a quarter of the cost of a private exercise facility. Many Ys are equipped with swimming pools, weight rooms, tracks and exercise rooms. You may also be able to take low-cost stretching and yoga classes, or join in a weekly basketball game for free.

Entertainment Activities At some Y facilities you may be able to see an inexpensive (or free) evening concert or play. Some also provide tours and travel opportunities. Others may have recitals of dance and music, or poetry readings involving the students who take classes at their facility.

Many Ys provide dance, music or art classes for less than a private tutor or local college would charge. But compare prices before you join to get the best deal.

Educational Programs Many Y organizations provide low-cost parenting, reading and writing, self-help, and personal growth classes, or spirituality classes at

BARGAIN FINDER

The Learning Annex, New York City and San Francisco's Entertainment Treasure

The Learning Annex offers inexpensive classes and workshops to residents of the New York City (212-371-0280) and San Francisco areas (415-788-5500). You can take writing and publishing classes, business classes, real estate classes, computer classes, health and spirituality workshops, or a seminar on how to be your own boss.

And after you have participated in two or more Learning Annex events per year, you can become a V.I.P. member for $29.95. Annual V.I.P. membership entitles you to reduced prices on seminars, discount coupons, home delivery of the Learning Annex catalog, and a waiver of the $10 per month registration fee for all classes for one full year.

Taking advantage of the Y for exercise classes is an investment your budget can handle. Your local Y probably offers low-cost yoga, swimming, weight and aerobic classes that will keep you fit and not empty your wallet.

The 92nd Street YMHA May Be NYC's Best Recreation Deal

The 92nd Street YMHA (212-996-1100; www.92ndsty.org) in New York City has comprehensive recreation choices, from lectures and health-and-fitness classes to concerts and art or music classes. You can take parenting classes or join a group for a travel tour. There are literary readings with famous authors and personal growth programs. The 92nd street Y is a Y like no other.

Most of the classes cost less than $20 a session (a bargain in New York) and the exercise program is much less expensive than a private health club. If you join the 92nd Street YMHA's health club you may pay one-third of the cost of a non-member at this club, and some of the exercise classes will be free.

Not all of the programs at this Y require membership. Usually you pay only the fees for the activities you choose, which appeals to tourists.

Membership programs are available for the **May Center for Health and Fitness,** the **Parenting Center**, the **Poetry Center** (writing center), the **Forum Club** (lecture program), and for the **Sixty+ Program**. The Sixty+ program offers bridge, singing, folk dancing, exercise, yoga, meditation, art, writing, drama, health seminars, world event seminars, literature and storytelling activities.

This Y offers something for everyone and is open to all.

a marginal cost. You may be able to learn how to speak a new language or rewrite your resume. Some Ys even offer classes on learning to use a computer.

How to Find a Y Near You There are many Christian and Jewish Y organizations across the country, and the best way to locate a local Y is to look in your yellow pages under YMCA, YMHA or JCC (Jewish Community Center). Many people learn of great Y activities and programs by word of mouth. If you have friends who take great low-priced jewelry or exercise classes, ask them where they go. Chances are they'll say the local Y.

Adult Membership Associations Cut Recreation Costs

Adult membership associations can really cut your recreation costs. If you are a member of AARP, AAA, or a senior community center you may be missing out on discounted recreation deals without even knowing it.

The American Association of Retired Persons (AARP)

The American Association of Retired Persons (AARP, 800-424-3410; www.aarp.org) offers anyone 50 and over the opportunity to receive a variety of membership discounts. For just $8 a year, you can join AARP and receive discounts on airfare, auto rentals, flowers, travel accommodations, and sightseeing tours and facilities.

Also, as an AARP member, you receive a copy of *Modern Maturity* magazine, a publication that focuses on the life, recreation options and welfare of adults over 50. You also receive a monthly AARP bulletin. AARP also offers a discount on America Online (an Internet access company).

Call AARP customer service toll free to become a member (800-424-3410). You can call the regional office of AARP to get a listing of local services, activities, programs and services that AARP provides.

- Northeast region of the U.S. (617-723-7600)
- Southeast region of the U.S. (404-888-0077)
- Midwest region of the U.S. (773-714-9800)
- Southwest region of the U.S. (214-265-4060)
- Western region of the U.S. (206-526-7928)

American Automotive Association (AAA)

The American Automotive Association (AAA; www.aaa.com) is a nationwide organization that offers more than travel and automotive-related services. For approximately $50 a year ($20 for each additional driver), AAA offers member roadside assistance, travel guides, maps and planning tips, and 10% to 30% discounts at restaurants and amusement areas around the country.

If you go to the Hard Rock Cafe and show your AAA membership card, you can receive 10% off your dining bill. You can also get discounts on limousine usage, tire store supplies, tuxedo rentals, eyewear and theater tickets. Many times you can receive discounts for specialty tours (such as at Radio City Music Hall).

Once you join, be sure to ask for a listing of participants so you can take full advantage of the discounts AAA offers.

Senior Community Centers

Many senior community centers issue membership cards that get you discounts at local establishments. Each center is individual, so you must ask about what it provides.

Also, many senior centers offer inexpensive recreational activities and programs. You can take a poetry course, join a nature club or go to a spring dance. Just because you're over a certain age doesn't mean you have to stop learning or having fun.

Look in your local yellow pages under Senior Services for a center near your home.

Take Advantage Of Your Local Library

If you haven't been to your local library in the past few years, you're in for a surprise. Libraries offer some of the highest quality, least expensive entertainment values around.

If you live near a city, be sure to check out the calendar of events for the central library as well as your local branch library, since each may have different offerings. For example, large central libraries are more likely to attract famous authors or film festivals, while local branch libraries are good places to find reading groups and children's after-school activities.

Here are some of the programs offered by many libraries across the country. Take advantage of as many as possible and you'll be getting a good value for your local tax dollars.

BARGAIN FINDER

Empire State Senior Games

The Empire State Senior Games (Syracuse, NY 315-492-9654) is an organized sports and leisure program for anyone age 50 and older. In addition to competitive sporting events, there is a wide variety of organized recreational events, including a **Wellness Fair** and game booths. There are no residency requirements for these games.

You can participate in archery, badminton, basketball, billiards, bowling, bridge, cycling, golf, handball, horseshoes, a race walk, a road-running race, softball, tennis, track and field and much more.

There is a $25 registration fee and a $15 non-competitor fee for those who don't want to compete but want to be a part of the recreational activities and social events. Some minimal additional activity fees are charged for golf, basketball, softball, volleyball and bowling.

Lodging information is provided in the registration brochure.

Virtual Card Catalogs

Over the past ten years, most libraries have put their card catalogs online (on computer). If you don't know anything about computers, it's a good idea to take one of the introductory courses libraries offer to show you how to use their online system. You can still use the card catalog to look up older books, but online systems offer far more information than card catalogs, telling you whether a book is in the library or not, when it's due (if it's checked out), or whether you can order it from another library through interlibrary loan.

Buy Your Local Library's Overstock

You may be able to buy bargain books for yourself and your family at your local library. Ask your local library if they ever sell parts of their collections. Many libraries sell their old copies as they receive new ones in better condition, or when they find that they have too many copies of one book. You may be able to buy books for much less than the cover price. Books sold can range from classic and contemporary literature to children's and non-fiction books.

Movie Nights

Many libraries show movies on a weekly or monthly basis. The films sometimes revolve around a theme, such as foreign directors, children's classics or movies based on famous books.

Stop by the library and ask for a schedule of upcoming films. You might even be invited to recommend your favorite movies or themes for upcoming screenings.

Concerts

Libraries have become popular venues for local musicians. Many libraries hold concert nights when you can enjoy free performances by classical or folk musicians, cabaret singers and local choirs. If you are a musician yourself, you might want to ask the librarian how you can apply to perform at the library.

Home Videos

In addition to books, many libraries now have a wide range of videotapes available for loan. The fee is usually $1 or less for an entire week, far less expensive than the $2 to $4 video stores charge for just one or two nights. Sometimes libraries offer their main collection of videos for free and charge only for new additions.

If you're renting more than one video, be sure to ask when each tape is due, because new releases are sometimes due back before other tapes.

In addition to popular feature films, libraries usually have a wide array of foreign films as well as informational videos on subjects like art history, child-rearing, the natural world and home improvement. This is a great way to introduce your family to movies beyond the New Releases section without spending a lot of money.

Audio

Library audio sections have grown significantly over the past ten years. Most libraries offer a selection of compact discs, cassette tapes and records that you can borrow to listen to at home. Although these may include folk, rock, popular and children's music, collections are usually dominated by classical music.

Even more popular than music are audio recordings of books. Originally intended for people with vision problems, books on tape have become incredibly popular with commuters and travel-

ers who listen to them in the car, train or bus. Most libraries offer a selection of new releases, non-fiction and classical literature on cassette tapes. Collections include both abridged versions, usually on two cassettes, and unabridged versions, which may come in volumes of eight to twenty or more cassettes.

Most people begin listening to the abridged versions and move on to unabridged novels as they become more familiar with the audio format. Listening to a book is a great way to pass the hours of a long car trip, especially if there are children along for the ride. And always check to see who's reading on the recording; you'll be surprised by the number of celebrities who have become involved in this medium.

Internet Access

If you don't have a computer and Internet connection of your own, you may be able to go online and explore the World Wide Web for free at the library. Most libraries have rules about the length of time you can stay on their computers and whether or not you can write and receive e-mail. If you are new to the Internet, your library may offer a beginners' class or worksheet to help you get started.

Often libraries provide handouts with addresses of interesting websites on a variety of topics, such as Government, News, Investing and Just for Fun. If you are not just surfing the Web but looking for specific information, these handouts can be a great help.

Newspapers and Magazines

Buying magazines at the newsstand can cost a fortune, and it's usually not practical to subscribe to enough magazines to cover all of your interests and hobbies. Fortunately, libraries subscribe to a large number of magazines and newspapers, including some of the most popular (*Vogue, National Geographic, Time*) and obscure (*Mother Earth Times, Fortean Times*).

The periodicals section of the library is a great place to browse through recent magazine articles on fashion, news or nature, as well as to check out some of the daily newspapers you don't get delivered to your home.

If you want to take your reading home, you can often check out actual copies of out-of-date magazines for a couple weeks. And, of course, you can look up even older articles on microfiche and microfilm.

DID YOU KNOW

Alumni Association Membership May Give You Entertainment Discounts

If you're a member of an alumni association, you may be able to get discounts on hotels, car rentals, theater and sporting events. For example, being an alumni association member of a state university may get you discounts to the school's football games or the state's symphony orchestra. If you contribute to the alumni association you are usually considered to be a member.

If you're an alumni member, call the alumni department of your school and ask about what discounts you may be missing out on. Or if you're not a member of your school's alumni association, call and ask how you can become one and if there are any member benefits.

FOR YOUR INFORMATION

Libraries Online

You can access the card catalogs (and other resources) of some of the biggest and best libraries directly from your home computer:

- **American Universities**
  (www.clas.ufl.edu/CLAS/
  american-universities.html)
- **Law Library of St. Louis**
  (tlc.library.net./lla)
- **The Library Corporation**
  (www.tlcdelivers.com)
- **Library of Congress**
  (www.loc.gov)
- **The New York Public Library**
  (www.nypl.org)
- **Orion System at UCLA**
  (www.library.ucla.edu)
- **The University of California**
  (www.lib.berkeley.edu)
- **United Kingdom Public Libraries on the Web**
  (dspace.dial.pipex.com/town/
  square/ac940/weblibs.html)

Reading Groups

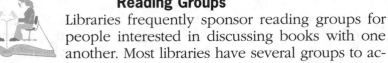

Libraries frequently sponsor reading groups for people interested in discussing books with one another. Most libraries have several groups to accommodate different interests (mysteries, world literature, best-sellers) and schedules (daytime or evening meetings). Groups usually create a reading list and get together once or twice a month to discuss the chosen book for that meeting. Ask about joining an existing group or starting a new one focusing on your particular interest.

English Tutoring

Most libraries sponsor volunteer tutoring programs teaching English reading and writing skills. Local citizens volunteer to work with other adults who want to improve their reading and writing skills, often because they didn't get to finish school or were born in another country. If you have some extra time (many tutors are retired), this is a great way to reach out to your community and meet people from a variety of backgrounds.

Children's Programs

Many libraries put a great deal of effort into their children's activities, sponsoring reading hours, holiday parties, movie nights, after-school activities, volunteer opportunities and educational programs aimed at all age groups. Often parents are requested to be present with their children during many of these activities. Check with the children's room at your library to get a schedule of upcoming events.

Stop by the information desk and check around the exits and borrowing desk to locate pamphlets and posters with details about upcoming events. It's more likely that there will be several pamphlets on different kinds of activities than one comprehensive calendar of events.

If you find certain programs that interest you, get in touch with the person in charge to find out even more about getting involved. And if your library doesn't offer the kind of program you're looking for, ask about finding other branches that might have the program—or starting the program at your own library.

Savvy Shopping Secrets

Here's how to find the best bargains on clothes, shoes, toiletries and more for you and your family by making the most of sales, discount stores, second-hand shopping and shopping on the Internet.

Bargain-Hunting Basics For Clothes Horses

Building a wardrobe of basics and staying away from trendy apparel are good strategies when you want to make the most of the money you spend. If you want quality without high cost, there are ways to find what you're looking for and not let the cost of clothing drain your individual or family budget.

First Things First

Finding bargains begins with knowing how to shop. Think about what you want or need to buy before actually approaching a store. Then make a checklist of the clothes you want to make up your basic wardrobe. If you shop with this list in hand you will be less likely to buy something you don't need or won't wear.

A Year's Worth of Sales

Most stores have clearance sales in January and July, and there are always sales around the holidays. For the best time to find bargains on specific items, find out when they go on sale.

January

is the best time to buy fall and winter outerwear accessories, such as hats, scarves and gloves. Winter boots, shoes and faux furs can have big markdowns during this month.

February

is the best month to find markdowns on resort wear.

March, April, May

are the best months to find sales on spring raincoats, dresses, suits and handbags. You may also find some pre-season sales on swimsuits and footwear in the month of May.

CHECKLIST

Identifying Good Quality

Remember that a low price is not a deal if you aren't buying a well-made item. If your inexpensive shirt falls apart the first time you wash it, for example, you wasted your money. If you want to make sure that the clothes you're buying are well made, follow this easy checklist.

❑ Tug gently on the zippers and seams to make sure they are sewn on completely.

❑ Be sure all seams are flat and even, with no puckering.

❑ Check for even, small stitching.

❑ Look at the shoulders and armholes of jackets to be sure they're wrinkle-free.

❑ Examine zippers to be sure they zip, lie flat and are sewn straight.

❑ Make sure the buttons fit into their button holes easily.

❑ Try on pants and skirts to make sure you can sit comfortably in them, and try on shirts to make sure that your arms and shoulders can move freely.

A little checking when you are shopping can save you the time, money and aggravation caused by not shopping wisely.

When considering an item in a store, ask yourself the following questions:

- Will it go with anything else in my closet?
- Do I have anything too much like it already?
- Will I wear it more than once?
- Will it wear well?
- Will it soil easily?
- Does it need special maintenance or dry-cleaning?
- Is it within my budget?
- Is it in the right price range for the type of item it is?

Where's the Sale?

Mass merchandise stores aren't the only places that have sales. Look for sale merchandise in fine boutiques or high-end department stores. And check every time you shop to be sure you don't leave a store without realizing a sale is in progress. It might be one you wouldn't want to miss.

Most major department stores have permanent sale racks or regular areas where they keep sale merchandise, though the sale rack or section may not be in plain sight. Not surprisingly, a store would rather have you pay full price. If a store does not have a sale section or rack, ask when their next sale will be.

A store does not have to have a store-wide sale to have sale items. You can find clothes on sale all the time, especially if certain items are overstocked. And you may find the greatest sales in small boutiques.

And don't be afraid to ask a high-end store if there are any items on sale. Many stores keep the past year's merchandise on sale for a fraction of the original prices. In fact, savings of 50% to 80% off of original (or sometimes off reduced) prices means that you can wear last season's haute couture for the same price as this season's bargain brands.

June, July	**August, September**	**October, November**	**December**

June, July are the best times to buy summer clothes, especially swimwear and summer dresses. Summer is also a great time to buy jewelry, especially winter stones like emeralds and rubies.

August, September are the months for fall pre-season sales, and in October you can find savings on fall suits.

October, November are the sale months for fall dresses, suits, sweaters, shoes and boots.

December is the month to find sales on winter evening wear, winter sportswear and sometimes great clearance sales on coats.

Finding Bargains on Clothes for the Whole Family

Various times of the year are better than others for buying certain items for your wardrobe. Sales are most prevalent when a new season of clothing is due into the stores. A great sale time is in January, just after the Christmas shopping rush and just before spring apparel arrives. Most department stores and boutiques have pre-season sales in July for fall clothing and March for spring fashions. Also, stores tend to hold theme sales during holidays such as Presidents Day or Mother's Day.

Women's Clothing

Women's clothing goes on sale year-round. During each sale period you can find markdowns of almost 50%.

Dresses December and January are the best sale months for holiday dresses, while February is the month for resort dresses and formal wear. Spring dresses usually go on sale in May, with even further markdowns in June and July. In August you can get big discounts on summer dresses, and October is the sale month for fall designs.

You can get great deals on designer dresses and other women's clothing at off-price stores. Most off-price stores sell not only this year's styles at less than retail cost, but also manufacturers' overstock, close-outs and last year's inventory items for up to 70% below retail prices. Overstock refers to items that the manufacturer or retailer expected to sell well, but didn't, creating surplus inventory.

The off-price chain, Loehmann's, is a great place to find selection and savings, with 68 stores across the country offering name brands at savings of up to 60% off retail prices. Check your yellow pages for a Loehmann's near you.

BUYER BEWARE

Sales Aren't Always a Bargain

Sales are so common that we often forget to check whether or not they are really a bargain.

Sometimes a markdown of 50% off is actually just a reduction in an artificially inflated list price. For example, if an item's original price is 150% higher than it should be, a 50% markdown still makes the item overly expensive and not a good deal. Ignore the promise of a discount and focus on the price you will actually pay.

To determine what a good price is, compare prices at different stores that offer sales on the same kind of merchandise. A store that is having a 20% off sale could have much better deals than one claiming to have a 50% discount. The best way to ensure you're getting a good price is to do your homework by researching prices and proposed markdowns before you buy.

Off-Price Doesn't Mean Off-Quality

When you hear that a store is off-price, don't assume that the merchandise it carries is damaged or made from lesser quality materials than what you can buy at a department store or designer boutique.

In fact, the definition of an off-price store is one that sells only name-brand, nationally known labels. The only difference between the items you buy at an off-price store and those at a fancy boutique is the price. So if you're looking to get the best buy without compromising fashion or style, off-price stores may be one of your best options.

At an off-price store, you can find designer, name-brand items marked 40% to 70% below retail prices. Off-price stores buy their merchandise from the same manufacturers as department and designer stores, and negotiate pricing so that they can then sell the garments to consumers at a discount.

Pre-season shopping is about the only thing you can't do at an off-price store. As part of their contract with manufacturers, off-price stores, such as **Syms** and **Burlington Coat Factory**, don't receive the new designs until the season begins. Designer-label shoppers know that you can buy fall apparel in traditional retail stores as early as June, sometimes even in May. But if you're willing to wait a few weeks, you can find the same styles for less at an off-price store.

Shoes Women's shoes go on sale twice a year, as the new shipments of seasonal shoes arrive. Department stores have pre-season sales in July for fall shoes and in February for spring fashions. At the same time they feature close-outs on shoes from the season that's ending. So you can find bargains on sandals in July and suedes in February.

Lingerie Valentine's Day is at the heart of lingerie sales, which run from mid-January to mid-February and provide up to 30% savings. Christmas and Mother's Day are also big sale times for intimate apparel.

Victoria's Secret (800-888-8200) is probably the most popular lingerie catalog around. You can receive great catalog savings right after Christmas, and the catalog prices are almost 20% lower than Victoria's Secret retail store prices.

Maternity Wear Discount chains, such as T.J. Maxx and Marshalls, usually offer maternity clothes at prices 10% to 40% lower than department stores. Or call Mother's Works (215-625-0151), a 40-store outlet chain that offers styles at prices almost 70% below retail, to find an outlet store near you.

The men's department is also a great place to buy inexpensive maternity wear. Men's large shirts and sweats, which are roomy and comfortable, can cost 10% less than traditional maternity garments. Over-sized clothing is another option that may be cheaper than maternity wear.

Men's Clothing

You can always find men's clothing discounted at department store holiday sales, but here are some other places to look for the really good deals.

Men's Office Attire The real deal on men's clothing is at off-price stores such as T.J. Maxx (800-926-6299), Marshalls (800-627-7425) and Syms (201-902-9600), which receive the most recent styles only eight weeks after the department stores do. You can regularly save 30% to 80% at these stores.

Name-brand and designer outlet stores are also great places to find discounted men's apparel. Sometimes you can find reductions as high as 70%. Call Brooks Brothers (800-444-1613) or J. Crew (800-562-0258) to find outlets near you. Or call Outlet Bound (800-336-8853) for information, brochures and discount vouchers from 170 outlet centers across the country.

A little planning and homework will pay off in big savings on clothing for the whole family.

40% off at off-price store

20% off through catalog

Wholesale price at kids' outlet store

50% off at end-of-season sale

60% off of irregular garment

35% off at June overstock sale

25% off during July pre-season sale

Men's Shoes Find great prices in men's shoes twice a year when wholesalers dump their overstock on retailers. June is the time for spring and summer shoes, and October for fall and winter shoes.

Men's Sportswear The Gap (800-333-7899) and Old Navy (800-333-7899) are great places to go to spend less for men's sportswear. And many men's designers have outlet stores. Sales, again, tend to be timed to take advantage of pre-season supply, end-of-season surplus and holidays.

Children's Clothing

Since children tend to outgrow their clothing quickly, it makes sense to hunt for the best prices you can find. Try these stores for high quality and low prices:

- OshKosh B'Gosh (800-282-4674) has 140 outlet stores that sell top-quality children's clothing at 30% below retail prices.

- Carter's Childrenswear has outlet stores in more than 30 states nationwide. Contact Outlet Bound (888-688-5382) for the Carter's outlet closest to you.

- Hanna Andersson (800-222-0544), a high-quality children's catalog company, has three outlet stores, in Oregon, New Hampshire and Chicago. You can find clothes at 20% off cat- alog prices, and get irregular and off-season clothing at big markdowns.

TRY SOMETHING DIFFERENT

Shop Outlets for Men's Shoes

Are there holes in the soles of your shoes? Almost every major men's shoe brand has an off-price outlet store. Each of them sells first-quality, in-season shoes at almost 40% off, and some sell irregulars at almost 80% off.

Irregulars are slightly damaged shoes that were never sent to the re- tail stores, or were returned for being imperfect. Damages usually consist of a slight stitching mistake, color error or size irregularity, but most often the imperfections are invisible to an un- trained eye. Call to find the nearest location of these outlet stores.

- **Bally** (800-825-5030)
- **Cole-Haan** (800-633-9000)
- **Timberland** (800-445-5545)
- **Florsheim** (800-808-1356)
- **Rockport** (800-762-5767) (factory irregulars only)

Women Pay More

You may or may not be surprised to find out that most women's clothing is more expensive than men's. Many women know the difference exists. They just don't have a solution.

Crossing the Fence

Consider evening the odds by shopping for women's clothes in the men's department. Except for dresses and evening attire, men's clothing departments may have what you need. Running shoes and general athletic wear are great items to look for, as are basics such as sport socks and gloves. Oxford shirts and sweaters may be as much as 20% less expensive, and casual slacks will be cheaper too.

Clothes for All Sizes

Larger-size women can often find a great selection of slacks and sweaters for a small percentage of the cost of clothing in the plus-size stores.

Petite-sized women may want to consider looking in the young men's or boy's department for smaller clothing that costs even less than in the men's department.

Coats and Jackets

The later in the season you shop for coats and jackets, the lower the price will be. After Christmas, discounts on winter coats can be as much as 70% off. And in February and March, you can find great deals on winter sportswear. What's more, you can save an extra 25% on ski jackets if you choose a man-made filling instead of goose or duck down. Man-made fillings will keep you just as warm and are machine washable.

For great savings on coats and jackets, check out Burlington Coat Factory (BCF, 800-444-2628). BCF, an off-price chain, has 230 stores in 41 states and sells brand-name coats, jackets, linens, baby clothes and accessories for one-third less than most department stores.

Athletic Shoes and Apparel

Road Runner Sports (800-662-8896) is one of the largest mail-order companies for running shoes, specialty footwear such as hiking shoes, and brand-name athletic wear such as Reebok and Champion. Road Runner sells post-season styles and current-season overstock items at prices up to 60% off retail.

Also, if you're an outlet shopper, consider checking out the sweats and other athletic clothing at one of the many Champion outlets (800-999-2249) located nationwide.

Swimwear

You'll get the best deals on swimwear at the end of the season, and since bathing suits don't take up much space, you can buy in the fall for the next year. If you look for classic styles, you'll always be in fashion. Buying ahead may not make as much sense if you're shopping for children, however, since it's very difficult to predict the right size ten months in advance.

If you're shopping by mail, Victoria's Secret (800-888-8200) offers some great swimwear options for women. And J. Crew (800-562-0258) sells fashionable and affordable swimwear for men and women. Don't forget to check out their catalogs and the catalogs of other sportswear retailers for big end-of-the-season clearance sales.

One advantage of buying from a catalog is that you can return a suit if it doesn't fit right—something you usually can't do if you buy a bathing suit in a store.

A second advantage is being able to try the bathing suits on at your own leisure. You can order three or four different styles and see which best compliments your figure—in the comfort of your own bedroom, not a group fitting room or tiny cubicle with harsh lighting.

Hot Tips on Accessories

Like most apparel, accessories are priced lowest toward the end of a season. But you can also find pre-season sales where you can save up to 30% off normal retail prices.

Gloves and Scarves

July is the sale time for chiffon scarves and straw hats. December and January are the times for big discounts on winter accessories such as wool scarves, gloves and hats.

Off-price chain stores such as T.J. Maxx, Syms and Marshalls may offer the largest savings on accessories. But small accessory boutiques are also great places to check for deals. Many boutiques have frequent sales and offer a wide variety of classic styles. If you stick with the basics for your wardrobe, you are less likely to waste your money.

Socks and Stockings

For slightly imperfect socks and stockings, One Hanes Place offers a variety of styles, sizes and colors at 50% off department store prices. Call 800-522-1151 for a catalog.

Fortunately for men, socks are not a pricey issue. But if you're looking for a deal, try buying socks at one of the many off-price department stores, like Syms, or at mass market stores like Wal-Mart or Kmart.

You can also buy socks and stockings at warehouse outlets such as Costco, Sam's or BJ's. They carry name brands at reduced prices, though they may feature different brands at different times.

Briefcases, Portfolios and Handbags

The best time to buy briefcases and portfolios is in January and July during the end-of-season clearance sales, when prices are 25% to 50% off. Father's Day and graduation season are also big sale times for briefcases and portfolios, although savings may be slightly less.

Leather products tend to be pricey, but you can find some high-quality, below-retail bags and cases at high-end leather outlet stores such as Coach (800-223-8647) and Bally (800-332-2559). The best prices tend to be on overstock or close-out items, including items in trendy colors.

Consider Man-made Materials The best alternative to buying a high-priced leather bag is to purchase one in canvas or a man-made material. Durable and generally waterproof, this type of bag is usually available for $50 or less.

IT PAYS TO ASK

50% Off of What?

If you see that an item is marked 50% off, always find out whether that means 50% off the original pre-sale price, or 50% off the lowest price on the ticket. Markdowns on sale prices can mean even greater bargains.

BARGAIN FINDER

Free Earrings

Do your ears sting, turn black or become agonizingly painful when you put on your favorite gold earrings? Here is the answer to those sensitive ear woes. Once more you will be able to wear those fashionable earrings you always dreaded to put on because of the allergic reaction they caused. **Simply Whispers** will send you a catalog of their exclusive earrings made of top-quality surgical steel with the look of silver and 24-karat electroplated earrings for gold lovers. But not only that. You will be sent a free pair of earrings to try as well. Best of all, the earrings are guaranteed for life. You have a choice of pierced or clip-on styles. Call them toll-free at 800-445-9088.

Best Bargain Beauty Tips

Beauty tips are a dime a dozen. Some of the best ones recommend using inexpensive items you have around the house, so they're bargains too:

- To erase the effects of a sleepless night, fill your sink with cool water and a few ice cubes. Gently splash your face for two or three minutes. Not only will it wake you up, but it may help you mask the tossing and turning of the night before.

- To treat puffy eyes, experts suggest tea bags. Wet the tea bags (herbal or regular) with hot water. Cool them with cold water, squeeze out excess water and then place the bags on your eyes. Then lie down and relax for a few minutes.

For well-made canvas or nylon totes with shoulder straps, Eddie Bauer (800-645-7467 for store locations, 800-426-8020 to order from the catalog) is a great place to shop. Or check out L.L. Bean (800-341-4341).

How to Buy a Handbag Handbags are usually 20% to 50% off during the end of July and August, and just before Christmas, when retailers are trying to make room for new merchandise. Sometimes, department stores and specialty stores carry a house brand that costs around 20% less than a designer label. Instead of buying a bag with a name you recognize, look on the shelf below for a no-name version or designer copy.

You'll also want to think about what size bag you need before you buy. The fastest way to destroy a purse is to over-stuff it with junk. If you know you carry a lot in your bag, don't buy a cute, petite bag that won't even hold your wallet. Consider buying a backpack or big shoulder bag and save yourself aggravation and money.

Great Ways to Save On Cosmetics And Toiletries

Statistics show that Americans spend more than $16 billion a year on personal beauty supplies. Did you know that instead of spending $15 for a lipstick at your favorite department store, you can spend only $5 at your local drugstore?

The best way to save money on cosmetics is to stop buying designer products. For a quarter of the cost, drugstore cosmetics are much better buys. Revlon and Covergirl use the same basic ingredients in their products as many high-end designers do, but they sell them in plainer packaging at a fraction of the cost.

The best way to save money on cosmetics is to stop buying designer products.

Bargain Beauty Supplies

Sally Beauty Supply (800-275-7255), a chain that has 1,550 stores in 46 states, specializes in low-cost beauty needs, from cotton balls to hair dryers and shampoo. Discount flyers advertising weekly specials are available at the individual retail stores. Sally Beauty Supply will match competitors' prices if they are below their own. But don't look for designer names. The chain sells generic equivalents.

Discounted Name-brand Cosmetics

If you love name-brand cosmetics, or if you want a favorite lip shade that no one else makes, you can find discounts on designer products that are easier on your wallet than department store prices. The Beauty Boutique catalog (440-826-1712) offers fragrances, cosmetics and skin care products from a number of major brands, including Estee Lauder, Elizabeth Arden and Yardley of London, at up to 90% below retail prices.

Between Drugstore and Designer

If you like scented lotions and shampoos, but hate designer prices, consider specialty stores such as Bath & Body Works (800-395-1001) or The Body Shop (800-541-2535), which offer special deals.

Bath & Body Works features daily specials in their stores, such as four items for $20, and publishes an annual, free newsletter that includes discount coupons redeemable in their stores. The Body Shop offers a discount if you return an empty container of the same product when you make a purchase. This can save you 10% or more.

Consider calling both chains for more information, or to order their products by mail.

Gender-blind Savings

Women can easily save 20% on toiletries like deodorant and disposable razors by purchasing products targeted at men. The ingredients are usually the same, although the scents or colors may be different. Compare prices before you buy.

Savings for Everyone with AARP

In addition to discounts on prescription drugs, the respected AARP Pharmacy Service offers over 10,000 drugstore items, including moisturizers and fragrances, at almost 40% less than drugstore prices. Even though the pharmacy exists in conjunction with the American Association of Retired Persons, the service is available to anyone. And AARP members are eligible for additional discounts. You can order a catalog by calling 800-456-2277. Product orders are usually shipped within 48 hours.

Drugstore Chain Labels

Another way to save money on your toiletries and drugstore items is by buying drugstore brands. Many drugstore chains offer their own versions of popular products, such as shampoo or hand lotion, which are often made by the same company that makes the name-brand versions. The advantage of the drugstore brand is that you will pay almost 60% less because the product doesn't have a fancy label.

BARGAIN FINDER

Where to Find Great Beauty Buys

Beauty and fashion magazines, such as *Glamour* (212-880-8800), *Cosmopolitan* (212-649-2000) and *In Style* (212-522-1212), have annual beauty bonus spreads.

Each year, these magazines list their favorite and most requested personal beauty items with information on prices and where you can find them. Look for articles highlighted as "Best Beauty Buys" in the spring months, or call the publication to find out when you can expect its next bargain beauty report. One warning: Not all of the items are inexpensive.

McCall's magazine (212-499-2000), includes a "Steal of the Month" in the Beauty Secrets section of the issue. The feature highlights a single beauty item, including the price and the 800-number you can call to buy the product. If you say you're a *McCall's* reader when you order, and that you read about the product in the magazine, you'll get a discount.

If you don't subscribe to these magazines, you can usually find copies at your local library.

Buying in Bulk

If you have a family, you should consider buying your toiletries in bulk. Most drugstore items cost less, sometimes as little as half the price, when you buy them in the larger sizes.

In many instances, drugstore chains will also have manufacturers' specials. This type of sale promotes name-brand products by offering large discounts, and makes bulk buying a particularly attractive option.

Also, the off-price superstores, like Price Costco (800-774-2678), offer great savings on bulk items such as shampoo and toilet paper. Look in your yellow pages under Off-price Superstores for the location of the store nearest you.

The Sweet Smells Of Saving

When you buy perfumes at a department store fragrance counter you spend up to 50% more than when you buy them at a drugstore or discount chain. The selection may be wider at a department store, but if the discount outlet carries the brand you wear, you can save a lot of money.

When to Use Department Stores

Department store perfume counters come in handy when you want to test a new fragrance. And department stores may be your only option if you want to receive free samples of fragrances. The small sample containers are great when you travel.

Shop Duty-free

You can cut fragrance costs significantly when you shop duty-free at shops in international airports or on some international flights. They tend to sell fragrances at 20% off department store prices, though selection may be limited, especially on the planes. Plan to buy duty-free items on your trip home, so you won't have to carry your purchases for your entire vacation.

Consider a Copy

Like many items that carry designer names, perfumes are cheaper when you purchase knock-offs, or copies, that smells the same as name brands. Essential Products in New York City (212-344-4288) offers duplicate men's and women's colognes at up to 90% off their designer-name prices. If you have a particular scent in mind, call to see if it's available. Chances are, they'll have it.

Buy the Big Size

Buying a larger-sized bottle is another way to save money on fragrances. You'll pay 20% to 40% less per ounce when you buy more ounces of a scent. For example, a 200-milliliter bottle that costs $50 is a better deal than a 100-milliliter bottle of the same scent that costs $35.

For All-around Savings

Perfumania (800-3-FRAGRANCE) sells brand-name manufacturer scents at up to 70% below retail prices. Call for a location near you. And don't forget to check designer outlet stores. In addition to savings on clothing, they offer designer-labeled scents at reduced prices.

Shopping for Shoes

Department stores and discount chains tend to have the lowest prices on shoes. But when you shop for shoes, comfort should be your number one priority.

Shoes made of synthetic materials, such as plastic or rubber, don't let your feet breathe the way leather does. And poorly made shoes will not wear well. They can even permanently damage your feet or posture.

You make out best buying good, medium-priced shoes that are comfortable and classic in appearance (so they won't go out of style for years to come).

Getting the Perfect Fit

Don't damage your feet by wearing a pair of shoes that doesn't fit well. A shoe fits well when your toes lie flat without being squeezed together, your heels fit closely, the sole of your foot rests comfortably on the sole of your shoe and the arch of the shoe is the same as the arch of your foot.

Don't make the mistake of believing that your shoes will stretch to fit if they're not comfortable when you try them on, or that they can be shrunk. If a store doesn't have your size, don't let yourself be persuaded to buy the next bigger or smaller size.

Here are some other useful tips:

- Most people have one foot that is larger than the other, and it's best to buy shoes the size of your larger foot.
- When you go shoe shopping, wear the socks or stockings that you are likely to wear with the new shoes. It's frustrating to find that you can't fit thick, warm socks into your new winter boots.
- Buy your shoes at the end of the day when your feet are a bit larger.
- If you haven't had your feet measured since you were a teen, your next visit to the shoe store is the perfect time. You might find you've been buying the wrong size.
- Finally, be sensible when you buy shoes. Most people have a closet full of shoes, but only one favorite pair they wear all of the time. When you find shoes you live in, buy an extra pair.

INSIDE INFORMATION

Salon Hair for Less

You can have hair that looks like a million without spending a million at the salon.

Model cuts have become a growing industry. Model cuts are haircuts and colors done by hairdressers-in-training. Most fine salons have special training nights for their newly recruited, licensed hairdressers, so they can update their cut and coloring skills. These hairdressers are learning to cut hair the way the salon prefers and are supervised by the top stylists in the salon.

You can get a $15 to $35 cut at a chain salon like **Super Cuts** or **Jean Louis David**. But, by attending a training night at a fine salon, such as **Vidal Sassoon** or **Jacques Dessange**, you can get a great cut at the fraction of the fine-salon price. For example, Vidal Sassoon charges $14 to $18 for a haircut on training nights, and $20 to $35 for color or a permanent. Look in your yellow pages for a Vidal Sassoon salon near you.

If there is a high-end, expensive salon in your area that you have always wanted to try, call to ask if they have training nights when you could sit in as a model. You will probably have to make an appointment for a consultation first, and will need to schedule your cut around when the salon has its training nights.

Making Athletic Shoes Last

To save money and get the most from your athletic shoes, air them out for 24 hours after each use. Pull out the insoles and stuff the shoes with newspapers or paper towels. Place the insoles in a well-ventilated area.

Never leave your athletic shoes in the sun or a hot car, and never toss them into a washing machine. Extreme temperatures will reduce their useful life-span.

Also, don't try to resuscitate worn-out shoes by adding new insoles. Most shoe breakdowns occur in the mid-sole, the wedge of cushioning between the outersole and the upper. Insoles are designed to provide support, not replace the mid-sole.

Fix Them or Toss Them?

If your best shoes are wearing out, find out how much it would cost to repair them before you buy a brand new pair.

Cost to repair shoes		Cost of new shoes
New soles	$25.00	
New heels	10.00	
New shoelaces	2.00	
Total cost	**$37.00**	**$100.00**

Shoes for Seniors

Walking shoes may be the safest shoes for seniors to buy. They provide good support and traction. And shoes that lace up, or tie, rather than slip on, are much safer and provide more support. What's more, shoes that lace can be easily fit for orthotics, braces or swollen feet.

People who aren't steady on their feet should avoid wearing slick leather soles on carpets, polished wood or tiled floors—or in the rain. And finally, shoes like slippers or ballet flats provide little support and can lead to falls and broken bones.

What You Can Repair—And What You Can't

Don't waste money by assuming that your shoes or boots have outlived their useful life. The following checklists will let you know if you can revive a favorite pair or if it's time to dispose of them.

Keep shoes and boots if:

- The problem is a broken zipper. Most shoe repair stores can replace broken zippers. And since boots are a little more costly than the average shoe, fixing them is worth the time and cost of getting them repaired.
- They have a flat, stitched-on sole. Stitched-on soles can be easily repaired by a shoemaker.
  - Your heel breaks. Heels, including stilettos, can be reworked by your neighborhood shoe repair shop.
  - The calf of a high boot has stretched. Some boots can be altered to fit by a repair shop. Sometimes the store where you bought the boots can send them to their own shoemaker or back to the manufacturer for alterations.

Throw them away if:

- The fabric covering the inside of the heel is damaged and cannot be mended. Foot support depends on how securely your heels are held, so don't keep shoes that are too loose.
- There's a hole in the upper, which is the part of the shoe you see. Unlike clothing, it is almost impossible to sew a torn shoe.
- The rubber sole molded to the upper of your shoe breaks. Rubber cannot be easily mended, and once the foundation of a shoe deteriorates, the rest is sure to go.
- There's a stain that cannot be removed. Examples are oil stains from the street, cooking stains and salt stains.

- Your sneakers still smell even after you have washed them. Saving smelly sneakers can lead to worse problems, such as the fungal virus called athletes' foot.

Returning Without Regret

Don't be afraid to return something you've bought if you find that you don't want or need it. Unless a store clearly states that there are no refunds or exchanges on an item, it is your right as a consumer to be able to return the item for a credit or refund.

Basic Return Strategies

Part of shopping smart is having a strategy for returns, especially if you tend to impulse shop.

If you're not familiar with a store's return policy, always ask what it is. If you buy an item that seems like a steal, it's no bargain if you decide you don't like it and you can't return it.

Always try on an item before buying it, so that you don't find out that it was a mistake only after you get home. But sometimes lighting in a store is different than at home, and the color or style of an item may not please you the same way at home as it did in the store's changing room.

Keep Your Receipts

Keep your clothing receipts to ensure that you'll get back what you paid if you decide to return something. It's a good idea to file them together so they're easy to locate.

If you buy an item at full price and it goes on sale before you return it, you'll need to have your receipt to get a full-credit refund. Otherwise, you'll get back only the sale price amount.

Check Out Return Policies

Stores set their own return policies, which tend to vary from place to place. For example, some stores have a "no questions asked, satisfaction guaranteed" approach, while others require evidence of poor quality or damaged goods. Here are some factors to be aware of:

- What the time limit on returns is. It's usually between seven days and six months.
- Whether the store offers a full refund or store credit only. Some stores allow no refunds or exchanges on sale items or clothing that's been worn.

HERE'S HOW

Extend the Life Of Your Shoes

Follow this easy checklist to make your shoes last as long as possible:

- Let your canvas shoes air dry. Drying them in the drier will speed up the aging process.
- Don't wear your leather shoes after the roads have been salted in winter. Salt can eat away at the shoes, as well as bleaching or discoloring them.
- Always waterproof your suede or leather shoes.
- Use a wire-bristle brush to keep your suede or nubuck shoes looking brand new.
- Put rubber soles on the bottom of your leather soles. Rubber will wear much more slowly than leather, especially on hard pavements or city streets.
- Don't wait until your heels have worn down completely to replace them. That will be too late.
- Use shoe trees to keep shoes in their proper shape.
- Keep your shoes in their original shoe box to protect them from dust and scuffing.
- Let your leather shoes dry naturally. Drying them on a heater can burn or destroy the leather.
- Stuff your wet shoes with paper or cloth so that they will retain their shape.

Athletic Shoes May Be Just for Athletics

Experts believe that some athletic shoes may not be safe in all environments. In fact, some feel that wearing the wrong kind of sturdy shoe can actually increase the risk of falling, especially for the elderly.

Bulky rubber-soled shoes, like some high-fashion sneakers, can be hazardous when worn on carpet. The heavy rubber toes can get caught in the pile and make it easy to trip. Similarly, flat or worn-down athletic shoes can be dangerous on wet surfaces because they increase your chances of slipping.

- If the store takes returns only if you have a receipt, or if a receipt is not necessary.

Return policies should be posted at the register or on your receipt, but if you don't see the policy anywhere ask the clerk to write it down for you. Salespeople and policies change frequently. You want to make sure you have proof of what you were told, so that if you do return the item there will be no room for disagreements.

A Higher Authority

If you want to return something and are told it's against the store's policy, don't take no for an answer. Ask to speak with the manager. If you offer a good explanation, most stores will go along with your request.

Take Advantage of Customer Service

If you are having problems dealing with a chain store's return policy, you have the option of calling nationwide customer service. Many companies have toll-free numbers. The company representative may accept a return that the individual store would not.

BUY | RENT

Cost to buy wedding clothes for bride and groom:

$8,000.00

Cost to rent same wedding clothes for bride and groom:

$1,000.00

Best Finds in Wedding Dresses and Formal Wear

Buying formal wear does not have to be a budget-breaking proposition, even though it tends to be the most expensive clothing there is.

Outlet Stores

The best advice for saving money on your fancy clothes is to shop at outlet stores. David's Bridal (800-399-BRIDE) is a 38-store chain that stocks wedding gowns, bridesmaid dresses and other apparel the wedding party may need. Sizes range from 4 to 26, and you can save almost 50% off what you'd pay at a regular retail store.

Bridal Bonanza

If you're in the market for a wedding dress, consider planning a February trip to Boston, Massachusetts. Filene's Basement (617-348-7934) in Boston has an annual blow-out wedding gown sale. The sale lasts for only one day, and runs from 8 a.m. to 7:30 p.m. Filene's suggests calling for the specific sale date.

Merchandise goes fast. The process is basically run and grab. When the store opens on the day of the sale, masses of women run for the racks, some grabbing 20 gowns or more. Popular sizes go fast, but selection and prices are incomparable.

Used Formal Wear

Consider buying second-hand formal wear if you want to save lots of money. But beware: If you're shopping for a special occasion, such as a wedding, you want to make sure that the amount of cleaning and alteration you'll need doesn't cost more than a new dress or suit would.

Renting Clothes

Renting clothes for special events or occasions can be very cost-effective, especially if you need to wear them only once. Renting designer clothes is also an affordable way to wear styles that would normally cost hundreds or even thousands of dollars.

Rental stores specialize in tuxedos, wedding gowns and general evening attire. Check your yellow pages under Bridal Shops or Tuxedo Rental and Sales for stores in your area.

Many rental shops also sell off part of their inventory, which means you can get substantial savings. If you find a rental shop that's having a sale, consider buying a used tuxedo. You'll save almost 80% off the price of a new one.

Alternatives to Retail Shopping

Garage sales, thrift stores, resale stores, flea markets, estate sales and swap meets are inexpensive alternatives to expensive department stores and fancy boutiques. Not only can you find items at give-away prices, but in some cases you can sell your old clothes and increase your shopping budget. When you decide to shop outside of traditional retail stores there are a few tips to remember:

- The earlier you arrive, the better. Smaller crowds mean more clothes to choose from and less hassle.
- Don't be afraid to negotiate price.
- Ask questions. The more you know, the better able you'll be to spot the real bargains.
- Don't haggle over a price too long. If it's a bargain and you really want it, don't battle the seller over pennies. You could lose out.

TRY SOMETHING DIFFERENT

Be Flexible On Fabrics

A pure silk evening dress may be the most luxurious option, but you can save hundreds by choosing a dress made out of a less expensive fabric. Consider polyester shantung, a fabric that looks and feels like silk, but costs far less. Polyester is also more durable, more stain-resistant and less likely to snag.

IT PAYS TO ASK

Wedding Dress Prices Are Negotiable

Competition among bridal salons is high. If you find a gown you like in a bridal magazine, write down the model number. Then call several bridal shops and ask for a price quote. Be sure to let each shop know the lowest bid you've been quoted.

Challenging each store to beat the lowest price can save you as much as 20% off the regular retail price of your dress.

Consignment and Resale Stores

Consignment and resale stores sell expensive clothes at rock-bottom prices. Although the terms resale and consignment are often used interchangeably, there are a few differences between them.

Consignment Selling

Consignment shops accept merchandise from individual owners to be resold. They then pay a percentage of the selling price, often 40% to 60%, to the owner after the item has been sold. Haggling over price is not as easy as it is at a garage sale because there is more than one party involved in the pricing.

Consignment stores may be a great way of reselling your own unwanted clothing as well as buying what other people want to sell. Ask the shop owner or manager what the buying procedures are. And, be prepared to wait awhile for your items to sell.

You may want to research which stores have a fast turnover. Stopping by as a buying customer a few times may help you identify a store that moves its merchandise quickly. If you don't think the salesperson you talk to seems professional or knowledgeable, ask to speak with someone else. If you are not confident that you can trust the store or that your clothes will sell, continue your search.

If you do decide to use a consignment shop, it is important to keep track of what you give and to whom. Keep your receipts and check in regularly with the stores to see if your things have sold.

Resale Buying and Selling

Resale stores buy items outright from previous owners. Resale stores also specialize in selling clothing from medium-priced department stores or very high-end department stores and boutiques. Most of the clothing you will find is secondhand, but you can also find brand new merchandise with the original tags still attached.

Many resale stores also carry manufacturer samples and last season's clothing from retail stores. Shopping resale for children's clothing can really be a bargain, since kids tend to outgrow their clothes before they're worn out.

While prices at resale stores are less expensive than at retail stores, don't expect thrift-store savings. Since resale stores pay for the clothes they sell, they have to charge enough to make a profit. But this also means they tend to have a more upscale selection.

Consignment and Resale Shopping Tips

When shopping in consignment or resale stores, it is important to keep these guidelines in mind:

- Look for well-organized stores. They tend to have better merchandise.
- Check whether the store launders or cleans the clothes before displaying them. Most stores do, but don't be afraid to ask.
- Pay special attention to cuffs, collars, pockets, armpits and crotches for stains and wear and tear.
- Make sure the garment has all necessary parts, such as zippers and buttons.
- Check for moth holes if the clothes are made of wool.
- Find conveniently located stores so that you can stop by frequently, since new merchandise is always coming in.

When you find a store that carries brands you prefer, ask the owner or manager to call you when new items of interest arrive. That way, you'll get first crack at the things you're interested in.

Thrift Stores

Thrift stores sell used clothing, housewares and other items at extremely low prices. They are usually run by not-for-profit organizations such as The Salvation Army, Goodwill or local charities and hospitals, and can charge low prices because they get their merchandise for free. Usually it is donated by people who no longer want the items. Any profits go to the organization that operates the shop.

Two Styles of Pricing

There are usually two types of pricing used in thrift stores. One is individual pricing of each item, and the other is straight pricing. An example of straight pricing is when all jackets cost $3. Thrift store prices usually change frequently, so if something looks too expensive one week, go back the next week. Chances are it will cost less.

Most thrift shops are located in the less fashionable parts of town or in suburban strip malls. Look under Thrift Shops in your local yellow pages to find a thrift store close to you.

Thrifting like an Expert

Don't mix thrift shopping with regular shopping. Regular stores will look over-priced, and thrift stores may look dirty and faded. Thrift shopping should be an event in and of itself.

A good day's thrift shopping could center around five or six stores. Sunday is usually a bad day to go thrift shopping because most shops are closed. Saturday is an ideal day because most of the merchandise that has come in during the week is on the floor.

When you enter a thrift store, begin by scanning the racks. Walk up each aisle and look for colors or styles that interest you. Don't be afraid to run your hands along the clothing. If the clothing feels good to your fingers, it will probably be a comfortable item to wear. If you find something you like, check for obvious defects. If you see any, decide if they are things you could fix for very little cost. If you don't sew, keep looking. Most thrift shops have lots of clothes to choose from.

Many thrift stores lack dressing rooms, so be careful about buying items you can't try on. There is a no-return policy at most thrift stores, so if an item doesn't seem like it will fit, don't buy it.

Thrift Tips

- Don't buy things you don't like just because they are cheap. A bargain is only a bargain if you'll use it
- Bring friends who look more than they buy. They may help you restrain yourself and give you an objective opinion.

BARGAIN FINDER

A Thrift Store Near You

The **National Association of Resale and Thrift Stores (NARTS)** provides consumers with lists of locally affiliated resale and thrift stores nationwide. You can request a listing of shops within your zip code by sending $3 (check or money order) and a self-addressed stamped envelope to NARTS, P.O. Box 80707, St. Clair Shores, MI 48080. Or check out their website at www.narts.org.

FOR YOUR INFORMATION

Books on Second-Hand Shopping

For more insight on the best possible bargains, go straight to the experts:

- *FLEA: The Definitive Guide to Hunting, Gathering and Flaunting Superior Vintage Wares* by Sheila Zubrod (HarperCollins, $14).
- *The Rummager's Handbook: Finding, Buying, Cleaning, Fixing, Using and Selling Secondhand Treasures* by R. S. McClurg (Storey Books, $12.95).
- *Thrift Score: The Stuff, the Method, the Madness* by Al Hoff (HarperPerennial Library, $12.95).

Quality Is Timeless

A well-made piece of clothing can last forever. Your goal in secondhand shopping is to buy quality at a low price. But never buy just for the sake of buying. And don't fret if you find nothing you want on a particular day.

Classic, timeless garments like a navy suit, a pair of **Levis** or a **Gucci** bag are the best buys. They always look stylish, they're made with good materials, and they're well-designed and constructed.

Natural and synthetic fabrics both wear well physically, but natural ones may look better longer than synthetic ones. Trust your instincts when you're bargain hunting. But remember, the more you look, the more you'll learn.

You can follow these tips to help you decide what to buy:

- Look for manufacturers and logos that you recognize.
- Watch prices and don't forget to compare.
- Inspect all items for damage.
- Determine cleaning and repair costs.
- Balance what you want with what you need.

- If you know seasoned shoppers, ask if you can tag along with them. They will have researched the best places for bargains and can teach you the tricks of the trade.
- Look for Thrift Shop, Consignment Store, Resale Store and Flea Market listings in your yellow pages under their respective titles. Consignment Stores are sometimes listed under Thrift Stores and vice versa.
- When you travel, look for thrift shops in the area you're visiting. The Salvation Army, Goodwill, churches and not-for-profit organizations have stores in many towns and cities.
- Finally, when you're considering an item, it is best to carry it around with you. If you don't hold on to to it, chances are it won't be there when you've made your decision.

An Eye for Quality

One advantage of buying used clothing is that if an item has been worn, yanked, washed and dried several times and it still looks good, it will probably keep looking good for a long time to come. Remember, though, that thrift shop clothes aren't always a perfect fit, since the clothes have already had a life before you. The real question is whether or not it's a fit that you can handle.

And finally, always wash the clothes you buy from a thrift store before wearing them. A lot of stores clean the merchandise before they put it on the floor, but it is safest to wash it again anyway.

Flea Markets and Swap Meets

You can find bargain-priced new and used items at flea markets or swap meets. Flea markets and swap meets are usually made up of groups of vendors in individual booths outdoors or under one roof.

A flea market is like a big yard sale where you can find clothes, housewares, jewelry, entertainment items and toys at low cost. Generally it's a mixture of junk, antiques and new merchandise.

Since you are usually dealing with the owner, haggling over the price of an item is part of the experience. If there is an item that you want but you feel it is too expensive, don't be afraid to ask the vendor if you can have the item at a lower cost. It is best to offer an alternate price to keep the dialog going. You don't want to let the vendor simply name another price.

Most flea markets are open every weekend, but the vendors can change weekly. Look in your local paper's classified section for flea market listings or ask your friends if they know of any good markets to attend. You may be surprised at how many people seek out shopping deals.

Flea Market Buying Tips

- Come prepared with a list of items you want to buy.
- Don't assume everything is a bargain.
- Be wary of fakes when shopping for brand-name items: Some imitations are hard to spot.
- Know when to bargain. Don't assume that the first price you see or hear is final, even if it's written on the price tag. Always offer a lower price because vendors are interested in moving their goods.
- Carry cash. Many vendors offer better deals for cash payments.
- Beware of pickpockets.
- Dress for comfort and convenience. Wear comfortable shoes and keep your hands free.

Some flea markets contain hundreds of stalls and are located in permanent (or semi-permanent) locations. Flea market stalls sell anything and everything you can think of—but they're not always a bargain, so know your prices.

FLEA MARKET
- Antiques
- Art
- Bicycles
- Books
- Chatzkas
- Clocks
- Clothing
- Flowers
- Fur Coats
- Hats
- Housewares
- Jewelry
- Junk
- Linens
- New Items
- Plants
- Records
- Sports Equipment
- Sporting Goods
- Tools
- Toys
- Used Items

EVERYTHING! EVERY WKND

Don't Get Carried Away

Don't be swept away by the flea market experience. If an item you're considering doesn't seem like a bargain, chances are that it's not. Some merchants choose to sell in flea markets because they know consumers think they'll get a deal. Junk is junk no matter what the price, and just because merchants have wholesale quantity doesn't mean they're selling at wholesale prices. The only true bargain is a smart buy.

Estate Sales

Estate sales are sales to liquidate a lifetime's accumulated possessions. Usually they are held at the home of the original owner, often after the owner's death.

The neighborhood where the sale is held may tell you a lot about the type of merchandise you'll find. For example, an estate sale in a wealthy neighborhood may have expensive, high-quality items in good condition. Sales in older neighborhoods may have more antiques, whereas those in modern neighborhoods may have more contemporary furniture and other merchandise.

BARGAIN FINDER

Markets Where You Can Make Out

It's not always easy to know where to find the best flea markets and swap meets. Expert shoppers have recommended the following.

- Swap Shop of Ft. Lauderdale, FL, 954-791-SWAP.
- The Flea Market at the Nashville Fairgrounds, TN, 615-862-5016.
- Rummage-O-Rama, Milwaukee, WI, 262-521-2111.

Take Your Time And Save

A good way to avoid overspending when you catalog shop is to mark the items that you like, and then put the catalog down for a couple of days. If you still like the items and feel they're a good buy when you look at them again, place your order. But if you change your mind, you have avoided buying something you may not really need or want.

The same holds true for store buying. Put an item on hold, and if you still like it when you go back to the store, you know you won't be wasting your money.

Auction houses sometimes take control of an estate sale and sell all of the merchandise through their auction house. At the auction houses you may have to purchase an entire lot (or collection) of merchandise to get the one item that you want. But if the price is right, as it often is, it may be worth your while to buy five items for the one or two you want.

Check your local or city paper regularly for nearby estate sales, and check into getting your name on a local auction house mailing list. Some houses charge minimal fees to send you their catalog or newsletter.

Shopping by Mail

Shopping by mail usually saves you time and can also save you money if you do some research before you buy. Always compare the mail-order price with the retail price of each item you're considering.

If the price is right, verify shipping and handling costs. They can make buying by mail more expensive than you think, especially if you order just one or two items at a time, or if the company uses an expensive delivery service and doesn't offer a more economical alternative. One strategy is to compare the shipping and handling costs printed in several different catalogs to figure out what's typical.

Also check return policies. You want to be able to get a full refund on any item you send back, including the cost of return shipping. Some, but not all, companies arrange to have their delivery service pick up your returns or provide postage-paid return receipts. Ask before you order.

Most of the information you need will be printed in the catalog, and most mail-order companies have customer service departments and toll-free numbers. Don't hesitate to call and ask questions.

Extra Savings

If you're looking for extra savings, check the pages near the order form, usually in the middle of the catalog. Companies frequently list their clearance items there. If no clearance or sale items are listed, ask the sales representative

THE MAILORDER CO.
TO: Tim Saver
Anyplace, USA

you order from if there are any discounted items available. But be sure to check sale prices against the regular prices in the catalog so you'll know whether or not you're really getting a good deal.

Many catalog companies publish clearance catalogs as well as their regular catalogs. If you're on their mailing list, you can order the items you want as they go on sale.

Tips for Better Mail-order Shopping

- Comparison shop. Compare similar items in different catalogs and with items in retail stores to make sure that you get the best price available.
- Read product descriptions carefully. Don't rely on photographs which may falsely represent the items. But remember that sometimes text can be as deceptive as pictures.
- Find out about the company's return policy before you order.
- Keep a photocopy of every order form you mail and date it for easy reference if there is a problem.
- Never send cash with an order.
- If you order by phone, write down what you ordered, the total cost of the order and the reference number (which the phone representative should give you).

Open-Air Bargain Shopping: Garage, Yard And Lawn Sales

You can find listings of garage, yard and lawn sales in the classified section of your local newspaper or shopping guide. It also pays to check under headings such as Auctions and Sales or For Sale by Owner. Driving around town is another way to find garage sales, since the people organizing the sale usually post signs advertising it.

Most garage sales are seasonal because they are held outside. Early spring to summer is a great time to start garage-sale hunting, and you should find good shopping until the weather turns cold, usually in mid- to late fall.

Garage-sale Strategies

Here are a few basic guidelines to help you get the best deals at garage sales:

- Get a detailed map of the area where sales are scheduled and plan your route to save time.

BARGAIN FINDER

Catalog of Catalogs

Say good-bye to in-store shopping. *The Catalog of Catalogs: The Complete Mail-Order Directory (5th edition)* by Edward L. Palder (Woodbine House, $24.95) offers access to over 10,000 mail-order companies in approximately 800 different categories catering to every interest. Chances are, your favorite brand or store has a catalog which will give you access to special sales and extra savings.

INSIDE INFORMATION

What You Should Expect to Pay

If you're new to garage-sale shopping, you probably have no idea what items usually go for. Is $1 for a paperback book a good deal or a ripoff?

Here are some of the most common garage-sale items and their typical prices:

Cassette tapes	50¢ to $2
Coats	$10 to $30
Compact discs	50¢ to $4
Designer clothes	under $100
Furniture	$5 to $100
Glassware	10¢ to $1/piece
Hardcover books	50¢ and up
Paperback books	5 for $1
Rugs/Carpets	$15 to $80
Silk blouses	$4 to $15
T-shirts	25¢
Toys	under $10
Trousers	$2 to $10

Garage sales in different neighborhoods tend to offer different kinds of items.

- Arrive early so that you have your pick of the best items before too many other people arrive. If you're late, you may get lower prices, but the choice of merchandise will be more limited.
- If you want to haggle, bring small bills. If you think the price is fair, don't bother to haggle. You could lose out on the item altogether if you try to make a great bargain better.
- Don't forget to check your merchandise for faults. Plug in all appliances if there's an outlet available. A bargain is only as good as the quality of the item.

Choosing Your Locations
- You'll usually find better quality merchandise in affluent areas, though you may have to spend more money to get the items you really want.
- Prices are generally cheaper at church or other not-for-profit sales than at people's houses, but donated items may not be of high quality.
- Group sales may offer a wider selection of merchandise. Some towns have official days for garage sales, so you can get your pick of bargains without having to make several trips to the same neighborhood.

Holding Your Own Garage Sale

Garage and yard sales can be great ways to clear out your family's old clothes, and make some cash for new ones. Holding a sale can be a very trying business, though, so make sure that you want to invest the time and energy required to make the sale worthwhile.

Where to Hold It
The first rule for a successful sale is to hold it in a populated area where you know other yard sales have flourished. If your best friend's neighborhood is a better area for a sale, ask her about doing a combined sale. More stuff could mean more customers.

DID YOU KNOW

Best Buys
You never know what you might find at a garage sale, but some items are consistently available at great prices:

Dishes and glassware: You'll find unbeatable prices on mix-and-match kitchenware for college students or a first apartment.

Records: Not available in most retail music stores, multitudes of albums show up at garage sales at low, low prices. These sales are havens for people who collect music from the 30s, 40s, 50s and 60s.

Costume jewelry: Whether you want to match a new outfit, fill a child's dress-up box or add to a serious collection, you'll probably find what you're looking for. Signed pieces usually go for higher prices, but you can often find a real steal.

Sports Equipment: Look for tennis racquets, golf clubs, bowling balls and other items at about one-third of the retail price.

You should only need an advertisement for your sale if you live off the beaten path.

When to Hold It

The best time to hold your sale is on one of the first sunny spring weekends. Do not hold a yard sale on a holiday weekend when most people are away. It is possible that your town may require a license. Check with your local town hall before you start the sale procedures. You don't want to do all of the work and then find out you can't hold the sale.

How to Advertise

Post signs advertising the location of the sale. Place them at all of the intersections near your home, out as far as the main road.

Stencil or write the words Yard Sale three to four inches high on a piece of cardboard and write the date and location in the middle of the sign. Put an arrow at the bottom showing which direction to turn.

You can use spray paint to make the job fast, but you will have better control with a thick, waterproof marker.

On the day of the sale, make the merchandise as attractive as possible: Large items tend to stop cars, so put those near the road. Hang up as much clothing as possible, and lay out clothing for children according to size. Group similar items together.

What to Charge

Remember, your primary purpose is to get rid of your old stuff, so price everything so it will go.

Consider pricing everything at one third of the price it would cost new. If someone wants an item but you aren't ready to lower the price, ask them to come back later. Save your negotiating for the end of the day, when you really want to unload any leftovers.

You should only hold things if a customer pays you first. If you hold an item that isn't paid for, and the customer doesn't return, you will lose profit from someone else.

Always guard the money you make at a sale. Keep it in your pocket or in a lockable box.

When It's All Over

Don't forget to take down all yard sale signs immediately. There are always stragglers who will ignore the date and time of a sale. If you still have items left, put them back in a box for next year.

Little Helpers

Yard sales can be a great way to teach your children or grandchildren about consumer buying and selling. If you have your kids work at the sale, let them keep the money they make.

IT PAYS TO ASK

Haggling Guidelines

Haggling is an added perk of shopping at flea markets and garage sales. Half the fun of buying secondhand items is ensuring that you get the best bargain possible. Not everyone is comfortable with, or sure of, how to haggle. Here are some hints to help you get the best deal you can:

- Decide the maximum price you are willing to pay for an item before you start haggling.

- When you make your first offer, don't make it your maximum price. There's a chance that you may get the item on your first offer, but if you don't, you want to leave yourself room for bargaining.

- Watch for a seller's signals. Sometimes while you are browsing a seller may tell you that the prices are negotiable. Take advantage of the opportunity to haggle.

- Be nice. No one is going to want to compromise on a price to an unappreciative, obnoxious customer. Good manners may help you get a lower price.

- You may have stronger haggling power at the end of the day. This is when sellers are eager to get rid of their stock.

Marcy Syms on Shopping for Quality—And Getting the Best Possible Value

Marcy Syms is the CEO of **Syms Clothing Store**, a nationwide chain of off-price stores that offer name-brand clothing and accessories at below retail prices.

How should consumers go about saving money on high-quality apparel?

I think most of it has to do with personal discipline.

Have a budget in mind. Look at your existing wardrobe and have an understanding of what your lifestyle needs are. Consider how you want to look. Sometimes it's best to write down what your wardrobe needs are. If you don't, you'll probably end up spending more money than you think you're spending.

Another thing you can do is carry swatches. If you want to buy something to match an outfit you already have, take a little swatch of the fabric with you so you don't have to spend your time returning something that doesn't work.

What's the biggest mistake people make when buying discount clothing?

Impulse buying. Planning ahead is very important when you want to save money.

With retail markups as high as they are, how can consumers tell if a sale is really saving them money?

Know whether a store is reputable. Have you noticed a trend of the store marking up its prices and then marking them down? How many times does one item get marked down? What percentage is the typical markdown?

Mid-season markdowns may mean something fishy is going on. End-of-season markdowns are safer. Learn the protocol for your favorite stores' sales. On any particular item, if there have been three markdowns in the middle of a season, you can come to only two conclusions: Either it had the wrong price on it to begin with, or the buyer is going to be fired.

Are there any insider tips for spotting quality in clothing?

I always look at linings. Turn a garment inside out to see how the seams are joined. See if the garment is fully or partially lined. Look at the stitching. It makes me feel good to wear something that has even hems and seams that match. Look for pieces that you can turn inside out and see a garment that's just as attractive on the inside as it is on the outside. These are the clothes that will last a long time and make you feel good when you're wearing them.

Are there any secrets to caring for quality clothes?

The secret is to try to minimize the amount of dry cleaning a garment goes through, even if the label says "dry clean only". That's because even the highest quality fabrics get slightly damaged each time you dry clean.

Try not to dry clean something after only two or three wearings. Let it air out instead. You can try steaming it next. And try spot cleaning before submitting the entire garment to the dry-cleaning process. Remember, too, that how you hang and store a garment will affect how it ages.

Do you have any other advice?

The best way to save money is to buy designers and brands you know and trust. Then you know how they're going to wear and how they're going to fit. And buy clothes in the size you are now, not in the size you want to be.

How to Find a Great Fur Without Spending a Fortune

If you want a fur, but aren't crazy about the cost, consider buying a coat that is a mix of real and faux fur. Many high-fashion designers are creating new styles using mixed furs. Mixed-fur coats cost almost 80% less than real fur coats, and it's often hard to notice a difference between them.

If you have your heart set on 100% real fur, your best bet may be to travel to New York City. New York is famous for furriers, many of them located along Seventh Avenue between 28th and 30th Streets. You can save 30% off what you'd pay at a retail store, and you may be able to make an even better deal.

Wherever you shop, summer is the best time to buy furs. Stores sell most of their furs during the cold fall and winter months, but by July the retailers are itching to move what's left in their inventory. You can find savings of up to 50% during July and August heat waves.

Same Coat, New Look

If your old fur coat is out of style, you can have it reworked by a tailor or furrier, sometimes for as little as one-third the cost of a new one. It's a great way to keep using your favorite fur or one that belonged to your mother or grandmother.

Some alterations are expensive, though, so make sure to check before you have anyone work on your coat. Get a firm price and a sketch of what the coat will look like before you give permission to restyle it, so that you're not surprised or disappointed at the outcome.

Find Furs outside of a Specialty Store

Before you consider buying a used fur, you should shop around and ask questions. Handle and inspect a few coats so that you will be more knowledgeable when you eventually find one you know you want to buy.

Where to Look Thrift shops may be great places to look for luxury items such as furs. Although they're secondhand, they're often in good condition. And believe it or not, you can often find great bargain furs at garage sales, especially if you are looking for a small size. Next time you go to a garage sale, check out the coats. Many people sell their out-of-style furs right in their own back yards.

FOR YOUR INFORMATION

What Furs Are Worth

The type of fur a coat is made of determines its price. And different types of fur have wildly different prices. While you should never pay more than $1,500 for a rabbit coat, a Russian sable could cost you more than your home.

Type of Fur	Price Range
Russian sable	up to $250,000
Mink	$4,500 to $30,000
Rabbit	$700 to $1,500
Faux fur	$250 to $795

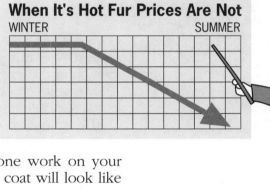

When It's Hot Fur Prices Are Not

WINTER   SUMMER

No matter what type of fur coat you want, you'll get the best price on it during the summer. As temperatures rise, fur prices drop. Look for the best deals on last year's styles as stores make room for new fall and winter collections.

Deals on Jewelry

Here are three places to call if you're looking for good deals on quality diamonds, gemstones and gold. Get the best price you can elsewhere and then see what they have to offer.

Rennie Ellen
(New York City, 212-869-5525)
   Rennie Ellen has a strong reputation in the diamond industry. She carries diamonds in a wide variety of shapes, sizes and qualities. And she charges up to 70% less than retail stores.

Maurice Badler Jewelers
(New York City, 800-622-3537)
   Call for their catalog, which features savings on all types of jewelry.

S. A. Peck & Company
(Chicago, 800-922-0090)
   Save up to 50% off retail prices when you buy from their catalog.

What to Look For When buying used fur, look for soft hides and full skins. Check out the lining to see if the pieces of fur are long and evenly sewed together. Brush the fur back and look for a difference of skin and fur color. If the skin and the fur are the same color the fur may be dyed rather than natural, which makes the coat less valuable.

When to Tailor If you find a fur coat that you like at a good price, but aren't crazy about its fit, you can probably have it tailored. You can't do much with a coat that's too small, but if it's too large or just not stylish, you should check with a local furrier or alterations shop to estimate how much it would cost to alter.

Bargain Diamonds Are a Girl's Best Friend

Here's how to get jewels fit for a king and queen (on a pauper's salary). As with all types of shopping, looking around for the lowest price will get you the best deal.

Costume Jewelry

Costume jewelry may be one of the best accessory bargains around. You can get jewelry that looks like the real thing—for a fraction of the price.

Save yourself even more money by buying costume jewelry in its off-season. Summer accessories, such as pearls and pastel-colored jewelry, are cheapest in the fall and winter, when you can save up to 30%. Dark colored jewelry, such as imitation rubies or emeralds, can cost 30% less in the spring and summer.

Providence, Rhode Island, is considered the costume jewelry capital of the world. Many manufacturers work in and near the city, in part because it has historically been a stopping place for immigrants who specialize in jewelry making. You can find savings of 50% to 90% off retail prices by visiting the wholesale shops there. For more information, call the state's visitor's bureau at 401-274-1636.

The Real Thing

The best advice in buying real jewelry is to stay away from the mall. Mall stores may charge 20% to 50% more than a discount jewelry warehouse. There are many discount jewelry warehouses located in metropolitan areas throughout the nation. Look in the yellow pages under Jewelry-Retail for their ads.

If you are going to shop at a discount jewelry store, you need to be aware of what you are buying. Gems are expensive and you want to make sure that you get what you pay for. When you shop at a discount or other off-price jewelry store, make sure you get a certificate of replacement. This certificate is an appraisal letter, or guarantee, that allows you to return the jewelry if it turns out to be worth less than what was promised.

Jewels of the Season Summer months, like July and August, are the best times to buy real gems. Avoid Christmas time and the pre-wedding season in the spring if you are looking for jewelry markdowns.

Hunt for Wholesale Consider looking in your yellow pages for a jewelry wholesaler. Wholesalers don't typically sell retail, but some may steer you to a low-cost jeweler, or sell you a stone you can take to a jeweler to have set. The gem is 90% of your cost for a piece of jewelry.

Pawn Shop Treasure Many jewelers sell second-hand jewelry at 25% less than the price of a new piece. But the best secondhand jewelry bargains are found in pawn shops. Although they are much less glamorous than Tiffany's, pawn shops often have the best deals on jewelry. You can save 30% or more when compared to buying new jewelry wholesale. But there's no guarantee about quality.

Estate Sales Estate sales are another great place to check for jewelry bargains. Most pieces of jewelry are marked well below their original value. Look in the classified section of your local newspapers for listings of sales near you.

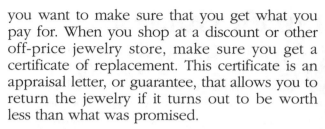

Government Auctions

Have you ever considered contacting the federal government to buy jewelry? The **U.S. Customs Service** holds auctions to sell jewelry and other valuables that have been confiscated. You can buy priceless gems at greatly reduced prices, but it isn't always easy to determine which auctions to attend. You can contact the U.S. Customs Service directly by looking in the blue pages section of your local telephone directory for the number. Often you can look at the merchandise the day before the auction is scheduled. It is best to check out an item before you make a bid.

Watches

If you want to buy an everyday watch, your best bet is to head to a discount chain store. Stores like Kmart carry lines like Seiko and Timex, and sell them for about 20% less than retail watch dealers.

While Christmas and graduation may be the worst times to find a deal on watches, just after these events, in January and July, may be the best time to get a discounted price.

For designer brand watches at discount prices, call for the Tourneau catalog (800-348-3332). Tourneau carries 45 brands of new Swiss watches as well as some pre-owned designer brands such as Rolex and Piaget.

A Quick Guide to Discount Shopping

BARGAIN FINDER

Outlets Are Us

Your best bet in finding what outlets are available and where you can find them is to call **Outlet Bound** (800-336-8853). Outlet Bound provides free information, brochures and VIP vouchers for 170 outlet centers across the country, as well as directions on how to reach the outlets. The vouchers can be redeemed for specific store coupons at each outlet center.

And if that's not enough, Outlet Bound publishes an annual nationwide guide for $13.45 (price includes $3.50 for shipping), which includes a discount coupon you can use at any one of the outlet store locations.

This 200-page guide includes an index to where outlet stores and centers are located, how to get to the outlet centers and how to find a particular store when you reach the center. It also provides more VIP vouchers and coupons, for use when you get there.

If you're online, check out their website at www.outletbound.com, where you can search for stores by brand-name, location or outlet center name.

Specialty chains, general merchandise stores, off-price stores and outlets are all good places to look for inexpensive apparel. Remember: Discount shopping doesn't mean lower quality, just lower costs.

Specialty Chains and General Merchandise Stores

You can save up to 50% or more when you shop at a specialty chain or general merchandise store. These no-frills stores sell brand-name products at discounted prices and have multiple locations at the national, state or city level. You can telephone the national headquarters of a store for a list of local locations. Also, check your local yellow pages under General Merchandise stores.

Types of Discount Stores Specialty chain stores, such as Burlington Coat Factory and Sally Beauty Supply, typically focus on one type of merchandise. In contrast, general merchandise stores like Wal-Mart and Target carry a whole range of different products including clothing. Both types of stores carry a variety of manufacturers and designers, and new products arrive daily and weekly. It pays to drop in often. If you see something you like, it is wise to buy it because not every item comes in every week. If you find an item at a good price, take it. It may not be there on your next visit.

Return Policies Return policies are usually liberal in these stores, but you should check the policy at each store you visit. There may be limits on the amount of time you have to return or exchange an item, and you'll probably need to have a receipt to get your money back.

Outlets May Be Your Best Bets

Outlets may be the most cost-effective clothing and accessory sources around. Most name-brand, high-fashion designers have at least one outlet store. By shopping in outlets, you can dress in expensive styles but pay discounted prices.

Outlets carry overstock, pre-season styles and irregular items at prices 20% to 70% off retail. Often, you can call an outlet to find out if they carry a particular item that you saw in a retail store. You probably won't be able to purchase the item over the phone, but some stores may hold the item for you until you can go in. Many experts advise you to stop buying at designer retail stores until you have explored the outlet option.

Tips for Shopping Outlets When you are shopping for outlet bargains, you need to remember some smart shopper techniques.

- Before you buy, find out the outlet's return policy. Ask if you can return an item, and if you'll receive cash or a credit. Some discount outlets have an all-sales-final policy.
- If you are searching for a particular item, perhaps shoes for a suit, take a fabric swatch with you.

Something for Everyone

No matter what you want to buy, there's a store that sells it at a discount.

Specialty Chain
UP TO 50% DISCOUNT ON OUR SPECIALTY

General Merchandise Store
DISCOUNT ON A WHOLE RANGE OF PRODUCTS
BUY NOW – THEY GO FAST

Outlet Store
- OVERSTOCK
- PRE-SEASON
- IRREGULARS
20%–70% OFF

Off-Price Chair Store
BIG DISCOUNTS ON BRAND NAMES

Clearance Center
- Discounts on brand names.
- Seconds, returns, floor models, last season's stock, and more!

- Look in the back of the outlet store. Many stores have a table or rack with clearance merchandise priced below the everyday discount prices.
- Don't forget to check the size of the clothing carefully. Tags get lost and mismarked all the time, so it's best to try on any item of clothing before you decide to buy.
- If you buy merchandise marked "irregular", make sure that the irregularity is something you can live with.
- Carefully check every item for faults before you pay. If a button is missing, or there's a frayed seam, talk to a salesperson or cashier. Sometimes an outlet or discount store will give you a further markdown on the already discounted price.

Appropriate Attire On a more personal note, always dress comfortably when you outlet shop. Sturdy, comfortable shoes are smart, because chances are you'll spend more time than you expect on your feet. Be prepared for a crowd (although during the off-season outlets may not be any more crowded than retail stores).

Off-price Chain Stores and Clearance Centers

At off-price chain stores or clearance centers, you can find brand-name merchandise at greatly reduced prices. Many non-discount stores and retail chains also have their own clearance centers. Check with your favorite department store to see if it has a clearance location. Many do.

Generally, all the unsold products from all of the company's stores go to one location to be sold at a discounted price. The items sold include seconds, slightly damaged goods, returns, floor models, previous season's stock and mismatched goods.

TRY SOMETHING DIFFERENT

Great Discount Catalogs

These catalogs specialize in luxury and faux-designer items at well below retail prices.

- **Essential Products**
  (212-344-4288) offers imitations of brand-name perfumes at a fraction of brand-name prices. Call for a list of available scents.

- **Alberene Scottish Cashmeres**
  (800-843-9078 or 212-689-0151) offers 40% to 50% savings on cashmere, free shipping and a 30-day refund guarantee.

- **Sportsware Clearinghouse**
  (513-522-3511) features overruns from a variety of manufacturers. You specify the size, color and style (of T-shirts, sweats, baseball caps, socks) and they send you the best match they have.

Outlets across America

Several companies own outlet centers all around the country, some of which contain over 100 different factory stores. Call to find the centers nearest you.

Belz Factory Outlet World (901-260-7290) has five outlets near major thoroughfares in Florida, Montana, Nevada and Tennessee, with two more planned for Florida and Puerto Rico.

Charter Oak Partners (888-SHOP-333, www.charter-oak.com) has 12 outlet centers in 11 states. Call for a free brochure and ask about their coupon book.

Chelsea GCA Realty (973-228-6111, www.chelseagca.com) has 19 outlet centers in 11 states. Ask about their coupon book when you call.

FAC Realty Trust (800-SHOP-USA, www.factorystores.com) has 36 outlet centers in 21 states. Call for free brochures and money-saving coupons.

Horizon Outlet Centers (800-866-5900) has 38 outlets in 20 states.

Hosiery Outlets (800-831-7489) has over 200 factory outlet stores selling L'eggs, Hanes, Bali and Playtex hosiery nationwide.

Prime Retail (800-980-SHOP, www.primeretail.com) has 52 outlets in 27 different states. Call for a free brochure listing outlet centers, store names, maps and area attractions.

Tanger Outlet Centers (800-4-TANGER, www.tangeroutlet.com) has 31 centers in 23 states. Call for complete store listings and a free coupon book.

VF Factory Outlet (800-772-8336) sells items at half off the lowest ticketed price on Vanity Fair, Lee, Healthtex and Wrangler products at 47 stores in 25 states.

Off-price Chain Store Listings

Bed, Bath and Beyond (212-255-3550) has 80 stores located in 21 states.

Burlington Coat Factory (800-444-2628) has 250 stores located in 41 states.

Clothestime (877-825-3266) has 400 stores located in 21 states.

DSW Shoe Outlet (614-497-1199, ext. 1413) has 23 stores located in 15 states.

Famous Footwear (800-403-2668) has 785 stores located in 44 states.

Loehmann's (800-366-5634) has 70 stores located in 22 states.

The Men's Warehouse (800-776-7848) has 385 stores in 49 states.

Target (800-800-8800) has 798 stores located in 39 states.

Sally Beauty Supply (800-275-7255) has 1,550 stores located in 46 states.

Wal-Mart (800-925-6278) has 2,234 stores located in 50 states.

Bargain-Hunting in Cyberspace

The World Wide Web has become one of the easiest ways to shop. You can order directly from your favorite brand-name or catalog company, or shop in a number of online malls.

What's easier than being able to price and product compare without leaving your home? Prices are competitive because there are lots of choices on the Web.

But if you're going to shop with your computer, there are things you should know before you pass your buck over the wire.

A Few Words about Online Security

Unsecured information sent over the Internet can be intercepted by an unwanted third party. This is why it is best to consider using a browser that will scramble purchase information.

Two protocols that comply with industry standards are Secure Socket Layer (SSL) or Secure Hypertext Transfer Protocol (S-HTTP). Most often they are included with your Internet connection services.

If you don't have the software to assure the security of your transaction, consider calling the company's 800-number, faxing your order, or paying by a check or money order instead of completing the order online. If you do decide to send your credit or charge card information into cyberspace, then it is good to know that you are partially protected by the Fair Credit Billing Act.

You should always avoid using established numbers for your password, such as your birth date or a portion of your phone number or social security number. Try to be as original as possible in creating your password, and use different passwords to access specific areas on the World Wide Web. And never share your Internet password with anyone.

Cyber-shop Smart

Here are some valuable tips for shopping online:

- Buy from online companies that you know and would shop with off-line. If you want to try new merchants, ask them to send you a paper catalog or brochure to get a better sense of their merchandise and services.
- Always find out a company's return policies before you make an order, just as you would when catalog shopping or shopping at a store.
- Pay attention when you are filling out the order form on your screen. You don't want to order 100 hats instead of 1, or a size 16 when you want a 6.
- Always check what the shipping charge will be and that all of your charges are calculated correctly. You usually have different shipping options, and if you're not in a hurry to receive the item, it pays to have your purchase sent for the lowest cost.
- The same laws protect you when you shop by phone, mail or cyberspace. If a company does not state how long it will take for you to receive your merchandise, you can expect to receive it within 30 days. Otherwise they must notify you so that you can determine whether or not you still want the items.
- Always remember to print out a copy of your order and confirmation number for your records.

Cybershopping eliminates the cost of the middleman, but make sure to factor in shipping costs before you buy anything online.

BUYER BEWARE

Don't Fall Victim To a Sweet Talker

Home-shopping channels often prey on lonely viewers. People who feel lonely or alienated can fall victim to sweet-talking order-takers, who may lure them to buy more than they could ever need.

Be careful of buying junk as well. Some channels sell low-quality jewelry, carpets and other accessories worth even less than the low price you pay.

Don't be fooled by shiny garbage. If you'll never use or need it, it is definitely not a bargain.

A Word of Warning

Always be cautious if anyone online asks for you to supply personal information, such as your social security number, to conduct a transaction. It is rarely necessary and should be taken as a warning sign. Scams are spreading very quickly on the Internet and as a smart consumer you'll want to safeguard yourself.

Shopping by Remote Control

Have you ever tried the convenience of home-shopping? You can find some unique and interesting items right from your own home.

Some TV networks, like Home Shopping Network (727-872-1000) and QVC (800-345-1515), offer clothing, jewelry, and household and gift items at prices that are often as much as 40% below the cost of comparable items from a retail store. Sometimes they offer special deals of the day, so look for them when you tune in, or ask about special sales when you call.

Many people are surprised to find out you really can find some good deals on home-shopping channels.

How You Can Save

Home shopping can be cheaper because it cuts out the middleman who tends to increase cost. If you want to shop at home, but you aren't sure of what's offered, ask the shopping station to send you a schedule of times when particular items are sold.

Be a Smart Shopper

It's important to beware of the ease of home shopping. Don't let an enthusiastic host convince you to buy low-quality merchandise, especially if you don't need it.

When you shop from home, it is best to use your credit card, because you are then guarded by a consumer protection policy. If there is a problem, contact the Consumer Protection Agency in your state that investigates shady operations.

Television shopping's return policies are similar to those at traditional stores. They usually offer a 30-day full-credit refund policy and refunds for damaged goods.

Care for Your Clothes, And Spare Yourself A Dime

Save yourself and your family lots of money by learning how to take good care of your clothes. How you clean and care for them when you're not wearing them is as important as how you treat them while they're on.

One reason people end up spending so much money on clothing is that they don't properly take care of what they have, and consequently their clothes tend to have very short life spans.

Your best bet in caring for your clothes may be giving them a vacation from cleaning. Before you decide it's time to launder or clean a garment, try airing it out for a couple of days. Then brush it with a lint removal or pet hair removal brush, which you can find for less than $10 at a drugstore or pet supply store.

Care Labels and Your Clothes

Did you know that if you follow the cleaning instructions on the care label of a favorite sweater, and it shrinks or the dye runs, you can return the item and ask the merchant for a replacement, exchange or refund?

The Federal Trade Commission's Care Labeling Rule states that manufacturers must tag their textile clothing with at least one safe cleaning method. Besides telling you how to clean an item, the care label should provide any necessary warnings about how not to clean the item. Labels are not, however, required on clothing, shoes or accessories made of leather. Many manufacturers provide care information on these items anyway.

Choosing a Dry Cleaner

Whether it's a matter of time, convenience or merely your choice of fabric, everyone has made at least one trip to the dry cleaners. But how do you know if you are sending your clothes to be refreshed or ruined?

Choosing a dry cleaner seems like a relatively easy thing to do. But experts believe that, like shopping for your clothes, doing a little homework can save you lots of money and time.

The first thing you may want to consider in choosing a dry cleaner is whether the cleaner has been recommended to you by a friend or co-worker. If you know someone who trusts their clothes to a cleaner, then you can be pretty sure that you can do the same with your own clothes.

Ignore claims of French cleaners. The term is meaningless. You should be more concerned with the quality of cleaning, such as

CHECKLIST

Store Your Clothes Carefully

Most people spend tremendous amounts of money replacing clothes that have not aged well. But you can save your money by taking proper care of your clothes.

❑ Store your clothes in a dark area that is protected from temperature extremes. Choose a closet or chest, not an attic or basement.

❑ When you use cedar chests or wooden hangers, make sure clothes do not touch the wood because it contains oils that can stain fabric. Try to build shelves or racks that let you store clothes at a fair distance (six inches or so) from the walls.

❑ Never starch clothing before storing.

❑ If you're using mothballs, keep them in loosely fastened cloth bags so the chemicals in them do not damage your clothes.

❑ Don't hang clothes in plastic bags because they can mildew. Instead, use an old sheet as a dust cover.

❑ To get rid of pilling that can make jackets and sweaters look old and worn, buy a sweater comb or sweater stone to pull pills off a garment without damaging it. They are available in department stores and catalogs. An alternative is masking tape, which can remove many pills. But never use a razor because it weakens fibers and can ruin a garment.

Clothing Care Basics

- Only one method of safe cleaning care has to be listed on the tag. It is usually best to use the method suggested by the manufacturer.

- If you followed the washing instructions and your red-and-white shirt is now pink, or if your garment was dry-cleaned according to the care instructions and is damaged, return it to the retailer and ask for an exchange or refund.

- If the retailer won't cooperate, ask for the manufacturer's name and address, and write to the company. Describe the garment and list information from the labels and tags. Estimate how many times you've washed the garment or had it dry cleaned. Include the full name and address of the retailer.

- Don't remove your clothing care labels. You risk losing important information about the best care for your garments.

whether or not garments are hand-finished, which is better for fine silks and detailed garments.

Don't use a cleaner until you know their pricing policies. There is no return policy if you take the item home and don't like the price!

Help Your Dry Cleaner Help You

If you are bringing stained clothing to your cleaners, it's best to draw attention to the stains yourself. Don't assume all stains will be noticed. If you have already attempted to remove a stain yourself, own up to it, because what you have put on the garment may affect what the cleaners can then try to do.

Always check your clothes before you remove them from the cleaning facility. A cleaner should redo an item at no charge if it was not cleaned or pressed to your satisfaction.

And finally, how you treat your clothes between cleanings will really make a difference. Make sure to blot up spills before they set into your garments. Allow your clothes to air out before you put them away in your drawer or closet. Don't leave your coat or pants pockets full of junk, which will ultimately stretch and ruin the garment. And don't forget to give your clothes a rest between wearings. It's not smart to wear the same pair of pants three times a week. Rotate your wardrobe.

Skipping the Dry Cleaner

A new option for cutting dry-cleaning costs is a product called the Home Dry Cleaning Kit (800-810-2340, request item #29092). For approximately $11.95, you can buy a kit which includes cleaning supplies for 12 garments. To freshen and clean your sweaters or dry-clean only clothing and cut your dry-cleaning bill costs, you may want to consider trying out this new product.

You place a cleaning sheet and approximately four garments in a reusable dryer-safe bag, and seal the bag. Then place the bag with your garments in the dryer, on a low temperature or permanent press, for approximately ten minutes. You will need to iron or steam your clothing to remove the creases that are usually removed by the dry-cleaning store. You can find the kit in most supermarket chains or drugstore chains.

Caution: This product includes a spot removal kit, but experts suggest using a professional cleaner to remove stains. If you want to try this kit's stain removal process, test it on one of your least favorite items of clothing first. There is always a chance that you can make a stain worse and possibly make it permanent.

Iron like a Pro

BUYER BEWARE

Dry Cleaning Can Be Hazardous to Your Health

Some experts advise that wearing your freshly dry-cleaned clothes can be hazardous to your health.

Consider letting your clothes air outside of their plastic dry-cleaning bags for at least 24 hours before wearing them or putting them in your closet. Some experts feel that airing them for at least a few days in a well-ventilated area, such as your garage, is the safest bet.

The solvent perchloroethylene (perc), used in dry-cleaning, is considered a hazardous air pollutant. Experts say, if your clothes are returned to you with a strong chemical smell, take them back and insist that your dry cleaner do a better job—or consider finding a different service.

You can save a lot of money by doing your own ironing, both at home and on the road. Most hotels and motels will provide an iron and ironing board if you request them.

Iron-clad Ironing Tips

Here are some very basic ironing tips your mother may never have taught you:

- Always hang items directly after ironing. This will ensure that wrinkles don't immediately return. Also, if you wear an item after ironing or steaming without letting it air out and cool down, you may increase the amount of puckering and creasing.
- Starch should be sprayed only on the underside of a garment. Allow the fabric to absorb the starch before you begin to iron. Consider rolling the garment into a ball to help the absorption process.
- If the iron sizzles when it touches the fabric, the iron is set too high.
- Most irons have temperature gauges which show the correct setting for certain types of fabrics. Pay attention to what your iron tells you.

Synthetics and silks should be ironed on low temperatures (approximately 350 degrees), wool should be ironed at medium to high temperatures, and cotton and linens should be set at the highest temperatures (approximately 400 to 425 degrees).

Ironing can make your clothes look their best—or ruin them before their time.

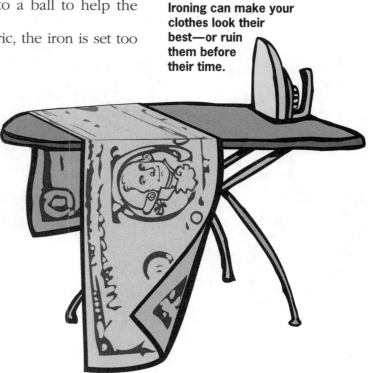

Pack Light

Space is money when you're traveling. Try to wear your bulkiest clothes on the airplane so you have less to carry. Save additional room in your luggage with these products:

- All-purpose travel soap instead of separate products for cleaning hair, skin and clothes.
- Polyester or polyester-blend travel clothes (instead of 100% cotton) that can be washed out each night and will be dry by morning.
- One multipurpose, waterproof coat with good breathability.
- Compact items that replace larger ones, such as fleece tops instead of bulky wool sweaters.

Tips from the Experts

Expert ironers/pressers suggest ironing sections of your clothes in the following manner:

- Shirts should be ironed starting with the collar, then the back yoke, then the cuffs, then sleeves and finally the body. Some say you should repeat ironing the collar once the shirt is completed for a fully finished look. And always take a second glance when you're done to make sure there aren't other touch-ups you need to do.
- Pants should be ironed starting with the pockets, then the waistline, followed by the inside portion of the legs, and ending with the outside portion of the legs. Using an old handkerchief as a press cloth can help avoid the shine some fabrics tend to get when ironed.
- If your clothes tend to get shiny or dulled by ironing, consider ironing them inside-out.

Packing Well Can Save You Money

Packing your clothing carefully and logically can save you money on pressing bills. For example, put your sweaters and jeans on the bottom of your suitcase because they are the sturdiest, and leave your socks and underwear for last so that you can use them to fill empty spaces and kept the rest of your apparel secure.

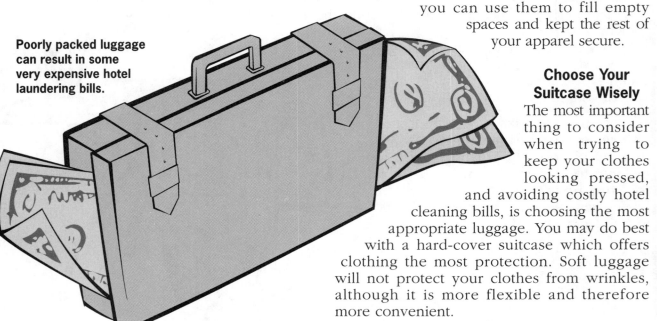

Poorly packed luggage can result in some very expensive hotel laundering bills.

Choose Your Suitcase Wisely

The most important thing to consider when trying to keep your clothes looking pressed, and avoiding costly hotel cleaning bills, is choosing the most appropriate luggage. You may do best with a hard-cover suitcase which offers clothing the most protection. Soft luggage will not protect your clothes from wrinkles, although it is more flexible and therefore more convenient.

Consider traveling with a small carry-on case and a garment bag. Most airplanes and trains have room to hold garment bags in their upright position, allowing your clothes to travel wrinkle-free.

Everything in Its Place

Believe it or not, the more tightly packed your garment bag is, the tidier your clothes will stay. Try to buy a garment bag that has extra zippered compartments where you can stash your shoes, socks and undergarments, and then you will only have to carry one bag.

The second thing to consider when packing is how you've packed your clothes. Packing silks, pants, skirts and dresses in plastic will protect them from creasing. Folding your clothing lengthwise will not only save space but protect the clothing from wrinkles.

And lastly, make sure you wrap your toiletries in leak-proof containers. If you don't have any available, or don't want to buy some just for a trip, put your shampoo and soaps into gallon-sized plastic bags. This way, if an item opens up due to the altitude of a plane or rough rails of a train, your clothes will be protected from spills.

Steam Away Dry-Cleaning Bills

To save money on costly dry-cleaning bills, consider stretching the time between cleanings by using an inexpensive garment steamer.

Steaming your clothing can remove wrinkles and unwanted puckering or creases. It can also help protect your clothing from dry-cleaning chemicals and the wear and tear caused by the cleaning process.

Using a steamer won't replace cleaning altogether. By steaming your clothing you are simply removing the evidence of excessive wear. You'll need to use dry cleaning to remove perspiration, dirt and stains. But you may be able to increase the life of your favorite suit or pair of pants by not taking them to the dry cleaners every week.

An Alternative to Ironing

Some experts believe that steaming is safer for your clothing than ironing. With a steamer, you aren't placing the extreme heat of an iron directly on your clothing. Therefore you are protecting your

---

HERE'S HOW

Make It Last

Following these simple laundry tips can keep your clothes looking like new for years to come.

Wash It Right

- Close all fasteners, zippers and buttons before you wash.
- Empty pockets before you wash.
- Handwash delicates or wash them separately in the gentle cycle.
- Separate colors (whites, brights, pastels and darks).
- Wash fabrics whose colors may bleed separately.
- Wash terry-cloth towels, robes and other lint-producing materials separately.
- Wash very dirty garments, such as those covered in mud or lipstick, in a separate load to keep them from staining other clothes.

Dry It Right

- Add a couple of clean, dry towels to small loads to speed up their drying time.
- Avoid ironing by using the dryer cycle recommended on care labels.
- Don't leave clothes in the dryer after they're dry.
- If possible, use a dryer with a moisture sensor, which automatically turns off the machine when your load is dry.
- Leave enough room for air to circulate through each load.
- Use the perma press cycle for garments that can be damaged by excess heat.

Cashmere in the Washing Machine

Did you know that some fine wool sweaters, even those made of cashmere, come out best when you handwash them in cold water? Cashmere can also be washed in the machine (inside out) and dried flat (not in the drier).

Believe it or not, a dry-clean-only tag can be wrong. Sometimes manufacturers place dry-clean-only tags on their apparel as a way of safeguarding themselves against complaints if something goes wrong in the laundry process.

If you are going to take a risk and launder a garment with a dry-clean-only tag, consider first experimenting with one of your least favorite sweaters. Then, if you aren't satisfied with the results, you haven't compromised your favorite sweater. One caution: Angora and fancy loose-knit sweaters should always be dry cleaned.

garments from burns and discoloration. Also, irons tend to make sharp creases in clothing that you may not want.

That doesn't mean you won't need an iron, however, especially when you want to smooth a tablecloth or other linens, or touch up the crease in your best slacks. But you may want to consider purchasing an iron that includes a vertical steam application, such as the Rowenta Professional Iron ($125). A vertical steam application will prevent the common water drips and spotting that other steam iron applications can cause. Such an iron can be expensive, although experts say it's highly effective.

What to Look for in a Steamer

Two types of steamers you may want to consider are the full-sized home steamer and the smaller travel steamer, which is easier to pack.

If you consider buying a full-sized steamer (which can run from $150 to $300), don't be put off by the seemingly high cost. The amount of money you will save in dry cleaning bills by using the steamer will save you money in the long run.

A full-sized steamer is what most clothing stores use to remove the evidence of creases from freshly unpacked garments. Placing the head of a steamer in the inside of a shirt can remove all the creases and wrinkles almost instantaneously. Experts say that this type of steamer is the most effective, and some prefer it to ironing.

But you may also want to consider a travel-sized steamer. Travel-sized steamers are small (so they're easy to pack), good for quick touch-ups and cost as little as $30. And they can come in handy when you're on business trips or vacation to help cut the expense of hotel dry-cleaning bills.

A Few Steamers Worth Trying

Here are a few steamers, both full-sized and travel-sized, you may want to consider. Prices are suggested retail, but you can probably find stores that have them at a discount. Call for local store information. If you order by phone, remember to ask what shipping and handling charges will be.

Rowenta DA-55 Steambrush (781-396-0600, $39.95).

Rowenta DA-56 Steambrush, with crease attachment (781-396-0600, $55).

Jiffy Esteem Hand-Held Travel Steamer (800-525-4339, $69).

Jiffy J-2 Jiffy Garment Steamer (800-525-4339, $189).

Brookstone Dual Voltage Garment Steamer for travel (800-846-3000, $39).

Brookstone Pro Garment Steamer (800-846-3000, $200).

Norelco Garment Steamer/Wrinkle Remover TS75 (800-243-7884, $26.99).

Norelco Garment Steamer/Wrinkle Remover with Dual Voltage TS85 (800-243-7884, $31.99).

The Many Faces Of Stains

Before you take a stained garment to the dry cleaner or throw it in the trash, make sure you can't remove the stain yourself using products you have around the house.

Stains, like people, come in many shapes and sizes. Learning how to remove a stain correctly the first time can save you money on cleaning bills. And it may mean you won't have to lay out extra money to replace damaged clothing.

Here are some insider tips on how to remove the most frequently appearing stains.

Kids are magnets for grass stains, but you can keep their clothes clean with a little bit of hot water, chlorine bleach and rubbing alcohol.

Grass Stains

If you notice a grass stain when you're doing the wash, you can still save your kids' clothes by rubbing detergent into the dampened stain. Wash the item in hot water with chlorine bleach. If the stain remains, try sponging the spot with alcohol.

Use bleach only on bleachable fabrics, or you may increase the damage. If the fabric is non-bleachable, omit the chlorine bleach. If you are worried about damaging the color of an item, dilute the alcohol with two parts water.

BARGAIN FINDER

Costumes for Non-Profits

Most theater and dance companies store and reuse their costumes. But, as their needs change and their wardrobes age, many theatrical companies donate what they can to children's performance companies and not-for-profit costume rental agencies.

If you are a member of a not-for-profit organization, such as a church or school group, and need costumes for a theatrical performance or dance recital, you can call **The tdf Costume Collection** (212-989-5855). The tdf Costume Collection rents costumes donated by world-renowned dance and theater companies like those at **Juilliard** in New York City and will deliver nationwide. (No retail or individual buyers are allowed.)

DID YOU KNOW

Babywipes Fight Stains

Use babywipes to erase small stains, such as lipstick or makeup on your collar. Babywipes are gentle enough to use on delicate fabrics, and can save you a bundle in dry-cleaning bills. Gently rub the stain with the babywipe until the mark disappears.

HERE'S HOW

Get Tough on Chewing Gum

Get rid of stubborn chewing gum by freezing it, either in the freezer or with ice cubes in a plastic bag, and then carefully scraping it off with a dull knife. Be careful not to pull too hard and tear the fabric.

If you get red wine on your clothes at a restaurant, immediately ask your server for some salt or hydrogen peroxide (if it's available) to draw out the stain.

Blood Stains

To remove blood from clothing, soak the stain in cold water and then rub the fabric with detergent and rinse. You can also use un-flavored meat tenderizer to break up fresh blood stains by applying it to dampened spots.

If the stain does not come out of cotton, polyesters, rayons and linens, try applying a drop of household ammonia and rinse. Blood stains in wool and silk are best treated by the dry cleaner.

Perspiration Stains

To remove perspiration stains, use a prewash stain remover or rub with a bar of soap. When perspiration changes the color of fabric, apply ammonia to a fresh stain and rinse. If the stain is old, try applying white vinegar and then rinse.

Stubborn perspiration stains may be effectively removed if you wash the item in hot water with a product containing enzymes or oxygen bleach. Never wash an item in water that is considered too hot for the type of fabric, however. Always remember to check the care label before washing.

Ink Stains

Some inks are impossible to remove, and trying to wash the stain out yourself may actually set it in deeper. If you don't know what kind of ink has stained your clothes, but you know the kind of pen it came from, try calling the manufacturer before you attempt to launder the item. The service department should be able to recommend a solution.

If the ink stains don't come from permanent markers, try pre-treating the fabric with dena-tured alcohol or a prewash stain remover and sponging the area around the stain. For re-moving ball point pen ink stains, hairspray may be the least expensive solution.

Red Wine Stains

Treat red wine stains with a thick layer of salt to draw out the stain. Then rinse the fabric in warm water. Red wine stains on wool and silk can be treated with hydrogen peroxide solution, rinsed and then washed.

Learning to Sew Can Save You a Bundle

Brushing up on your old sewing skills or learning how to sew is a great way to save money on children's clothing. You can also save on hefty tailoring bills by learning how to fix your own hems and zippers.

If you think that making your own clothing is an occupation of the past, you'll be surprised to know that there are many resources to help you make this a worthwhile venture.

Pulling all Your Threads Together

You may want to consider beginning with a sewing class. Sewing classes are frequently given, for minimal cost, at your local high school or community center. Call the adult education department of the high school and inquire about their evening classes or weekend workshops.

If the high school in your town doesn't offer sewing classes, call the high school of a neighboring town. Don't be afraid to ask for suggestions from the schools. Most people are happy to help.

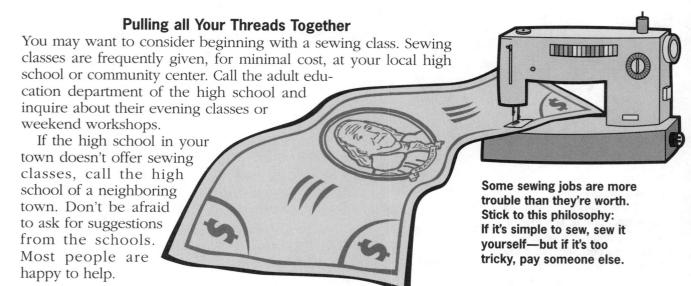

Some sewing jobs are more trouble than they're worth. Stick to this philosophy: If it's simple to sew, sew it yourself—but if it's too tricky, pay someone else.

When You Need a Little Help

If you are a beginner or a seasoned sewer who wants to use your skills to make a little extra money, You Can Make It Inc. may be what you're looking for. You Can Make It Inc. is a free referral service for teachers and students of sewing.

For approximately $36 a month, You Can Make It Inc. will set you up with a local sewing instructor who will teach you to sew, help you find appropriate patterns and supplies for your sewing level, and teach you the basics for achieving your sewing goals.

Or, if you would rather work alone, You Can Make It Inc. will supply you with a series of seven different instructional video tapes, for $36.95 a tape (plus $3 shipping and handling).

You Can Make It Inc. works in conjunction with most of the major pattern companies, such as McCalls and Butterick, so you can learn how to make quality clothes at a reasonable price.

Contact You Can Make It Inc. toll-free at 888-576-2739, or check them out at www.youcanmakeit.com.

Places for Patterns

There are a number of magazines and pattern companies that provide monthly publications which include sewing tips, free patterns and information on resources.

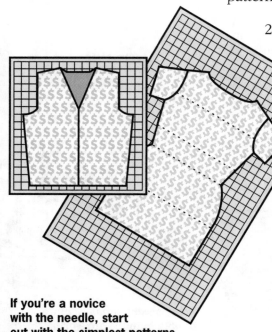

Butterick (800-766-3619, mail order division or 800-766-2670, technical help line) is one of the best-known pattern companies. They publish two pattern magazines, *Vogue Patterns* ($3.95) and *Butterick Home Catalog* ($3.50), which you can find at your local newsstand or pattern store. You can also call them toll-free for a yearly subscription or for a listing of other publications they offer, like special sewing books and video tapes.

Butterick also publishes two knitting magazines, *Vogue Knitting* ($4.95) and *Family Circle Easy Knitting* ($4.99), which you may want to look into for making your own sweaters and accessories.

If you're a novice with the needle, start out with the simplest patterns (using only one or two pieces of fabric) and work your way up to more complicated ones. Sleeveless dresses and children's jumpers are great projects for first-timers.

Cutting Back Travel Costs

Here's how to find rock-bottom airfares,
free hotel rooms, bargain vacation packages,
inexpensive car rentals, last-minute deals and more.

Finding a Great Travel Agent

A good travel agent can save you a great deal of time and money, but a disreputable one can leave you stranded with no tickets and no money in your pocket. Since there are relatively few regulations governing travel agents, you need to take responsibility for finding a good one yourself. The search is worth the time you put in, since a good travel agent can save you 10% to 15% on the price of your trip.

Where to Look

The secret to finding a good travel agent is to get references from friends, family members and business associates who like to travel the same way you do. Favor local agents who have been in the business for at least a few years and who use the most up-to-date computer systems. If the agent you like best is popular (and therefore hard to reach), ask the person who referred you to call the agent on your behalf to introduce you.

What to Look for In a Travel Agent

❑ Membership in the **American Society of Travel Agents (ASTA)** or the **Association of Retail Travel Agents (ARTA)**.

❑ **Certified Travel Counselor (CTC)** certification.

❑ A 24-hour toll-free hotline for emergencies.

❑ At least four Computer Reservation Systems (CRSs).

❑ A computer system that ranks flights according to cost.

❑ Use of consolidators to book international tickets.

What to Avoid

❑ Inexperience or inattention.

❑ Preference for airlines that pay commissions to agents.

❑ Membership in a particular airline's incentive plan.

❑ Generic information you could find on your own.

Background Check

Beware of using the services of an inexperienced or fly-by-night travel agent.

When you find an agent you like, check to see if the agent is registered with one of the two main professional travel organizations: the American Society of Travel Agents (ASTA) or the Association of Retail Travel Agents (ARTA). Both require member agencies to post bond to protect their clients.

Also check with the Institute of Certified Travel Agents (ICTA, 781-237-0280) to confirm that the agent is a Certified Travel Counselor (CTC). CTCs have at least five years' experience as travel agents and have completed ICTA's two-year, graduate-level program.

Refunds and Payments

Ask your agent upfront about any extra service charges you should expect for faxes or long distance calls. Also ask whether the agency will provide a refund (or partial refund) if a tour operator or airline goes out of business before your vacation. For added security, make sure you get commitments on cancellations and refunds in writing.

Find out how your travel agent is paid by the airlines. In the past, most agents received a 10% commission on the cost of each booking, which encouraged them to sell more expensive tickets. Recently, however, airlines have been cutting back agents' commissions to maximums of $25 per one-way flight, regardless of the ticket price. In response, some travel agents have started charging customers a service fee of around $35 for each booking. Find out in advance if your agent charges a fee.

Agent Expertise

Your agent should take the time to get to know you and your travel preferences, such as your favorite airlines, the hotels you like and your first choice for airplane seating. Good customer service means your agent should accept no calls and avoid interruptions while talking with you.

A good agent should be personally familiar with the trips and vacations you are considering, rather than just reading descriptions to you from a brochure or computer screen. You could find that information on your own. Agents in the know can give you suggestions about the best attractions, restaurants and shopping areas. Plus, since the photographs and descriptions in travel brochures can make even the dingiest hotel look like an elegant resort, you need to be able to rely on your agent to make sure you get your money's worth.

A Good Travel Agent Defined

- **Gets to know your travel preferences.**
- **Uses a variety of sources for information.**
- **Is personally familiar with many destinations.**
- **Makes money-saving suggestions.**

Getting the Best Service

It pays to establish an ongoing relationship with your agent. When booking your first trip, let the agent know that you plan to come back for your next trip if everything works out well. The prospect of future business is the only real incentive a travel agent has to find you the cheapest fares, particularly if the agent gets a percentage of what you pay for your tickets.

It helps to be courteous as well. Try to give your agent at least four weeks' notice before you travel so the agent has the time to search for the best deals while there are still many options available. And if the trip goes smoothly, give your agent a call or write a short thank-you note.

Lower Airfares

Travel agents use Computer Reservation Systems (CRSs) to search among all the airlines' available fares. The best agents use four or more CRSs to stay on top of last minute price changes. CRSs can search for the best prices, fastest flights or particular airplane models (if, for example, you prefer jets to propellers).

Your travel agent should be able to suggest ways to save on your airfare, such as buying consolidator tickets, booking overnight flights or choosing weekend departures. Make sure your agent knows your top priority (whether it's saving the most money or avoiding layovers), because it may change your agent's search method dramatically.

You probably have multiple priorities, however. Many people would rather pay an extra $100 than have two four-hour layovers. Finally, ask your agent to keep searching for cheaper flights even

DID YOU KNOW

Specialty Travel Agencies

Most travel agents specialize in a particular type of travel. The most basic categories are business and leisure travel, but agents also specialize in areas like cruises, charters, up-scale resorts or bargain vacations. Get the best deal on your vacation by choosing a travel agent who specializes in your area of travel preference. Some larger offices have several specialties. Check the ads and stories in your local newspapers to find agents with a particular specialty.

after you purchase your ticket. If she finds one at a significant discount, it may be worth the cancellation fee to rebook your flight. For example, most airlines charge a cancellation fee of $30 to $50 per ticket, but if the new flight saves you $200, it's certainly worth paying the fee to save $150 or more.

Your computer could be your best bet for finding inexpensive domestic and international flights.

Great Travel Websites

Here are some travel websites full of free information and money-saving travel tips. If you don't have Internet access at your home or workplace, most libraries have computers you can use. Ask the librarian to help you find what you're looking for, or attend one of their introductory sessions to learn how to use the computer on your own.

Arthur Frommer's Outspoken Encyclopedia of Travel, www.frommers.com

This is one of the all-time best budget-travel websites from one of the all-time best budget-travel experts. Find information on practically any travel-related issue you could dream up, including bargain airfares, all-inclusive vacations, inexpensive resorts and group tours.

Budget Travel, www.budgettravel.com

Budget Travel was developed as a central Internet location full of information for "all of us who don't want to pay 5-star prices."

Centers for Disease Control, www.cdc.gov

Here's a good place to check with if you want to stay healthy on your next vacation, especially if you're traveling to a particularly exotic location.

Eurotrip, www.eurotrip.com

A clearinghouse of information for people traveling to Europe, Eurotrip offers tips for Eurailers, inter-railers, students, backpackers and other budget travelers.

Izon's Backpacker Journal, www.izon.com

Based on Lucy Izon's book, this site is packed with bargain information aimed at young travelers who aren't afraid to rough it in order to see the world.

BUYER BEWARE

Internet Travel Scams

Internet travel scams are on the rise as more people look for travel deals on the World Wide Web. Take these precautions when ordering tickets online.

- Get the company's policies on refunds and cancellations in writing.

- Refuse to do business with any firm that asks for personal information that is not needed for the transaction.

- Don't respond to pressure. Legitimate offers do not require instant responses.

TravelShop, www.travelshop.de/index-e.html

TravelShop features over 100 pages of information on airlines, airports, hotel chains, cruises, worldwide travel agents, rail travel and destinations grouped by continent.

U.S. Department of State, travel.state.gov/travel_warnings.html

Get instant reports on the current political situation and tourist dangers in any country around the world.

Save on Airfare

The most frustrating thing about airfares is that, like stock prices, they refuse to stay put. Of course, you can get a great deal if you buy when fares are at their lowest, but you can likewise spend a fortune when prices are up. If you know what factors affect the price you pay, however, you can get a good deal almost every time you fly.

Factor 1: How Flexible You Are

It's easiest to find a low airfare when you have plenty of time to do some research. One of the reasons business travelers pay so much more for airline tickets than leisure travelers is that they don't have time to call around for the lowest fare. In order to keep their businesses running smoothly, they need the most convenient and punctual flight with the least number of restrictions, and they pay heavily for that privilege.

As a leisure traveler with fewer time restrictions, on the other hand, you can pay a much lower price.

Factor 2: When You Fly

Prices vary greatly depending on when you want to fly. Ask your ticket agent if flying at a particular time of day or day of the week would save you money. You will probably get the best deal on flights shunned by business travelers, such as:

- Late-night flights.
- Flights on holidays.
- Round-trip flights that include a Saturday night stay-over.
- Weekend domestic flights.
- Weekday international flights.

You can also save a good deal of money by flying during the off-season. This means traveling to the Bahamas or Hawaii in the summer, and to Europe or Canada in the winter. Since there is less demand for airplane seats at these times, prices are lower.

The time of day when you call the ticket agent can also affect your price. If you're calling the airlines directly, try calling after

It Pays to Be Flexible

You can get plenty of discounts on airline tickets if you can be flexible about when you fly. Here are some ways to reduce the cost of your ticket:

- On a different day.
- At a different time of day.
- During a different week of the month.
- At designated off-peak times.
- During special seasonal deals.
- On another airline.

Promotional Tickets

Some airlines offer Promotional Tickets (for standby travel) to travel agents as a bonus for booking a certain number of flights with them. Agents sometimes sell these tickets to customers looking for a really cheap flight. Ask your agent if this is an option.

Money-Saving Alternative to Flight-Accident Insurance

Flight-accident insurance is expensive—but the chances of dying in a plane crash are slim. It's a much better deal to make sure you have a standard life insurance policy with coverage enough to take care of your family no matter how you may die than to buy a one-time policy every time you board a plane.

7 p.m. or on weekend mornings, when they receive the fewest calls. You'll wait for a shorter time before you are helped, and the agent will have more time to find you the flight with the best price.

Factor 3: Where You Fly to and From

Consider flying in and out of small airports located within a one or two hour drive of larger hubs, such as Milwaukee instead of Chicago or Oakland instead of San Francisco. Flights from these smaller airports often cost less because they have to stay competitive with those flying in and out of the bigger airports.

The smaller airport might also be closer to your destination than the hub is. If not, a $200 savings might be worth an hour's car ride. Make sure you have your ground transportation worked out before you fly, however. You don't want to spend all the money you save on your flight paying for a one-hour taxi ride.

Factor 4: What Airline You Fly

Start-up airlines generally charge less than larger, established companies because they are still trying to make a place for themselves in the industry. They frequently have smaller fleets and fly to and from fewer locations, but if they offer the flight you're interested in, they can be a good deal.

Don't just assume that you're getting the best fare when you book with a small company, however. You should still call around to see what prices the other airlines offer, especially during air-fare wars when established airlines drop their prices substantially.

Here are a few discount airlines for domestic and international travel that offer everyday low prices on their flights.

Domestic Discount Airlines
   Southwest Airlines (800-435-9792)
   Western Pacific (800-930-3030)

International Discount Airlines
   Air Jamaica (800-523-5585)
   Cathay Pacific (800-233-2742)
   City Bird (888-248-9247)
   Icelandair (800-223-5500)
   Singapore Airlines (800-742-3333)
   Thai Airways (800-426-5204)
   Virgin Atlantic (800-862-8621)

Factor 5: Who You Are

Status fares are cut-rate tickets for people who fit into certain groups that wouldn't normally pay for a full-price airline ticket.

You can get up to 75% off your ticket price if you are a full-time student, a senior citizen, a youth under age 26, an active-duty member of the military (or a dependent), a child traveling with an adult, part of a family flying together, a member of the clergy or a teacher. To get a status fare, you've got to let the booking agent know you're eligible.

Factor 6: How Resourceful You Are

You can find airline discount coupons in some unexpected places. Look for money-saving coupons in places such as:

- Supermarket bulletin boards.
- Banks and credit unions (for members only).
- Computer supplies, camera film and other products' packaging.
- Travel clubs.
- Credit card offers.
- Coupon books like *Entertainment*, sold by charities and other groups as fundraisers.

These coupons may feature offers such as two domestic flights anywhere for $130 each, friend-flies-free discounts, or 20% off any ticket. These offers usually come with a number of restrictions, but they can still save you a good deal of money.

How Seniors Can Fly for Less

Most of the major airlines offer a 10% senior citizen discount for people ages 62 and up. This isn't the only way seniors can save money on flights, however. Here are two other options that could save you even more.

Airline Coupons

If you take at least two round-trip flights a year, consider buying a book of flight coupons good for travel anywhere an airline flies within the continental United States. Travel to Hawaii usually requires twice as many coupons. A book of four one-way coupons good for one year costs around $550 to $600, depending on the airline. That's only $138 to $150 per ticket, a pretty good deal if you are flying a good distance.

Call around to see which airline has the best offer. Ask about blackout periods and any limitations on the number of seats that can be filled by coupon holders per flight.

DID YOU KNOW

Know the Code

Use on-time performance codes to choose between similar flights. A flight's on-time performance code is a number between zero and nine that indicates how frequently that flight arrived on time during the past month. Flights rated nine arrive like clockwork, but you'll be lucky to arrive at all on a flight rated zero. You can find a flight's on-time performance code by asking the reservations agent.

BUYER BEWARE

Be Wary of Classified Ads

People who buy nonrefundable airline tickets they can't use sometimes sell them through the classified ads. These tickets are non-transferable. If you buy one, you will have to fly using that person's name, which will obviously be a problem if you have to show a passport or other form of identification before boarding (as is now required on most domestic as well as international flights).

Bruce Northam on Taking Great Vacations on a Low Budget

Bruce Northam is a travel writer, popular university lecturer with **Lecture Literary Management** in New York City and author of *The Frugal Globetrotter: Your Guide to World Adventure Bargains.* His love of travel has driven him to seek out bargain vacation opportunities around the world.

What's the best all-around travel bargain available today?

If you've got the time, around-the-world airline tickets from consolidators are great deals. If you're planning on taking a lengthy journey with stops at many destinations around the world, this is by far the least expensive way to fly. My favorite around-the-world broker is Ticket Planet (800-799-8888).

How can people cut back on their vacation spending without cutting back on their enjoyment?

Have a mission or develop a quest. Perhaps you'll want to focus on a particular hobby or interest, such as birdwatching, festival hopping, learning new dance steps, attending religious services, seeing native animals or attending theater performances. Devise a hobby-inspired crusade.

Begin your quest as soon as you arrive at your destination. Find out where the local gurus on your topic work or hang out, and start exploring. Instead of spending your time at overcrowded tourist traps, you'll be wandering through local neighborhoods, meeting interesting people, eating at local restaurants and traveling more like an adventurer than a tourist. And, while tourist attractions are notoriously expensive, exploring the true heart of a new city can cost next to nothing.

What tips do you have for people interested in low-cost adventures in another city or country?

Be your own travel agent. If you have time and flexibility, you can create your own adventure focused on your interests. Use guidebooks only to get yourself around town. Once you get to the area you're interested in, such as the historical district or bohemian part of town, put the guidebook away and wander around on your own. If you have your nose in a guidebook the whole time, you'll miss the best parts of your vacation.

If you're feeling brave, pitch the guidebook away and go up to the roof of the place you're staying. Look around and pick an interesting direction to go for an all-day walk.

If you pass an interesting factory, school or business, go in and check it out. In many places, particularly in underdeveloped countries, people are happy to let you watch their daily work.

What do you suggest for cheap souvenirs?

Don't buy another baseball cap or T-shirt. Instead, go for local specialties, such as inexpensive street art or regional crafts. Occupational tools such as bamboo fish traps or handmade backpacks can be purchased (though they may not be for sale) at a fair price. Even a newspaper or magazine in another language (with interesting photos) can be a hit back home.

What has been your favorite frugal vacation?

Walking 190 miles, coast-to-coast across Northern England with my father. We walked along towering shoreline cliffs, through dense forests, and in and out of remote villages, meeting people and seeing landscapes tourists rarely see. Nothing gives you a real sense of the countryside like walking through it. You have time to encounter wonderful people and locales that would be only a blur through the window of a bus or train. And the bed & breakfasts were very reasonable and walking was free.

If you are only going to fly a short distance or there is a fare war going on, you might be better off paying for each trip separately and taking the senior citizen discount. Check prices of both options before you decide how to buy your tickets.

If you're using a coupon, you must confirm your flight 14 days in advance or fly standby. Children are sometimes allowed to use senior coupons if flying with a senior.

Freedom Trips and Freedom Flight Club

Continental Airlines also has special deals for travelers ages 62 and up. Their Freedom Trips and Freedom Flight Club allow you to fly domestically and internationally at substantial discounts. Freedom Trips offers 4 or 8 trip certificates for one-way domestic trips. Freedom Flight Club is a membership program for discounted domestic ($75 membership fee) and international flights ($125). Call 800-441-1135 for further details.

The Lowdown on Airline Consolidators

Consolidators have been around longer than almost any other source of discount airline tickets, and they are generally a safe place to look for a good deal.

What They Are

Consolidators buy airline tickets in bulk at a discount and then re-sell them to the public. They usually buy leftover, unsold tickets which airlines are happy to sell cheaply in order to fill their planes. Because they buy leftover tickets in bulk, consolidators are able to sell their tickets at low prices, often saving you between 20% and 50% off the regular ticket price.

Consolidators deal primarily in international tickets on established airlines for departures within the next month or so. That means you can plan your vacation a month or so in advance, but not much more than that. If you have a relatively flexible schedule, consolidators can be one of the best sources for a good deal on your international airfare.

Where to Find Them

Many consolidators advertise in the travel sections of *The New York Times*, *USA Today* and *The Los Angeles Times*. Also take a look in the travel section of magazines and your local paper.

Some travel agencies double as consolidators, and are happy to sell you consolidated tickets. Other agencies may be less forthcom-

FOR YOUR INFORMATION

Airfare Consolidators

Consolidators deal mostly with international flights, but some have begun offering deals on domestic flights as well. Many consolidators work primarily with travel agents. Here are a few consolidators who work directly with the public. Companies book flights all over the world unless otherwise noted.

- Air Brokers International (800-883-3273)
- Brendan Air (800-491-9633 or 818-785-9696)
- Cheap Seats (800-451-7200)
- Council Travel (800-226-8624) books trans-Atlantic flights only.
- Magical Holidays (800-228-2208 or 212-486-9600) specializes in flights to Africa, the Middle East, Europe, and some destinations in the Far East.
- STA Travel (800-777-0112) The lowest rates are for ages 30 and under.
- Ticket Planet (800-799-8888)
- TRAVAC (800-872-8800 or 212-563-3303)
- Travel Bargains (800-AIRFARE; www.1800airfare.com) books flights within the U.S. and all over the world.
- TFI of NYC (800-745-8000 or 212-736-1140)
- 800-FLY-CHEAP (800-359-2432) books flights within the U.S. and to Mexico.

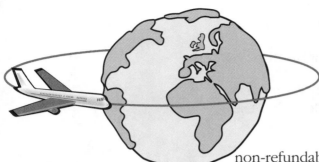

Consolidators are a good source for round-the-world tickets. These are tickets for travelers who want to keep traveling around the world in same direction, and usually require you to fly exclusively with two or three designated carriers.

Round-the-world tickets can save you big money over individual tickets. Prices range from around $1,600 to $6,000, so check around for the best price.

BUYER BEWARE

The Rate Bait and Switch

During one study made by the **New York Better Business Bureau**, officials chose 20 airfare consolidator ads from the newspaper at random and called to purchase an advertised fare. They were unable to get the advertised price from even one company.

ing with information about consolidators. If you have this problem, ask your agent to look at *Jax Fax*, a publication for travel agents that lists all consolidators and their rates, both for flights and ground packages.

Potential Problems

Unlike full-fare tickets, consolidator tickets are non-refundable and not honored by other airlines. Some experts say that you need to save at least $100 per ticket to make consolidator tickets worth your while. The majority of travelers using consolidator tickets, however, don't experience any serious problems.

Misleading Advertisements Your tickets will almost always cost at least $20 higher than those in the consolidator's newspaper advertisements, which operators usually say are sold out when you call. And during price wars, consolidated tickets might cost more than tickets purchased directly from the airline. You need to pay attention to make sure you get a good deal.

Slim Service Since they usually operate on narrow profit margins, consolidators don't offer the same kind of personal service that travel agents and airline representatives do. If you don't know exactly where and when you want to go, you might be better off buying your tickets from a travel agent.

Tricky Schedules Consolidator tickets can be difficult for people with tight schedules, because flights are rarely direct and often have several lengthy layovers and tight time restrictions. Be sure you're going to have enough flexibility to handle the flight schedule before you buy.

No More Miles Many consolidator tickets don't earn frequent flyer miles, which may or may not matter to you. These miles could be worth $300 or more toward a future ticket, so take your frequent flyer status into consideration before you choose a consolidator ticket.

Missing Tickets Some consolidators don't deliver your tickets until they receive your payment. At that point, you could find out you're only wait-listed on the flight. Others consolidators don't deliver the tickets until you're at the airport.

Protect yourself by calling the airline to make sure it is familiar with the consolidator. Then call the airline again 24 hours after you make your reservation to see if you have a reserved seat. Also, consider paying with a credit card to protect your purchase, even though the consolidator will probably charge you an extra 2% to 5% to do so.

Low-Cost Flights in Foreign Lands

Air passes are either coupon books or passes for an unlimited number of flights, both good within specific countries for limited periods of time. Airlines sometimes limit air-pass holders to flying only on certain, less busy days of the week and stopping only once in each city (with the exclusion of the airline's hub). Passes for unlimited travel are sometimes standby travel passes, meaning you get a seat on a flight only after all the ticketed passengers are seated. Standby passes are best for people who have more time than money.

You have to buy air passes from a travel agent outside the country you'll be visiting, usually from the same airline that flies you into the country. Some air passes are available only in the U.S. to citizens going abroad, and you might have to show proof of U.S. residence before making your purchase. Contact a country's major airlines for more information.

BARGAIN FINDER

Consolidator News for Californians

Californians should consider buying consolidator tickets only from agencies registered with the state as travel sellers. These agencies show a registration number in their sales materials. If you buy your tickets with a registered agency and it fails, you have access to statewide reimbursement funds.

Ask your travel agent about air passes if you're planning to visit multiple locations in a single country or geographical region.

Air Passes around the Globe

Here are a few airlines around the world that have offered air passes recently. Before you buy your pass, though, make sure the rate of exchange doesn't make it cheaper for you to buy each ticket separately.

Indonesia: Garuda Indonesia Airlines, 9841 Airport Blvd., Suite 300, Los Angeles, CA 90045, 800-342-7832.

The Visit Indonesia Decade Pass entitles holders to between three ($300) and five ($500) flights within Indonesia. You can add on up to ten additional flights for $110 each.

Drive One-Way

Consider flying one-way and driving the other. You can often save up to 50% on a rental car when the companies have a directional imbalance. This means they have a number of cars in New York that really belong in Washington, and vice versa. Call or stop by local car rental offices to compare deals and prices.

Air Hitch and Air Tech have rock-bottom airfares if you're willing to hitchhike—which means being flexible about where and when you fly.

Malaysia: Malaysian Airlines, 800-552-9264

The basic Visit Malaysia Pass costs $99 and is good for five flights within the main island of Malaysia within 28 days.

Thailand: Thai Airways International, 800-426-5204

The Amazing Thailand pass costs $199 for four flights within Thailand.

United States: United, Delta or US Airways

Several airlines offer air passes within the United States for foreign tourists. If you have friends or relatives coming to visit from another country, tell them to call several airlines and ask about their offerings. Delta recently offered one pass with unlimited travel for 30 days for $500, and another for 60 days for $800.

Hitchhike Your Way To Europe, The Caribbean...

If you have a flexible schedule, consider hitchhiking your way onto a plane flying to Europe, the Caribbean, Mexico or any one of the 50 states. Two little-known companies, Air Hitch (212-864-2000, 310-574-0090 or 415-834-9192) and Air Tech (800-575-8324 or 212-219-7000), give you access to last-minute empty seats for very low prices.

You choose a departure city, one or more possible destinations, and a three- to five-day window of time during which you are willing to depart. Then you receive a voucher to exchange at the airport for boarding passes. On the eve of your multiple-day window, you contact the company to find out what flights are available. Travelers get their first choice dates and destinations over 70% of the time.

This type of flying gives leisure travelers the flexibility to fly in and out of different European cities and make last-minute changes in their itineraries, options that are usually extremely expensive. If you want to get away to Europe or the Caribbean and aren't particular about your exact destination, air-hitchhiking may be the best deal for you.

Prices to Europe range from around $175 one-way from the Northeast to $269 from the Northwest. Similar airfares are available to the Caribbean and Mexico. And a limited number of flights within the United States cost even less.

These fares are hard to beat, but fare wars have been known to drop prices for round-trip tickets to London down to $150, so be sure to check around before you buy.

The Newest Ways to Save With Charter Flights

When you book a charter flight, you're buying your ticket from a wholesale tour operator, not from an airline. Charter companies make deals with airlines to use their planes to fly specific routes at specific times. Then they sell tickets for these flights through travel agents or their own retail outlets.

Although charters used to be for tour groups only, individual travelers can now take advantage of charter fares without purchasing an entire vacation package. The savings are usually competitive with flights booked through a consolidator, and the best deals go to those who book the furthest in advance.

Like consolidator flights, charters are almost exclusively for international travel.

Who Can Fly on a Charter

You can usually save around $50 to $400 on a trans-Atlantic coach flight by flying on a charter. The savings for first-class tickets can be even greater, with seats often costing less than half as much as comparable seats on a regular flight.

Charter companies are able to charge less than most airlines because they don't keep up regular schedules, flying only when there is enough demand to easily fill their flights. For example, a charter company might only have flights to Europe during the summer (when the most people are free to travel) or to the Caribbean during the winter (when the most people want to be at the beach). And even during peak vacation seasons, charters tend to fly less frequently than major airlines.

If you're planning far in advance to visit a popular vacation destination during tourist season, you should have no trouble finding a good deal on a non-stop charter flight. Your chances of finding a charter flight decrease significantly, however, if you're planning at the last minute to fly to an unusual destination for an odd time period or during the off-season. You will also be unable to find a charter flight if your destination country (like several in the Far East) has protectionist policies for its national airline.

Flying One-way on Charters

While most people use charters for round trips, it's sometimes possible to purchase one-way tickets (known as half round trips) from a charter company for slightly more than half the round-trip ticket price.

It may even be possible to by two half round trip charter tickets arriving and departing from different cities. For example,

Finding a Charter Flight

Travel agencies are usually a good source for information on charter flights. Charter companies also advertise directly in the travel sections of major newspapers like **The New York Times**, **USA Today**, and **The Los Angeles Times**.

Contact these companies for more information on charter flights. Note that many companies that used to fly charter flights now offer standard flights at discount rates.

- **Balair/CTA** (800-322-5247 or 305-751-5108) flies charters to Zurich and has connections to other European cities on Swiss Air.
- **Council Travel** (800-226-8624) flies charters to Europe in the summer.
- **Martinair Holland** (800-366-4655, www.martinairusa.com) flies to Amsterdam and has connections to other European cities.

Tag Along And Save

If your college or local church group is arranging a charter flight for a group vacation, ask whether there are any extra seats. You might be able to grab a great deal on a flight to Europe or another destination.

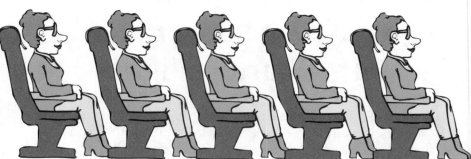

You can sometimes get a great deal by tagging along on a charter flight with a local club or religious group.

you may be able to fly from New York to London on one charter flight, travel around Europe, and then fly from Paris back to New York on another charter flight. Ask your travel agent or the charter company if this could be a money-saving option for you.

Possible Drawbacks

There are several drawbacks to flying on a charter. Make sure the money you're saving is worth any extra hassles or worries you'll have.

Inflexibility Since they have fewer flights, charters give you less flexibility in your vacation schedule. If a charter makes only one round-trip flight weekly to your chosen destination, for example, you have to be prepared to arrive and depart only on those days.

Cancellations Charter companies make their money by booking each flight to capacity, so they might cancel your flight at the last minute if they don't receive enough reservations. Since other airlines are not obligated to honor your ticket, you may have to choose between being stranded until another charter flight is available or paying out-of-pocket for a ticket on a different airline.

Long Lines Charters are notorious for having understaffed check-in lines, and sometimes ask you to arrive three to four hours before your flight to be sure you get checked in.

Short on Comfort Charter flights aren't known for luxurious conditions or gourmet food. Expect a full cabin and a tight squeeze in your seat. This drawback is far more troublesome on a long flight to Southeast Asia than a short flight to the Bahamas.

    Best Choice: Wide body Boeing 757s are the most comfortable charter aircraft to fly.

    Worst Choice: DC-10s and L-1011s that have been specially configured for charter flights are the least comfortable charter aircraft to fly, especially when filled to capacity.

Late Departures Operating on a tight budget, charter companies tend to have relatively small inventories of aircraft. Therefore, if your plane has a mechanical difficulty, you might have to wait hours, even days, until another plane is available. And you won't receive any compensation for your time unless you wait more than 48 hours.

Rebaters: Travel Agents Who Pay You Back

Rebaters are travel agents who reimburse you for part or all of the commission they are paid by airlines. To cut costs, they generally offer no-frills service, expecting you to do any vacation research and trip planning on your own. You should know where and when you want to go before you call your rebater, and let the agent know if you have any airline preferences.

In return for this cut-rate service, rebaters charge their customers a standard fee of around $15 per ticket for making reservations and booking a domestic flight (or $25 for an international one). You usually must pay a minimum ticket price of around $350 for domestic flights in order to receive a rebate.

Most agents will book additional passengers at a discount, and may stop charging extra after three or four people on the same trip.

How It Works
If a round-trip flight from New York to Helsinki costs $900, the rebater would charge you $835:

$ 25	Rebater fee
+ $ 900	Ticket price
$ 925	
– $ 90	Rebater's discount
$ 835	Your cost

Naturally, the savings increase as the price increases. While you may not want to give up the full service of your normal travel agent to save $30, it might be worth it when the savings reach $300.

Some rebaters will book hotel and car rentals for you, but many rebaters deal only in airline tickets. If you plan to buy tickets from this type of agent, you'll have to take care of booking accommodations and ground transportation on your own.

Discount Travel Agents
Some travel agencies (known as discounters) use coupons and other deals to offer prices comparable with rebaters. What really matters is the final price you pay, not whether it comes from a rebater or discounter.

BUYER BEWARE

Travel Agents' Secrets

Travel agents use computer systems created by airline companies. Although these systems search for all available flights, they may favor their mother airline by listing it first, updating its fares more quickly or making it more time-consuming for a travel agent to book with another airline.

Ask your travel agency which airline created their booking system and always question if a flight on that airline is really the least expensive option.

Airline incentive programs are another reason your travel agent may favor a particular airline. Using a concept similar to the frequent flyer miles programs, incentives reward agents for booking more tickets on the same airline.

INSIDE INFORMATION

Virtual Tickets

Save yourself the cost of the airline's service charge by telling your ticket agent you want virtual tickets (also known as e-tickets). The agent will send you your itinerary and a confirmation number. When you get to the airport, use the confirmation number and your credit card to get your ticket and seat assignment from one of the airline's automated ticketing machines. There is rarely a line at ticketing machines, so virtual tickets also let you avoid a long wait at the ticket counter.

Internet Fares

The Internet is the home of today's most exciting new ways to save on travel. If you're online or can get access through someone who is, you can save a bundle. Ask about free Internet access and instruction at your local library.

There are thousands of travel-related websites, but you'll get the most useful information if you find a few you really like and start your search with them every time.

Last-minute Weekend Getaways

Several of the top airlines, starting with American, have made certain low-cost, last-minute tickets for weekend trips available exclusively online. Destinations and costs become available each Wednesday for round-trip flights departing the following Saturday (occasionally Friday) and returning Monday or Tuesday. A wide variety of domestic and even some European destinations are available each week.

The best deals fill up fast, such as a recent February deal for a round-trip flight from LaGuardia, New York to Tampa, Florida for only $159. Many airlines let you sign up on their website to have these deals e-mailed to you once a week when they come out. If you're interested, sign up for all the airlines who have departures at an airport near you.

Other Online Deals

In addition to last-minute weekend fares, many airlines offer other Internet-only steals like fare reductions, buy-one-get-one-free deals and online ticket auctions (during which tickets are sold to the highest bidder). Airlines change the rules and regulations governing these offers all the time, so be sure to read the fine print.

Websites for Cheap Tickets

These websites feature great deals and free information on air travel and a wide variety of other budget travel topics. Or visit an airline's own website for more information on their offerings.

Airlines of the Web (www.itn.net/cgi/get?itn/cb/aow/index:XX-AIRLINES)

You can get general information on flying inexpensively, find links to most of the airlines that have Internet websites, and make online reservations.

Best Fares (www.bestfares.com)

This electronic version of *Best Fares* magazine features Internet-only deals, hidden travel deals, a currency exchange, ATM locator, ski resort information and travel articles. Some sections are free, but you have to be a *Best Fares* subscriber to access many parts of the site.

Expedia (expedia.msn.com)

Expedia searches multiple airlines to find the lowest fares for your chosen destination. To use their Fare Finder service, type in the cities you want to travel to and from and it will e-mail you the best current fares it finds on a weekly basis. (These are not always the best you could find on your own, but they are usually pretty good.) You can also book flights, rental cars and hotels, check the weather around the world, read travel columnists' opinions of different destinations and more.

Internet Travel Network (ITN) (www.itn.net)

ITN offers frequent-flyer information, news on popular travel destinations, travel guide reviews, weather reports and the option to bid on or buy cruises, air fares and travel packages.

TRAVAC (www.travac.com, 800-TRAV-800)

TRAVAC (TRAvel VACations) issues over 75,000 tickets (through 15,000 travel agents) every year. Most flights are on major, scheduled carriers. TRAVAC services over 100 international destinations using 20 major airlines.

Travelocity (www.travelocity.com)

Make last minute plane, hotel, car rental or cruise reservations at this interactive site powered by the SABRE reservation system (used by travel agents). Also see their currency converter, vacation packages and activity information by city.

Travelsites (www.travelsites.com)

Bookmark this site. Travelsites is a great central location to start any travel-related search on the Web. It has pages with easy links to over 100 airlines' webpages and 25 or so sites where you can get airline ticket price quotes and make reservations online. There are also pages devoted to links to cruise lines, hotels, trains, individual countries' tourism offices and general travel information.

Travelweb.com (www.travelweb.com)

Travelweb uses the travel agents' Pegasus computer system to let you find low airfares and make reservations online. Look into hotel rates, weekend getaways and airplane fares.

Once you've found a few good travel websites, look for their recommendations (usually in the form of hot-links) for other websites to visit. Chances are you'll like those sites too.

Flying as a courier isn't the great deal it used to be—but you can still find some pretty cheap flights.

The Mysteries of Air Courier Travel...Revealed

Air courier travel is one of the most talked about, least understood ways to fly. The truth is that today, most courier flights don't offer enough savings to be worth the hassle. Once you understand how they work, however, you can sometimes get real deals—if you are an adventurous traveler who is willing to fly alone, leave at the last minute and travel light.

Here's how courier travel works.

The Courier System

If a business needs to send a small package or document overseas quickly, it has two choices: 1. Send it as air cargo, which can be held over for a day by the foreign country's customs department, or 2. Use a courier company that gets someone (known as a courier) to fly on a passenger airline and check the package as personal luggage, which is not held over in customs.

Businesses frequently choose the second option and hire a courier service because it allows them far more control over how quickly the package arrives in the hands of the recipient.

What You Get

Almost anyone 18 or older can get a flight as a courier, but you should know that fabulously inexpensive courier flights are mostly a thing of the past.

Low prices and even free tickets are not unheard of, however, especially if you're willing to fly to any of a variety of destinations on last-minute notice. For example, you could pay $100 for a round-trip ticket to Tokyo from Los Angeles for which the passenger sitting next to you paid $1,800.

The average courier ticket runs around one quarter of the cost of a full-price economy class ticket. Tickets to popular destinations may not offer significant savings over charter flights and other bargain tickets, however. If you're thinking about flying as a courier, first find out how much standard tickets to your chosen destination cost so you will know what kind of savings you are really getting.

The Best Deals

The best deals for couriers are on last-minute deliveries. As deadlines approach, companies become more anxious to find couriers

for flights that aren't booked, and start dropping what they expect you to pay. Your cost tends to be lowest from January 1 to March 15 and highest during the summer, when many students are on vacation and available for courier duty.

If you can fly on short notice, you can get a great deal–especially if you're not picky about your destination. Let the courier company know what destinations you are available to fly to on short notice so they have your information on hand when last minute deals or the rare free flight turns up. The best deals usually go to reliable couriers who have established a relationship with the company.

If you want to make a reservation in advance, try calling early in the morning at the beginning of the month for a better chance at getting a good deal.

The Drawbacks

There are quite a few restrictions on traveling as a courier. Make sure you are comfortable with these limitations before you buy your tickets. And always ask the company when you will receive your actual ticket. You may not get it until you meet the courier agent at the airport on the day of your flight, a condition which makes some travelers rather nervous.

Unreliable Schedules Courier flying is only for people with flexible schedules, since it is practically impossible to book a courier flight more than one month in advance. Most flights have a mandatory one- or two-week stay, although it is sometimes possible to make other arrangements.

One-passenger Travel Only one courier is sent per delivery, so you must travel alone—although you can sometimes arrange with a friend to be couriers on consecutive days (or on the same day with another courier company).

Baggage Limits You must travel light (often with only one carry-on bag) because couriers usually have to forfeit their right to check any bags since the space will be taken up by the package they are escorting.

Extra Fees In addition, courier companies often charge extra if you pay by anything other than money order (check, credit card…), and tickets are non-refundable and non-transferable.

Finding a Flight

Once you've decided you want to be a courier, the first thing you need to do is find a courier company that flies out of an airport near you. The cities with the most courier flights are New York, Los Angeles, San Francisco, Miami and Chicago.

DID YOU KNOW

Bereavement And Medical-Emergency Discounts

Almost all airlines offer price reductions to people requiring last-minute flights to attend funerals or visit seriously-ill family members. Discounts range from around 50% to 70% off of full coach fares. Simply call the airline and be prepared to supply information, including the deceased's name, your relationship, and the funeral home's address and phone number, or the name and phone number of your sick relative's hospital. Discount airlines rarely offer discounts on top of their already lower fares.

BUYER BEWARE

Vacation Loans

Beware of the vacation loans made by some tour companies. For example, a cruise line might offer you a 24- or 48-month loan to cover the cost of your cruise at an annual interest rate of up to 27%. Some firms will even give you a loan for a second vacation while you're still paying off the first.

In the long run you could end up paying an extra 50% or more for your vacation. For example, a four-year $5,000 loan at just 20% interest ends up costing about $7,300.

HERE'S HOW

Get the Best Seat For Your Money

You'll have the most options if you get your seating assignment and boarding pass in advance, but airline and travel agents cannot issue these more than 30 days before a flight. So, if you purchase your ticket earlier, have your travel agent arrange for the boarding pass to be sent to you when it becomes available. If you purchase your tickets directly from the airline, you can only get your boarding pass at the airport or city ticket office.

DID YOU KNOW

Renew Your Passport by Mail And Save

Plan ahead. Renewing your passport by mail is quick and $35 cheaper than requesting a rush at the last minute. **The Passport Agency** has a new 888 telephone number, not free. For information, call 888-362-8668.

Your departure city will, in part, determine your destination options. Flights from East-Coast cities, for example, fly mostly to Europe, while those from West-Coast cities fly mostly to Asia and Australia. If you live on the East Coast and are looking for an inexpensive flight to Tokyo, however, it might be worth it for you to fly out to the West Coast on your own as cheaply as possible in order to fly to Japan as a courier.

Look for courier services in your yellow pages under Air Courier Svce. or borrow a book on courier travel from the library. Some popular titles are:

- *Air Courier Bargains: How to Travel World-wide for Next to Nothing* by Kelly Monaghan (Intrepid Traveler, $14.95).
- *How to Fly Around the World Almost for Free as an Air Courier* by William Halken (Magni Co., $12.95).
- *The Courier Air Travel Handbook* by Mark I. Field (Perpetual Press, $12.95).

A few, but not many, flights require you to escort a package on the way home as well. If you're not acting as a courier on that leg of the trip, you're free to check your luggage.

Locating a Courier Company

Here are a few courier companies that can help you become a courier. Find out what their fees are ahead of time and make sure the costs don't add up to more than they would with a consolidator flight.

Jupiter (310-670-5123)

Jupiter arranges courier flights from the West Coast to Seoul and Bangkok on Japan Air. There is a $35 registration fee. Most flights are for up to one-month stays.

Now Voyager (212-431-1616; www.nowvoyagertravel.com)

Now Voyager charges travelers $50 a year for access to lists of courier flights as well as its own charters, which are sometimes just as inexpensive. They list flights with American couriers originating in New York, New Jersey, Detroit and Los Angeles.

Flights to Europe require an additional $28 airport departure tax on your day of departure. Pick your tickets up in their Manhattan office or get confirmation information over your fax machine. The least expensive fares are available between January 1 and March 15.

Courier Associations

The Air Courier Association (IACA) (303-278-8810 www.aircourier.org)

IACA offers members information on courier flights. There is a one-time Lifetime Membership Fee of $29. Annual dues are $39. First year total is $68. Renewal dues are $39.

International Association of Air Travel Couriers (IAATC) (561-582-8320, www.courier.org)

IAATC charges members $45 a year for access to up-to-date courier flight information. Members receive a bimonthly bulletin of international travel opportunities, tips and bargains from courier agencies around the country, although IAATC itself sells no tickets. You can also get a list of last-minute courier flights (updated twice daily) 24 hours a day over the fax or on the Internet. IAATC tracks over 70,000 courier flights a year.

BUYER BEWARE

Delayed Flight Myth

Many travelers believe that airlines are required to compensate passengers when their flights are canceled or delayed. In fact, the government only requires compensation when passengers are bumped against their will from an oversold flight, which happens very rarely.

When Getting Bumped Is a Bargain

When a flight is overbooked, meaning there are more people with confirmed tickets than there are available seats, the airline has to bump (remove) people from the passenger list. Airlines routinely sell more tickets than there are seats because they can predict the average number of ticket-holders who routinely don't show up for departure. In fact, these predications are becoming so accurate that passengers are rarely bumped from a flight against their will.

If you do wind up on an overbooked flight, however, and have a reasonably flexible schedule, getting bumped can actually be a great deal. Here's what you need to know to take advantage of being bumped.

Getting bumped can be a good deal—if you're not in a hurry to get somewhere.

Who Gets Bumped?

The flights most likely to bump passengers are those flying heavily-traveled routes at the most popular times of day. It is, for example, far more likely that you will get bumped on a noon Sunday flight from California to New York than a 5 a.m. Tuesday flight from Denver to Anchorage, Alaska. Find out from the airline ahead of time whether your flight is routinely overbooked.

How to Avoid Getting Bumped

If you definitely don't want to be bumped, here are a few precautions you can take to make sure you're on-board when your plane takes off.

1. Check with the Department of Transportation. Find out which airlines flying your intended route have the best record for not bumping passengers. Be aware that the statistics include involuntary bumping only.

2. Take the least crowded flight possible. The less likely your flight is to be overbooked, the less likely it is that anyone will be bumped.

3. Make sure you have a confirmed ticket. The status box on your ticket should read "OK" not "Standby." Check the status box as soon as you purchase your ticket.

4. Get to the gate on time. Do this even if you already have a seating assignment and a boarding pass. Although deadlines for domestic flights are often only ten minutes before departure, they can be as early as an hour before departure (or three hours for an international flight). If you're not there by the official check-in deadline, the airline assumes you're not coming and can give your seat to someone else. And, even if you are on time, the last passengers to check in are the first ones to get bumped.

How It Works

If your flight is overbooked, the airline representatives will ask for volunteers to take a later flight. As an incentive, they frequently offer volunteers a free voucher for a future round-trip domestic ticket on their airline. This can be a great deal, but make sure you know the details before you accept. Ask about any restrictions, such as blackout dates, expiration dates or required Saturday night stays that might make it difficult for you to use the ticket. Also ask how far in advance you can make a reservation.

If not enough people accept the free ticket offer, the airline may begin offering cash payments in addition to the voucher, up to a couple hundred dollars. The price goes up once passengers are actually on board. If you volunteer to be bumped at the gate and then the airline later makes a better offer to someone on the plane, ask the airline to increase your deal to match the later offer. They may or may not agree, but it can't hurt to ask. There are no regulations on how much the airline has to offer volunteers, and payments may vary from one airline to another.

Some people try to get bumped on purpose, making reservations on flights that are consistently overbooked and packing only carry-on luggage. While this is a very unreliable way to travel, there's no reason not to try to get bumped if you have the time. If you want to be bumped, get to the gate early, ask to put your name on the top of the volunteer list, don't check any bags and stay near the desk just before flight time.

Get the Facts

There are a few things you should consider before you accept an airline's bumping offer. First, find out how long the wait will be until the next flight. Are you willing to wait that long? Ask if you will have a confirmed reservation for that flight or be flying standby, in which case you might not get on that flight either. If it's the last flight of the day, ask yourself if you are willing to spend the night in a hotel and whether you can get in touch with anyone who's supposed to meet you at your final destination.

Also ask the airline if they will pay for any meals, phone calls, hotel stays and other incidentals you may need while you wait. Otherwise you may wind up spending any compensation you receive before you even get into the air.

Denied Boarding Compensation on Domestic Flights

 NO compensation if you arrive within one hour of schedule.

 $200 compensation if you arrive between one and two hours late.

 $400 compensation if you arrive over two hours late.

Involuntary Bumping

On the off chance that the airline can't get enough volunteers and you are bumped against your will, you should know what to expect. Involuntary bumping is one of the few areas of air travel still controlled by the federal government, and the Department of Transportation requires airlines to give involuntarily bumped passengers a written statement describing their rights.

Basically, if an airline can find a way to get you to your destination within one hour of your scheduled arrival time, it is not required to reimburse you for your trouble. If, however, the airline can't get you there until between one and two hours of your scheduled arrival time (one and four hours on international flights), it must reimburse you on the spot the amount of your one-way fare, up to $200, for the inconvenience. This is known as denied boarding compensation. And if they can't get you there until over two hours after you were supposed to arrive (over four hours on international flights), they have to give you double the one-way fare, up to $400.

The airline is still responsible for getting you to your destination, even after paying you denied boarding compensation. If you'd rather find another way to get there, however, you can request an involuntary refund and try to make your own flight arrangements with another airline. This is a risky option unless you know you can get yourself there faster on your own.

Denied Boarding Compensation Limitations

Unfortunately, there are many circumstances under which the airline does not have to pay you denied boarding compensation:

1. You don't have a confirmed reservation (the status box on your ticket doesn't read "OK").
2. The flight you're confirmed on holds fewer than 60 passengers.
3. The flight originates outside the U.S. (Only the first half of a round-trip ticket to another country is covered).
4. You arrive at the gate after the check-in deadline.
5. The airline gets you to your destination within an hour of your scheduled arrival time.
6. You are bumped because the airline has to substitute a smaller plane for the original.
7. You are flying on a charter flight.

INSIDE INFORMATION

Who Bumps The Most?

The Department of Transportation keeps records of how frequently different airlines bump their passengers. To get a copy of their most recent *Air Travel Consumer Report* containing information on voluntary bumping, denied boarding compensation, lost, damaged or delayed luggage complaints, and flight delays by airline, flight and airport, write to the Office of Consumer Affairs, Department of Transportation, 400 Seventh St. S.W., Rm. 10405, Washington, D.C. 20590, 202-366-2220. Or, read this and other publications online at www.dot.gov/airconsumer.

Winning with Frequent Flyer Programs

The airlines launched the first frequent flyer programs in the mid-1980s as a way to encourage customer loyalty. Today, over one trillion frequent flyer miles have been earned, although most are never actually redeemed—much to the delight of the airlines.

In the long run, the airlines want you to spend more money. Your goal, on the other hand, is to make frequent flyer programs work to your advantage. Here's how.

How It Works

After you sign up to be part of an airline's frequent flyer program, you earn mileage points every time you fly with that airline. When these points add up to a certain number (often a minimum of 25,000) you can redeem them for free flights, upgrades and other rewards. Since you must fly with a particular airline to earn points in its program, airlines hope you will fly regularly with them instead of searching around for the best deal every time you fly.

You don't have to be a frequent flyer to earn miles toward a free flight.

Getting Started

It's free to sign up for these programs, so take a few minutes to fill out a form whenever you fly on a different airline. This is easy to do if you ask for the forms while you're waiting for departure and fill them out then or during your flight. From then on, every time you make a flight reservation with that airline, give the travel agent or airline representative your frequent flyer number so the miles will be added to your account.

You'll earn the most rewards if you fly frequently on the same airline (your primary carrier) because your miles will be concentrated in one program. Choose an airline that has most of the following qualities to be your primary carrier:

- Flies in and out of your local airport.
- Has frequent flights with reasonable rates to the cities you visit most frequently.
- Offers high mileage points for the trips you plan to make.
- Has tie-ins to earn extra points with credit cards, car rental agencies and hotels you already use.
- Has tie-ins with other domestic and international carriers you already use.
- Has no expiration date for miles (there are fewer and fewer plans like this).
- Requires the least miles for the most benefit.

HERE'S HOW

Accumulate Frequent Flyer Miles...Fast

Build frequent flyer miles quickly by paying for large expenses such as college tuition with airline affinity credit cards if the institutions accept them. These big-ticket items produce mileage points rapidly. Be sure to pay off the charges within the grace period, however, to avoid paying high interest rates.

Try to fly with your primary carrier as often as possible, but don't let this keep you from looking around for the best deal. Each time you fly, call around or ask your travel agent what the least expensive flights are for when and where you want to go. If your primary airline offers one of the best deals, great. But if another airline has a less expensive flight, ask yourself if the miles are really worth the extra $100 or more you might have to pay. Chances are, they're not.

Earning Mileage Points

Flying is the most obvious way to earn frequent flyer miles. Airlines award their program members a certain number of miles for each of their flights. The number of miles you earn is usually, but not always, related to the distance you are flying. Ask the agent how many miles you will be earning before you buy your ticket. And make sure you use exactly the same name that's on the plan when you buy your tickets to be sure that the points are awarded to your account.

There are, however, many ways to earn frequent flyer miles without getting on an airplane. It's possible, in fact, to accumulate enough miles to earn rewards without taking a single flight. Over the past few years, the airlines have made numerous deals with other companies so that members can now earn free miles every time they use their credit card or make a long distance phone call.

The airlines send out information on all kinds of mileage deals with your monthly mileage update mailing. They frequently offer bonus miles as an incentive to get you to join their clubs or use other services. For example, one TWA offer gave members 5,000 bonus miles for taking out a one-year membership in its Ambassador's Club.

You can also earn extra miles from other companies the airline has arranged tie-ins with, such as car rental companies, cruise ships, long distance phone companies, credit cards, dining cards, florists, ski resorts, hotels and even stock brokerages and car-buying services. Typical offers are several hundred bonus miles with your rental car or hotel room, one mile per dollar spent on your credit card and two or three miles per dollar spent on other offers. Many major airlines are also making deals with smaller, regional airlines so that your miles from both go to the same account.

These special deals are constantly changing, so always ask if the mileage offer is still good when you call. Also ask if you're getting the best deal. There are sometimes multiple offers available at the same time for the same service. For example, your frequent flyer newsletter might include an offer of 2,000 bonus miles for signing up with MCI, while an advertisement

TRY SOMETHING DIFFERENT

Pool Your Frequent Flyer Miles

Consider pooling your frequent flyer miles with other people to make a free trip possible, even if your own mileage falls short. **British Airways** (800-955-2748) lets up to four household members add their miles together. **Japan Airlines** (800-525-3663) lets family members enrolled in the Family Club combine miles. Rules change frequently, so check with your airline for an update. Combined miles can be redeemed on partner airlines even when those airlines do not allow pooling of miles.

INSIDE INFORMATION

Log On for More Miles

In an effort to encourage more people to visit their websites and purchase tickets online, airlines sometimes offer 1,000 or more bonus miles to members of their frequent flyer clubs—for simply signing up to get a PIN for their website or filling out a questionnaire.

From time to time, visit the websites of any airlines whose frequent flyer program you belong to and look for special offers.

Frequent Flyers Should Check in Early

If you're flying on frequent flyer miles, make sure you leave yourself enough time to check in. **United Airlines** recently enacted a rule that requires frequent flyer passengers to check in at the departure gate at least 20 minutes prior to their flights—and at least 30 minutes before international flights. Other airlines are expected to follow. This new rule replaces the old 10-minute requirement.

Frequent flyer award redeemers who lose their seats will have to get on a stand-by list for open seats on later flights—with no guarantee for when seats will become available.

IT PAYS TO ASK

Free Flights from Your Job

Business travelers get more out of frequent flyer programs than anyone else, particularly if their company pays for their tickets. Since they tend to travel long distances frequently and pay high prices, business travelers rack up miles quickly and are treated very well by the airlines.

If you travel for your company, you can probably keep the frequent flyer miles from your trip—even if your company pays for your tickets. Ask your supervisor for more information.

you receive directly from MCI offers you 5,000 bonus miles on the same airline.

Reaping Your Rewards

The number of restrictions on frequent flyer miles has been creeping steadily higher ever since they were introduced. It is still possible, however, to find a good deal. You just need to keep your eyes open and plan ahead.

Most airlines send out a monthly statement including your current number of frequent flyer miles and advertisements for special deals. This statement should also list the number of miles required to receive different rewards, which changes fairly frequently. Currently, most plans require 25,000 miles for a round-trip domestic coach ticket, the most popular award by far because it requires the least miles. A round-trip international coach ticket might cost 50,000 or 60,000 miles.

Get the most for your money by using your miles to buy the most expensive tickets they can. For example, if you're planning on taking two domestic round trips this year and only have enough miles for one free flight, plan to use the miles for the flight that you expect will cost more.

Airlines sometimes send out merchandise catalogs featuring stereos, magazine subscriptions and other items you can purchase with your miles. The merchandise usually requires far fewer miles than the least expensive plane ticket. If you don't have enough miles for a plane ticket and the expiration date is approaching, call your program and ask if there are other ways to spend your miles so you can avoid losing them altogether.

Virtual Deals

The Internet offers a wide range of special offers. Frequent flyers who aren't already Internet-savvy might find this is a good time to learn.

For example, Continental (www.flycontinental.com) and Northwest (www.nwa.com) advertise last-minute weekend-travel specials for frequent flyer program members—but only on the Internet. Every week, Continental posts a new special frequent flyer offer. Recently there was a weekend flight from Colorado Springs to New York requiring just 12,500 miles—half the miles that ticket would normally cost.

Sometimes these special Internet prices are as low as 7,500 miles, instead of the customary 25,000 miles. Web-Flyer (www.webflyer.com) posts all current frequent flyer deals from a variety of airlines. Internet deals are frequently valid only for an upcoming weekend, so you can't really plan ahead. But if you're looking for something to do over the weekend, they offer great opportunities.

Flyer Beware

The airlines count on most people never redeeming their frequent flyer miles, and continue to make it harder to cash them in. Here are a few of the problems you may encounter when trying to redeem your miles for airline tickets.

1. Expiration Dates Most airlines put a time limit on their frequent flyer miles of two to five years. That means you have to collect enough miles to receive an award before they expire or you will lose them completely. This can make it hard for infrequent travelers to benefit from frequent flyer programs. If the expiration date is approaching and you are only a few miles short of your desired reward, you can usually get the miles you need from a credit card or other tie-in, or make up the difference in cash.

2. Blackout Dates Make sure you will be able to use your miles when you want to. Airlines have many blackout dates, often during the Thanksgiving and Christmas holidays, when it's impossible to use your miles for a free ticket.

3. Sold-out Flights There are usually a limited number of seats available on each flight for people using frequent flyer rewards, especially on popular flights. If you want to use frequent flyer miles to fly to a popular destination, plan ahead and book the flight well in advance. Don't be surprised if, even then, the airline says there are no more seats available for frequent flyers. If this happens to you, ask to be put on the waiting list and look for another flight.

Another approach is to use your frequent flyer miles for a companion fare or upgrade, since airlines always prefer to have a paying customer. Or try a totally different approach and pay cash for your airfare, using your miles instead to pay for your rental car and accommodations.

4. Missing Miles Sometimes the miles you've earned don't show up on your statement. Always save the bottom sheet from your ticket and all your boarding passes until you're sure you've been credited for the correct number of miles. If a dispute occurs and you need to provide the airline with proof of your flight, send photocopies of your records and keep the originals for yourself.

Airlines prefer to have paying customers on their flights rather than people using frequent flyer miles, so they don't make it easy to redeem your reward miles. To get the best deal, pay close attention to the fine print when you book your reward flight.

Be an Elite Frequent Flyer

Frequent flyers with elite-level status are eligible for more benefits than regular members, including:

- Bonus mileage
- Faster upgrades
- Preferred boarding privileges
- Special check-in

To obtain elite-level status, which requires accumulating a large number of miles within a given year:

1. Choose the airline with the most generous program, and take as many flights on a single airline as possible. Within reason, stick with that airline—even if another carrier has a more convenient departure schedule or a more direct flight.

2. Read program mailings carefully to learn about special offers of bonus miles on specific routes.

3. As the year's end approaches, examine your program balance. If you're near elite-level status, consider taking a flight or two earlier than you planned in order to put you over the top.

5. Spending Too Much for Too Little Don't get so caught up with mileage bonuses and tie-ins from other companies that you spend more money accumulating miles than they are actually worth. For example, most credit cards that earn frequent flyer miles charge an annual fee and have higher interest rates than comparable cards. It may cost less to use a fee-free card with a lower rate and look for a bargain-priced airline ticket. If, however, you routinely spend $25,000 a year on your card, it's certainly worth a $40 fee to get a free round-trip domestic ticket.

Selling Your Miles

The airlines will usually only agree to issue your frequent flyer awards in your name or the name of an immediate family member.

It is not actually illegal to buy and sell frequent-flyer flight coupons, but most airlines don't allow it. If you use an award issued in a different name and the airline finds out, your ticket could be confiscated and the program member's account penalized. Confiscation of a ticket could leave you stranded in a foreign country.

Some people are willing to take this risk for a great price, however. If you're a risk-taker looking for a good deal, consider buying flight coupons from a broker or from FlyerSource (www.smartflyer.com) on the Internet. To post or view Flyer-Source ads, you must register at a cost of $10 for 30 days.

Best Websites for Frequent Flyers

The Internet is the best source of information on frequent flyer programs, since printed material goes out of date almost immediately.

Most airlines have a website with up-to-date information on their own programs. Some of these sites allow you to join the program online, check on the status of your account, find out how many miles you could earn on different itineraries, redeem your points for rewards, and even earn extra miles by answering questionnaires, entering sweepstakes or booking online.

Here are a few sites to interest any frequent flyer.

Clickrewards (clickrewards.com)

Earn frequent flyer miles on the Web by shopping, entering sweepstakes or registering software. Current participating shopping sites include Macy's Online, Golfweb and Microsoft Plaza. Visit the site to find out who the newest participants are.

Frequent Flyer Program Site (www.theffpsite.org)

Get up-to-date information on numerous frequent flyer programs, links to many airlines' websites, and tips on little-known ways to accumulate miles and how to maximize your benefits on any plan.

Travel Discount's Frequent Flyer Programs (www.traveldiscounts. com/discount/airlines/freqfly.htm)

Links to a variety of frequent flyer sites.

Travel.Com (www.TRAVEL.com/aviation/airline/alff.htm)

Links to a variety of frequent flyer sites.

WebFlyer (www.webflyer.com)

Sponsored by *Inside Flyer* magazine, WebFlyer is a good source for all kinds of information on frequent flyer programs. The site features editor Randy Peterson's reviews and rankings of the different programs, details on affinity credit cards, up-to-date information on programs' last-minute fare deals, links to over 60 frequent flyer programs' websites and an online version of *Inside Flyer.*

Frequent flyers who aren't online can subscribe to *Inside Flyer* at 1930 Frequent Flyer Point, Colorado Springs, CO 80915, 800-209-2870, $36 for 12 issues.

The Scoop on Airport Transportation Worldwide

A useful little book for airline travelers is *Salk International's Airport Transit Guide*, which tells travelers "how to get from the airport to the city worldwide." This pocket-sized guide lists local transportation choices and prices for over 420 airports in the U.S. and around the world, from Los Angeles, California to Reykjavik, Iceland. Find out whether your destination's airport has car rentals, taxis, shuttle vans, scheduled buses, hired limousines, light-rail or subways that will take you to your destination, how much they cost and how to locate them quickly upon arrival.

You'll find that many cities offer public transportation that can save you a great deal of money over a private taxi or limousine. And if you do decide to take a taxi, the *Airport Transit Guide* gives you the going rates in each city, so you don't pay more than you should. It also lists the general information phone number and website (if available) for each airport.

DID YOU KNOW

Comparing the Frequent Flyer Programs

Randy Peterson, editor of *Inside Flyer* magazine, has been following the growth and changes in frequent flyer plans since their inception. In a recent analysis of the most popular programs, he came up with the following ratings.

B+ Northwest WorldPerks
(800-225-2525)

B+ American Airlines AAdvantage
(800-433-7300)

B US Airways Frequent Traveler
(800-872-4738)

B United Mileage Plus
(800-241-6522)

B America West Flight Fund
(800-235-9292)

B Alaska Mileage Plan
(800-426-0333)

B Continental OnePass
(800-525-0280)

B– Delta Frequent Flyer
(800-323-2323)

C+ TWA Frequent Flight Bonus
(800-325-4815)

C Southwest Rapid Rewards
(800-445-5764)

Best Cheap Sightseeing Tips

On your next trip to a new country or city, don't spend all your time on bus tours. You'll part with your money without getting a real taste of the local culture. Instead, take advantage of all the inexpensive and free things there are to see. Here are some low-cost sightseeing ideas that will give you a real feel for the area:

❏ Spend an afternoon lazily strolling through one or two residential neighborhoods.

❏ Search out a restaurant that's popular with the locals.

❏ Visit an outdoor bazaar.

❏ Spend an afternoon people-watching in a local restaurant or cafe.

❏ Rent bicycles, or ride the bus or subway.

❏ Ask about community theater productions, singing groups or local sports events.

❏ Visit the smaller, less expensive museums.

❏ Use a guidebook to take your own walking tour.

The *Airport Transit Guide* is generally sold in bulk to travel agents and corporate travel managers who pass it along to their clients as a gift or special promotion, so ask your travel agency if they have any available. If you absolutely can't get your hands on a free copy, you can buy it for $9.95 a copy.

Great Deals, Just for Seniors

There are several respected travel companies that specialize in vacations for seniors. Unlike most tour companies, these organizations prefer to work with individuals rather than travel agents. That means that you have to contact them directly to receive their catalogs and information.

Since these companies cater to seniors, they understand your budget restraints and usually have very reasonable prices. And, since most of these groups are relatively large and have been around for some time, they have the influence and know-how to help you plan a great (active or relaxing) trip for less.

One way they do this is to plan many of their trips during the off-peak seasons when prices are lowest. Their customers, most of whom are retirees, are flexible about when they travel but always want to pay a reasonable price. As always in travel, you'll get the best deals if you have a flexible schedule.

Elderhostel

Over 300,000 seniors (ages 55 and up) take part in Elderhostel's educational trips every year. For a very reasonable price, you can choose from a fantastic selection of courses offered at hundreds of different schools around the world. You stay with other seniors in student accommodations or youth hostels, and eat in the school cafeteria or other group facility.

You'll receive around four and a half hours of instruction a day, depending on your field of study. The courses cover a wide array of liberal arts and health-related topics as well as the local culture and geography. Some recent offerings just in Arizona included "Native American Spirituality: From Peyote to Catechism", "Tempting Your Palate: Foods of the Southwest", "Natural Forces at Work: the Sonoran Desert", and "Glass Design and Technique". Most courses offered in the U.S. last one week, while overseas and foreign-language courses usually last for three weeks. Book early in the season for the best selection, although 95% of applicants get enrolled in their first-choice course.

One price (currently $345) includes room, board and tuition costs per person in the U.S. courses. Overseas trip prices include airfare and cost an average of $2,500 per person for a three-week course.

More Information: Elderhostel, 75 Federal St., Boston, MA 02110, 617-426-7788.

Gadabout Tours

Gadabout specializes in tours in the U.S., with a few going to Europe and other overseas destinations. Ask about their Unpack Once trips, on which you stay at one hotel for the duration of the tour, taking a bus to and from different destinations each day. These vacations are popular with people who don't like to live out of their suitcases, staying at a different hotel each night. Prices average around $100 a day. Also ask about seniors' cruises.

More Information: Gadabout Tours, 700 East Tahquitz Canyon Way, Palm Springs, CA 92262, 800-952-5068 or 760-325-5556.

Grand Circle Travel, Inc.

This company has three main divisions: Grand Circle Travel, Overseas Adventure Travel and Vermont Bicycle Tours. The main Grand Circle Travel agency offers a wide variety of trips. Their popular live-abroad, extended-stay vacations include round-trip airfare to an overseas destination plus accommodations in an efficiency or studio apartment, organized entertainment and some meals for around $100 a day or less. And you can choose to stay for anywhere from a week to several months. An extended stay in Costa del Sol, Spain is one of their best deals for as little as $65 a day.

Grand Circle's Overseas Adventure Travel offers light adventure trips for groups of seniors. And recent addition Vermont Bicycle Tours has bike tours traveling all over the U.S., Canada and Europe.

Request brochures on areas of the world you are interested in traveling to as well as a free copy of *101 Tips for Mature Travelers*.

More Information: Grand Circle Travel, 347 Congress St., Boston, MA 02210, 800-248-3737 or 617-350-7500.

There are low-priced tour companies that specialize in taking groups of older adults to exotic destinations all around the world.

BUYER BEWARE

Cruise and Tour Lengths

Cruise and tour lengths are not always as long as their advertising suggests. A seven-day cruise really lasts six nights. Tours with late-night departures and early-morning return flights count both departure and return days as tour days, even if you are not really on the trip either day. Cruises that leave at night and arrive early in the morning may also count both departure and arrival as full days.

Always count the number of nights a cruise or tour lasts, not the days. When reading ads, watch for phrases like "subject to change" and "restrictions may apply." Get details before you book any trip that includes them.

Saga International Holidays

This large British company serves over 250,000 traveling seniors (ages 50 and up) a year, mostly from the United Kingdom, the United States and Australia. Saga deals mostly in bus tours, some of which combine tourists from all three countries. The most popular destinations are in the U.S., Canada and Europe, but Saga also offers tours in Mexico, South America, Australia and the Far East, as well as cruises.

More Information: Saga Holidays, 222 Berkeley Street, Boston, MA 02116, 800-343-0273 or 617-262-2262.

Volunteer Vacations

A service-oriented vacation is a great way to combine travel with personal growth and community service. As a volunteer, you gain access to lesser-known areas which are rarely seen by the average tourist, and you have the chance to give something back to the community or environment. Best of all, service-oriented adventures are available at a fraction of the cost of most adventure trips, and the fees you do pay are sometimes tax deductible.

Here are some organizations that offer a wide range of exciting volunteer-travel opportunities in the United States and around the world. Most organizations require volunteers to be 18 or older, and many have trips especially for seniors.

American Hiking Society

The American Hiking Society (AHS) sponsors two-week expeditions in all 50 states. Teams of 10 to 12 volunteers help build and restore hiking trails for the National Park Service. This is an inexpensive way for nature lovers to see remote and beautiful parts of the country. There are trips for both novice and veteran hikers. Volunteers provide their own camping gear and should be in good enough physical condition to hike five miles a day. The registration fee is $65, and the volunteer season runs from March through October.

More Information: Send a self-addressed stamped envelope to AHS Volunteer Vacations, P.O. Box 20160, Washington, D.C. 20041-2160 or visit www.americanhiking.org.

Volunteers for Peace

International volunteer excursions are sponsored by organizations in over 60 host countries, including Belgium, Guatemala, Spain and the Czech Republic. Groups of 10 to 20 volunteers live in workcamps and assist in community

development and international education. Programs cost $175 for two- to three-week sessions. Meals and lodging (but not airfare) are included.

More Information: Volunteers for Peace, 43 Tiffany Rd., Belmont, VT 05730, 802-259-2759.

Sierra Club Service Outings

In addition to its hundreds of regular expeditions, the Sierra Club sponsors about 45 service-oriented trips around the United States each year. Groups of ten or so volunteers join a Sierra Club cook and leader for week-long treks into the wilderness to maintain and repair trails and picnic areas, or work on documentation and conservation projects. Most trips alternate between work and recreation days, so there is plenty of time to hike, fish and enjoy the scenery. Possible destinations include Buffalo National River in Arkansas, St. Croix in the U.S. Virgin Islands and Redrock Canyon near Sedona, Arizona. Service trips cost much less than regular excursions, running around $325 for most week-long outings. Volunteers range in age from 20 to 70 and up.

More Information: Sierra Club Outing Dept., 85 Second St., 2nd Floor, San Francisco, CA 94105, 415-977-5630, www.sierraclub. org/outings/.

Alaska State Parks Volunteer Program

For those interested in longer expeditions, Alaska State Parks offers full-time volunteer positions for adults interested in assisting park rangers, giving natural history talks or working with trail crews. Lodging is included, and most positions supply meals or pay an expense allowance of $100 to $300 a month. You must provide your own round-trip transportation to Alaska.

More Information: For a booklet describing volunteer positions, write to Volunteer Coordinator, Alaska State Parks, 550 W. 7th Ave., Suite 1390, Anchorage, Alaska 99501-3561, 907-269-8708, www.dnr.state.ak.us/parks.

Appalachian Mountain Club

The Appalachian Mountain Club (AMC) has 11 chapters throughout the northeastern United States, each offering a variety of volunteer-vacation opportunities for ages 16 and up. For a program fee of $75 to $95 a week, you can join a Volunteer Crew responsible for maintaining and improving conditions along the trails.

Benefits of Volunteer Travel

- Deep savings on food and lodging.
- Unique destinations you don't see as a tourist.
- Chance to get involved in local communities.
- Possible tax deduction on the price of your trip.

You must have prior backpacking experience and your own camping equipment, but AMC will train you in hand tool techniques, safety procedures, and trail construction and maintenance techniques. Crews usually consist of a leader and six to eight men and women of assorted ages. AMC has recently added special Crew programs for teenagers, seniors and women-only. Most excursions include food and shelter, but specifics vary. AMC chapters also offer shorter trips, educational weekends and one-day events.

More Information: Call your local chapter or contact AMC at 603-466-2721.

Earthwatch Expeditions

Earthwatch volunteers assist in a wide range of scientific expeditions all over the world. Earthwatch offers many different educational trips, including 20 or so that cost less than $1,500 (not including airfare). Fees cover your food and lodging expenses and support project research. Recent inexpensive one-week trips included excavating Pueblo ruins in Arizona ($695), studying disappearing species of migrating songbirds in Puerto Rico ($995) and exploring the mysterious Mammoth Caves of Kentucky ($695).

Willing volunteers can find low-cost travel opportunities aimed at helping improve the standard of life in countries all over the globe.

More Information: Earthwatch, P.O. Box 403-RE, Watertown, MA 02272, 800-776-0188.

Amizade

Amizade Ltd. sponsors volunteer programs at four international sites: 1. Santarém, Brazil, 2. Cochabamba, Bolivia, 3. Pevas, Peru and 4. Yellowstone National Park in the United States. Volunteers get involved in community projects like building schools and health posts or replanting trees in depleted forest reserves.

Programs are open to ages 18 and older, although children ages 12 to 17 may attend the Yellowstone program with their parents. Amizade handles flights, accommodations, volunteering and recreation activities at reasonable, but not rock-bottom prices. For example, a two-week program in Brazil costs around $2,650. Part

of the price pays for your travel and accommodations, and the rest keeps the program running. Amizade also runs programs in conjunction with Elderhostel (877-426-8056).

More Information: Amizade, 367 S. Graham St., Pittsburgh, PA 15232, 888-973-4443.

Savings Especially For Singles

Traveling alone (because you're single, divorced or widowed) can be expensive—and sometimes lonely. Solo travelers usually end up paying significant surcharges, from 25% to 100%, on hotel rates and other prices which are normally listed for double occupancy.

If you're a single traveler, however, don't despair. There are quite a few newsletters, networks and travel agencies that specialize in finding great, inexpensive trips for singles. There are also services that help you find a travel companion with whom you can take advantage of double-occupancy prices. If you want more information on thrifty ways to travel alone, help finding a travel companion, or updated news on tours with other singles, you can start by contacting one or more of these companies.

Connecting Solo Travel Network

For $25 a year, this organization offers tips for solo travel, single-friendly travel listings, ads for travel buddies and a hospitality exchange (a network of traveling singles who are willing to host other traveling singles around the world). Members communicate through a bi-monthly, 20-page newsletter.

More Information: Connecting Solo Travel Network, P.O. Box 29088, 1996 W. Broadway, Vancouver, BC V6J-5C2, 800-557-1757 or 604-737-7791.

Saga Holidays

Saga links up single seniors to share accommodations by matching criteria (such as female, non-smoker) on their computer. Send for a free brochure listing their wide variety of available tours.

More Information: Saga Holidays, 222 Berkeley Street, Boston MA 02116, 800-343-0273, 617-262-2262.

Singles travel networks and clubs help you

- Avoid single-travel surcharges
- Meet new people with similar interests

HERE'S HOW

Do's and Don'ts For Singles

It's simple to enjoy a great vacation while traveling on your own. Just follow a few simple guidelines:

- **Do** look into singles-oriented travel clubs and tours.

- **Don't** go to couples-oriented resorts where you'll feel awkward being on your own.

- **Do** stay at hostels and other accommodations that foster a group atmosphere.

- **Don't** stay at impersonal hotels that require you to pay a single-room surcharge.

- **Do** expect to meet lots of new and interesting people.

- **Don't** expect to meet the man or woman of your dreams.

T.G.I.F.

This singles club for travelers ages 35 and up has over 600 members. Events include Get-away Weekends, river rafting, sailing, cruises and other longer trips. Ask for a complimentary calendar of events when you call.

More Information: T.G.I.F., 977 Wellington Drive, North Vancouver, BC, Canada V6K-1L1, 800-661-7151.

Travel Companion Exchange

Travel Companion Exchange (TCE) is the largest and most successful travel companion company in the United States. Jens Jurgen established TCE 18 years ago because of what he calls Noah's Rule: "All travel bargains are based on double occupancy." Today, TCE offers two important services: one of the best bargain-travel newsletters available and a means for single travelers to find partners to accompany them on vacation. Age groups range from 20-somethings to 80 and up, but most TCE members are over 50.

Members of TCE pay $159 a year to receive the bi-monthly newsletter and thousands of short descriptions of other singles looking for travel partners of the same or opposite sex. Members submit a profile of themselves that is summarized in this listing, including hobbies, travel interests and the like. Each member can then request a full profile and contact information for any listing. Members can request one free profile a month and pay $2 for each additional request.

Travelers not looking for travel partners can subscribe to the newsletter only for $48 a year (includes five back issues). Request a sample newsletter for $6.

More Information: Travel Companion Exchange, P.O. Box 833, Amityville, NY 11701, 800-392-1256 or 631-454-0880.

Alternate Accommodations: When You Don't Want to Pay Hotel Prices

Hotels aren't the only places you can spend the night while you're on vacation, and on the whole they're not the best deals for overnight stays. Consider these money-saving alternatives to high-priced hotels.

Vacation Rentals

Renting a house, condo or apartment can really cut the cost of your vacation. As hotel prices continue to rise, rentals become more attractive, especially since they offer more room for families and large groups. And a rental can save you more money if you make your own meals in the kitchen—or just shop for beer and soda at a local supermarket and keep it in the refrigerator instead of spending $2 a Pepsi in the hotel bar.

Rentals are usually an option only if you are planning to spend a week or more in your location, since most are rented on a weekly basis. You may also have to follow the traditional Saturday-to-Saturday rental cycle, although alternate deals can usually be arranged during off seasons.

For a great deal on an off-season getaway, look into renting a condo in a Vermont or Colorado ski area in the summer. The mountains are beautiful, the weather cool, and there's plenty of hiking, swimming, mountain biking and other sports for the whole family. Plus, your rental will probably cost you less for the month than it does for a week during the peak winter season.

Ask your travel agent about rentals or look in the travel section of your local newspaper and in the classifieds of cultural and travel magazines. If you know

Vacation rentals let you feel right at home. And you don't pay for expensive hotel extras such as hotel breakfasts, drinks at the bar, tips for the bellboy and high prices at the hotel newsstand.

Better Car Rental In Europe

Book your European car rental through a U.S. firm that you know and trust, through an experienced travel agent or through **Auto Europe** (800-223-5555) or **Rail Europe** (800-438-7245), two respected firms specializing in European rentals.

It is hard to compare car-rental rates in Europe on your own. Basic rates and the value added tax (VAT) vary, car models are likely to be unfamiliar and there may be unexpected restrictions on rentals. For example, automatic-transmission cars are scarce and expensive, and many models may not be driven into Italy or Eastern Europe.

Credit Card Use Abroad Can Cause Problems

Let card issuers know before you travel, so they will not think charges are unauthorized if your spending pattern changes. The card issuer may be unable to help if a store overseas refuses to fix or take back defective merchandise, because local law overseas governs those transactions. Try to get written guarantees from overseas merchants or make the assumption that there is no guarantee before you buy an item.

where you want to go, call the town and ask for a copy of their local paper, or check with a Realtor in the area.

Hostels for All Ages

Most people think of hostels as cheap accommodations exclusively for college students and other young travelers. But today's hostels serve a much wider population, housing guests of all ages.

Hostels are generally the least expensive accommodations available to travelers. Originally intended for young people, the typical hostel has common sleeping areas and bathrooms. Guests sleep in rooms with other members of the same sex, often in twin or bunk beds. You also share any additional facilities, such as kitchens and common areas. In return for giving up a little luxury and privacy, however, you pay rock bottom prices, often under $10 a night.

Hostels come in all shapes and sizes. There are thousands of hostels in Europe, and several hundred in North America and around the world. Most don't accept reservations but will do their best to squeeze you in.

Consider joining Hostelling International-AYH (733 15th St. N.W., Suite 840, Washington, D.C. 20005, 202-783-6161, www.hiayh.org). Annual membership is free for ages 17 and under, $25 for ages 18 to 54, and $15 for ages 55 and up. Membership includes a membership card entitling you to a variety of travel discounts, and a listing of 150 hostel facilities throughout the United States. Listings of almost 5,000 more hostels in Europe and the Mediterranean, or Africa, Asia, Australia and New Zealand are available for an additional $13.95 each.

Home Swaps

One great way to save money on accommodations, especially for a large family, is to find someone who has a home in the place you want to visit and agree to trade a vacation at their home for one at yours. If you arrange a swap with someone who has a home comparable to yours, you'll get the comfort you are used to at little or no cost, saving yourself a bundle on hotel fees. Most home exchanges last at least a month, particularly for retirees and Europeans who receive five or six weeks of vacation a year.

If you know someone with a home in a different state or country, ask them if they'd be interested in swapping with you. If not, look into joining one of the vacation exchange clubs that list thousands of homes all over the globe. Most clubs cost only $65 a year to join, a small price to pay for free accommodations.

Once you find a potential home exchange, make sure you and the other owner agree on the terms before you make the trade. Decide whether you also want to swap cars, whether

A home exchange lets you try out a new part of the world, while another family gets to try out your home town.

you're willing to take care of plants or pets, and whether you'd like to introduce your guests to some of your friends.

Finding a Home Exchange Club

These organizations offer different ways to find potential home exchanges around the world.

HomeLink P.O. Box 650, Key West, FL 33041, 800-638-3841

A one-year membership in HomeLink costs $98 for five catalogs listing homes around the world, mostly in Europe. Request a free information packet.

Intervac U.S. 800-756-HOME or www.intervacus.com

Intervac offers two types of memberships: Web-only ($50) for one-year listing online and in the big January Book. Web-only members do not receive Home Exchange Books. Printed-Web ($93) for a listing in the big January Book and online for a year and copies of Home Exchange Books. Homes are primarily located in the U.S., Western Europe and Canada, with a few in Eastern Europe, South America and Asia as well.

The Invented City 41 Sutter St., Suite 1090, San Francisco, CA 94104, 800-788-2489 or 415-252-1141, www.invented-city.com

The Invented City charges $75 to $125 annually for six to nine catalogs (although you can only list your house once). The majority of listings are in North America, Britain, Scandinavia, Switzerland and Australia.

Trading Homes International P.O. Box 787, Hermosa Beach, CA 90254, 800-877-8723, www.trading-homes.com

Trading Homes International charges members $65 a year for three directories of around 3,000 listings each. You can also

Little-Known Hotel Discounts

- Shareholder rates may be available if you own stock in the company that owns or manages the hotel.
- A frequent flyer rate may be available if you fly on an airline with which the hotel has a partnership.
- Emergency-situation rates are given to people traveling because of family illness or stranded by natural disasters.
- Family package rates, often available at resorts, include breakfast or recreational discounts.
- Corporate rates are often available if you have a business card, even if you are not traveling on business.

Questions to Ask Before Booking a Room

- ❏ Can I cancel my reservation, or check out a day early, without penalty?
- ❏ How late can I arrive without having paid for my room in full?
- ❏ Is there room service, and if so, during what hours? (Some hotels have reduced the hours for room service or cut it out entirely.)
- ❏ Does the quoted rate include tax and service charges...breakfast...parking?

choose to join via the Internet for the same price or get both Internet and paper listings for $95. Locations include South Africa, the Caribbean, Australia and New Zealand as well as Europe and North America.

Worldwide Home Exchange Club 202-588-5057; www.wwhec.com

For $60 to $75 a year, you get two directories listing over 1,500 homes in the U.S., Canada, Europe, South Africa, Australia, New Zealand and sometimes Asia.

Finding Great Hostels

A good guidebook can be your best bet for finding guest hostels. Begin your research in the library, but consider buying your favorite book to take on your trip with you so you can make notes and not worry about bringing it back in perfect condition.

Here are a few good guides to hostels around the world.

- *At Home in Hostel Territory: A Guide to Friendly Lodgings from Seward to Santa Cruz* by Janet Thomas (Alaska Northwest Books, $12.95).
- **The Berkeley Guides Series** (Fodor's Travel Publications, around $17.95 each).
- **Cheap Sleeps Series** (Chronicle Books, around $12.95 each).
- *Japan for the Impoverished: A Travel Guide* by Jim Richman and James Richman (Borgman Corp., $24.95).
- **Let's Go Series** (St. Martin's Press, around $13.99 and up).
- **Lonely Planet Shoestring Guides Series** (Lonely Planet, around $19.95 each).
- **Moon Travel Handbooks Series** (Moon Publications, $19.95 each).

If you're online, check out **The Internet Guide to Hostelling** at www.hostels.com. This website offers backpackers a wide variety of information on budget travel and hostels. Their hostel database, the Worldwide Hostel Guide, has a giant list of hostels around the world, searchable by country and city. If you're a first-time hosteller, you should check out the FAQ (frequently-asked questions) sheet on hostels to see what you're getting into. There's also a Bulletin Board to meet travel companions and share information, links to bargain travel sites and other money-saving information.

Don't Pay Full Price For That Room!

There are plenty of ways to find a hotel room for less than the listed price, whether you want to stay at a local motel or the Four Seasons.

Ask Your Travel Agent

Your travel agency is a good place to start looking for ways to save on accommodations. Ask your travel agent about any unpublicized sales going on in hotels in the area you're planning to visit. Travel agents often have good tips on how to pay less at resort and business hotels.

Travel During the Off Season

Hotel prices drop significantly during the area's off season, so consider booking your trip then. Weekend rates are usually much lower than weekday business rates. And try not to stay in a city during a major convention, when hotel prices go through the roof.

Request a Status Discount

Most hotels offer 10% discounts for people over age 60, and the discount increases for members of AARP, National Alliance of Senior Citizens or Silver Keys. Many hotels will also give you a discount for being a student, veteran, young adult or a member of AAA, a business organization or other group.

Call Hotel Chain 800-numbers

Before you make your reservations, you can call a few of the larger hotel chains to find out if they have hotels in the area, how much they charge and whether they have any current sales or discounts.

Call the Hotel Directly

You'll almost always save money by calling the hotel directly instead of booking through the chain's 800-number. Book your room well in advance, so the hotel agent knows you have time to shop around. And don't accept the first rate offered to you. Many hotels have a fall-back rate that they will quote if, and only if, a customer is reluctant to accept the standard rate.

Pay Cash

Some hotels will give you a discount for paying cash instead of using a credit card.

Consider going south in the late fall or early spring, instead of mid-winter. Hotels give discounts of half-off or more during the off season.

Get Cleaner Travel Facilities

If you are sensitive to smoke or just want a cleaner environment, ask for a smoke-free hotel room, transatlantic flight and car. The car-rental companies, notably **Budget**, and the **American Lung Association** have cooperated to eliminate cigarette lighters in some vehicles. Ask your travel agent to enter this preference on your personal record, so it will be requested every time.

Hotel Chain 800-Numbers

Although rarely the least expensive way to book a room, hotel chain 800-numbers can be very useful for finding out the local phone numbers of chain hotels in a particular area.

- **Days Inn** 800-325-2525
- **Econo Lodge** 800-446-6900
- **Embassy Suites** 800-EMBASSY
- **Hampton Inns** 800-HAMPTON
- **Holiday Inn** (Ask about Great Rates Program) 800-HOLIDAY
- **Marriott** (Courtyard) 800-321-2211
- **Marriott** (Residence) 800-331-3131
- **Motel 6** 800-4MOTEL6
- **Novotel** 800-NOVOTEL or 212-315-0100
- **Choice Hotels** (Central reservation service for **Rodeway Inn**, **Quality Inn**, **Sleep Inn**, **Comfort Inn**, **Clarion**, **Friendship Inn** and **Econo Lodge**) 800-221-2222
- **Radisson Hotels** 800-333-3333
- **Red Roof Inns** 800-THE-ROOF
- **Sheraton** 800-325-3535
- **Super 8** 800-848-8888
- **Travelodge** 800-578-7878

Book through Your Airline

If you're traveling overseas, consider booking your hotel through your airline. Many international carriers have established relationships with foreign hotel chains that can save you money. For example, American Airlines (800-832-8383) sells vouchers for 20% to 30% off at several hundred Best Western hotels in Europe, while British Airways (800-359-8722) offers air and land packages. Check with your airline to see if it has a similar program.

Join a Discount Club

There are several discount clubs that offer card-carrying members up to 50% off the list price of mid-range hotel rooms across the country and around the world. Request a club's list of hotels to see where they are, and what type they are, before you join. The details of these programs change frequently, so be sure to read the small print before you sign up.

- **Encore** (800-638-8976 or 301-459-8020) lists 3,000 hotels around the world at varying discounts for an annual $69.95 fee.

- **Great American Traveler** (800-548-2812) offers 50% off at 1,500 hotels like Ramada Inn for $49.95 the first year and $29.95 for renewals.

- **Hotels at HalfPrice** (800-648-4037) offers 50% off at over 4,000 hotels, plus a one-time free room certificate, airline-savings vouchers, rebate travel agent services and other frequently-updated services for around $60 a year.

Call a Hotel Consolidator

Consolidators, also called discounters, book blocks of rooms months in advance—and at steep discounts. In exchange for agreeing to buy rooms on slow nights, consolidators get their pick of rooms when the hotel would otherwise be sold out. Unlike discount-card companies, consolidators deal primarily with deluxe properties, but agree not to heavily advertise their names.

Here are some hotel consolidators and the areas they cover:

- **Accommodations Express** (800-444-7666) Major U.S. convention and resort cities, including Boston, Las Vegas and Chicago.

- **Capitol Reservations** (800-847-4832) Washington, D.C.

- **Central Reservations Service** (800-950-0232) Boston, Atlanta, Orlando, Miami, San Francisco, New Orleans and New York City.

- **Express Hotel Reservations** (800-356-1123) New York City and Los Angeles.

- **Hot Rooms** (773-468-7666) Chicago.

- **Hotel Reservations Network** (800-964-6835, www.hoteldiscount.com) New York, Chicago, San Francisco, Los Angeles, New Orleans, Orlando, Washington, D.C., London, Paris and more.

- **Quikbook** (800-789-9887, www.Quikbook.com) New York City, Washington, D.C., Atlanta, San Francisco, Boston, Los Angeles and Chicago.

- **Room Exchange** (800-846-7000, 212-760-1000) Over 22,000 hotels and resorts in the U.S., the Caribbean, Mexico, Canada, Asia, Europe and the Far East.

- **San Francisco Reservations** (800-677-1550) San Francisco and surrounding areas.

- **Washington, D.C. Accommodations** (800-554-2220) Washington, D.C.

Great Deals on Top-Notch Cruises

Often thought to be only for the rich and famous, cruises have become one of the most affordable vacation options.

Cruises aren't only for the rich. In fact, if you know how to go about it, you can probably pay less for a cruise than almost any other vacation.

First, never pay the price listed in the cruise brochure. Hardly anyone does. Cruise companies are known for selling a large number of cabins at discount prices through travel agencies and cruise consolidators, so you should expect a discount of at least 25%. And if you have a flexible schedule, you can sometimes save up to 75% by filling empty cabins at the last minute.

Your best source of discounts is one of the many cruise-only travel agencies that make a business of selling deeply-discounted cabins. Savings are always greater in the off season, so consider traveling to Alaska or the Caribbean in the spring or fall. You'll save even more if you don't have your heart set on a particular ship or destination, and if you're flexible about when you embark.

Cruises are usually all-inclusive, so that one price covers your accommodations, meals and most entertainment. Find out about additional costs (such as alcoholic beverages or special island excursions) ahead of time so you can estimate your total cost.

163

Cruise-Ship Health Scorecards

You can request health scorecards for any cruise ship in the U.S., since **Centers for Disease Control and Prevention (CDC)** personnel check the ships' food, water quality and cleanliness regularly. Look for a score of 86 or better. To request a free copy of a ship's most recent scorecard, contact Vessel Sanitation Program, National Center for Environmental Health, 1015 N. American Way, Room 107, Miami, FL 33132. Or visit the CDC website, which is linked to the inspection program at www.cdc.gov/travel/.

Best Cruise Deals

Know a good buy when you see one. The best deal you'll find on a cruise is about 70% to 80% off the rack rate. Two-for-one deals are also good bargains, particularly if they include round-trip airfare.

Find the Best Cruise for You

Here are some of the larger travel agencies that specialize in cruises, good bets for finding a great cruise at a low price.

The Cruise Line, Inc. (800-777-0707 or 305-653-6111).

Open seven days a week, The Cruise Line offers an average savings of $600 to $2,000 off list prices on cruises all over the world. Request one of The Cruise Line's guides to first-time, senior, family, ultra-deluxe, or wedding and honeymoon cruises. Last-minute savings are updated weekly on the 24-hour recording at 800-777-0707, ext. 2610, and at their Web site, www.mytravelco.com/cruises.

Cruises of Distinction (800-634-3445 or 248-332-2020).

Get on their mailing list to receive catalogs of cruise discounts four times a year, or ask about their last-minute cruise specials.

Cruises International, Inc. (888-255-7447 or 847-891-8820).

Cruises International prides themselves on their customer service, creating custom client profiles to find the best cruise-match within each client's budget. Call and get on the mailing list for their seasonal catalog, their magazine about cruising, *Cruise Trends*, and their six annual *Cruise Savers Guides*, each of which focuses on a different cruise line.

Cruises Only of Orlando (800-683-7447).

Known as the world's largest cruise-only travel agency, Cruises Only of Orlando offers low-priced cruises around the world.

Spur-of-the-Moment Cruises, Inc. (800-343-1991 or 310-521-1070).

Calling itself "America's clearinghouse for last-minute and unsold cruises," Spur-of-the-Moment offers discounts of up to 80% on cruises for travelers with flexible schedules. Their cruise hotline (310-521-1060) features an up-to-date recording of last-minute cabin openings.

Travel Services International (www.mytravelco.com).

This 35-year old company offers up-to-date information on cruise deals and expert cruising advice on its new Internet site.

Canadian Province Tourist Information

Like American states, each Canadian province has a travel office that will send you free tourist information. The type and amount of information varies, but items are similar to those from American states: free maps, calendars of events, travel guides and brochures containing information about accommodations, campgrounds, restaurants and attractions, and recreational activities. Tell the operator if you are interested in a particular city or type of vacation (such as hiking, fishing or museum-browsing) to receive information tailored to your preferences.

It usually takes three to four weeks for the information to arrive.

Travel Alberta 17811 116th Ave., Edmonton, AB T5F-2J2, Canada, 800-661-8888 or 780-427-4321. www.discoveralberta.com.

Tourism British Columbia 1803 Douglas St., Victoria, BC V8W-9W5, Canada, 800-663-6000 or 250-387-6309. www.hellobc.com.

Explore Manitoba 21 Forks Market Rd., Winnipeg, MB R3C-4T7, Canada, 800-665-0040 or 204-945-3777. www.travelmanitoba.com.

Tourism New Brunswick P.O. Box 12345, Campbellton, NB E3N-3T6, Canada, 800-561-0123. www.tourismnbcanada.com.

Newfoundland and Labrador Tourism Branch P.O. Box 8700, St. John's, NF A1B-4J6, Canada, 800-563-6353 or 709-729-0862. www.gov.nf.ca/tourism.

Northwest Territories P.O. Box 610, Yellowknife, NT, X1A-2L9, Canada, 800-661-0788 or 867-873-7200. www.nwttravel.nt.ca.

Prince Edward Island Tourism P.O. Box 940, Charlottetown, Prince Edward Island, C1A-7M5, Canada, 800-565-0267 or 902-368-4444. www.gov.pe.ca/.

Ontario Travel 800-668-2746 or 416-314-0944. www.ontario-canada.com or www.travelinx.com.

Tourisme Quebec 800-363-7777, ext. 997. www.bonjourquebec.com.

Tourism Saskatchewan 1922 Park St., Regina, SK, S4P-3V7, Canada, 800-667-7191 or 306-787-9600. www.sasktourism.com.

Tourism Yukon P.O. Box 2703, Whitehorse, Yukon, Y1A-2C6, Canada, 867-667-5340. www.touryukon.com.

Going to Canada is one of the most affordable ways to travel internationally, especially when there's a favorable rate of exchange.

Your Passport to Savings At U.S. National Parks

The United States National Parks' $10 Golden Age Passport is one great benefit of growing older. But young people can get in on the action too, with the $50 Golden Eagle Passport.

There are several special passes available for visitors to United States National Parks: the Golden Eagle, Golden Age and Golden Access Passports. Passport holders can enter any national park without additional charge, which is a great deal for frequent visitors. Passports are non-transferable and can only be used by their owners.

1. Golden Eagle Passport

Cost: $50
Validity: One year from date of purchase.
Requirements: Anyone can purchase a Golden Eagle Passport.
Benefits: Gains entrance to all national parks, monuments, historic sites, recreation areas and national wildlife refuges that charge an entrance fee. Admits cardholder and any passengers in same vehicle. Also provides a 50% discount on federal use charges for swimming, parking, boat launching, cave tours and other facilities and services.
Purchase at: Any National Park Service (NPS) entrance or by mail: National Park Service, 1100 Ohio Dr. S.W., Rm. 138, Washington, D.C. 20242, Attn: Eagle Passport.

2. Golden Age Passport

Cost: $10
Validity: Your lifetime.
Requirements: Anyone 62 or older who is a citizen or permanent resident of the United States. Must show proof of age.
Benefits: Gains entrance to all national parks, monuments, historic sites, recreation areas and national wildlife refuges that charge an entrance fee. Admits cardholder and any passengers in same vehicle.
Purchase at: NPS entrances only.

3. Golden Access Passport

Cost: Free
Validity: Your lifetime.
Requirements: Any citizen or permanent resident of the United States who is blind or permanently disabled. Must show proof of medically-determined disability and eligibility for receiving benefits under federal law.
Benefits: Gains entrance to all national parks, monuments, historic sites, recreation areas and national wildlife refuges that charge an entrance fee. Admits cardholder and any passengers in same vehicle.
Purchase at: NPS entrances only.

Get the Best Deals In Real Estate

Here's the inside story on how to find the best deal on a new home, what to look for in a real estate agent, how to make an offer, when to buy a fixer-upper, ways to save on closing costs and how to sell your home for the best profit.

Before You Buy a New Home

A home is the largest purchase most people will ever make. This decision will affect your life for many years, so you want to make sure that you get the best deal you can.

Once you have made the decision to buy a home, it's tempting to run out, grab a real estate agent and start shopping right away. But in order to find the right house and get the best deal on it, there are several things you need to do before the search begins.

Know What You're Looking For

Your first task is to decide exactly what you want in a new home: a two-bedroom condominium, an older house in a historic neighborhood or perhaps a recently built home in a newly developed area.

The Pre-Approval Advantage

Pre-approval could give you the upper hand when competing against other buyers for the house you want. If the market is good and a seller receives several similar offers, your pre-approval may be the crucial plus in your favor. You will look like the more prepared buyer and promise an easier sale process, giving you the inside track.

How to Find a Buyer's Agent

There are two associations that can give you referrals to buyer's agents in your area:

- **Real Estate Buyer's Agent Council** (800-648-6224) maintains a list of its members. Look for an agent who holds an Accredited Buyer's Representative (ABR) designation. The Council awards this designation to agents who have passed a two-day training program, a written exam and have been buyer's representatives in at least five closed sales. You can search for agents in your area on the Internet at www.rebac.net.
- **The National Association of Real Estate Buyer Brokers** (650-655-2500) will also help you find a buyer's agent in your area.

The more thought you've given to what kind of home, neighborhood and amenities you're interested in, the easier it will be to weed through all the homes that are available. You may want to make a list using columns to rank details in the order of their importance to you.

Know What You Can Afford

The most important thing you need to figure out is how much money you can afford to spend on a house. For most people, this means how much money a lender will let you have in the form of a mortgage. Keep in mind that no matter how much a lender approves you for, only you know how much money you spend each month and what your lifestyle is. Don't over-stretch your limits, or you could wind up in financial trouble before you realize what's happening.

Pre-qualification

Pre-qualification is the easiest and least time-consuming way to determine your price range. To pre-qualify, visit a lender and honestly answer questions about your income, debts, savings and credit. The lender will perform some quick calculations and tell you about how much money you could get on various loans. This whole process only takes ten or 15 minutes, after which you'll have an idea of what the maximum is you can spend on a new home. There may be a fee, though, so ask first.

Pre-approval

Lenders aren't required to give you a loan just because they say you're pre-qualified for it. They are obligated to give you loans you're pre-approved for, however, and pre-approval makes you more attractive to sellers who won't have to wonder if your loan will come through.

So when you're seriously ready to buy, consider applying for pre-approval for a specific loan. Do your homework and interview a few lenders. Some lenders will pre-approve you for free, while others may charge you a fee. (Paying for a credit report is fairly standard.) Then bring all the information the lender requests to complete the application. Approval can take from a few days to several weeks.

If you find a good rate, you can lock it in, which means you get that rate even if rates in general go up. Be sure to ask what happens if the rates drop even further before you buy your home. Usually you can negotiate to get the lower rate. Some lenders require a deposit (which will be returned to you at closing) to lock in a rate. But remember that you'll lose your deposit if you don't close on the loan.

When to Buy

There are a couple of factors you should consider before deciding when to purchase your new home.

Time of Year Believe it or not, the month of the year you buy your home in can affect the deal you get. The best time to buy is close to the holidays in December. Statistics show that there are fewer home sales between Thanksgiving and New Year's than any other time of year. Most buyers are busy with the holidays and put off shopping for a home until after the new year. Sellers realize this and many take their homes off the market. The ones who keep their homes for sale during this time are usually desperate to sell. This is a big advantage for the buyer in negotiations.

If you choose to buy a home in spring, however, sellers have the advantage. The majority of buyers are shopping then, generally because families with children prefer to move at the end of the school year. More buyers mean more competition for you and less chance of a low bid being accepted.

Real Estate Climate Is it a buyer's or seller's market? Take the time to learn about the market you are entering. It will help you determine your negotiating strategy and give you a better idea of what to expect when you begin looking at homes. You will also learn how the market will affect the value of the home you buy.

In a buyer's market, you may be able to get a lower price or better terms from the seller. However, what's known as a buyer's market is actually a declining market. Be careful. Home prices are going down and no one can predict how far they will fall before they start to climb again. If you buy in a declining market, you may find a few years later that you can't sell for what you paid.

In a seller's market, there will be fewer homes for sale and more buyers competing for them. Chances are that you will pay close to asking price for your home and have less negotiating room on the terms. In very hot markets, you may even have to pay more than the asking price.

A seller's market is a rising market. Your new home will be a better investment if you buy in the initial stages of a rising market. But don't make the mistake of buying a home at the top of a rising market. When prices are at all-time highs, the market usually peaks and begins its decline. Remember, real estate markets run in cycles and no one market lasts forever.

Who's Who In Real Estate?

- **Real Estate Agent:** A real estate agent is paid by the seller but spends most of the time with the buyer. Agents show you several different homes in an area and help you begin negotiations on the ones you're interested in.

- **Buyer's Agent:** Buyer's agents usually show you a larger selection of homes, provide more information about the sellers and fight more for concessions in your favor. They are paid through the listing agent, but you may have to pay them an up-front retainer based on the purchase price of your new home.

- **Realtor:** A Realtor is an active member of a local board of Realtors affiliated with the National Association of Realtors.

- **Broker:** Brokers are people who have a real estate broker's license, who can not only make real estate transactions for others in exchange for a fee, but can also operate a real estate business, and employ salespeople and other brokers.

Costco Real Estate Service

Costco, the company that operates Costco and **Price Club** warehouse stores, also has a real estate service that will rebate home buyers and sellers thousands of dollars in broker commissions and mortgage fees.

Buyers and sellers must be executive members of Costco, which currently costs $100.

Once a member, you can work with a Costco-referred real estate agent to buy or sell your home. At closing, members receive a rebate based on the negotiated sales price. Find program details online at www.cost co.com. (888-295-5352)

If you use the Costco mortgage broker service to find a loan, you will also receive a rebate of nearly 1% of the mortgage amount.

The Scoop on Schools

SchoolMatch (800-724-6651, www.schoolmatch.com) is a service that provides current, objective information on all U.S. public schools and accredited private schools. You can order varying levels of information by phone or on the Internet.

SchoolMatch's **Snapshot** is a brief summary of key school district statistics ($19 by phone or fax, $10 on the Internet). The **Report Card** is more detailed, taking into account 22 different factors ($49 by phone or fax, $34 on the Internet).

Finding the Best Agent

Choosing the right agent is an important task for homebuyers, yet many people don't take the time to make sure they get a top-notch one. You want an agent who will work hard to help you find the perfect house and be a strong advocate for you in negotiations.

What to Look for in an Agent

The best agent is one who is active and very familiar with the area where you want to buy. Look for agents who have a number of properties listed and can demonstrate they've made a number of sales in the past few months.

Be sure to ask about particular neighborhoods to see how much the agent knows. A good agent should be able to tell you about the school system, the price range of homes and how many are for sale in a particular neighborhood.

Feeling comfortable with your agent is equally important. You want one who will listen to you, inquire about your needs and wants, offer suggestions and pleasantly answer all of your questions.

Consider a Buyer's Agent

Most agents have a responsibility to the seller. That's right. The agent that is helping you find and negotiate the purchase of a home does not work for you. That means you should keep all information that would help the sellers to yourself, such as how much you're willing to pay for a home and how quickly you need to buy.

Luckily, there is a better way. Buyer's agents work solely for you. They help you negotiate the best possible price and loan terms, appraise the value of the house you choose and find the best mortgage.

To find a buyer's agent, look in newspapers, ask friends and relatives, call agencies or contact one of the buyer broker associations for referrals in your area. It's a good idea to speak to several before deciding which one to hire. Ask for the names of recent clients and contact them to see how satisfied they were.

When you have chosen an agent, be sure to sign an agreement that legally obligates the agent to put your interests above all others, including sellers represented by others in the same agency. Also, determine up-front how the agent expects to be paid.

Typically, your agent will split the commission with the seller's agent. Be aware that if you decide to buy a home not listed with an agent (For Sale by Owner), you may end up paying the commission (usually 3%) out of your own pocket. Some agents may ask for a retainer that will be returned only if you buy. Check around, because not all require this.

House Hunting

When you begin house hunting, take the time to find out as much as you can about the areas you are interested in. Nearly every city has neighborhoods on the upward swing that promise increased home values in the near future. Here are some signs of a growing neighborhood:

- An increasing number of homes are being sold to people from other areas of the city or from out of town.
- New and existing homeowners in the neighborhood are investing in home remodeling and renovations.
- The majority of homes are owner-occupied, not rented. The neighborhood has an active community association.
- Transportation projects (new roads, bridges, mass transit) are under way to improve access to the area.

Schools

Even if you don't have children, it's wise to buy a home in a strong school district. It will be much easier to resell and will appreciate more quickly. Try to find out what local test scores are, where the high school graduates go to college and whether the district has a good reputation statewide.

Crime

For concrete information on crime, call the local police precinct. Ask for crime statistics for both the city and the particular neighborhood you are considering. The police should be able to give you the current figures as well as comparisons with previous years—listed by type of crime as well as by neighborhood.

Commute

Don't rely solely on the commute times given by neighbors you talk to on the street or the owners of a particular home you are looking at. Make the actual commute from the neighborhood to your place of work (and back again) during rush-hour to find out how long it's really going to take.

Walk the Streets

The best way to get a feel for any neighborhood is to park your car and walk. Talk to the people you meet and try to collect as much information about the area as possible. Here are some questions to ask:

- What is the general opinion of the local schools?
- Is there much crime in the neighborhood?
- How close are grocery stores and other conveniences?
- What kind of commute is there to the main areas of the city?
- Is there much traffic in the area?
- Are there any excessive noises, such as nearby railroads or airplanes?

House Hunting On the Internet

Shopping for a home on the Internet is becoming increasingly popular. It saves time and helps buyers become familiar with the real estate market. An excellent site for real estate resources is **RealtyGuide** (www.xmission.com/~realtor1), which offers a resource library and newsroom, links to Realtors and lenders, and even a chat room.

To look at homes on the Web, begin with the **International Real Estate Digest** (www.ired.com). This website contains links to sites that list homes in a wide variety of areas. Most of the linked sites are local real estate agencies that showcase the homes they are selling.

Other good sources for homes are the national websites that offer selected homes from multiple-listing services. While most cover many areas of the country, there is no one complete listing, so you still have to search around. Websites you may want to visit include:

- **The National Association of Realtors** (www.realtor.com) Probably the largest source of listings.
- **Cyber Homes** (www.cyberhomes.com)
- **Homes.com** (www.homes.com)
- **HomeScout** (www.homescout.com)

Homeowners' Associations

The neighborhood you are interested in may have a homeowners' association. It usually charges dues and comes with a set of rules that all homeowners must follow. Ask for a copy of the rules before buying and make sure you can live with them.

Zoning and Developments

It's a good idea to check whether any zoning restrictions apply to the area you are considering. For example, building and home additions are tightly restricted in coastal zones and historic districts.

You should also examine the area with an eye to what could be. If you see an undeveloped area, such as empty lots, woodland or farmed fields, check with the local zoning board or planning department to see if development is pending which might lower home values.

Making an Offer On a Home

You've found the home you want to buy. Now it's time to make an offer (in the form of a sales or purchase agreement). If you submit a sales agreement and it is accepted and signed by the seller, it is a legally binding contract. So make sure that your initial offer leaves nothing out.

All agreements should set a time limit (no longer than 48 hours) within which the seller must respond in writing or the offer will be void.

Decide What Price to Offer

Making a bid on a home requires an educated negotiating strategy. Ask your agent to give you as much information as possible about the selling prices of comparable homes in the area. Try to determine the average percentage the selling price was below the asking price.

Low-ball offers are tempting to make. If the seller agrees to it for whatever reason, then you will have gotten a terrific deal. Be careful, though. Sellers tend to be emotionally attached to their homes and an overly low offer may insult them. You should try to keep your offer within reasonable limits that will encourage the sellers to respond with a counter-offer.

Elements of a Good Sales Agreement

You will probably want to include these terms in your offer.

Earnest Money Deposit Protection   The sales agreement should specify who is to hold your deposit, such as the real estate agent, a title company, an escrow service or an attorney acting as an escrow agent. Never hand your deposit over to the sellers. No matter how honest they seem, you are opening yourself up for problems. Be sure to spell out how the deposit will be returned to you if the sale does not go through.

Settlement and Possession Dates   Your sales agreement should specify the date of settlement and when you are to take possession of the house. It's a good idea for the agreement to state that the sellers are to be out of the house one day before closing, or actual signing, of the sale documents. This will help eliminate any problems getting the sellers to move.

  If the sellers are not sure they will be able to move by that time, you may agree to rent the home to them for a certain number of days. Make sure that the sales agreement includes the amount of daily rent and acceptable length of time for the sellers to stay.

Personal Property   List all items you would like to receive included with the home, such as appliances, carpeting, light fixtures, fireplace screens, sheds and fences.

Physical Inspection   Include in the sales agreement your right to a final inspection. The wording should specify the time of inspection as "one to three days prior to closing." If a specific date is written in and escrow takes longer than expected, your inspection could be worthless.

  Remember, the final inspection is not the time to find problems with the home. This is simply to ensure that everything is in working order, no recent damage has been done and the sellers have removed all of their belongings. This is also a good time to check that all personal property written into the contract has been left there as agreed.

Financing   Contingency clauses make the entire sales agreement subject to a certain action. Making the purchase contingent on your getting satisfactory mortgage financing is a popular clause. If you have been pre-approved, there is no need for this contingency.

  It's possible to negotiate for the seller to pay all or part of the expenses involved with financing, such as discount points and appraisal fees. You may also ask the seller to finance a portion of the purchase price. Be sure that all information and terms are outlined in the agreement.

HERE'S HOW

Choosing a Home Inspector

Ask your agent, lender, lawyer or friends for referrals to home inspectors. Most states don't require home inspectors to be licensed, so keep these tips in mind when searching:

- Ask if the inspector belongs to the **American Society of Home Inspectors (ASHI)** or the **National Association of Home Inspectors (NAHI)**.

- Find out how long the inspector has been in the home-inspection business.

- Ask what qualifications the inspector has. Retired county and city building inspectors often make excellent choices.

- Get the names of several past clients. Call these people to see if they were satisfied. If they've been in their home at least six months, they will have had enough time to see if something unexpected came up that wasn't discovered by the inspector.

- Look for an inspector who has errors and omissions (E and O) liability insurance, which will protect you if it can be proven that the inspector was negligent.

Tag Along with the Home Inspector

One of the best ways to get to know the home you're buying is to accompany the inspector on the house tour. Listen carefully to all comments and don't be afraid to ask questions. You'll learn a lot of useful information that probably wouldn't be included in the report. You may even get suggestions on how to repair minor problems that the seller will not be responsible for.

BARGAIN FINDER

Buying Foreclosures

Foreclosures are pieces of real estate being sold to repay a debt. They can be tremendous bargains for a buyer. There are many ways to buy a foreclosure property. You can buy directly from a distressed owner before foreclosure, at the foreclosure auction or through government agencies and lenders who have taken over foreclosed properties.

Finding opportunities takes a bit of effort. You can ask a real estate agent to track down any foreclosures on the Multiple Listing Service or contact lenders and government agencies. Another, perhaps easier, way is to use a service that gathers information from a variety of sources and makes it available in one place, such as **Foreclosures Online** (www.4close.com).

Buying a foreclosed property requires some extra work and thought. You should research the process before giving it a try. There are many books available that can help you form a strategy to get the best bargains, tell you what to watch out for and direct you to sources that will help you find properties.

Home Inspection You should definitely include a contingency clause making the purchase subject to your approval of a home inspection. Your approval is an important point. You can refuse to approve the inspection until the sellers come to terms with you on repairs.

Termite Inspection Require a termite inspection along with language that allows you to void the agreement or negotiate with the seller for extermination and repairs.

Environmental Hazards You may want to include environmental inspections as a contingency of sale. Hazards to test for include asbestos, lead paint, radon and buried oil tanks. You can negotiate who pays for these inspections and what will be done if any hazards are found.

The Scoop on Mortgages

There are so many different varieties of mortgages that there is sure to be one that suits your needs. The trick is to find it. You can read mortgage and real estate books, explore options on the Internet and talk to different lenders to find out what mortgage is right for you. Another option is to hire a mortgage broker.

Comparing Loans

You have to learn a whole new vocabulary when you shop for a mortgage.

The two most popular loan types are fixed rate mortgages and adjustable rate mortgages (ARMs). With a fixed rate mortgage, your interest rate stays the same throughout the life of the loan (and so do your payments). An adjustable rate fluctuates according to the

terms of the loan, and usually means your payment changes from time to time. Make sure when you look at rates that you are comparing apples to apples. To compare the benefits of one loan to another you may need the help of a lender or mortgage broker.

When comparing rates from different lenders, people commonly look at interest rates and points. Interest rates are fairly easy to understand, but points are a bit more confusing. Basically, a point is an up-front payment of interest that lowers the interest rate. Each point equals 1% of the loan and lowers your interest rate a certain amount, usually ¼%. The best deal is a combination of the lowest interest rate and the least number of points.

The annual percentage rate (APR) is the most accurate device for comparing loans. The APR is the cost of your loan expressed as a yearly rate.

Penalty Clauses

There are two penalty clauses to watch for in loan agreements: refinancing and prepayment penalties. Make sure that your agreement doesn't charge for either. You will always want the option of refinancing at a lower rate in the future. Prepayment penalties will prevent you from paying extra money toward your loan that could save you a substantial amount of money in interest.

Low Down Payments

If you are short of cash for a down payment, you have several options: You can look into government-backed loans and learn more about the special programs offered by Fannie Mae, Freddie Mac or individual states. You might also buy private mortgage insurance (PMI). With the last option, you receive a regular loan but insure it against your default. The cost of private mortgage insurance can be added to your loan amount and will increase your cost of buying. Once the amount of equity in your home exceeds 20%, you will no longer need insurance. Make sure that your lender eliminates PMI when enough equity is built up.

Special Loan Programs

FHA and VA mortgages are government-insured loans. FHA loans are guaranteed by the Federal Housing Administration and VA loans by the Veterans Administration. To qualify for a VA mortgage, you must have been on the active list of the armed forces during certain periods of time. Check with the Veterans Administration for the specific requirements.

FHA and VA loans require low down payments and may have lower rates. There are limits on the amount of money you can borrow, however, which vary by region. FHA and VA loans are also assumable, provided the buyer who wants to take over the loan is qualified for the mortgage and meets all requirements.

Peter G. Miller on Getting the Best Deal on Your New Home

Peter G. Miller is the creator of the **Our Broker's Consumer Real Estate Center** website (www.ourbroker.com) and author of six books on real estate.

Is there a way to ensure that the home you're buying is going to be a good value for your money?

You want to make sure that the purchase price is reasonable and that the terms of the purchase offer are reasonable. So, unless you're a real estate expert, use a buyer broker: someone who represents purchasers in the market place, not sellers or property owners. It's good to have a professional involved in the transaction who works for you and who is obligated to get the best price and terms for your interests.

The next thing to do if you don't have a buyer broker (perhaps even if you do) is use an attorney or legal clinic to review any documents before you sign.

And don't buy any property unless the purchase is contingent on a home inspection by an independent inspector, whom you select and pay. Don't expect the home to be in perfect condition, but make sure that you understand its current physical shape, what repairs it's likely to need in the next few years, and what they will probably cost.

These professional services are cheap when you consider the alternatives. For example, if you buy a home that turns out to have hidden damage, that can be very expensive. If you buy a home and you overpay, that's very expensive too.

Is there such a thing as bargain real estate?

I think that from time to time there are real estate bargains. To get a real bargain, look for are homes in the path of future growth—not in the areas that are hot today, but the areas that have potential to be hot in a few years. Look for a community with a growing job rate.

Secondly, look for homes with cosmetic problems that have repelled other buyers. Keep an eye out for a well-built house where the painting is terrible (the front door is puce) the rugs are falling apart and the grass is not mowed. You're going to paint the place and mow the lawn when you move in anyway.

How can people find the best, most affordable mortgage?

There is an enormous number of lenders competing for your business. Borrowers have enormous leverage in the market place, but you have to help yourself. Think ahead a year or two and develop a budget. Have a sound financial profile and good credit. A couple months before you go house hunting, check your credit. Make sure that you don't have any items on your credit report that are out-of-date or factually incorrect. If you do, complain and get them corrected. Then speak to as many lenders as possible, shop around and let the lenders compete for your business.

You should also learn more about the special programs offered by Fannie Mae and Freddie Mac, such as Fannie Mae's Community Home Buyer's Program and Freddie Mac's Home Steps service. These programs help first-time homebuyers and low-income families finance homes.

If you belong to a union, check to see if it participates in the Union Privilege loan program offered by the AFL-CIO. Union Privilege loans require as little as 3% down and usually have interest rates at or below national averages.

Reduce Your Closing Costs

Your lender is required under the Real Estate Settlement Procedures Act (RESPA) to give you a good-faith estimate of what your costs for the loan will be within three days of when you make a formal application. While costs for a loan are not your only closing costs, they make up the largest percentage. There are some areas where you can cut these costs.

The time to negotiate is right after receiving the good-faith estimate, not on the day of closing. If some costs seem unreasonable and the lender refuses to negotiate, you can shop for a new lender. If many people are buying homes, creating a high demand for mortgages, you may not be able to negotiate the fees down very much. But when there are fewer buyers, you may have more leverage.

Following are closing costs for a loan that you may be able to negotiate:

Document Preparation Fee You shouldn't pay more than $50 for your lender to prepare documents. You can refuse to pay at all, but your lender can also refuse to loan you money if you don't.

Loan Fee A high loan fee is ridiculous if you are paying points and a document fee. Try to find a lender who either doesn't charge a loan fee or charges only a minimal amount.

Account Setup Fee This is another fee you should negotiate to lower.

Impound Account and Setup/Service Fee Some lenders require you to set up an impound account to hold and pay tax and insurance on your home. Negotiate to lower the charge.

Attorney Fee This is a fee for the lender's attorney. Since most lenders have an attorney on staff, this should also be negotiated.

FOR YOUR INFORMATION

Internet Mortgages

Technology has made it possible to shop and apply for a loan without ever leaving your home. Obtaining a loan over the Internet can benefit you by saving time, especially if you live in a rural area and would have to drive long distances to see a lender. It can also save you money by cutting mortgage costs.

Even if you don't want to go through the mortgage application process over the Internet, there are many websites that offer a wealth of easy-to-understand information about shopping for mortgages. You can also compare rates and calculate what size mortgage you qualify for.

One interesting site is **CASA** (Characteristics and Sales Analysis), run by the consulting firm **Case Shiller Weiss** (www.cswcasa.com). It provides analyses of prices and market trends in major areas around the country.

Here are some other websites to check out:

- **Countrywide** (www.countrywide.com)
- **Homebuyer's Fair** (www.homefair.com)
- **Irwin Mortgage** (www.inlandmortgage.com)
- **HSH Associates** (www.hsh.com)
- **Iown.com** (www.iown.com)
- **Bank Rate Monitor** (www.bankrate.com)

Cleaning house is one of the most important ways to prepare your home for sale.

Getting Your Home Ready to Sell

If you want to sell your home quickly and for the most money, you've got to make it a hot commodity by making a few preparations. There are four areas to concentrate on: repairs, curb appeal, indoor appeal and home information.

Repairs

Look at your home objectively. Make notes of all repairs, major and minor, that need to be done. Then you can determine which repairs to make and which ones not to make. You want to do the minimal amount of fix-up work required to get the maximum price for your home. However, any repairs that aren't made could be potential bargaining points for buyers. So carefully weigh the cost of repairs you make yourself against the discounts buyers may want for them.

Curb Appeal

The goal is to make your home appealing to buyers on first sight. To pique their interest immediately, keep the grass cut and landscaping neat. You may want to paint the front door, even if it doesn't really need it, and place pots of colorful flowers on either side. Keep the lights burning, so your home looks inviting to people who happen to drive by at night.

Indoor Appeal

Cleaning house is one of the most important ways to prepare your home. Everything should be spotless and should stay that way. If someone wants to view your home, you will only have a few minutes to straighten up and make things look perfect. Nothing will turn off buyers quicker than an untidy or cluttered home.

Here are some tips for making the inside of your home as appealing as possible to buyers:

- Re-arrange or store some of your furniture to make the house seem larger. Also, clear out closets and remove some of the clothes to make them appear more spacious.
- Try hanging a mirror in a small foyer or hallway to make it seem larger.
- Clean all light fixtures and install the maximum wattage in them.

BARGAIN FINDER

Hire a Sitter for Your Vacant Home

If you move into a new home before you sell your old one, you are at a disadvantage. An empty home is much harder to sell and you are probably paying two mortgages, which means you want to sell quickly. Consider finding a friend to stay in your house or hiring a housesitter.

Caretakers of America/America's Home Tenders (303-832-2313), currently available in 14 states, provides a pre-screened housesitter to live in your home at no cost to you. The housesitter pays all utility costs and is responsible for trash removal, minor repairs and keeping the home in ready-to-show condition. Caretakers and the housesitter provide furniture for a model-home look. Caretakers' sitters not only maintain your home and help it sell faster and for a better price, but they are prepared to move out within ten days on written notice.

- Remove heavy curtains and open windows if weather permits. Light, sheer curtains will emphasize the spacious, airy feeling you are trying to create.
- Make the house smell good and fresh. Try boiling cinnamon sticks on the stove, placing fresh flowers throughout the house or lighting candles.
- Buy new shower curtains and throw rugs for the bathrooms.
- Create counter space in the kitchen by removing all unnecessary items.
- Keep in mind that when it comes time to actually show your home, you should store all valuables in a safe place that cannot be accessed by potential buyers.

Home Information

Make a binder of neatly organized information available for interested homebuyers to view. The following is a list of documents you should include:

Property Tax Statements Even if property taxes are re-assessed in your state upon sale, this will give buyers an idea of what to expect.

Utility Bills Include copies of the past year's bills for gas, electric, water, sewage, garbage collection and any other utilities. If you don't save your bills, contact the utility company and ask for a printout of the past year's worth of invoices.

Maintenance Records This shows the care you have taken with your home. Of special interest to buyers will be records of roof repair, appliance repair, plumbing service and electrical work.

Warranties Include all warranties still in effect on any part of your home.

DID YOU KNOW

Comparison Home Sales

If you are having trouble finding comparable sales to help you set your asking price, try **Home Price Check** at www.domania.com. Here you'll find the largest free online archive of United States home sales. Want to know what your neighbor sold his house for? You can search the database by specific street address and find out.

Pricing Your Home

Choosing a listing price for your home is extremely important. You don't want to charge too much or too little. If you ask more than the market value of your home, it will take longer to sell—and you will probably have to lower your price in order to sell at all. If you ask less, you won't get the best deal.

Look at Comparables

The selling price of comparable homes is the key to pricing your home. Your agent should be able to supply you with a list of comparables. If you are selling your home on your own, you can still get this information from agents. Simply call several and ask for it. Inform the agents that you are selling by yourself, but will

The Scoop on Hiring an Agent

Hiring a selling agent is like choosing a work partner: You want someone who will do the absolute best for you. To begin your search, look to see what names appear most frequently on For Sale signs in your neighborhood. Then, call several real estate brokers active in your area, and ask who their award winners or top performers are. Invite at least three who work regularly in your neighborhood to come by separately and give a listing presentation.

Here are a few things to do when you meet each agent for the first time:

- Ask how many properties the agent has listed in the past six months. Then ask how many have been sold.

- Ask for a list of clients whose homes the agent has sold recently. Contact them to see if they were satisfied with the agent's performance.

- Find out how long the agent has been in the real estate business— the longer, the better.

- Inquire about professional organizations the agent belongs to. Look for membership in the local real estate board, a multiple-listing service and the State and National Association of Realtors.

- Ask what kind of marketing plan the agent proposes for your home. A good agent will be able to give you an immediate, direct and comprehensive plan of action.

- Find out how knowledgeable the agent is about your neighborhood. You'll want to know about recent selling prices, competing properties, market value in your area and anything else that will affect the selling price.

keep them in mind. Most will be happy to oblige you in the hopes that if you eventually decide to use an agent, they will get the listing.

Do Some Legwork

Don't trust that the homes on the list you receive are truly comparable. Check them yourself. If a home has a different number of bedrooms or bathrooms or other amenities, you can rule it out. Next, look at only the most recent sales. Lastly, drive by the homes that seem truly comparable to see how yours stacks up.

Evaluate the Numbers

Once you have a list of accurate comparables, look at their prices. If one price is substantially higher or lower than the others, discard it. Special circumstances were probably involved. Now you should have a range of prices to base your asking price on. It's generally safe to go with the average list price, hoping that a buyer will offer the average selling price.

Offers and Counter-Offers

When you receive an offer for your home, you have three choices: You can either accept the offer as is, reject it completely or make a counter-offer. If the offer is close to what you want in price, terms and other areas, by all means accept it. It's usually best not to reject an offer completely. You stand to lose nothing by making a counter-offer that doesn't give much away on your part. If the buyers are serious, they will accept or make their own counter-offer.

While any part of the sales agreement is negotiable, there are four areas that most people counter on: price, terms, occupancy and contingencies.

Price

How far is the offer from your list price? Is it near the average selling price on your list of comparables? If it is lower than you hope to get, counter with something lower than your list price but more in line with what you expect. Never reveal the rock-bottom price you will sell for.

Terms

You can use terms that favor the buyer to get a price offer that's closer to what you're asking. For example, if the buyers want seller financing, you might consider it. But, in turn, negotiate for a shorter mortgage or higher interest rate than a lender might offer.

Occupancy

The key to occupancy disputes is to be flexible. You don't want a good deal to fall apart over when you move out and the buyers move in. Be creative and try to come up with a compromise that will suit everyone.

Contingencies

You will likely run into several contingencies. These are useful to buyers because they provide an out. Consider whether each contingency is reasonable or not. If it's not, you can counter by crossing it out as unacceptable. However, an easy way to deal with contingencies is to set a time limit and keep it as short as is reasonable.

For Sale by Owner

Selling your home by yourself and saving the substantial amount of money normally paid to agents in commission is a tempting prospect. However, it requires a good deal of work, preparation, and real estate know-how—and a concrete plan of action.

Before you make the decision, do a little research. Use all the resources you can find, including books with worksheets and sample documents as well as the Internet.

Learn about Loans

Agents often help buyers arrange financing. To make buyers feel comfortable buying without an agent, you should learn a bit about the different types of mortgages. It's also a good idea to contact several lenders in the area. They can provide you with information and pre-qualification forms to give potential buyers.

Protect Yourself

When selling on your own, you can protect yourself by hiring a real-estate lawyer to look over and prepare documents. Be sure to negotiate the fee in advance. Another option is to pay an agent a set price to handle the paperwork.

A real-estate lawyer can also inform you of the laws in your state concerning disclosures of problems with your home.

Consider Partial Commissions

Most buyers go to agents when they begin looking at homes. This makes it very difficult for people selling their own homes to attract buyers' attention. Offering a partial commission to buyers' agents is one way to reach all of those buyers. Here are several different ways you can make this offer.

If you're going to sell your own home, it's important to do a little research and create a concrete plan of action.

New Type of Mortgage for Fixer-Uppers

Fannie Mae's (800-7-FANNIE, www.fanniemae.com) new **Homestyle Mortgage** lets buyers borrow based on the appraised value of their house after renovations. The renovation portion of the loan is held in an escrow account (similar to a deposit) from which their lender pays contractors directly. Adjustable rate and 15- and 30-year fixed rate mortgages are available, and interest rates should be on par with the national average.

For homeowners who have already purchased, Fannie Mae also has a home equity line of credit, which lets you borrow as much as $50,000 (or 90% of the value of your home after repairs). But beware: You could be stuck with a mortgage that is worth more than your house if renovations go awry.

The Assessor: A Valuable Advisor

The assessor is the person who appraises real estate in your community. That assessment determines what taxes you pay. This person can orient you to the various zoning laws and building codes, and tell you what financing is available (including government grants) for renovating.

Hire a Discount Broker Some agents offer limited services for a small commission (1% to 2%). Others provide certain services, such as listing your home on the multiple listing service, for a flat fee. The listing usually requires you to pay a 3% commission to the agent bringing the buyer.

Sign a Temporary Listing Contract This is an agreement with an agent who has an interested buyer for a reduced commission, usually half the going rate (2% to 3%). The agreement should specify the name of the prospective buyer, the time limit for the agent to bring you a purchase offer and the asking price for this transaction. You may decide to raise the price a bit to help cover the cost of the commission.

Advertise an Open Listing To do this, specify in your ads that you will pay a reduced commission, usually 3%, to any agent who brings you a buyer. You will sign an agreement with each agent who comes by. It's not necessary to specify a particular buyer, but you should write in an expiration date in case you later decide to sign an exclusive listing with one agent.

Condos and Co-ops

Many people choose to buy condominiums and cooperative housing. These options are especially popular for first home purchases and retirement homes because they usually cost less than single-family homes and require little maintenance.

A condo or co-op is a unit within a building or complex. In both housing types, you share the common areas of the building or development with other owners. With condos, you own your unit outright, but with co-ops you purchase shares in the cooperative that entitle you to live in one of the units.

Market Values

Though condos and co-ops are often less expensive alternatives to single-family homes, their values are more volatile. They are usually the first to feel the effects of a declining market and the last to gain the benefits of a rising market. This means that condos and co-ops are harder to sell and do not appreciate as well as single-family homes. Units located in major metropolitan areas, such as New York City, Boston and Chicago, or near perennially popular resorts, are exceptions.

When buying, beware of complexes that contain a large percentage of absentee owners who rent their units. The more renters there are, the lower your unit's value can slip.

Maintenance Fees and Regulations

In both condo and co-op dwellings, the board of directors handles the maintenance and upkeep of all shared areas, inside buildings as well as outdoors. All condos and co-ops charge owners a monthly maintenance fee to pay for upkeep, taxes and management. Generally, the more amenities a complex has, such as a pool, playground or community center, the higher the maintenance fee will be. Owners of this type of housing are also subject to the rules set by the board of directors.

Financing the Purchase of Condos and Co-ops

Buying a condo or co-op is similar to buying a single-family home. When figuring the size mortgage you can afford, remember that a maintenance fee will be added to your monthly costs. In co-op purchases, you will receive shares and a certificate of occupancy instead of a deed to a unit.

In the past, co-ops were difficult to finance because they could not be purchased with a mortgage. Now, however, in areas where co-ops are popular, many lenders have developed special financing for them.

Manufactured Homes

TRY SOMETHING DIFFERENT

The Modular Alternative

For better quality and durability than with manufactured homes, look into modular homes. They are more expensive than manufactured homes, but are made to meet the highest state building codes. All the parts are transported to the building site by truck and then put together by a contractor. Once constructed, the finished homes are difficult to distinguish from regular homes. Modular homes are financed with conventional mortgages.

Modular homes and manufactured homes that are designed like conventional houses and situated on owned land will appreciate in value the same as site-built homes. Even manufactured homes on leased lots can appreciate if the land rents are stable and the location is desirable.

Manufactured homes, upscale versions of mobile homes, are becoming increasingly popular. The houses are built in factories, moved on trailers to the site and installed.

Financing a manufactured home is more expensive, however, because manufactured home buyers usually must get a personal property loan instead of a conventional mortgage. The exception to this is if the home sits on a permanent foundation and you own the land beneath it.

Another expense to factor in is the cost to buy a piece of land or rent a lot. Many dealers operate manufactured housing sites. If you lease a site, be sure to sign a binding rental agreement to prevent tenancy conflicts.

One problem with manufactured homes can be shoddy installation. If your home is not attached to the ground properly, it will be very vulnerable to storms such as tornadoes and hurricanes.

Today's manufactured homes offer good quality and designs that rival conventionally built homes—for much lower prices.

Make the Most Profit Buying Fixer-Uppers

Knowledge and experience are the most important skills in buying fixer-uppers and selling them for a profit. Experts look for the following:

- **The house must be damaged.** Better yet, if it is a defect that most people agree is horrible, the price will be reduced considerably.

- **The house must be repairable.** Know whether the horrible problem is readily correctable or something that can be lived with indefinitely. Be innovative with repairs.

- **There must be a true profit margin.** This is the difference between the purchase price plus estimated repairs, and the actual market value. The profit margin will be greater when buying more expensive homes.

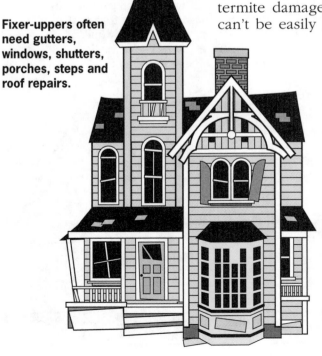

Fixer-uppers often need gutters, windows, shutters, porches, steps and roof repairs.

Fixer-Uppers

Homes that have been damaged—this can range from holes in the walls to property that has been flattened by a tornado—are often referred to as fixer-uppers, handyman specials or damaged properties.

People buy fixer-uppers for a variety of reasons, most commonly because they can be potential bargains (since the property has been damaged, the price is reduced). Other people who love the creative process of renovation work with Realtors who show them only distressed properties. And some people aren't looking for a fixer-upper at all, but happen to fall in love with an older home that needs a lot of work.

For whatever reason you buy a fixer-upper, it can be a good financial deal and a rewarding experience if you go into it with your eyes open and have a plan for repairing the damage.

Sometimes It's Just Not Worth It

Renovation is a good investment—per square foot, you can't build for the price you can restore for. A family can restore an old home for half of what it can cost to buy a new home. The problem is, though, that many families spend the bulk of their available cash to buy a fixer-upper, and are left with nothing to pay for fixing it up.

What to Watch Out For

Avoid houses with damaged roofs, water in the basement, termite damage, off-level foundations and sagging floors that can't be easily straightened (no matter what the bargain price is) unless you're sure you can handle the repairs. Keep in mind that if the building doesn't qualify for a Certificate of Occupancy, you'll have to get a building loan, which costs more than a mortgage.

If the house's price and contractors' bids are too high, and it doesn't add up to a financially sound investment, wait for something better to come along. There are a lot of opportunities out there.

If This Is Your First House

If you're buying your first house, it is usually wise not to take on a major renovating job. Get experience, get to know prices and learn a little about plumbing, heating and electricity before making your first renovation. If the price is right, however, you might want to take a chance.

Before Buying a Fixer-Upper

Picking out the right home is tricky. Picking out the right home that needs work is doubly difficult because old houses almost always come with surprises. Remember the first rule of renovation: It always takes longer and costs more than you expect. Before you buy, take a good long look at the following.

Yourself

- How much of the work are you prepared to do?
- What tasks do you have the skills, time and desire to do?
- Are you flexible enough to own a house that will be full of surprises?
- If you are going to live in the house while it is being renovated, can you live in a dusty, dirty environment?
- Do you want to live in the home, and if so, for how long? Or will you resell as soon as possible for profit?

The House

There are basically three categories of fixer-uppers: those needing a face-lift, those requiring cosmetic surgery, and those destined for major surgery. The last category requires new plumbing, heating, electrical systems, footings and siding. Have an engineer (or someone familiar with old houses) look over the structure with you. Pay particular attention to the basics: foundation, plumbing, wiring and roof. Try to inspect the home just after a rainstorm. Keep in mind that it is harder to renovate a building that already has been poorly remodeled. If others tried and it didn't work, don't burden yourself with their problems.

Your Finances

You don't have to repair your home all at once. However, be sure that you will have a way to finance your repairs once you've closed on your home. Get quotes from several contractors who work on old homes. Be prepared to spend twice the highest amount because of inevitable surprises.

The Neighborhood

Financially, the location may be more important than the home itself. Is the area on the upswing? Is the house in a historic district where you will need to comply with certain regulations? Is it zoned for single-family dwelling or can you subdivide? The potential gain—as well as the risk—is more if you buy in a fringe area that hasn't been gentrified yet, as opposed to buying in a more established area.

DID YOU KNOW

To Do, or Not to Do It Yourself

The single best way to control costs on your fixer-upper is to do it yourself. Even if you are not a skilled tradesperson, there are demolition, cleaning, stripping and many other jobs you can do. The more you can do yourself, the better off you'll be.

If you are not skilled or handy it can often be best to NOT do it yourself. An amateurish renovation, or one that's professionally done but poorly thought out, detracts dramatically from the value of a home and makes it more difficult to sell.

But when considering whether or not to do your own renovations, consider this: If you make more money an hour than it would cost you to hire a contractor, it could actually cost you more money to do it yourself.

BARGAIN FINDER

Save Treasures For Reuse

As you demolish, don't forget to save removable pieces such as doors, windows, doorknobs, porch balustrades, mantels and moldings to reuse. Once stripped, shined or repainted, they can add character and remain part of your home's history. When the time comes to put your house back together, you'll have a hard time buying these treasures at any price.

Turn Your House into a Money-Maker

Look for an existing house that can be converted into a multi-unit. There is tremendous appreciation through this type of renovation. An older one-family house is more valuable with several rents coming in. Look for a building in which each apartment will be about 800 square feet. A third-floor apartment can be as small as 500 square feet.

If you move into the house, you can renovate unit-by-unit and do all the work in your spare time. As you convert each apartment, you'll have more money coming in to help pay off the mortgage. And, because it's investment property, half the costs of renovating, improving and repairs can be applied as an income write-off. If you don't reside in the other half, it's all deductible.

Measure Your Own House

Take the measurements of your house yourself, rather than paying an architect to do this. This is the preliminary step of drawing plans. It is time-consuming, unskilled labor that can be done by any careful adult with a measuring tape.

If you do hire someone else, try to negotiate an hourly fee and insist on a cap that can be exceeded only with your explicit approval.

Fixing Up Your New Fixer-Upper

Once you buy, put together a plan of action before anyone lifts a hammer. It is all-important that you think through the big picture before beginning work on any individual projects.

The Plan

Structure a plan of attack for your new home, regardless of whether it needs extensive rehabilitation or just some cosmetic work. The most important factors in the plan are establishing what work needs to be done and realistically determining what you can (and will) do yourself—and what you should hire someone else to do.

Creative Visualization

Walk around the building and figure out how the space can be used more efficiently. What rooms can be opened up? Where can extra storage be created? Can some of the rooms be better utilized?

Beware of Over-renovation

Over-renovation is any improvement to a structure that costs more than the value it adds. If you are going to live in the house, an expensive project could be worth it if it brings enough pleasure into your life to justify the cost. But don't price your property beyond its value and the value of the other properties in the neighborhood. Once you've reached the level of adjoining properties, stop.

What an Architect Can Do for You

If your fixer-upper requires more than cosmetic work, a professionally-drawn set of comprehensive plans and specifications prepared by an architect will save you money and frustration in the long run. Here's what an architect can do.

Make Structural and Aesthetic Decisions Even if you know how you want your home to be renovated (where the walls and windows will go), an architect can make sure that everything fits (from your plumbing pipes to the refrigerator), comment on your design, give you advice on the latest materials available and let you know if the building will be structurally sound. Architects know building codes, and can subcontract an engineer if needed.

Put Your Vision on Paper The architect's clear and scaled-to-size drawings will be invaluable for you. Contractors will have something to bid on, and, as work progresses, you can return to the drawings again and again to answer your questions.

Eliminate Any Potential Bureaucratic Hassles In most municipalities, any time you are going to make any structural changes, the local building department must be notified. And you must get a building permit before work can begin. Even if not absolutely required, the architect's signature on an application for a building permit will often smooth the approval process.

Owning Your Own Home As You Get Older

Despite ever-rising costs and more space than is needed, most seniors continue living in their own homes. There are options to make this more affordable.

Rent out Rooms

Many senior organizations are beginning to establish programs to match older people who need good affordable housing with other retirees who have extra space in their homes. Ask your local senior center for more information. But be sure local zoning laws permit renters.

Move to a Less Expensive House

If you move to a significantly smaller, less costly house or condominium, you can invest remaining profits from the sale of your original house and use the income it produces for living expenses.

Try a Reverse Mortgage

If you are living in a home that is paid for, you can turn it into a reliable source of income through a reverse mortgage. Instead of paying a monthly check to the bank, the bank pays you. But remember, it's a loan and will eventually have to be repaid. How much money you can draw out is based on the amount of equity in your home, an annual percentage rate applied against that equity and your life expectancy.

For more information, check The National Center for Home Equity Conversion Web site at www.reverse.org. Or contact AARP (800-424-3410) for their free guidebook called *Home-Made Money: Consumer's Guide to Home Equity Conversion.*

DID YOU KNOW

Tax Savings When You Sell

You owe no tax on profits of up to $250,000 ($500,000 if you're married and filing a joint return on the sale of your house) when you sell your home.

You must have owned and lived full-time in the home for at least two out of the five years leading to the sale, and can't take advantage of the savings more than once every two years. For more information, request the publication **Selling Your Home** from the IRS Forms Line (800-829-3676).

HERE'S HOW

Retirement Communities

When you are looking for a community to retire to, consider the following criteria. Take a special look at college towns, which tend be full of social opportunities, have a reasonable cost of living and be generally safe places to live.

- Climate
- Cost of living
- Distance from family and friends
- Housing
- Medical care
- Nourishment for your interests
- Public transportation
- Senior services

Helpful Resources For Seniors

- *The Consumer's Directory of Continuity Care Retirement Communities* is a 600-page book listing retirement communities in all 50 states. *Cost:* $35 plus $3.50 shipping. Call 800-508-9442 to order.

- For help in locating an assisted-living facility, call **The Assisted Living Federation of America** at 703-691-8100 or visit www.alfa.org.

- For help in finding an attorney who specializes in elder law, contact the **National Academy of Elder Law Attorneys** at 520-881-4005. You can search a directory of Elder Law attorneys at www.naela.org.

- For a free copy of **Your Home, Your Choice** *(Living Choices for Older Americans)*, call the **Federal Trade Commission** at 202-326-2222.

Ways Seniors Can Save On Housing Costs

As you get older, your income tends to be less than it used to be. So if you want to continue living in your home, you may have to find alternate ways to finance it.

Tax-postponement Programs

Many states have adopted over-65 property tax postponement programs. These allow older people to put off paying property taxes on their residences until after death. At that point, the taxes are paid before heirs take their inheritance. For information, call your local property-tax assessor's office.

The Home Energy Assistance Program

You can save on expenses through this program which helps low-income homeowners and renters cut their energy costs. Some states limit assistance to heating expenses, and others help with lighting and cooking costs as well. File an application with your local department of social services early in the year.

Supportive Housing for the Elderly

If you meet certain income guidelines, your rent will be no higher than 10% to 30% of your adjusted income. Plus, many of these buildings offer coordinators to help with senior needs. Call your local public housing office for information.

HOME Repair/Modifications Program for Elderly Homeowners

Funds are available to low-income seniors for home repairs. To locate the closest program and application information, contact Community Connections at 800-998-9999.

Housing Voucher Program

Low-income senior tenants may be eligible for coupons worth the difference between 30% of their income and the market value of the apartment. Check with your local housing authority for more information.

Other Senior Housing Options

Continuing-care retirement communities or assisted-living facilities might offer you the security, help and companionship you need. In general, those sponsored by religious organizations, fraternal groups and other nonprofit agencies tend to be more reasonably priced.

Household Bargains

Here's how getting better deals on your telephone service, utility bills, appliances, home computers, furniture and household repairs can add up to super savings.

Phone Bill Basics

With fees for monthly service, charges for extra services and long distance prices, phone charges can add up. Fortunately, there are ways to lower those costs.

Start by examining your phone bill. Extra services such as speed dialing, call waiting, caller ID and call forwarding can add quite a bit of money. Evaluate your needs for these services and cancel any that aren't necessary.

Maintenance

You may also want to rethink your need for an inside wiring maintenance plan. Problems covered by these plans rarely occur. Call an electrician instead of the phone company for maintenance on wires or jacks. It's usually much cheaper.

Dual Lines

If you have more than one phone line, determine whether you really need both. If so, consider a second-ring service instead. This allows you to have two telephone numbers, each with a

distinctive ring, while using only one line. You'll save money by avoiding the basic service fee for a second line as well as a second installation.

Moving Bargain

When moving, arrange with the previous tenants or owners to switch the name on their phone bill to yours. You'll keep their phone number and avoid paying a new hookup fee. The only downside may be answering calls intended for them for a while.

Cut the Cost of Your Long Distance Phone Bill

In the early 1980s, the Bell monopoly was deregulated, creating business opportunities for other companies and an enormous amount of confusion for consumers. With hundreds of long distance companies in existence, there has been an ongoing price war featuring a barrage of different marketing techniques.

Sometimes it's easier to just ignore it all and stick with the company you already have. But there are big bargains to be found, even if you don't want to make a major effort. And the more homework and haggling you're willing to do, the bigger your savings will be.

Determine Your Needs

The long distance company and specific calling plan that's right for your neighbor may not be right for you. Everyone has different calling patterns, and to get the best deal you need to determine what your pattern is.

- Do you make most of your calls during the day, in the evenings or on the weekends?
- Do you make most of your calls within the state, state-to-state, or to another country?
- Do you have a fax machine? If so, when and where do you fax the most?

Shop Around

The quickest and easiest way to save money on your phone bill is to call your current long distance company and ask what the best discount plan is for your calling patterns. If you are one of the 60% of long distance customers who are still paying the basic rate for your long distance service, then this step alone can save you lots of money. You may also want to check with the other major companies and compare their best savings plans.

If you are interested in what smaller, emerging carriers are offering, look for their ads in your local yellow pages. Alternative carriers do less marketing and advertising, but they use mailings, newspaper ads, magazines, the Internet and word of mouth. So keep your eyes and ears open.

Pros and Cons of the Major Carriers

While some smaller companies may save you a bit of money, there are some definite pros to choosing one of the major carriers:

- If customer service is particularly important to you, the larger companies are your best choices. Smaller companies have lower budgets and usually can't afford the kind of round-the-clock customer service large carriers can.
- The big three, AT&T, MCI and Sprint, offer special tie-in offers, such as linking with different airlines' frequent flyer mile programs. When signing up for a special offer, however, make sure your discount calling plan is not affected.
- The main reason to choose a smaller long distance carrier is cost. If you do your homework, you can almost always find a small carrier who offers lower prices than the big three. Plus, calling cards from the big three have higher per-minute rates and usually have a surcharge per call. Smaller companies offer lower rates with no surcharge and you can often sign up for one of their calling cards without switching to their long distance service.

IT PAYS TO ASK

Bargaining Is Key

It's cheaper for long distance carriers to keep old customers than to attract new ones through special offers and advertising. So carriers have started rewarding customers with big discounts—if they ask.

They key is to bargain and haggle. Shop around, at least among the major carriers, then call your current carrier armed with this discount information. Ask what they'll do for you. Don't hesitate to mention what another company has offered you and that you are prepared to switch companies if you cannot get the rates you want.

More than likely, you will get a great rate from your current provider with only a little bit of work and some bargaining savvy.

Alternative Carriers

Before choosing an alternative company, be sure to get all the facts. Then watch your phone bill to make sure you are getting the deal you agreed to.

Small, Nationwide Providers	Resellers	Dial-around Services
These companies offer similar services to AT&T or MCI, but are often less expensive and may have less reliable service.	Resellers lease lines from major carriers. By buying calling time in bulk and advertising mostly through the mail, they are able to offer low rates.	Dial-around services let you use an access number to bypass your current carrier. They advertise large savings and low rates, but often have time requirements or monthly fees.

DID YOU KNOW

Quick Ways to Save on Water Heating

There are many things you can do to cut your water-heating costs besides buying a more efficient heater. Try the following suggestions:

- Do as much cleaning as possible with cold water.

- Repair leaks in faucets and showers.

- Turn the faucet off when shaving.

- Install a low-flow showerhead. They provide a low-cost way to reduce hot-water consumption by 30%.

- Lower your water heater thermostat. Most heaters are automatically set at 140 degrees, but 120 degrees is sufficient for most household needs. Check your dishwasher first, however. If it doesn't have a booster heater to raise the temperature of incoming water, you should not lower your water temperature.

- For electric water heaters, try installing a timer that will automatically turn the heater off at night and on in the morning.

- Wrap exposed hot water pipes with insulation to minimize heat loss, especially in unheated areas such as basements.

- If you have an electric hot water heater, place an insulation jacket or blanket around it. Insulation is easy to install and widely available. Check with your local utility company. It may offer the blankets at a lower price, give you a rebate or even install them at no cost. Installation is more difficult on gas and oil-fired heaters. Ask your local furnace-installer for instructions.

Before You Sign Up

- Find out if there are restrictions on when or where you call. Ask if you are required to spend a certain amount per month in order to get the advertised rate. Finally, make sure that the rate is permanent and not good only for a few months before jumping to a much higher rate.

- Inquire about a carrier's billing increments. Many alternative carriers bill in six-second increments instead of rounding up to a full minute. Some even bill in one-second increments.

- Make sure you are aware of any monthly fees. If the rate is low enough, it may be worth paying a small monthly fee, but in general, it is better to choose a carrier that charges no monthly fee.

- Ask about rates and surcharges applied to calling cards. A large percentage of carriers impose a surcharge or per-call fee for using a calling card—and charge high rates.

- Beware of carriers that require you to use their service for a certain length of time before their low rates apply. You are most likely to encounter this policy with dial-around services.

- When you find an offer you want to accept, ask the customer service representative to confirm your agreement in writing.

Save Big on Utility Bills

The best way to save money on utility bills is to conserve energy. Most everything you do in your home drains energy in some way. Cooking, cleaning, heating, cooling, lighting your home and running all of your major appliances use power. Saving energy can mean big reductions in your monthly electric and gas costs.

There are basic energy-saving techniques that everyone tries to employ, such as turning off lights when they aren't in use and not staring blankly into the refrigerator with the door open. But there are many ways to save energy that are often overlooked. A small amount of effort around the house can lead to a noticeable difference in your monthly bill.

Water Heaters

Water heating is the second largest household energy user after heating and cooling your home. Fortunately, there are a number of things you can do to lower your water-heating costs.

The most important cost-saving measure is to make sure your hot-water heater is energy efficient. If your heater is very old, you may want to consider purchasing a new model.

Refrigerators and Freezers

Refrigerators and freezers consume about one-sixth of all electricity used in a typical American home.

Out with the Old These appliances have become more efficient in recent years, so the first step to saving money is to get rid of old, inefficient models. If you need to update and are considering buying a new model, check out the section on buying appliances later in the chapter.

Do the Dollar Test If you already have an efficient model, be sure to keep it that way. Clean the condenser coils, set the temperature on a medium setting and make sure the door seal is airtight. To test the seal, close the door on a dollar bill and try to pull it out. If the dollar slides out easily, kiss that dollar good-bye because you're wasting energy and money by letting cold air leak out.

Don't Overwork Your Appliances

- Don't place the refrigerator or freezer near heat sources, such as ovens, dishwashers, radiators or heating vents, washers or dryers, furnaces, or in direct sunlight. Heat causes the appliances to use more energy to keep cool.
- Regularly defrost manual-defrost models. Frost buildup increases the amount of energy needed to keep the motor running.
- Keep your refrigerator full. It retains cold better. If your refrigerator is nearly empty, store water-filled containers inside. (Be careful not to overfill the containers.)
- Allow hot foods to cool before refrigerating them. Also, try to thaw frozen foods inside the refrigerator. This will help cool the interior and eliminate the use of energy to thaw them in an oven or microwave.

Cooking and Cleaning

A surprising amount of energy is used daily in cooking and cleaning your home, especially when you use appliances such as stoves, ovens, dishwashers, washing machines and dryers. Here are some ways to save energy (and money) while you're cooking and cleaning:

Keep your refrigerator and freezer away from the stove. Heat causes appliances to use more energy to keep cool.

CHECKLIST

When You're Going Away

Here are a few simple ways to save money while you're away from home:

- ❏ Use timers on lights for safety and savings.
- ❏ Consider turning off the refrigerator if it's empty.
- ❏ Turn the thermostat for the heating system down. In cold weather, keep enough heat on to prevent bursting pipes.
- ❏ Turn air conditioners off.
- ❏ Turn your water heater down or off.

Lighting Your Home

When most people think of electricity, their thoughts usually turn first to lights. And even though lighting doesn't use as much energy as heating, cooling and refrigeration do, there are still ways to save energy when using lights. The first step is to turn off lights when they aren't needed. Also, don't over-light a room. Try turning off a light or two to see if you miss them.

Replace old incandescent bulbs with new compact fluorescent bulbs. You'll get the same amount of light for a quarter of the cost. Plus, fluorescent bulbs lasts up to ten times longer.

Keep all of your bulbs, lighting fixtures and lamps clean. Dirt blocks light and increases heat.

When you're away from home, use timers to turn lights on rather than leaving one lit all the time. It's safer and cheaper.

Add Energy-Efficient Repairs To Your Mortgage

The **Department of Housing and Urban Development's (HUD's) Energy Efficient Mortgage (EEM)** program allows you to add $4,000 to $8,000 on to the end of your mortgage—as long as the money is used for repairs to improve the energy efficiency of your home. Contact the **Federal Information Center** (800-688-9889) to locate the HUD office nearest you for more information.

Stoves and Ovens

- Keep stovetop burners and reflectors clean to reflect the heat better and save energy.
- Select the right-sized pan for the right burner. Larger burners use more energy than smaller ones.
- If you have an electric stove, get in the habit of turning off the burners several minutes before the allotted cooking time. The heating element will stay hot long enough to finish the cooking without using more electricity. This works with oven cooking too.
- Don't preheat your oven unless you're baking.
- Cook several items at the same time when using your oven.
- Resist the temptation to peek in the oven every few minutes. Every time you open the door, the temperature drops about 25 degrees, causing the oven to work that much harder to heat back up.
- If you have a self-cleaning oven, clean it only when necessary, and clean it right after cooking a meal to take advantage of the heat already in the unit.

Washing Dishes

- When washing dishes by hand, use a sink stopper or dishpan and run the hot water as little as possible.
- Use cold water—not hot—to operate your food disposal.
- Scrape dishes before loading them into the dishwasher instead of wasting water by using the dishwasher's rinse-hold setting.
- Wait until you have a full load to run the dishwasher.
- Experiment with your dishwasher to determine which cycle best meets your needs. Short econo-cycles use less water and energy than heavy-duty cycles. Do not use a more powerful energy cycle than you need.
- Let your dishes air-dry. It works, and it won't cost you a nickel in energy.
- Clean the filter at the bottom of the dishwasher regularly to keep the machine running efficiently.

Washing Machines and Dryers

- Wait until you have a full load before using the washing machine and dryer.
- Shake out wet clothes before placing them in the dryer.
- Clean the filter in the dryer before every load to ensure maximum efficiency.
- Check the dryer vent to the outside of your home regularly to make sure it is not obstructed by lint or other materials. Also check that it is not blocked by overgrown shrubs or plants.
- Hang clothes out to dry on the line. Sunlight is free.

Take Advantage of Deregulation

You may have heard about the deregulation of the electric power industry. It's already begun in some states and will be instituted in all states over the next few years. The big question is whether deregulation will make electricity cheaper. The answer is still up in the air. Power generation is the only part of the industry being deregulated. Supply and distribution could still cost the same.

Deregulation will probably bring a small amount of savings to the average consumer and is guaranteed to bring about a good deal of confusion. Some power companies have already begun marketing efforts to hold on to their customers. Their offers may include money credits toward your electric bill, frequent flyer miles and tie-ins with long distance telephone carriers and credit cards for special offers.

For now, your best bet is to stay informed about the changes in your state, and to take advantage of incentive offers if they benefit you.

IT PAYS TO ASK

Cost-Saving Programs

With deregulation, electric utilities will be forced to offer special programs (similar to the calling plans long distance carriers offer) to make their companies more enticing to consumers.

Check with your electric company about cost-saving programs such as load management and off-hour rate programs. Many utilities already have these programs. You just have to ask.

Heat and Cool Your Home More Efficiently

Controlling the temperature in your home makes up a substantial portion of your utility costs. The trick is to keep your home comfortable without wasting money on energy.

Control the Temperature

Begin with your thermostat. Keep it as low as is comfortable for your family—usually around 68 degrees. When you're going out or to bed, turn it down to 60 degrees or install a timer to turn it off and on automatically.

The same applies for your air-conditioner. Operate the unit on a medium setting and use a thermometer to see that it goes no lower than 78 degrees. Turn the temperature up when leaving the house. If you have a window unit, turn it off when you're out. It costs less to re-cool a room than to keep it cool all day. Try using a timer to turn the air conditioner on half an hour before you return.

Insulating your attic and sealing around outside doors and windows is an easy, cost-effective way to keep your home warm all winter.

Keep Warm and Cool Air Inside

One-third of your heating and cooling costs may be going out of the window—literally. Air escapes through your attic, windows and doors. Adding insulation to your attic if you don't already have it is the most cost-effective, energy-saving measure you can take. To seal additional air leaks, use weather-stripping and caulking around outside doors and windows.

Another opening that's often overlooked is your fireplace damper. Keep it closed unless a fire is burning. An open damper on a four-foot-square fireplace can let up to 8% of your hot or cool air out the chimney.

Using ceiling fans and portable fan units to cool your home costs far less than an air conditioner.

Know When to Use a Fan

Ceiling fans or small fans help circulate the air in summer. They can make a room seem four degrees cooler, so you can set the thermostat at a higher temperature and still feel comfortable.

Only use the continuous fan operator on your air conditioner when it is really necessary to maintain a comfortable temperature. In most cases, using the fan intermittently provides enough air movement.

Use kitchen, bath and other ventilating fans sparingly. Turn them off as soon as they are no longer needed. In about one hour, these fans can pull out an entire houseful of warm or cool air.

Keep It Clean

Periodic maintenance can reduce your heating and cooling costs by up to 10%. Clean and replace filters on air conditioners and furnaces regularly. Similarly, oil-fired boilers should be professionally cleaned and tuned once a year. Gas-fired equipment needs to be checked every other year.

Get a Little Help from Nature

Sunlight is a great way to heat your home, and, best of all, it's free. Open drapes and blinds during the day in winter to maximize the heat gain.

In summer, shade is a low-tech, low-cost way to cut your cooling bills. Using exterior or interior shades as well as trees and other vegetation can reduce the temperature indoors by as much as 20 degrees on a hot day.

Shades and Awnings About 40% of unwanted heat that builds up in your house comes in through windows. Although both exterior and interior shades can control this heat gain, exterior

INSIDE INFORMATION

Home Energy Audits

A home energy audit can identify ways to save up to hundreds of dollars a year on home heating and air conditioning. Ask your electric or gas utility if they can do this audit for free or for a reasonable charge. If not, ask for a referral to a qualified professional, or ask if a do-it-yourself kit is available.

shades—such as awnings, louvers, shutters, rolling shutters and solar screens—are more effective, since they block the sunlight before it enters the windows.

Awnings rate high because they are attractive and they block direct sunlight without disturbing the view from your window. You will want to remove awnings for winter storage or buy retractable ones so that when the heat from sunlight is desirable, it can enter.

Plants and Trees Trees, shrubs and vines all provide valuable shade to cut down on the heat entering your home in the summer. Plants create a cool climate that can dramatically reduce the temperature in their surrounding area.

- Deciduous trees (ones that lose their leaves in winter) offer one of the best ways to cut home cooling costs. When selectively placed around your home, they shade the roof, walls and windows from the sun. Plus, when the leaves drop in autumn, they permit the winter sunlight to reach and warm your house.
- Shrubbery planted a few feet away from the house will provide extra shade without obstructing air currents.
- Vines grown on trellises can shade windows or a whole side of a home. Set trellises away from the wall to allow air to circulate.
- Try planting trees or shrubs to shade the outside portion of window air conditioners and increase their efficiency. Be careful not to obstruct the air flow around the unit.

HERE'S HOW

Choose the Right Shade Plants

Before buying and planting vegetation for shade, read up on different trees and plants. Also, take advantage of the advice and know-how of nursery employees.

Factors to consider when choosing trees and plants include height, growth rate, branch spread and shape. Then think about placement. Experts recommend planting trees between directions. For example, plant a tree on the northeast side of your home, instead of on the north or east side. When selecting a planting site, notice the size and direction of shadows at the site, especially during summer months.

Save Money on New Appliances

Major appliances require a sizable investment, so take the time to research the options before you buy. A more expensive unit may have special features that make it a bargain in the long run.

What Do You Need?

The first step in buying appliances should be to determine exactly what you need. Decide on the size of the product. Appliances that are too large for your needs will waste energy and cost extra money to operate.

Check the availability of a gas hookup for the appliance you are buying. Gas appliances are almost always less expensive to use than electric ones.

Decide what features you will really use. Consider the possibility of adding features at a later date, such as installing an icemaker in a refrigerator.

BUYER BEWARE

Misleading Names

Don't be misled by names when you look for energy-efficient appliances. Names such as Energy Miser, Energy Saver or Fuel Saver don't necessarily guarantee savings. The best way to determine energy efficiency is to compare the information provided on **EnergyGuide** labels.

CHECKLIST

Which Appliance Is Right for You?

❑ Make sure that all the appliances you look at are energy-efficient. Most will come with **EnergyGuide** labels for easy comparison.

❑ Be sure to compare service terms as well as prices. A slightly more expensive item may have a better warranty.

❑ Read the warranty carefully before finalizing your decision. Does the warranty cover the entire product or only certain parts? Is labor included? How long does the warranty last?

❑ Ask your salesperson for the appliance's use and care manual and read it carefully before buying the appliance. The salesperson should have available manuals from the floor models. Reading the manual will help you ask pertinent questions. Plus it will tell you how the product operates and inform you of any special care the product needs.

❑ Make sure that authorized factory service is readily available in your area for the brand you select.

❑ Establish the cost of delivery and installation. They may be included in the price of the appliance.

❑ Once you have made your purchase, make sure you save your sales slip. You never know when you'll have to return faulty merchandise.

When you have decided what you need, plan your purchase. Never buy on impulse. Shop around and compare prices, but be careful to compare apples to apples.

Where to Look

Check newspapers, flyers and store advertising for sales and special offers. Sale prices at nationwide department stores are sometimes competitive with the prices at discount stores.

Discount stores and warehouse clubs (if you are a member) generally have the best deals. It's still a good idea, however, to compare prices and be sure you are getting the best price instead of assuming you are because you are shopping in a particular kind of store. If you decide to buy at a discount store, stick with brand-name appliances that you can evaluate by reading reports from independent testing services such as *Consumer Reports* and *Consumer Digest*.

Read the classifieds. You may find just the item you want. Be sure you know how old the used appliance is and that it has only had one owner. Ask if there is still time on the warranty. If the warranty is still in effect, be sure to read it carefully to see that it is not restricted to the original purchaser.

Some Specifics

While all of the preceding information applies to any appliance purchase, there are some specific things to look for when buying particular appliances that will help you make more energy-efficient choices.

Refrigerators and Freezers

• Top-freezer models use approximately 7% to 13% less energy than side-by-side ones.

• Choose a model with manual defrost when possible. Automatic defrost freezers can consume 40% more electricity than similar manual defrost ones.

• Chest freezers (with the lid on top) are far more energy efficient than upright models. They tend to do a better job of keeping cold air inside when the freezer door is open. And chest freezers tend to have manual defrost.

Dishwashers

• Choose a dishwasher with a booster heater so you can set your hot water heater on 120 degrees to save money.

• Look for a dishwasher that uses as little water as possible. Some models require almost twice as much water per cycle as others, and 80% of the energy required to operate a dishwasher is used to heat water.

Stoves and Ovens

- If you have the choice of a gas stove, it will cost less than half as much to operate as an electric one, provided it is equipped with electronic ignition instead of a pilot light. All new gas ranges are required to have electronic ignition.
- Conventional burners require more energy than induction or halogen cooktops.
- Don't rule out a self-cleaning oven. Although they use energy during cleaning, self-cleaning ovens are generally better insulated than regular ovens, which means they require less energy to cook food.

Washers and Dryers

- Select a washer that lets you control the water level and temperature.
- Look for a dryer with a sensor that will automatically shut off the machine as soon as it stops sensing moisture. It is preferable to a timer, which often keeps the machine running long after the clothes are dry.
- Check for a cycle that includes a cool-down period, sometimes known as a "perma-press" cycle. In the last few minutes of the cycle, cool air, rather than heated air, is blown through the tumbling clothes to complete the drying process.
- Gas dryers are generally more energy-efficient than electric dryers.

Hot Water Heaters

- Natural gas, oil and propane water heaters are less expensive to operate than electric models.
- Choose the most energy-efficient model you can. The more efficient it is, the more money it will save you.
- Determine the size water heater you need based on your First Hour Rating (estimated cost of operating for one year). Salespeople should be able to help you calculate this rating, which you can then compare to various heaters' EnergyGuide labels.

EnergyGuide Labels

EnergyGuide labels are the best source of information on the efficiency of appliances. They also make it easy to compare different models. For example, when shopping for a water heater, you can check the **First Hour Rating**, the estimated cost of energy needed to operate the water heater for a year, and the range of yearly costs of comparably sized water heaters from the least expensive to the most expensive.

Since 1980, EnergyGuide labels have been required on all new refrigerators, freezers, water heaters, dishwashers, clothes washers, room air conditioners, heat pumps, furnaces and boilers. The labels are not required on kitchen ranges, microwave ovens, dryers, on-demand water heaters, portable space heaters or lamps.

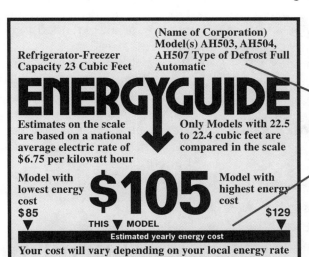

Every EnergyGuide will cite the manufacturer, model number and appliance type.

Listed will be the national average cost of running the appliance for a year. This is measured on a sliding scale and is relative to other models which use higher and lower levels of energy.

Some EnergyGuides (such as this one for a refrigerator) will display the actual cost of running the appliance based on the different energy rates (cost per kilowatt hour) in the country.

IT PAYS TO ASK

Energy-Efficient Rebates

Check with your electric utility company about rebates or programs to help reduce the costs of any appliance purchase that is energy-efficient. When you're shopping, ask salespeople if they have rebate information from your local utility company.

JOHN A. BUYER

BETTY B. BUYER

Double the Length Of Your Warranty

Approximately 120 million credit cards, including **American Express**, **Optima** and **Visa Gold cards**, automatically double the length of the manufacturer's warranty by adding up to six additional months when you use that card to buy a product. Check with your credit card companies to see which ones offer this benefit.

Extended Warranties

Nearly all appliances and electronic devices on the market today are sold with optional service contracts, which augment the protection of the product's warranty. However, you should carefully consider whether a service contract will actually benefit you.

The Difference Between Warranties and Service Contracts Warranties are included in the purchase price of a product. They cover certain repairs for a period of time. The type of coverage and time period varies from warranty to warranty. Service contracts, even when they are called extended warranties, cost extra and must be purchased separately.

The Value of Service Contracts In most cases, service contracts are not worth the money. They often duplicate the same contract period as the manufacturer's warranty or overlap it by only one year. According to consumer sources, if something is going to go wrong with your product, it will most likely happen right away and be covered by the factory warranty, making the need for an extended warranty practically nil.

Before Purchasing a Service Contract Ask the following questions.

- Does the included manufacturer's warranty sufficiently cover repairs for an extended period of time? If so, a service contract may be a waste.
- What will the service contract cover? It may cover only certain parts of the product or specific repairs. If the contract does not list something as specifically covered, assume that it is not.
- Is the product likely to need the repairs covered by the service contract? If the product is unlikely to need servicing, or if the cost of repairs is very low, a service contract would not benefit you.
- What are the requirements or conditions for obtaining repairs under the service contract?

Furniture Bargains

According to consumer advocate Kimberly Causey, author of *The Furniture Factory Outlet Guide* and *The Insider's Guide to Buying Home Furnishings*, now is a great time to buy furniture.

Nearly every furniture manufacturer now sells directly to the public through factory outlets and discounters, Causey says. Virtually every furniture brand on the market can be purchased directly from the manufacturer at 50% to 80% off retail prices. There are actually hundreds of such high-end brands as Drexel-Heritage, Henredon, Baker, Pennsylvania House, Maitland-Smith and Century. Nobody should pay retail for furniture.

Hallmarks of Quality Furniture

Although Causey does recommend that consumers save money by shopping directly at the source, she does not recommend sacrificing quality in order to cut costs. Well-built furniture is an investment. The average piece of furniture will be used for at least 15 years by the original purchaser. By carefully choosing the right woods, fabrics and methods of construction, consumers can make sure that their new furniture still looks like it just came off the showroom floor when it's time to hand it down to their children.

In her book, *The Insider's Guide to Buying Home Furnishings*, Causey gives these tips on how to make sure the furniture you buy is the highest-quality and offers the best value for your money.

General Quality Checks

- Look for sturdiness, a finish that is not rough to touch, and smoothly moving doors and drawers.
- Gently lean against the furniture. It should feel solid and sturdy.
- Make sure drawer pulls are attached with a screw that goes completely through to the inside of the drawer, not simply tacked or glued to the drawer front.
- Heavy furniture should have small concealed castors to help in moving it around.
- Look underneath furniture. You should see a small wooden brace in each corner. This adds strength and stability.

Wood Furniture

- Choose wood that is strong, hard, and doesn't warp. Solid wood is best. Avoid particle board, which is made of pressure treated, glued together sawdust.
- Look for the highest quality woods: cherry, mahogany, oak, teak and walnut. The middle range includes maple and birch.
- Understand veneers: beautiful wood that is used for exterior portions of furniture. They're fine as long as they are over quality wood and not particle board. Check for hidden pieces of exposed wood, such as under a table, on the back of a drawer, or the ends of a shelf to see what the veneer covers.
- Look for corners of drawers that are interlocking, not simply nailed-together, pieces.

Upholstered Furniture

- Check durability by sitting down. Get up and look behind you. Can you still see where you were sitting? A quality sofa or chair should spring right back to its original shape.
- Check the continuity of the fabric. Patterns should line up.

CHECKLIST

What to Bring When Furniture Shopping

- ❑ Drawing of your whole room, including placement of walls, height of ceiling, and location of doors and windows.
- ❑ Swatch of fabric from any existing furniture, as well as colors of carpets and walls.
- ❑ Measuring tape, notebook and pencil to write with.

FOR YOUR INFORMATION

Two Invaluable Books

The Insider's Guide to Buying Home Furnishings by Kimberly Causey (Home Decor Press, $24.95, 800-829-1203)

Get the best quality and the best prices on furniture, custom draperies, fabrics, wallcoverings, lighting, carpeting and decorative accessories. Addresses and phone numbers of over 1,200 factory outlets, discount sources for most brands of furniture and home furnishings at 50%–80% off retail.

The Furniture Factory Outlet Guide by Kimberly Causey (Home Decor Press, $24.95, 800-829-1203)

Very detailed information on hundreds of furniture factory outlets for nearly every brand on the market at 50%–80% off retail: Baker, Century, Henredon, Pennsylvania House, Drexel-Heritage, Bernhardt. Photos, directions, available discounts, special sales and more. Indispensable for travel to the factory outlets and ordering furniture by phone.

INSIDE INFORMATION

Save on Shipping

Let the outlets and discounters arrange return freight for your purchases. Freight lines normally give businesses a 50% discount off the prices they charge the general public. They will deliver your purchases right to your door, and put your furniture exactly where you want it, just as local furniture stores do. You save little or nothing by renting your own truck, not to mention having to move all the furniture by yourself.

- Check that chair and sofa seat cushions have zip-off covers for cleaning.
- Make sure the frame is built from a strong hardwood, not poplar or fir, and especially not particle board.

Beware of Phony Sales at Local Retailers

Sometimes a discount isn't really a discount. Often, what looks like a deep discount at a local furniture store is actually full retail. For instance, a local retailer may take a sofa that has a manufacturer-set retail price of $2,000 and mark it up to a retail of $3,000 right before putting it on "sale" for $2,000. Customers at the sale think they are saving one-third off the retail price, when in actuality they are saving absolutely nothing.

One major national furniture retail chain was recently sued by the state of California and seven other states for this type of false advertising. Although the chain admitted no wrongdoing, it was fined $1.2 million.

Causey recommends that furniture buyers carefully compare actual prices, not percentages off, among different sources when shopping for furniture. As long as you ask every source, retailers and factory outlets, to give you a written quote of the actual price, including any sales tax or freight charges, you can be certain of never being ripped off by a phony sale.

Shop During Slow Seasons

Retailers and manufacturers get the most business in the fall and spring, and the least business during the summer and winter. January and July are the slowest months for home furnishings sales. You'll have the best luck bargaining for a discounted price if you shop during the slow seasons, Causey says.

Big Furniture Savings in North Carolina

You'll get the best deals (50% to 80% off retail) if you go to the furniture outlets in person, most of which are located in North Carolina. There are outlets for Thomasville, Henrendon, Drexel-Heritage, Baker, Hickory Chair and Bernhardt, among hundreds of others. And your travel costs are usually offset by your savings on just one sofa or armoire.

Where to Go

Causey recommends researching what type of furniture each outlet carries before you leave on your trip. Then, you will know which cities in North Carolina (or various other states) you will want to focus most of your attention on.

Travel to North Carolina for Free

Some retailers will pay your travel costs if you buy a certain amount of furniture at their store. For example, if you buy $2,000 worth of furniture, they will arrange for your free airfare and hotel stay. Other discounters arrange savings on airfare and hotel costs no matter how little you buy.

Be sure to call ahead to find out which discounters are running special deals when you're ready to go to North Carolina, because free travel arrangements must be made in advance.

Shipping Costs

Here's a good rule of thumb for freight expenses: The cost to ship your furniture normally runs approximately 5% of the retail price. So, even including the freight costs, if you save more than 5% off retail at a North Carolina outlet, you're still getting a good deal.

Telephone Furniture Ordering Services

If you only need to buy one or two pieces of furniture, going to North Carolina in person isn't cost-effective. However, there are many North Carolina discounters that sell over the phone. Prices will vary, so call a number of discounters before you decide where to buy.

Request a Catalog If you don't know the stock number of the furniture you wish to buy, or if you just want to browse, many discounters will send you catalogs of the lines they carry. Also, many manufacturers have 800-numbers for consumers to call and request catalogs, Causey says.

Telephone Ordering Tips

- Compare prices among various phone sources.
- Always use your credit card.
- Don't forget to ask about freight charges.
- Buy from companies that aren't required to charge you sales tax.
- Buy shipping insurance when ordering breakables.

BARGAIN FINDER

Outlet Bonus

Let the furniture outlets help you plan your trip. Many furniture factory outlets have special arrangements with local hotels and airlines that can save you money if you let them book your trip for you. These discounts usually apply whether or not you actually buy any furniture at the specific factory outlet that arranged your trip.

Some factory outlets can even arrange free meals, discounts on local entertainment, and free seminars on interior design and furniture construction.

When you decide which factory outlets you wish to visit, call as far in advance of your trip as possible to find out how the outlets can help you cut your travel costs.

ASK THE EXPERT

Kimberly Causey On How to Get The Best Bargains On New Furniture

Kimberly Causey is a nationally-known TV and radio expert on consumer issues and the author of the best-sellers *The Insider's Guide to Buying Home Furnishings* and *The Furniture Factory Outlet Guide.*

Do you have any other advice for furniture shoppers?

Shop at the source, preferably a factory-owned factory outlet. Virtually every brand on the market has at least one, and many sell by phone.

Hire design help if you need it. It only costs about $200 to have a professional designer visit your home for the afternoon and give you a basic game plan for redecorating your home. When you consider how much money you're about to spend for furniture and how many years it will be in your home, the $200 you would spend for sound decorating advice is a good investment.

However, never ever use the so-called "free" design services available through local retailers. The designer is paid through markups on everything you buy. People who use these "free" services normally end up paying much too high a price for the design help they actually receive. It's much better to pay a local independent designer about $200 for her advice only and then buy all of your furnishings directly from the manufacturer's outlet or other wholesale source.

Make good use of all the free design advice that is available to you. Take time to look through design books and magazines at your local library or bookstore. Don't be afraid to simply copy the room arrangements and window treatment designs pictured in them. That's what most professional interior designers do.

Anyone Can Get a Good Deal on a Computer

Computers have become a regular feature in many households. Whether you already have one in your home or are a first-time buyer, navigating the computer marketplace can be daunting and overwhelming. But, armed with the knowledge of what you need, good sources of information and a few good buying tips, you can get a great deal on the right computer.

Buying a New Computer

Before you purchase a new computer, it pays to do your homework. You need to decide whether to buy a PC (an IBM-type computer) or a Macintosh. Next, you should determine what you need and want in a computer. The final step is to compare prices and determine where to buy.

Along the way, make sure you use the many sources of information available. Talk to friends, coworkers, neighbors and teachers about what systems and components they use. Also ask which brand names they have found most reliable. Look for articles in newspapers and magazines, and information from

INSIDE INFORMATION

Employee Discounts

Find friends, family members or neighbors who work for computer companies, computer stores, colleges or universities. They can often get you an employee discount on computer equipment.

consumer groups that rate different brands based on such things as reliability, cost, performance and quality of technical support.

PC or Macintosh? For the most part, the decision to buy a PC or a Macintosh is based on personal preference. Here are a few factors to consider before choosing:

- PCs are cheaper than Macs. While the price for Macintosh computers has been dropping, PC prices are still lower. Apple's recent decision to license its technology may eventually make Macintosh computers truly price competitive.
- The PC market offers many choices and options. There are thousands of PC manufacturers available to choose from because the technology has been licensed for so long.
- More software is available for PCs than for Macs.
- Translation between the two systems has vastly improved over the years, but it is still easier to share files with a like system. Know what you'll be using the computer for and whether you need to exchange files with other PCs or Macs.
- Macs are easier to set up and learn to use than PCs. The Windows operating system has helped make PCs user-friendly, but Macs are still more popular with beginners.
- Macs top the charts in user satisfaction and reliability.

What You Need To help you figure out what hardware you'll need, think about what you'll be doing with the computer. Are you using it for work, play, desktop publishing or as an educational tool for children? For example, if you want to have Internet access, you'll need a good modem. If you want to play games or use multimedia educational programs, your sound and video needs will increase.

A good way to get an idea of the computing power you'll need is to visit a computer store and read the minimum requirements on the sides of software boxes that interest you. Once you have a rough idea of what you need, salespeople will be able to help you with the details and technical information.

Computer Stores

The salespeople in a good store can advise you on what hardware and software will serve you best, how to put the pieces together and get started, and how to solve problems that arise as you use your system. It's a good idea to visit several stores to compare prices and service. Pay attention to how friendly, helpful and knowledgeable the sales staff is and always ask how long a store has been in business.

There are two basic kinds of stores that sell computers: retail outlets that stock name-brand computers and custom stores that build computers to your specifications. There are advantages to both.

CHECKLIST

What to Ask The Salesperson

❏ Do you use name-brand internal components?

❏ When is your technical support available?

❏ What does the warranty cover? For how long?

❏ Do you offer training for customers? What does it cost?

❏ Can this computer be upgraded in the future? Will it require proprietary hardware?

❏ Is the equipment new? (Believe it or not, an increasing number of consumers are paying for new equipment but are being sent home with used or refurbished machines.)

BARGAIN FINDER

Proprietary Hardware Trap

To save manufacturing costs and produce smaller units, many computer makers create special components for their machines combining different elements in one piece. This is called proprietary hardware.

Upgrading proprietary hardware can be expensive at best or impossible at worst. For example, if you have proprietary hardware and want a faster modem, you may have to buy an entirely new motherboard. Plus, most proprietary hardware upgrades must be special ordered from the manufacturer.

Matching Prices

If you have purchased through mail order in the past and have a favorite company, consider applying the following strategy. Find the best price for the product you want in **PC Today** or **Computer Shopper** and challenge your favorite mail order house to meet or beat the price. Many mail order houses advertise that they will make every attempt to match legitimate advertised prices.

Surplus Computers

Local colleges and universities sometimes have surplus computers which are offered at sales open to the public. Call the facilities or materials department to ask.

Buying a new computer may well cost less than repairing or upgrading your old one—if you've had it for four years or longer.

Retail Stores Retail stores offer models on display that can be tested, brand-name equipment, and a larger technical support staff. (Most stores also offer training.) But you are generally stuck with choosing from what's on the shelves and may get a system that's difficult to upgrade because it uses proprietary hardware.

Custom Stores Custom stores allow you to choose the components that you want to tailor your computer to your needs. They usually use brand-name internal components, but be sure to ask. The technical support and training available usually depends on the size of the store. There are large chain custom stores that offer all the support and training that retail outlets do, but small local custom shops may fall short in these areas. Keep in mind that custom computers are generally easier to upgrade.

Whichever store you decide to buy from, be sure to ask about warranties and return policies.

Buying through the Mail

Most people who buy computers through mail order do so over the Internet. But computer magazines are also chock-full of ads. By shopping the ads carefully, you can get great bargains. Plus, established mail-order companies have a very high standard of customer service, good satisfaction guarantees and well-informed salespeople.

Beware, though: Using mail order is not for the timid. It can be a good choice if you are familiar with computers and have purchased computer equipment before. First-time buyers are better off buying from a store that can help them get their system up and running.

If you think buying a computer through the mail could be right for you, here are some tips to keep in mind:

- Buy only from firms that sell equipment with full manufacturers' warranties.
- Buy only from firms that offer at least a one-month, complete satisfaction, 100% money-back guarantee.
- Check that a company has been advertising consistently for a year or more to ensure it is reliable.
- Pay by credit card if you have one. This will arm you better to deal with disputes.
- Ask about shipping and handling charges.
- Buy a well-known brand name unless you are familiar enough with computer equipment to be comfortable taking it apart and replacing internal components.
- Learn about any product before you order it so you can specify exactly what you want.

IT PAYS TO ASK

When to Upgrade Your Computer Instead Of Buying a New One

If you already have a computer at home, but it is suffering from symptoms of old-age (such as slow response, crashing, rejecting new software or not communicating well with the Internet), you're probably considering getting a new one or upgrading. Before making your decision, do a little research.

Just about any computer can be upgraded in some way, but it may not be worth it. In fact, trying to upgrade a very old system could end up costing more money than buying a new one. The two key issues in determining whether to upgrade are the age of your computer and the number of components you would need to get the system to perform the way you want it to.

Age Matters

Computer performance and speed tend to double about every two years. If your system is more than 4 or 5 years old, you will probably find that buying a new computer is the best bet.

Do the Math

If you only need one or two components, upgrading will probably be the best deal. For example, if adding more memory and a faster modem will bring your system up to speed, you won't spend much money. Most experts agree that it makes little sense to spend more than $1,000 to upgrade. Carefully weigh the cost of any upgrades against the performance they will give you.

The best way to find out what you need and if it's cost-effective is to do some research. Computer magazines often have articles about upgrading which list specific technical details. The Internet also offers plenty of advice for upgrading.

Don't Be Afraid to Ask

Computer retailers are a good source of information, though their views will probably be slanted toward selling you a new computer. Take advantage of computer-knowledge-able friends and colleagues. Also, check out local computer user groups. Many members have been down the upgrading path before and are excellent sources of information.

If you do decide to upgrade, compare prices and store reputations the same as if you were buying a new computer. Retailers often have different prices for performing the same upgrade.

Buying a Used Computer

While used computers don't have all of the power or technology available in new computers, they are a much cheaper option. Many parents buy used computers for their children and they are also good for people with budding computer interests who aren't sure if they will actually use a computer once they've bought it.

Research carefully to be sure you get what you want. Be sure you stick to established used-computer businesses that offer refurbished equipment, warranties and technical support. Don't buy through swap meets or classified ads. The equipment may not operate properly, usually comes with no guarantees or warranties, and may be overpriced.

Upgrading your old computer may cost less than buying a new one—if all you need is more memory and a faster modem.

Pauline Guntlow On How to Decorate Your Home without Spending a Fortune

Pauline Guntlow is a home decorator and author of *Your Own Home Decorator: Creating the Look You Love Without Spending a Fortune.*

On a small budget, what one thing can you do to make the biggest improvement in your home?

Painting a room can be the most rewarding, least expensive redecorating option. You can totally change the look and feel of the room with paint. A boring white room can be brought alive with bright green paint, or made sunnier with bright yellow. You can use paint to create the atmosphere you want in any room.

Where can you find high-quality, low-cost decorating materials?

Tag sales (garage and yard sales too) are a great place to find furniture, glassware, wall-coverings and art work. The Salvation Army and Goodwill are also great for furniture and fabric pieces. Then check out bargain stores such as Home Depot or low-cost furniture stores which have good deals—if you're a careful buyer and compare prices. Consider buying damaged or used pieces of furniture that you can repair yourself. You can often sew up a small tear or conceal a non-conspicuous stain.

What are some low-cost redecorating options?

- Hanging mirrors on your wall can really open up a room.
- Instead of buying a new piece of furniture, have slip covers made. Make sure you consider the color and durability of the fabric you choose.
- Making your own drapes is a great idea. It's not hard to do and can be less expensive and less time consuming than searching for the perfect ready-made drape. And it gives you more freedom on how you want the room to look. Bring a sample of the room color to the fabric store so that your drapes can incorporate the colors of your room and get you the right look.
- Tile an old coffee table for a new look. You can find tile and buy imperfect pieces for around $10 at a tile store. Then create a great rim for the table with rope.

What are the biggest mistakes that people make when redecorating their home?

Not having a focal point, such as a major piece of furniture or a wall display, is a major mistake. A focal point sets the stage for the room and gives you guidance on how to arrange the rest of the room (other pieces of furniture, paintings). The focal point doesn't have to be expensive, but it should be interesting.

A second mistake is not establishing a color scheme for the room you're redecorating. If you pick a scheme, you can make everything match and blend. You're better off buying things that will complement, not detract from, the general color scheme.

Finally, you need to consider how a room will be used. If you have children or pets, you can make a big mistake choosing a delicate fabric or light color for your couch. You'd be better off with something durable, even if it wasn't your first choice of cloth or pattern.

Pay Less for Home Repairs

It's up to you to keep your home-repair or renovation experience safe from outrageous cost overruns and shoddy work. It is a front-loaded work assignment: Initial research will pay off in the long run. If you've taken the time to protect yourself and put the right measures in place, problems shouldn't become major crises.

Establishing Relationships

There are long-term benefits to becoming someone's customer. Once you have found a contractor you are comfortable with, this relationship can benefit you as long as you own your home. You will have access to a network of other contractors, and you will have someone who is already familiar with your home to call in case of an emergency.

General Contractors

Assess your job: Do you need one contractor or a team? Often one job requires you to use several different contractors: architect, engineer, plumber, electrician, carpenter, roofer, tiler, asbestos removal, painter. Because the coordination of all of these services can be a full-time job in itself, it makes sense to hire a general contractor if you're doing a substantial building or renovation job.

The decision hinges on how you feel about your time, knowledge, budget and interest in managing the project yourself. With a general contractor, you maintain a relationship with just one person. On many jobs, the plumber, electrician or mason doubles as the general contractor.

Finding a Reliable Contractor

The process of working with contractors has a bad reputation—and legitimately so. However, if you educate yourself, use certain screening steps, trust your instincts, and include specific expectations and checkpoints in your contract, you will be fine. Not that the job will go as expected: There are always unforeseen circumstances!

The important thing to remember is that contractors who get through your screening process want the job to go as smoothly and quickly as you do. Contractors' reputations and clean records are their most important assets. Happy customers are their most valuable means of getting work in the future—both from you and your friends.

BUYER BEWARE

Never, but Never...

- Hire a contractor who solicits door-to-door, has no known address, operates from a post office box, or "just happens to be in the neighborhood."
- Put "Lifetime Guarantee" in a contract. Whose life is this referring to?
- Sign that work is acceptable before the work is done to your satisfaction. Take your time reviewing the work without your contractor present.
- Pay the bulk of your money up front. Withholding payment is your best leverage with your contractor.

DID YOU KNOW

Contractor Licenses

At least 38 states now require that all home-repair contractors be licensed. Be aware that a license may only ensure insurance coverage. There is no standard for the number of complaints that would get a contractor's license revoked. In most municipalities, the mechanical trades (plumbers, heating and boiler companies, electricians) are the only contractors that must meet certain requirements pertaining to education and hours on the job before obtaining their licenses.

Using an unlicensed contractor might be less expensive initially, but you might be liable if there is an accident at your job site, and you would have less legal recourse if there were problems with the work. A contractor's license number must be displayed in all advertising and on all correspondence.

Elements of a Smart Contract

Home-improvement contracts must be in writing. Two copies should be countersigned by the customer, with one copy kept by each party, before any work is done. Know that legally you may cancel any contract within three business days. Make sure any contract includes the following:

❑ The contractor's name, address, phone number and license number.

❑ The approximate start and completion dates, including any contingencies that would change the completion date.

❑ A specific description and design of the work and materials, including the phrase "to code."

❑ Who is supplying appliances. If the contractor is purchasing appliances, include brands, model numbers and other identifying information, along with the price.

❑ The payment schedule, and how it is tied to work completion.

❑ Who is responsible for obtaining permits.

❑ The length of warranties for workmanship and product.

❑ Who is responsible for clean-up.

Educate Yourself

Information is your best resource and your best protection. This can range from looking at pictures in home-design magazines to speaking with your local building inspector. Your research goal is to be able to:

- Refine the scope of the job you want done.
- Have a hands-on feel for the products you will be using.
- Determine what types of contractors you need.
- Draft a realistic budget.
- Ask the contractors the right questions.
- Know how to judge workmanship.

Develop a Plan

Think through all the related parts of the job you set out to do. Remember that it will cost less to do it all at once than to hire contractors a few years down the road for another round of work.

Visit showrooms, home centers and lumberyards that sell furniture or materials for the specific room you are working on. While you take in ideas, see if there is a designer on staff who could give you a free consultation.

Relevant government agencies, industry trade associations and manufacturers are all important sources of information on permits and codes, hiring remodelers, products and design ideas. The following organizations provide consumer information such as planning steps, checklists and helpful brochures.

- National Association of Plumbing-Heating-Cooling Contractors (800-533-7694) www.naphcc.org
- National Association of the Remodeling Industry (703-575-1100) www.nari.org
- National Kitchen and Bath Association (800-401-6522) www.nkba.org

The Screening Process

Your chances of finding a reputable contractor greatly increase if you follow these recommendations.

Find Likely Candidates

- Get remodelers' names from people who've gone through the process before: friends, family, neighbors. A personal recommendation is the best reference. If you don't know someone who's recently completed the kind of job you need, names from professional associations are a better bet than the phone book. If the same names keep coming up, they are the ones to interview first.
- Interview several contractors on the phone. Talk over the project in general. Pay attention to their phone manner. Do they

have listening skills? Do they return calls quickly? Reject anyone using high-pressure sales tactics.

- Check references. Ask for current customers as well as prior customers to get a sense of how the contractor handled the routine parts of the job—as well as the problems. Try to get a feel for what it was like working with the contractor. Examine the work to see if it meets your requirements.
- Verify that the contractor is licensed to work in your town and carries general liability insurance and workers' compensation. Write down the contractor's license number.
- Follow up by calling the Better Business Bureau or Consumer Protection Agency in your area to ask if the contractor has a good track record.

Screening Interview Questions You'll want answers to these questions for all potential contractors:

- How long have they been in business, and at what address?
- How long has the current crew been with them?
- How many other jobs are they doing simultaneously?
- At what number can you always reach the boss directly?
- What's their policy on change orders—yours and theirs?

Getting Quotes

Here's the standard procedure for the initial appointment:

1. Make an appointment to meet the contractors at the job site to fully explain the job.
2. Be prepared to discuss budget. This is the starting point for design as well as product selection.
3. Don't be surprised if you are asked to pay a consultation fee, to be charged up front but credited to the job if you choose that company. Ask questions. You are paying for their professional expertise.
4. Assess their work habits. Are they on time for the appointment? What is their personal appearance like? Do you sense a mutual respect?
5. As a follow-up to the appointment, contractors will submit their quotes in writing. Pay attention to how long it takes them to get this done. Expect a flat fee for the job.

FOR YOUR INFORMATION

Utilize Your Building Inspector

Every municipality has a building inspector, paid for with your tax dollars. Before starting any major building project or renovation, make an appointment with your building inspector to talk about the project. The inspector will tell you what permits or code requirements you need to understand. Ask for a list of the plumbers and electricians who are licensed to work in your town. Many times the building inspector can also recommend other contractors in good standing.

It's important to do things to code, and with the proper permits. While strictness varies greatly from town to town, if you do work without the proper permits, building inspectors are within their jurisdiction to ask you to rip new work out at your expense. If it states "to code" in your contract, your contractor is entirely responsible for the cost of all work that is found not to be to code.

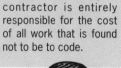

The time-honored phrase is "Get three quotes." The full phrase should be "Get three competent, legitimate quotes!"

When It's An Emergency

If you don't have a relationship with any contractors and disaster strikes, your best bet is to pick up the phone book.

1. Look in the yellow pages under the specific need that you have (roofer, carpenter). Call only those people who display their license numbers in their ads. When calling those who are just line-listed, ask for their license numbers and write them down.

2. Call local contractors first: They are the most likely to be licensed in your community.

3. Judge attention to detail and customer service by their phone manner. If it is after hours, rate the answering machine message. Answering services get even higher marks.

4. Expect to pay a fixed fee for emergency service to begin, plus materials. After you describe your situation, ask what the premium is for emergency calls.

Dealing with Quotes You should get several quotes to choose from. As you assess them, keep in mind that you are probably not comparing apples to apples. Look at the design and product ranges, and select the one that represents what you want. Remember that it is not always a bargain to go with the lowest quote. Sometimes contractors will low-ball a bid to get the job, and it can cost you in service, punctuality and lack of expertise. Discuss what can go wrong and how much more it might cost under a worst-case scenario.

Be prepared to pay a fairly large down payment, perhaps 30% to 50%. This amount can be negotiated, however.

Who Buys the Appliances? Either the homeowner or the contractor could buy appliances. It comes down to the balance among money, headaches and time.

The contractor typically buys an appliance at wholesale, marks it up and passes the cost to you. Yet in this age of discount shopping, a smart shopper can buy appliances for not much more than wholesale. The person who buys the appliances, however, assumes responsibilities of shopping, delivery, coordination as far as fit and compatibility, and returning the appliances if they're damaged.

Staying Healthy For Less

Staying out of the doctor's office and away from hefty medical expenses isn't as difficult as you think. Here are some bargain ways you can get fit, lower your medical costs, save on health insurance and stay healthy for less.

Low-Cost Tips to Keep You Fit

Keeping fit is the least invasive, least drastic and least expensive way to stay healthy. In fact, many health experts say that the most effective treatment is keeping your mind and body healthy on an everyday basis.

Most experts also believe that many common illnesses respond well to simple lifestyle adjustments. If you treat your mind and body well, you can take advantage of the greatest type of medicine, which is the body's ability to heal itself.

Secrets of Staying Healthy

Reduce your risk of premature illness. If you recognize how your mind and body interact to create health or become vulnerable to disease, you can build a lifestyle to help protect yourself from health crises.

Water Purifiers

Bottled water is an unnecessary expense. If you want cleaner water, think about installing a home water-purifying system that attaches to your faucet or under the sink, such as a reverse osmosis or carbon-KDF system. Or (if space is an issue), you can purchase a **Brita Filter System** which allows you to keep your purified water in a gallon-sized container.

It's also beneficial to flush your water system daily by running the water for about five minutes when it has not been used for four hours or more. And don't use hot water for drinking or cooking. Impurities from plumbing and hot water tanks can readily leak into the water.

Purify Your Drinking Water Consider purifying your drinking water. Drinking water is a major source of environmental toxins. Experts say that more than one million Americans drink water that contains significant levels of cancer-causing chemicals, such as arsenic, radon and chlorine by-products. Similarly, the U.S. Centers for Disease Control and Prevention report that millions of Americans become sick from water-borne microorganisms every year.

Take Your Vitamins Think about taking daily vitamin supplements. Some experts believe that vitamins may improve healing and wound repair, decrease heart disease and reduce the body's ability to produce free radicals (negatively charged ions that cause tissue damage and promote cancer). Check with your doctor to be sure which supplements are appropriate for you.

Exercise Try to exercise at least five days a week. The key is to find a way to use your body that is sensible and not traumatic.

Any type of exercise that raises your heart rate is beneficial. You may wish to start with a brisk ten-minute walk, working your way up to 45 minutes.

But if you already have an exercise routine that gives you a workout, there's no need to change.

Sweat for Success Consider taking a weekly sauna or steam bath. In addition to its ability to cool the body, sweating is one of the most important self-healing mechanisms because it allows the body to rid itself of unwanted or excess minerals and toxins.

Sweat in dry heat (sauna) or wet heat (steam), or a combination of the two. If you don't belong to a gym, try steaming in an enclosed shower for 15 to 20 minutes. Be sure to drink plenty of water before you enter the sauna or steam room, and drink enough afterward to replace lost fluids.

Eat Right Think about getting potentially unhealthy foods out of your refrigerator and pantry. Certain foods are suspected of inhibiting your body's ability to heal itself. They include polyunsaturated oils (safflower, corn, sunflower), artificially hardened fats (vegetable shortening, margarine), artificial sweeteners (aspartame, NutraSweet, saccharin) and artificial colorings.

Experts believe that polyunsaturated oils oxidize rapidly when exposed to air. Oxidized fats can damage DNA, promote cancer development, and speed aging and degenerative changes in body tissues. Use olive oil in moderation instead.

Consider adding fruits and vegetables to your diet, especially cruciferous vegetables (broccoli, cabbage), dark-colored fruits (red grapes, blueberries) and cooked greens (Swiss chard, kale, collards). In addition to their high fiber and vitamin/mineral content, cruciferous vegetables and dark-colored fruits have been shown to have significant anti-cancer properties.

Try to eat more whole grains and soy products. Data show that a diet rich in fiber can enhance digestion, reduce the risk of colon cancer, help lower cholesterol and slow the absorption of sugar into the bloodstream. Whole-wheat bread, brown rice and buckwheat are particularly beneficial.

The addition of soy products not only increases your overall fiber intake but also provides a form of protein that is lower in saturated fat than animal products.

The Art of Breathing

Focusing attention on your breathing can enhance your ability to relax and promote your body's good health and self-healing. Breathing exercises may help make your visit to the doctor's office something to smile about.

Here are some breathing exercises that experts suggest:

Inhalation Breath Observation Sit in a comfortable position with your back straight and eyes closed. Focus attention on your breathing, noting the point where you inhale. Do this for five minutes each morning.

Exhalation Breath Observation Sit in a comfortable position with your back straight and eyes closed. Focus on your breathing, but concentrate on when you exhale instead of when you inhale.

Relaxing Breath Sit in a comfortable position with your back straight and eyes closed. Touch the tip of your tongue to the inner surface of your front teeth and then slide it upward slightly to rest on the ridge between the teeth and the roof of your mouth.

Keeping it there, inhale through your nose for four seconds. Hold your breath for seven seconds. Exhale through your mouth. Repeat four times. This can be done in the morning or evening.

Stimulating Breath Sit in a comfortable position with your back straight and eyes closed. Touch the tip of your tongue to the inner surface of your front teeth and then slide it upward slightly to rest on the ridge between your teeth and the roof of your mouth.

Breathe in and out rapidly through your nose, keeping your mouth closed slightly. Your breathing should be audible. Try this exercise for 15 seconds, and then increase the time by ten seconds each time until you can do it for up to one minute. This exercise is best practiced in the morning.

HERE'S HOW

Fend Off Diseases Naturally

You can save money by fending off disease with natural substances. Consider adding garlic, ginger and green tea to your diet. A number of important and interrelated benefits are associated with these three foods:

Garlic has been shown to lower blood pressure and cholesterol levels, and reduce the risk of clogged arteries. It also appears to boost the immune system and stimulate your body's natural defenses against cancer. One to two cloves a day is ideal. If eating them raw or sliced in food doesn't appeal to you, add fresh garlic to food you're cooking a few minutes before the dish is ready.

Ginger can be a great help for upset stomachs. Ginger works by interrupting the nausea signals sent from the stomach to the brain, perhaps by absorbing stomach acid.

For motion sickness, ginger is even more effective than Dramamine. Two 500-mg ginger capsules (available at drug and health-food stores) every few hours can help upset stomachs, stomach discomfort caused from traveling, and pregnant women dealing with morning sickness.

Ginger can be consumed raw, cooked or pickled (which is how it is served at Japanese restaurants).

Green tea contains substances called catechins, which lower cholesterol, improve lipid metabolism and reduce cancer risk. Experts recommend one to two cups of decaffeinated green tea a day.

Tax-Free Medical Funding

Many companies give you the opportunity to set aside pretax income to pay for medical expenses your insurance doesn't cover. You have to use the amount you've set aside within the year, or you'll lose it. But if you have a sense of the minimum you're likely to spend each year on deductible or uncovered expenses (such as contact lenses), it can be a smart move.

Check with your employer or the human resources department of the company you work for to find out whether this is an option for you.

COBRA Insurance

If you leave your job, you don't have to worry about paying for the expensive costs of an individual insurance plan right off the bat.

COBRA (the Consolidated Omnibus Budget Reconciliation Act of 1985) gives you the right to continue your group insurance for 18 months after you leave a job, whether you quit, are laid off or retire (and for 29 months if you're disabled). The general rule is that you can buy coverage for 102% of your employer's cost.

Your employers cannot deny you coverage, except by ending health insurance for all employees.

Deal with Health Insurance The Economical Way

Health insurance may be one of the most economical investments you make. Without health insurance, every cent you save could be exhausted by a serious illness. Most health insurance plans cover hospital care and medical treatments, including visits to the doctor, medical tests and similar expenses.

Group vs. Individual Plans

Group insurance plans cost, on average, between half and two-thirds of what an individual plan costs. Many types of group plans are available. The most common ones are those offered by your employer. Religious organizations, labor unions and private organizations frequently offer their members group insurance plans as well.

If you don't have access to a group plan, your alternatives are buying an individual policy or joining a managed health care plan, such as an HMO.

Choosing a Higher Deductible

Health insurance is vital to maintaining economic stability and a sound financial future, but it's generally rather expensive. There is a way, however, to cut your costs.

In most cases, choosing a higher deductible lowers your insurance costs. A deductible is a dollar amount you must pay before the insurance kicks in (a typical deductible is approximately $300 a year per individual).

If you have a choice of several deductibles, you may want to opt for the highest one you can afford, say $1,000. This way you can use the insurance as a protection against major expenses rather than as a way to pay for everyday health care. Be sure, however, that the deductible is applied to the annual total of your expenses, not against each individual expense.

Indemnity Plans

Don't fall prey to what seems like the cheap cost of indemnity plans, because they may not be the best value for your money.

Indemnity plans guarantee that they'll pay a specific amount per claim (for example, $100 for every day you're in the hospital), but in general they are not a smart use of your insurance dollar. The amount they pay often covers only a fraction of the actual cost of any care you receive. And once you buy the policy, you may find hidden restrictions.

Managed Care Can Be A Great Deal

Managed care has become the preferred solution to expensive health care costs, and HMOs are the leading type of managed care organization.

Instead of charging for each service or visit to a doctor or hospital, Health Maintenance Organizations (HMOs) charge you an annual fee that covers all the care you receive. A big plus of prepaid care is that you never have to remember to file insurance claims or wait to be reimbursed for money you've paid out for treatment. And an even bigger benefit is that all the care you get is covered, so you won't be faced with an enormous bill for medical care you can't afford.

Types of Managed Care

Get to know the other types of managed care plans.

Preferred Provider Organizations (PPOs) PPOs are networks of doctors that provide discounted care to members of a sponsoring organization, such as an employer or union. If you use a participating doctor, you pay a small copayment at the time of your visit (approximately $10 or 10% of the bill).

But if you go to a non-participating, out-of-network doctor, your share of the bill jumps dramatically.

Open-ended HMOs Open-ended HMOs cover visits to the doctor of your choice. You will probably have to pay a larger premium (monthly fee) for this option, but you may want the flexibility to use a particular practitioner.

DID YOU KNOW

Medical Savings Accounts Can Save You Money

Investigate new **Medical Savings Accounts (MSAs)** if you work for yourself or for a small company (fewer than 50 employees). To qualify you must buy a health plan with a big deductible ($1,500-$2,250 for a single and $3,000-$4,500 for a family plan). In 2000, the figures are $1,550-$2,350 for a single and $3,100-$4,650 for a family plan. Then you can deposit pretax money into the MSA and withdraw tax-free amounts that you can use to pay qualifying medical expenses.

After age 65 you can use the money for any reason without penalty.

Ask the financial institution that handles your IRA account, or check with one of the following institutions:

- **Merrill Lynch**
  (800-637-7455)

- **Medical Savings of America**
  (800-853-7321)

Comparing Costs

PPOs
Premiums range from **$3,000–$9,000** a year for an individual

Network Provider
$10 copayment

Out-of-network Provider
$300–$1,000 deductible and 20% copayment

Open-ended HMOs
Premiums range from **$2,400–$7,200** a year for an individual

Choose Any Provider
20% copayment

Research before You Join

Before you join an HMO, you should consider checking whether it has been accredited by the **National Committee for Quality Assurance** (NCQA, 800-839-6487). NCQA is an independent nonprofit organization that rates HMOs on their medical treatment, physicians' qualifications, preventative health services, record keeping and more. At least 50% of all HMO enrollees have been rated. You can call NCQA for a free **Accreditation Status List**, which is updated on the 15th of each month.

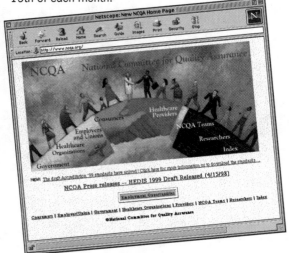

Questions to Ask before Choosing

Choosing a managed care plan will cost you less than buying a traditional fee-for-service policy. But if you are trying to decide among various plans, it pays to ask a few questions about each before selecting one:

- Can I choose which doctor I want to see, or are they assigned by availability?
- How long is the average wait for an appointment?
- Can I see doctors outside the network? How much will it cost?
- Is there a cap on the total coverage the plan will provide?
  - How much will each visit cost? Is there a limit to the number of visits?
  - Is there a copayment?
  - If a specialist is needed, will consultation be paid by the plan?
  - Can I be dropped if I need lots of care or make frequent visits to the doctor?
  - Are medications paid for? How many times can I refill them? Can I buy in bulk? Do I copay each time or just for the first prescription?
  - What hospitals can I use? Are there any limitations on the length of hospital stays?
  - What are emergency hospital care costs?
  - Are there any health services for home nursing?
  - Are orthopedic shoes, eyeglasses, syringes, blood-glucose meters and similar equipment covered?
  - Are health classes, weight-reduction seminars, exercise clinics or special services reimbursable?
  - Are there discounts for nonsmokers or people involved in fitness programs?

Pinch Your Pennies by Avoiding Common HMO Traps

Since HMOs are increasingly common sources of health insurance, it's good to know how to avoid any traps that can increase your costs.

Traps that Can Cost You Money

Here are the most common HMO traps that can cost you money, and ways you can avoid them.

Trap: Not realizing you can change primary care physicians only at specified times.

Every plan has its own rules, but generally you can only switch doctors at certain times or frequencies. Some plans allow you to change once a quarter, others three times a year. With some plans, you can switch only at the beginning of the month—while with others you can change only at the end of the month, even if you move or your doctor relocates, or if your doctor is away or unavailable.

Possible Solution: Check the language of your contract first to make sure you are making the change at the right time. Otherwise, you may be disqualified from coverage and have to foot the bill yourself. You may be better off staying with your old doctor for the time being.

Trap: Slow referral procedures.

Because you must obtain a referral in order to get a specialist's care paid for by an HMO, the process can sometimes be agonizingly slow and result in a delay in diagnosis.

Possible Solution: If you believe that it is urgent for you to see a specialist and your doctor disagrees, ask for a written explanation of why your condition is not urgent. If the doctor turns out to be wrong, you'll have documentation for bringing a legal case. Putting the opinion in writing may also cause the doctor to think twice.

Beware: If you pay for a visit to a specialist yourself without your HMO's approval and you cannot prove it was an emergency, you will probably not be reimbursed.

Trap: Allowing your physicians to make benefits decisions, rather than medical decisions, on your behalf.

This may seem like quibbling, but there's an important difference.

Solution: To protect yourself, ask your doctor to explain to what extent a decision is being influenced by contracts with your health plan. The key is making the distinction between decisions about payment and decisions about health and well-being.

If your doctor is overly influenced by HMO policy, you should be concerned about decisions affecting your health and well-being. So in every situation, ask your doctor this question. If the doctor's decision is based on policy instead of your health, ask what your next step should be to receive the best care.

HERE'S HOW

Ask Questions Before Switching Your HMO

While low out-of-pocket costs make HMOs attractive, you still need to ask hard questions before switching from one plan to another.

Here are some key questions you may want to consider asking before you sign on the dotted line:

- Will the HMO physician you want to use as a primary-care doctor be able to see you as a new patient?
- If you have a chronic condition, how does the HMO handle it?
- How easy is it to get appointments and referrals to see specialists?
- Can you get a standing referral to see a specialist without having to go through a primary physician each time?
- Will the HMO allow a specialist to be your primary physician? If so, will the specialist be able to see you for ailments and checkups unrelated to the specialty?
- Does the HMO offer a variety of benefit packages?
- How far will you have to travel to see a primary-care physician or specialist?
- How does the health plan cover an emergency? Does it require prior authorization for an emergency visit? What is its definition of an emergency?

Find the Person In Charge

Take the matter to a higher authority if you're not satisfied with what your insurer's customer service representative tells you. That person has a supervisor who may be able to help you.

If you feel you are being wrongly denied care by an HMO, ask for a medical director, a customer relations vice president, or someone whose job it is to oversee such problems. Most HMOs are required by law to have an appeals process.

If your medical insurance is provided by your employer, complain to your company's employee benefits people. Since they're the ones who choose and pay for the health insurance coverage, they may have more clout with the insurer than an individual employee does. Insurance company executives should be notified if employees are getting poor service.

If you still can't get satisfaction, try your state insurance commissioner's office. Most allow that any claim can be challenged as long as it is done in writing. Just threatening to contact the state insurance commissioner's office will likely cause your insurer to review your claim.

Filing like a Trained Professional (Without Paying for One)

Getting the money your insurance company owes you may just be a matter of filing a claim properly the first time. To do so, you've got to pay attention to detail.

Filing a claim is so complex that it provides many opportunities for errors and misunderstandings. When mistakes occur, insurers, already under pressure to hold down costs, are likely to question, deny or reduce the amount you're claiming.

In response, a new type of service has emerged to help people file claims and battle insurers.

Claims assistance professionals (many of whom formerly worked for insurance companies as claims administrators), charge anywhere from $25 to $90 per hour, and with their help, an estimated 50% of the claims that are challenged end up being paid by insurers.

Here are the effective strategies of claims assistance professionals that you can use yourself instead of spending the money to hire one.

Avoid Clerical Errors

A significant number of claims are rejected because of clerical errors. When you send in your claims, clerks may have to key them into computer systems, raising the risk of error. Even electronic claims can be problematic. Insurance group or Social Security numbers can be transposed.

These days, every diagnosis and procedure performed by a doctor is given a code number. Insurers look to the codes to decide if the doctor overcharged or used an inappropriate treatment, so if the numbers are wrong, claims will be unpaid.

Your insurer should tell you why a claim is denied or reimbursed at a lower level, so that you can correct any claim error that may be the cause. If the insurer says that treatment was not related to the diagnosis or was inappropriate, it could be a sign that the codes are wrong.

Keep Detailed Records

When challenging your claim, do it in writing and keep careful records of all contacts with your health insurers. Send copies to your doctor or hospital and the insurance company, and keep a copy for yourself. Keep notes about any telephone conversations you've had with the insurer detailing with whom you spoke, when you had the conversation and what was said—in case you need to refer to those conversations at a later date.

Enlist Your Doctor's Help

Enlist your doctor's help if your insurer won't pay what your doctor is charging. An insurer may feel the charges are more than the usual, customary and reasonable fees.

It's in doctors' best interest to prove that their tab isn't out of line, and they should be willing to send a letter to your insurance company detailing the facts.

In other cases, the doctor may need to submit a more detailed explanation of treatment and services. The procedure you received may be more complicated than the insurance company realizes.

Provide More Information

Provide more information about your symptoms if your insurer says the treatment wasn't medically necessary. Additional details may help to explain why you needed the treatment.

If your insurer protests that your treatment was experimental and not eligible, have your physician write a letter. Or, if you write it, have your doctor add to it citing medical studies or discussing how commonly the treatment is used.

Keep Track of Policy Changes

Keep careful track of policy changes and of what you've spent that qualifies against your deductible. Carefully read any memos and booklets from your employee benefits department or health insurer.

Keeping carefully organized records of your medical claims, doctor's bills and policy information will help you get the reimbursement your insurance company owes you.

Medigap, the Supplement To Medicare

Medigap policies cover a variety of services, including nursing home copayments, foreign-travel emergencies and prescription drugs. The best time to buy Medigap insurance is within the first six months after you begin your Medicare coverage. Otherwise, it may be more expensive.

Getting Free Advice on Medigap

You can get free advice on your insurance options and answers to your Medigap questions through your state's insurance counseling office. You can find the number in your telephone book or in the Health Care Financing Administration's *Guide to Health Insurance for People with Medicare*, which is available from your local Social Security office.

BUYER BEWARE

Pay Attention to The Codes

When a doctor's office gives you an insurance form filled with codes, ask for the meaning of each code. Incorrect codes are a major reason insurers reject bills, which then become the patient's responsibility.

If you are hospitalized, insist on an itemized bill, even though it may be lengthy. Make sure you understand all charges. Look carefully at pharmacy and medication categories and equipment-and-supplies listings, areas where errors are common.

Pay Attention to Your Medicare Treatments

When you get **Medicare** treatments, keep a log of all your medical visits and any procedures that are done. This will help you check if you are billed incorrectly, and make it easier if you have to file an appeal for additional payment.

Review every bill carefully. Medicare bills from hospitals and doctors often contain errors.

Also, it usually takes 35 to 45 days for Medicare to pay a claim. If you do not get an explanation of Medicare payments within 45 days, contact the Medicare carrier in your region.

Before traveling outside the U.S., find out what Medicare covers you for while abroad.

You might not be smiling when you find out you're not covered for disabilities through your work.

Another option is to check with the agency in your state that coordinates information and services for older residents, such as the Office or Department of Aging, Elder Affairs, or Adult Services. You can find their numbers in the *Guide to Health Insurance*, in the telephone book, and from groups such as the United Seniors Health Cooperative.

Remember that each state's insurance rules are a little different, so if you move after you retire, you may need to revise your Medigap coverage.

Medicare Opportunity

Many HMO insurers are working to provide in-network medical care to retirees that's much cheaper than regular Medigap coverage. If retirees are willing to commit themselves to visiting only network physicians, they won't need to purchase Medigap coverage. Instead, they will pay only $10 per doctor's visit and Medicare will reimburse other expenses. If this is an option open to you, it's worth considering.

Disability Insurance

It has become tougher to find a generous disability policy these days for a reasonable price. Among other things, insurers are limiting the amount of benefits they'll pay on new policies if you can't return to work at your present job or won't work at a job they deem comparable. Some insurers are no longer offering policies that promise never to raise your premium.

Make Sure You're Covered

Don't assume that you have adequate coverage through work. Most people who have group coverage at work for long-term disabilities are complacent and think they don't need to purchase individual policies.

The problem with most employer-sponsored policies is they have provisions that reduce benefits if you are eligible to receive benefits from Social Security, worker's compensation and other state programs.

Even though it is difficult to qualify for government benefits, most company policies say the insurer can offset these benefits as long as you are eligible for them, regardless of whether you actually receive them.

Workers who make between $1,500 and $3,500 a month may find that their long-term disability benefits from their company plans are only $50 a month. This can be devastating.

Look for Non-cancelable and Guaranteed-renewable Policies

Try to look for a non-cancelable and guaranteed-renewable policy. It will be hard to find a policy with both provisions.

A non-cancelable policy is one that the insurance company can't cancel unless you die or fail to pay your premium on time. This type of policy has fixed premiums throughout the life of the contract.

A guaranteed-renewable individual policy means the company cannot cancel or change the terms of the policy even if you change occupations or your health history changes as long as you pay your premiums on time. But the insurer can raise your premium if it raises premiums on all policies like yours.

If you own a non-cancelable guaranteed-renewable policy that pays if you are disabled from your own occupation to age 65 or for life, don't trade it in or let it lapse even if you have trouble getting a claim paid.

To safeguard your rights if the company contests a disability claim, pay the premium on time and write on the check, "contested premium," so that the insurance company cannot say you agreed that you were not disabled.

Compromise on the Waiting Period

Consider compromising on the waiting period. This is the period you must wait before you can start collecting benefits. The longer the waiting period, the cheaper the premium.

The typical waiting period is 90 days. But if you have the resources to support yourself for a longer period, the premium can be dramatically lowered.

Extending the waiting period to 180 days will cut your premium by around 20% to 25%.

Beware: You may lose more money if your extra expenses are higher than the cut on your premium.

Be Thorough and Accurate When You Apply

Try to be thorough and accurate when you apply. When an insurance company representative takes your medical history, list all the physicians you have visited and the ailments for which you have been treated. Take the application, read the medical questions yourself, and respond fully.

Otherwise, the company may be able to rescind or cancel your policy, alleging you lied on the application, if you become disabled within a certain period after applying for coverage. A company can cancel your coverage for any fraudulent misstatement, even if the information has no bearing on your disability.

BUYER BEWARE

Before You Retire Early, Check the Small Print

Before taking early retirement, check to see if your company can cut retiree health benefits. More and more firms are reducing them as cost-cutting pressures increase. Even companies that promise to provide retiree health benefits often include reservation clauses stating that they reserve the right to make benefits changes. Consider negotiating guaranteed health coverage as part of your retirement package.

Retirees age 65 and older can rely on Medicare, but that does not cover spouses under 65 or children.

FOR YOUR INFORMATION

Health Hotlines

You can get a free copy of **Health Hotlines**, a directory of the addresses and toll-free numbers of 250 helpful organizations that deal with asthma, Parkinson's disease, migraines and more. Write to Hotlines, National Library of Medicine Information Office, 8600 Rockville Pike, Bethesda, MD 20894, for your free copy. www.nlm.nih.gov

Avoid the Emergency Room

Prepare yourself for minor illnesses and injuries with a home first aid kit.

Keep your first aid supplies in a sturdy container with a lid, such as a tool box. Place a piece of masking tape on the outside of the box, with your local emergency phone number and the number of the poison control center.

Keep the kit in a dry area (not the bathroom), and out of the reach of small children. All household members (except small children) and your babysitters should know the location of the kit.

Supplies for Your First Aid Kit

❏ Ace bandage (3-inch width)
❏ Adhesive bandages (various sizes)
❏ Antibiotic ointment
❏ Antiseptic washes
❏ Bar of plain, non-scented soap
❏ Calamine lotion
❏ Cotton-tipped swabs and cotton balls or absorbent cotton pads
❏ First-aid manual
❏ Flashlight with extra batteries
❏ Hydrogen peroxide
❏ Individually packaged, sterile gauze pads
❏ Large safety pins
❏ Large triangular bandages
❏ Oral or rectal thermometers
❏ Petroleum jelly
❏ Roll of adhesive tape (1-inch width)
❏ Rolls of gauze bandages (2-inch and 4-inch widths)
❏ Safety matches
❏ Scissors
❏ Small bottles of aspirin and acetaminophen
❏ Tissues
❏ Tweezers and sewing needles

Savvy Ways to Cut Your Medical Bills

You'll be happy to know that there are ways to cut the cost of your medical bills without sacrificing top-quality care. All it takes is a few extra minutes to plan ahead.

Avoid Office Visits

You can save a lot of money by avoiding unnecessary visits to the doctor's office. Consider calling your doctor's office for answers to questions about medications, reactions to treatment, or recurring problems—instead of paying for a full visit.

You may want to ask if there are particular times of the day or week which are better for phone consultations, and make sure to ask if there is a charge for such calls.

Stay Away from the Emergency Room

Emergency rooms are extremely expensive for non-emergency care. You may pay up to ten times more than you would for the same treatment at your doctor's office. Many insurance plans, such as HMOs, are refusing to pay bills for visits to the emergency room that aren't life threatening.

If you're concerned about a child's earache or sore throat, call your doctor to find out how serious the problem is, and if it can be treated at home.

Or you may want to consider using an ambulatory care center for basic medical care, such as cuts, sprains, broken bones and sore throats. Most centers cost considerably less than hospital emergency rooms, and many are open 24 hours a day.

It's best to stay away from the emergency room unless it's really an emergency, or you may wind up paying as much as ten times more than what you'd pay in your doctor's office.

Buy a 90-day Supply of Drugs

If you buy drugs with a copayment, you may want to consider asking your doctor or pharmacist for a 90-day supply instead of three 30-day supplies. This way you will only have to pay one co-payment instead of three. Many plans cover only a 30-day supply at a time, however.

Long-Term Care Insurance

To offset the expense of a nursing home or home health care, many people over 50 consider long-term care insurance. Long-term health care can cost $200 a day or more, and is usually not covered by regular insurance plans.

Long-term care insurance provisions are complicated, and you may want to get some advice on how to choose the best policy from a fee-only insurance planner or your state's insurance office.

Fortunately, recent tax laws make the premiums partially tax deductible for people who spend more than 7.5% of their Adjusted Gross Income on health care expenses that are not reimbursed by either health insurance or Medicare.

Helpful Hints to Lower Your Hospital Bills

To lower your medical costs, make sure every procedure, test or hospital stay is absolutely necessary. This means staying on the ball while you're in the hospital.

Outpatient Procedures

Many procedures that used to require an overnight hospital stay can now be done on an outpatient basis, which can cost 50% less than a regular hospital procedure. Ask your doctor about new, minimally invasive surgical techniques, which may be less expensive and less traumatic than their predecessors.

A Second Opinion

Before admitting yourself to a hospital for surgery, you should always get a second opinion. Unnecessary surgery is a physical and economic risk most people can't afford to take.

DID YOU KNOW

Economy-Sized May Cost More

Buying the large economy size of an over-the-counter drug isn't a good deal if its expiration date arrives before you use it up. Consider buying only the amount of medicine that you'll use in one year. And check the expiration date on an over-the-counter drug before you make a purchase. You don't want to buy something that will only be good for one more month.

HERE'S HOW

Avoid Being Overcharged on Your Hospital Bills

You can avoid being overcharged on your hospital bills by requesting a fully itemized bill and reviewing it carefully.

Since billing mistakes are common, you may want to document all of your medications, procedures, tests and services throughout your stay. You can compare your log to the hospital's bill.

Here's what to look for when reviewing your bill:

- Duplicate billings (often for tests or x-rays).
- Unauthorized tests (especially if you have asked for advance approval).
- Phantom charges (often for medications that have never been administered to you).
- Bulk charges (if there is a broad heading, such as Pharmacy, you can't know if the total is accurate. So ask for a more detailed breakdown of the charges incurred).

Double the Strength of Your Pills and Save

You can save money on prescription medicine by asking your doctor to prescribe double-strength pills and then cutting them in half with a pill cutter. Half doses of larger-dosage pills are usually cheaper than full doses of smaller-dosage pills. (Don't try to divide capsules or time-release preparations.) You can buy a pill cutter for about $5.

Prevent Colds by Reducing Stress

Did you know that people under stress are more likely to catch colds? You can save money on cold medicine and missed work by learning how to reduce everyday stress.

Experts have found that people who suffer stressful periods lasting more than one month, or who suffer several minor stresses in one day, are more likely than others to be infected when exposed to cold-causing viruses.

Stress weakens the immune system, increasing susceptibility to colds. Stress-management techniques such as meditation and relaxation may improve your physical and emotional well-being, and consequently save you money on over-the-counter cold remedies.

Discuss Your Hospital Options

Don't allow a hospital to be chosen for you. Most doctors are affiliated with more than one hospital, so you should discuss your options. Many community hospitals may be 25% cheaper than for-profit hospitals, which may order more tests and have bigger markups on procedures and services. Be sure, however, that the reputation of a less expensive hospital is just as good as a more expensive private facility.

Question Testing

Ask your doctor why each hospital test must be done. And consider insisting that the hospital get your advance approval for all tests and procedures.

Don't Pay Hotel Prices

Hospitals have check-in and check-out times, just like hotels. If you arrive early or leave late you will be charged for an extra day. Consider calling ahead to find out the check-in time. When you're ready to leave, check out promptly.

Also, you may want to avoid weekend admissions if possible. In many cases, specialized medical care won't be available and you may be charged premium rates for basic care.

Make sure you check to see what the hospital charges for various services, like filling out forms for you, health and beauty aids, and the cost of medication you may need when you leave. Instead of paying $50 to $100 for these incidentals, ask to fill out your own paperwork, bring your own toiletries, and consider filling new prescriptions at a pharmacy outside the hospital.

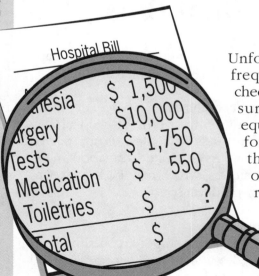

Inspect and Dissect Your Hospital Bills

Unfortunately, hospital bills are frequently inaccurate. Consider checking with your surgeon after surgery to find out if all the equipment that you were billed for was used. Make sure that there wasn't any medication on your bill that you did not receive. And if you do find discrepancies, call the hospital billing department and ask that your bill be reduced.

Save Money on Medication

Medicine can be one of the most expensive health care costs, but there are ways you can save money. Just make sure that reduced-cost doesn't mean reduced quality.

Generic Drugs

Consider asking your doctor if a generic version of your medicine is available. Generic drugs are cheaper (often half the price), and they're as safe and effective as name-brand medications.

Drugs sold under their generic names contain the same active ingredients and dosages as brand-name drugs, but the inactive ingredients may differ. This may alter an individual's reaction to the drug. It is important to make sure none of the inactive ingredients will cause an adverse effect before you start taking a generic prescription.

Over-the-counter Generics

Over-the-counter generics, such as ibuprofen, can also cost as little as half the price of their brand-name equivalents. If the labels list the same ingredients in the same amounts, you can be assured of the safety of your purchase.

Prescription Drugs

You may be able to order your prescription drugs through a mail-order pharmacy and get considerable savings, especially if you take long-term medication. Mail-order won't automatically be less expensive than your cheapest local pharmacy, but it's worth pricing along with your other options.

Some mail-order firms deal only with patients belonging to specific insurance plans, but others sell directly to the general public.

Medi-Mail (800-331-1458) is one of the country's largest mail-service pharmacies. It provides substantial savings on vitamins, prescription drugs and over-the-counter pain relievers. Doctors' prescriptions are verified and filled within 48 hours. You can receive a 90-day supply within one week.

The American Association of Retired Persons (AARP, 800-456-2277) also provides low-cost alternatives to retail pharmacy prices (almost 40% less). Even though the pharmacy exists in conjunction with AARP, the service is available to people of all ages. AARP members are eligible for additional discounts. Product orders are usually shipped within 48 hours.

BUYER BEWARE

Ask Questions Before You Sample The Latest Drug

Drug companies spend millions to influence the prescribing habits of doctors. Typically, they try to get doctors to recommend brand-new drugs with high price tags (and profit margins). What you want, however, is the best drug for your condition.

Ask your doctor if there are any drugs that have been on the market longer and whether it would be acceptable to take those drugs instead. In general, older drugs have longer track records of safety and are usually less expensive than new ones.

Be careful if a doctor wants to give you free samples of drugs that he normally would not prescribe. Most patients love getting free samples. But drug companies give most of these samples for the newer drugs that they're trying to promote. These are often drugs with which doctors aren't too familiar yet.

Before accepting a sample, ask your doctor how good the new drug is and whether there is another drug that is more established and less expensive.

INSIDE INFORMATION

Speed Up Your Headache Relief

You may be surprised to learn that caffeine can speed up the effectiveness of aspirin. If you have a headache, consider taking two aspirin with a cup of coffee or a caffeinated soft drink. You may be able to cut the waiting time in half, and it's a lot cheaper than using stronger headache remedies.

Using One Pharmacy Can Help You Stay Healthy

Using one pharmacy for all of your prescriptions can help you to stay healthy. Pharmacists keep a record of their customers' medications so that they can warn you when a new prescription may interact dangerously with one that you are currently taking.

If you use one pharmacy, you can also create a relationship with your pharmacist that will enable you to ask questions that may help you save money.

You can ask a pharmacist about a new drug that your doctor has prescribed for you, how the drug will help you, how you should take it, and what the possible side effects may be.

Also, you can ask your pharmacist for advice about non-prescription medications such as cold and stomach-ache remedies. Most pharmacists will be able to recommend over-the-counter treatments that will save you money in doctor's bills.

You don't have to give up being a pet owner if you have allergies. There are low-cost remedies that can relieve your nose and keep your dog out of the dog house.

Pharmacy Savings

Don't hesitate to call several pharmacies to find which one has the prices that will save you the most. Some pharmacies will charge as much as they can for medications, while others sell below cost to get customers into their stores.

Once you find a pharmacy that has costs you can live with, most experts suggest using that pharmacy for all of your prescriptions.

Yogurt Is a Natural Remedy For Women's Health

Yogurt relieves recurrent yeast infections. Experts have found that women who began eating five ounces of yogurt daily (containing the live bacteria lactobacillus acidophilus) had two-thirds fewer cases of recurrent vaginosis (yeast infections) than before.

Bacteria in the yogurt are believed to protect against infection either by maintaining an acidic environment in the vagina or by producing compounds such as hydrogen peroxide that kill bad bacteria. Yogurt is also a great source of calcium that can be helpful in preventing osteoporosis.

Hooray! Low-Cost Allergy Relief…Just In Time!

The over-the-counter antihistamine chlorpheniramine maleate offers effective, inexpensive allergy relief. This substance is the active ingredient in Chlor-Trimeton. Taken at bedtime, a four-milligram tablet, which costs less than 20¢, usually relieves symptoms for 24 hours and does not cause daytime drowsiness under these conditions.

For a stuffed-up nose, try the non-prescription decongestant pseudoephedrine, which is the active ingredient in Sudafed.

Health Club Money Savers

To save money when joining a health club, don't join an expensive club that offers more equipment or activity options than you will ever use. For example, if you want to lift weights or take an exercise class, a health club with a sauna or pool may be an unnecessary additional cost.

Also, before you join ask about new member perks, such as a free session with a personal trainer.

And, if you may need to take a long-term break for travel or other reasons, find out if the club can freeze your membership and start it up again on your return. Then you won't have to pay for the time you're not using it.

Judging Whether a Club Is Worth Your Money

One of the best ways to choose a quality health club that's worth your money is to thoroughly inspect its facilities. Good health clubs will be equipped with certain features, such as:

- Trainers and instructors who are certified by agencies like the American College of Sports Medicine (317-637-9200) or the Aerobics and Fitness Association of America (800-445-5950).
- Orientation sessions for new members.
- Staff members who monitor the exercise areas.
- Classes at several levels of skill.
- Clean and updated equipment and locker rooms.
- Safety and club rules clearly posted.

If you are still unsure whether to join after you thoroughly inspect a club's facilities, you may want to check with your state or local consumer protection agency or the Better Business Bureau to find out if any negative reports have been filed against the club, and what they were about.

Before You Commit

Before making a commitment to an annual membership, consider whether you're investing your money in the right place. Here are some tips on how to safeguard your money:

- Consider trying out a club before you join.
- Visit the club on the day that you would want to work out. Notice if the club is too crowded, and if the equipment or class you want is accessible.
- Think about joining a health club that offers several free visits or a short, low-cost trial membership.

FOR YOUR INFORMATION

Who to Call For Help

If you are questioning the reputation of a health club or its instructors, it is good to know that there are professionals you can contact:

- **Aerobics and Fitness Association of America** (800-445-5950) for information on certified trainers and fitness instructors.
- **American College of Sports Medicine** (317-637-9200) for information on certified trainers and fitness instructors.
- **American Council on Exercise** (800-825-3636) for general health and fitness information as well as information on certified trainers and instructors.
- **International Health, Racquet & Sports Club Association** (263 Summer Street, Boston, MA 02210) for news of complaints against clubs (to ensure that they meet minimum standards).

DID YOU KNOW

Thirty Minutes A Day...

Thirty minutes of some physical activity three times a week (even if it's walking), and getting enough sleep each night can contribute to long-term physical and mental health.

- Try to arrange paying for your membership on a monthly basis, or join a club that offers a 90-day trial membership.
- Try to negotiate your membership fees. You may be able to join the club at a price that is lower than the initial offer.
- Always check out the club's refund policy before you sign up. You don't want to find out after you join that your satisfaction is not guaranteed for more than one or two weeks.

Health Clubs to Check Out

Many health clubs are individually run and owned, but there are a few chains that have facilities nationwide.

Here are some nationwide chain facilities you may want to check out:

- Gold's Gym (310-392-3005; www.goldsgym.com)
- World Gym (800-544-7441; www.worldgym.com)
- Bally Total Fitness (800-348-6377; www.ballyfitness.com)

Some chains, such as Bally Total Fitness, offer a two-week guest pass, and others have newsletters with free health and fitness information. Your best option may be to join a club that offers the perks that suit your own interests and fitness goals.

Work Out at Home

To boost motivation and sense of purpose, consider trying health-club techniques at home:

- Sign in whenever you exercise.
- Install a mirror so you can check form.
- Use a floor mat for stretches and strength training such as abdominal crunches and side-lying leg lifts.
- Buy a rubber mat to place under your equipment in order to cut noise and vibration and protect the floor.
- Wear appropriate exercise clothing, such as breathable, lightweight sportswear.

How to Find Them To find health clubs near you, look in your yellow pages under Fitness Clubs or Health Clubs. Once you find some that are conveniently located, you can then do some inspecting and make some cost comparisons.

Don't Rush to Sign Up Don't be in a hurry to sign up for a membership. Make sure that the club you choose to join is the best investment for your money.

Consider the YMCA/YMHA Many YMCA/YMHAs across the country offer low-cost, quality health and fitness programs.

If you are interested in swimming, running or walking around a track, or joining a low-key exercise class, you may want to opt for joining a YMCA/YMHA program. Joining a Y will give you the opportunity to make a small investment for a fitness program before you invest money in a private health club. Some are at least as good as private clubs. And many Ys have senior health programs that enable people over 50 to work out with their peers.

Fitness Guidance For Seniors

You are never too old to become physically fit, and with medical bills as high as they are for seniors, staying healthy and out of the hospital can help you avoid paying high doctors' bills.

You may be surprised to find out that becoming and staying physically fit can be accomplished for very little money.

First Things First

Before beginning a fitness regime, it is essential to see your doctor to make sure that you don't have a condition that would make exercise a harmful activity.

Next, it's important to give your muscles a good warm-up before strenuous exercise. Begin with a slow walk, or do some simple stretches.

After you exercise it is also important to cool down before you collapse onto a chair. Stopping abruptly after a vigorous workout may give your heart an unwelcome shock. Try to move around for at least five minutes after you work out. Consider taking a slow walk as your cool-down option.

You may also want to take a warm shower or bath after exercise. This can help prevent your muscles from stiffening.

Workout Options

Aerobic exercise may provide the maximum health benefits. Keeping your heart rate up for approximately 20 to 30 minutes, three or four days a week, can keep your heart healthy. Aerobic exercise is also good for weight loss.

Speed-walking is a great alternative to paying for an aerobics or exercise class. You can speed walk around your neighborhood for free. You can also take advantage of shopping malls that open early, and walk in a weather-protected environment for free.

Lifting weights is a great way to keep aging bones strong. If you don't want to spend the money on two- or five-pound weights, you can lift 12- or 28-ounce cans instead.

Dental Discounts

The best way to save money on your dental care is to prevent a problem before it occurs. Experts believe that how well you take care of your teeth will determine how much money you will need to spend on them.

BARGAIN FINDER

Fifty-Plus Fitness Association

The **Fifty-Plus Fitness Association** (650-323-6160; www.50plus.org) is an organization that provides a combination of information about aging, exercise and a variety of fitness activities.

For $35 per year, you can become a member of Fifty-Plus and enjoy social gatherings such as talks, seminars, walks, bicycle rides, runs, swims and other exciting adventure events. You'll be notified of health improvement programs (which have an additional participation fee of $75), athletic and health club incentives (such as a free week's use of a selected club), seminars and an annual fitness weekend (including sporting events and a health fair).

If there isn't a Fifty-Plus group in your home town, you can become an ambassador and help to hold events and develop a local membership. By becoming a member you can learn how to bring the Fifty-Plus program to where you live.

DID YOU KNOW

Dehumidifiers Can Help Arthritis

Dehumidifiers used in the home can greatly reduce the frequency and severity of arthritic flare-ups. Changes in humidity are a big factor in pain flare-ups, and removing moisture from the air can help your bones be pain-free. Most dehumidifiers cost around $150–$300.

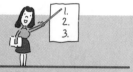

Get the Most Out of Your Dental Visit

To get the most out of your dental visit, you may want to follow this simple advice:

- Always ask about cost, and how and when you are expected to pay. Does the dentist participate in your health plan (if you have one)? Make sure that you understand the fees, and the method and schedule of payment before you agree to any treatment.

- Call around your community to compare factors like location, office hours, fees and emergency arrangements. If you're comparing fees, ask for estimates on full-mouth x-rays and preventative dental visits that include an oral exam and tooth cleaning.

- Ask about your treatment options. Which treatments are absolutely necessary and which are elective?

- If you don't understand any part of what your dentist recommends, don't be afraid to ask for more information.

Free Dental Insurance Guidance

You can call the **American Dental Association Council on Dental Benefit Programs** (312-440-2746) for free information on individual dental insurance, dental plan exclusions and employee dental insurance plans.

Dental Home-care

Did you know that many dentists advise brushing your teeth twice a day for at least two minutes? Many people don't brush for a long enough time to kill all of the germs and odor. Other people brush too vigorously, which can lead to gum recession and expensive dental repair.

How to Brush Dentists say that if you brush for two minutes (at a 45 degree angle) with soft, rounded, polished bristles, you will clean your teeth the best and save your mouth from gum disease.

Remember to clean the inside teeth surface where plaque deposits are heavy, and to clean the back teeth and tongue.

Dentists also advise replacing your toothbrush once every three or four months, or as soon as the bristles become worn, splayed or frayed. Replacing your toothbrush is important because a hard, brittle brush can injure your gums. Children's brushes may need to be replaced more often, because they wear out more quickly.

Flossing Flossing your teeth thoroughly once a day can be as important as brushing your teeth, since you are defending your teeth against plaque buildup that your toothbrush can't reach.

Sealants Sealing your teeth, to protect the enamel from plaque and acids, will cut the costs of your dentist bills. Toothbrush bristles cannot reach all the way into the depressions and grooves to extract food and plaque. Sealants protect vulnerable areas by sealing out plaque and food. Sealants cost about $25 a tooth, not much compared to the cost of filling and refilling cavities.

Fluoride Toothpaste Fluoride toothpaste can also add to prevention of dental disease. If you use a fluoride toothpaste or mouthwash, you are helping to inhibit the growth of bacteria in your mouth and keep plaque from sticking to your teeth.

How to Find a Quality Dentist

The American Dental Association suggests these simple ways to find a good dentist near you:

- Ask family, friends, neighbors or co-workers for recommendations, or ask your family physician or local pharmacist.
- Call or write to your local or state dental society which is listed in the telephone directory under Dentists or Associations.
- Ask your current dentist to make a recommendation if you're moving to a new area.
- Call or visit more than one dentist before making a decision.

Employee Dental Insurance Plans

Most dental coverage is the result of an existing insurance package that employees receive from their employer.

Employee dental plans vary. Some employers offer more than one dental plan. In fact, in some states the right to choose between two plans is the law. If you have a choice, the types of coverage are generally grouped into the following categories:

Direct Reimbursement Programs reimburse patients a percentage of the dollar amount spent on dental care, regardless of the type of treatment. This plan usually does not exclude particular types of treatment, and lets patients to go the dentist of their choice.

Usual, Customary and Reasonable (UCR) Programs usually allow patients to go to the dentist of their choice. These plans pay a percentage of the dentist's fee or the administrator's reasonable or customary fee, whichever is less.

Table or Schedule of Allowance Programs offer a list of covered services with assigned dollar amounts. The dollar amounts represent just how much the plan will pay for those services that are covered. Most often, the dentist's full charge is not covered for each service. The patient pays the difference.

Preferred Provider Organization (PPO) Programs are plans under which contracting dentists agree to discount their fees as a financial incentive for patients to select their practices. A patient must choose a dentist in the plan to receive a reduction of benefits.

Capitation Programs pay contracted dentists a fixed amount (usually on a monthly basis) per enrolled family or patient. The dentists agree to provide specific types of treatment to the patients at no charge (some treatments may require a patient copayment).

Dental Plan Exclusions

Some dental plans exclude treatments such as sealants, adult orthodontics, pre-existing conditions, specialist referrals and other dental needs. Some also exclude treatment for family members.

The American Dental Association highly recommends that patients not let the exclusions and limitations in their dental plans determine their treatment decisions.

Individual Dental Insurance

Although dental insurance can help pay a portion of dental costs, experts do not recommend purchasing individual dental coverage. Dental coverage is not economical for those in individual plans because the premiums you pay are often more expensive than the cost of the dental treatment you receive.

However, a few companies offer dental benefits for individuals. Most of these plans are referral plans or buyers' clubs. Under these types of plans, an individual pays a monthly fee for access to a list of dentists who have agreed to a reduced fee schedule. Payment is made from the patient directly to the dentist.

Dental School Clinics

You can get quality dental care at low cost from dental school clinics or centers. Costs are almost always lower than private services: An average checkup runs about $35 to $135. And some schools, such as **New York University Kriser Dental Center**, offer fee discounts of 10–20% to patients over 65. If you live near a university with a dental school program, consider calling to find out about their clinic hours, procedures and costs.

Most dental schools have an experienced dentist on hand to assist the students with all procedures.

Here are some examples of dental schools that have out-patient facilities.

- **NYU Kriser Dental Center** (New York City, 212-998-9800)

- **Indiana University School of Dentistry** (Indianapolis, 317-274-7957)

- **Oregon Health Sciences University** (Portland, 503-494-8867)

- **University of Florida College of Dentistry** (Gainesville, 352-392-8014)

- **University of North Carolina Dental School** (Chapel Hill, 919-966-1161)

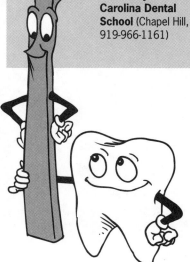

Charles B. Inlander On Getting The Best Deal On Quality Health Care

Charles B. Inlander is a faculty lecturer at the Yale University School of Medicine and president of the People's Medical Society, the largest consumer health advocacy organization in the U.S.

In your opinion, is there a particular type of health insurance that provides consumers with the best care for the lowest cost?

There's no question that an HMO is by far the most cost-effective plan. With an HMO, you know on January 1 of every year exactly how much your annual health care bill is going to be, regardless of how often you use the system, how sick you might get or how catastrophic or long-lasting the illness may be.

How can a person find high-quality health care providers?

Shop around. First look at public documents that list the success rates of local doctors in specialties you're interested in. Then ask friends and family for recommendations of board-certified physicians.

Look for a doctor's hospital affiliations and whether those hospitals have good reputations. You want to find hospitals that have strong reputations in specialties you may need (heart disease, maternity). Ask nurses which hospitals they would go to.

If you have a chronic ailment or anticipate certain types of problems because of your family history, look for doctors who are well-known in that specialty.

It's essential to find a doctor you're compatible with, but don't be swayed by bedside manner. If you have to pick between having a nice person or a competent person, pick the competent person.

What's the best way to find quality, low-cost health insurance?

If you want an HMO, for example, check out the public report card. Look for an HMO that has been certified or accredited by the National Committee for Quality Assurance (NCQA). Ask HMOs for third-party assessments, which are good for comparing one HMO to another.

Then look at the plans themselves. Compare apples to apples. What practitioners are in the plan? What facilities? What are the referral arrangements? Look to see who gives you the most benefits for the lowest price, with the providers you are most satisfied with.

In terms of other insurance models you have to compare coverage. What's covered—and what's not? What are your costs? What are they paying for? Are there copayments or deductibles or both? What are the premiums?

Are there any money pits in paying for health insurance that you can avoid, or that too many people don't pay attention to?

Never buy specialty health insurance, such as cancer insurance, or hospital insurance that pays you $50 or $80 a day. You're much better off putting your money toward comprehensive health insurance.

Be careful of plans that allow for lower premiums with a higher deductible. If you get sick it could really cost you.

If people are really having problems with premiums, copayments and deductibles I absolutely advise them to join an HMO. As long as you can pay the monthly premium, you'll get all the coverage you need.

How can you keep costs down in a fee-for-service plan?

Use the system prudently. Don't go to a specialist when a primary doctor can do the job. If you have heart disease, you don't need to go to your cardiologist when you have a cold or the flu. The other thing you can do is negotiate costs.

Start Walking for Your Exercise—It's Free!

Walking is a great way to exercise for free. While a leisurely stroll has only minimal health benefits, studies show that moderate to brisk walking at a three- to five-mph pace can significantly improve your fitness level.

Stretch before and after You Walk

To avoid any injuries that would increase your medical expenses, it's important to stretch before and after you walk.

At the start and finish of your workout, spend two minutes stretching your calf muscles, the hamstrings in the back of your thighs, the quadriceps in the front of the thighs, the inner thigh muscles and the lower back.

Be careful not to overstretch, particularly when muscles are not warmed up. Stretch only to the point of gentle tension in the muscles.

Mall Walking is Weather-friendly Walking

You can walk in a mall for free and be protected from the trials of unpredictable weather. Many shopping centers open early so people can walk there in the mornings. Also, you don't have to worry about potholes or oncoming traffic. Mall walking is a great activity for beginners who want to walk at a relaxed, moderate pace.

Cure Your Heel Pain Inexpensively

Inexpensive shoe inserts often work better for heel pain than custom-made arch supports. For people on their feet all day, custom-made supports may actually do more harm than good.

If you have heel pain caused by inflammation of the plantar fascia (the band of connective tissue stretching from the ball of the foot to the heel), consider using an off-the-shelf silicone or rubber heel pad. The cost is generally $10 to $40 for over-the-counter products, compared with $180 to $500 for custom-made ones.

FOR YOUR INFORMATION

Free Information On Aging

Free information on aging issues is available from many sources. You can contact federal and private agencies that operate for the benefit of older Americans. Every state, for example, has an **Office** or **Department of Aging**, and another for insurance. In addition, **Social Security** provides information and assistance on a variety of issues. Contact your local office, or call 800-772-1213.

Here are some other organizations you may want or need to contact:

- **Administration on Aging** (202-619-0724) is a federal agency that is a part of the department of **Health and Human Services**.

- **AARP Legal Services Network** (800-424-3410; www.aarp.org) provides easy access to attorneys across the country who reduce their fees for AARP members.

- **National Council on Aging** (800-424-9046) offers free information on family caregiving, senior employment and long-term care.

- **National Institute on Aging Information Center** (800-222-2225) provides free information about healthy aging. Ask for literature and referrals to organizations dealing with specific age-related illnesses.

Meditation Is a Free Way to Relax

A great way to reduce stress, pain, anger and anxiety (for free) is to turn inward and meditate.

There are many ways to meditate and many thoughts on how to do it. But most experts agree that, no matter what your reason or method, spending 10 to 20 minutes (twice a day, every day) relaxing your mind may help you lead a healthier and happier life. Try this simple technique:

- Choose a word, sound, prayer or phrase on which to focus.
- Sit in a quiet, comfortable place.
- Close your eyes and begin to breathe slowly and deeply while relaxing your muscles.
- Repeat your focus word, prayer or phrase silently to yourself as you exhale.
- As your mind starts drifting, acknowledge it—and return to your repetition.

Don't Be Rash

If your child comes down with a rash, do some investigative work on your own before you spend money on hefty doctor's fees. Ask yourself—Did you just change laundry detergents? Was last night the first time your child ever ate shellfish? Many rashes are simple reactions to a new food, lotion or sunscreen with PABA. If you answer no to the above questions, or your child's rash is accompanied by a sore throat or joint pain, it's time to call your doctor.

Pediatricians' Home Remedies

Parents will be happy to know that there are some low-cost home remedies to treat your child's colds, fevers and sunburns. You can also try these home-style treatments on yourself and other adults.

The Common Cold

Decaffeinated Spice Tea Add lemon and honey, and wait until it cools slightly. The tea is soothing and hot, which will combat stuffiness and open up the nasal passages. The honey in the tea can help soothe a sore throat as well. The lemon soothes and coats your throat with vitamin C.

Old-fashioned Chicken Soup Or use low-sodium canned soup. Not only will it make your child feel better, but making the soup keeps you too busy to worry.

Fun Fluids Make colorful Jell-O water by doubling the amount of water in the Jell-O recipe, offer enticing flavored ices, or serve watered-down Gatorade. The more fluids a sick child can drink, the better. The fluids help clean out the child's system.

Fever

Fever is not usually as dangerous as most parents believe it to be. It is a sign that the body is fighting infection. If you're concerned, take your child's temperature and make sure to tell the doctor how and when you obtained it.

If a high fever is not responding to the fever reducer prescribed by your doctor, try a warm bath, which will dissipate body heat. There is no reason for the water to be cold. Besides being unpleasant for the child, a cold bath can be dangerous and cause the child's body to go into shock or seizure. Alcohol rubs should be avoided for the same reason.

Sunburn

For sunburn relief, try tea bags. Let the bags steep in boiled water for five minutes. After they cool, remove them from the water and apply the wet bags to burnt skin.

Cheap Eats

Here's the recipe for paying less to get high-quality fruits and vegetables, meats, wines, breads, herbs and spices, teas and even dinners out on the town.

Navigating The Supermarket

The majority of Americans shop for their food in supermarkets. This is true whether they live on farms or in cities, are young or elderly, single or in families—and with good reason.

These retail food centers, which run from mid-size to very large, buy food and other household goods in huge allotments, so they have distinct price advantages over small grocers. Shopping at your local convenience store or specialty market may be quick and easy, but ultimately you will lose big by paying consistently higher prices.

So it's just sound economics to understand how supermarkets operate in order to stretch your food dollars.

Develop Basic Consumer Skills

To really save money when you food shop, you have to know what a good price is. First, you need a baseline cost, or starting point, for each item. Begin by comparing prices of particular food

One-Stop Shopping

Learn to put a value on your own time. Shopping at different stores for different items may save you money on sale items, but it takes considerably more time and gasoline than doing your entire list at one supermarket. Of course, there will be the occasional sale of something you want and use regularly at a store other than the one you most often frequent. But this may be the exception, not the rule.

Stick to Your List

Be sure to make a shopping list. And don't start it just a few minutes before your trip to the supermarket. Keep a running list in your kitchen. That way, when you discover you're running out of an item, you add it then and there.

Avoid shopping without your list and try to buy only those items you've listed. This will eliminate the danger of impulse buying, one of the most deadly threats to economical food shopping.

staples such as milk, bread, cereal and meat at several local supermarkets. Bring a calculator and take notes as you go.

You will see that some supermarkets have consistently better prices than others across the board. Some will have better prices on particular items but not on others. Others may have higher quality produce, meats or dairy products, or offer a wider selection than their competitors (though their prices may be higher).

Gradually, you will build your own price vocabulary and become better and better at determining what is or isn't a good deal.

Unit Pricing Is There for You

Unit pricing is a critical tool for determining what an item costs. With unit pricing, the price of a specific quantity or amount of a product, such as ounces of spaghetti sauce, pounds of butter or quarts of milk, is given on the shelf above or below that product. With that information, customers can compare costs between one product and another based on a common quantity.

For example, if one bag of potato chips is priced at 10¢ per ounce, and a second is 15¢ per ounce, obviously the first is the better buy. Beware: If the price marked on the package with the higher unit cost is lower, it means that the package contains less of the product than the other one.

Unit pricing is now mandated by law in many states, and reputable supermarkets in those states will display item-by-item information. This information is designed to help you, the consumer, get what you want at the best price. Take advantage of it.

Supermarket Circulars Are for You

Nearly all supermarkets announce food and product sales in weekly circulars, which may also contain coupons for that week. There is always meat, poultry or fish on sale, as well as fresh or frozen vegetables, fruits or a particular brand of orange juice. As your knowledge of prices increases, you will quickly recognize that many of these offerings are excellent buys.

Usually effective from Sunday through the following Saturday, these circulars are widely distributed by mail or as fillers in newspapers. If for some reason you miss a particular circular, you can pick one up at the supermarket, usually from a stack near the entrance or by the cash registers. Be sure to ask if you don't see one.

Use Your Coupons Wisely

Coupons are paper tickets entitling the holder to a discount, usually cents off, on a particular item. They are issued by manufacturers as well as supermarkets. Sources of coupons in addition to supermarket circulars are magazines, product packages, publication inserts, and general mailings by coupon distribution companies.

Coupons are issued for all kinds of merchandise in addition to food and food products. If used wisely, they can bring surprisingly good savings.

The key is wise usage. Don't buy an item you neither want nor need just because you have a coupon for it. An unneeded carton of flavored cottage cheese is useless if you don't routinely eat cottage cheese. It will probably spoil, resulting in a loss. On the other hand, purchasing a product you often use and want to keep in stock is a very sensible addition to your refrigerator or pantry.

More Coupon Smarts

Double or Triple Your Savings Some supermarkets and grocers periodically offer double or triple coupons, which means they give you two or three times the value of any coupon. A 25¢ coupon doubled would save you 50¢, and tripled would save you 75¢. Many establishments have a $1 ceiling on doubling or tripling. But whatever the store rules, this is definitely the way to make the most of your coupons.

Organize Your Coupons Lost or unfiled coupons sitting in a drawer or crumpled in the bottom of a handbag are useless. Coupons need to be organized and categorized. Expired ones need to be discarded.

Be sure to have your coupons with you when you shop. Small, wallet-size coupon folders are available with tabbed separators for filing by subject. Use this file when finalizing your shopping list—you'll find it a winning combo. Need Cheerios? Check your coupon file before you buy.

Supermarkets Issue and Accept Plastic

There's more than one way to pay for food for your family.

Get Your Own Card Supermarket cards, issued after a check on your credit, let you cash checks and give you automated, at-the-register deductions for sale or coupon items. This is what stores mean by clipless coupons (coupons that you don't have to cut out of a circular). This automation saves time while guaranteeing you the lowest prices available.

Credit, Debit and ATM Cards In many supermarkets, you may now charge your order on your credit card or debit it against your bank account using your ATM card. More and more shoppers appreciate this handy, quick means of paying for purchases.

However, some experts question the wisdom of charging or debiting food bills. Hefty additions to your credit card balance will increase your monthly carrying costs if you don't pay your bill in full. And you may be charged transactional fees on your

Sales Are the Time to Experiment or Stock Up

Supermarket sales give you great opportunities to be creative. An expensive brand of ice cream is on sale—this gives you a chance to try it at a reasonable price. Beef brisket is on sale—this might be just the moment to try that new recipe your neighbor gave you. Boneless, skinned chicken breasts are on sale—this is the time to stock your freezer with multiple packages for summer chicken salads.

Summer Turkey Sale

Aunt Dotty's Special Stuffing
1 Medium Apple
2 Onions
3 Cups Bread Crumbs
1 Tb. Ginger

INSIDE INFORMATION

Take a Rain Check

If for some reason your supermarket is out of stock on a sale item, you can usually get a rain check, entitling you to the sale price on that item at a future time. In some states, rain checks are the law. But required or not, most supermarkets are happy to provide them if you ask.

Formulating a Budget

List-making and record-keeping ultimately lead to budget-making. You will be able to see patterns of costs, and this will help you to anticipate your expenses. You may notice that certain categories of food seem to cost far more than you thought. Take meats, for instance—usually the costliest line item in the food budget. Perhaps you could save more by taking better advantage of announced supermarket sales to stock up for future meals or parties.

Value Means Getting the Most For Your Money

Price divided by quality equals value. Think about this formula as you shop. For example, marked-down, pre-packaged fruits and vegetables, or baked goods past their prime, may be considerably reduced in price. But check carefully to determine that these sale items are really usable. A bruised pear, wilted head of lettuce or stale cake is no bargain at any price.

ATM debits. Check with your card issuers as well as your supermarket to determine whether you could be losing money.

Timing Is Everything

Avoid shopping just before a meal, when you're hungry. Many things will look delicious, and you'll find yourself purchasing items you might not otherwise consider. Shopping when you're tired at the end of a hard day's work may tempt you to buy expensive, prepared food.

Try to food shop when you're free of such distractions as small, restless children or an unhappy dog barking in the car. These situations are stressful and may impair your normally sound judgment because all you want to do is get out of the store as quickly as possible.

Try to plan major shopping trips when your spouse or a friend can watch your children. You'll enjoy the freedom to focus on the task at hand and are more likely to come home with wiser selections.

Sniffing Out Merchandising Strategies

The goal of any supermarket is to keep the consumer in the store as long as possible, extending a shopper's exposure to displayed goods in the hope of increasing purchases. In contrast, the consumer's goal is to spend as little money as possible in the shortest time.

Supermarkets, like all stores, have spent years doing in-depth research on how to get their customers to spend more money. If you familiarize yourself with the following merchandising ploys, you'll be less likely to fall victim to them.

Endcap Sales: Look and Compare

Endcap sales or displays of products at the end of an aisle may not be bargains. They may be displayed before an announced sale begins, so that you end up paying full price because you purchased pre-sale.

Further, these products, though advertised as on sale, may still be more expensive than the competition. The endcap locations, placed some distance from similar products, make it difficult for you to comparison shop.

Endcap products often cost more because supermarkets charge the manufacturer for prime exposure—and those charges are passed on to you.

Look High and Low

Statistics have proven that products displayed on eye-level shelves are purchased much more frequently than those on lower or higher shelves. With this in mind, supermarkets charge food manufacturers to have their products placed in these prime locations. Better deals for the food shopper are often those brands banished to upper and lower shelves: They don't have added marketing costs to pass on to the consumer.

A Face Isn't Everything

The facing sides of a particular product, such as the front of cereal boxes, displayed in several side-by-side rows, give that product an advantage over a competitor who may have fewer front facings. The more facings a particular product has—five rows of one brand versus two rows of another—the better the product is likely to sell.

Look beyond this marketing technique. Some of the best deals might not be obvious to the eye. Consider all your options and compare prices carefully before making your choice.

Don't Succumb to Display Trickery

A half-empty shelf doesn't necessarily mean that a product is popular. Supermarkets sometimes remove a few products from a display so you won't think you're the first to buy. Purchase the products you want and don't be influenced by the decisions of others (or sneaky supermarket tactics).

By the same token, loss leaders (large displays of sale items near the door), or other big display sales elsewhere in the store, may be good deals. But that doesn't mean that all items in that particular supermarket are economically priced. Take advantage of these bargains but keep up your guard as you go through the rest of the store.

Pay Attention to Your Sense, Not Your Senses

Studies have shown that shoppers linger longer and buy more groceries if their supermarket plays background music. The same is true of certain smells. You are more likely to buy cakes and breads if you can smell their fresh-baked aroma.

Be aware that everything from lighting and music to aisle layout and eye-catching displays is carefully planned to encourage impulse spending.

Don't let your senses run your shopping trip. Stick to your list.

INSIDE INFORMATION

Get-One-Free Deals Aren't Really Free

The word "free" can hook you. Don't let that happen. "Buy one, get one free" really means two for the price of one, or 50% off. "Buy two, get one free" means 33% off. That's great as long as you understand what you're getting and what you're saving—and as long as the store hasn't raised its customary price on the product.

Likewise, stores that display signs reading "limit one to a customer" know that consumers buy more when there's a limit imposed. Watch yourself on that one.

The Great American Food Bill

According to the U.S. Department of Labor, the average American household spends nearly $4,300 a year on food. Most consumers could reduce this figure by 25% simply by eating more meals at home, buying fewer processed foods, selecting supermarket brands over nationally advertised ones and reducing the amount of meat in their diets.

Cereals by You

Stop paying extra for cereal with such added ingredients as dried fruit or nuts. A better buy is basic corn, oat, wheat or rice cereals to which you add your own fruit, nuts, sugar or honey. You'll eventually save big (and have the fun of custom designing your own breakfast).

What's in a Name?

The price differences among name-brand, store-brand and generic foods can range from small to significant, and there are often contrasts in quality as well. When comparing brands, consider both price and ingredients. Read labels and pay attention to the amount of fillers and additives.

Here is some general information on the three basic types of labels you'll find in the supermarket.

Brand Name Products

Brand-name products are usually the most expensive items in a supermarket. Most consumers believe brand-name products are of the highest quality. Bear in mind, when you buy a brand-name product, you are not only paying for the contents, but also for fancy packaging, store placement and advertising campaigns. However, purchasing a brand name with a coupon or on sale is a good way to get your favorites at good prices.

Store Brand Products

Store brands usually cost around 15% less than name brands, yet frequently they are manufactured by the same company that makes the name brand. But since store brands are not heavily advertised, stores can charge less for them and still make a profit.

If a store brand is significantly cheaper, give it a try. You may discover that your family likes A&P peanut butter just as well as the well-known Skippy or Jif, for example.

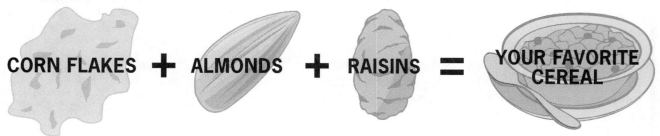

CORN FLAKES + ALMONDS + RAISINS = YOUR FAVORITE CEREAL

Generic Products

Generic products come in basic, no-frills packaging, usually labeled in black lettering that states simply what the product is, such as dishwasher detergent, sugar or napkins. Generic products are usually the least expensive, but can also be of lower quality or contain additives not found in brand- or store-name products.

You probably won't notice if you switch to generic sugar or chlorine bleach, but you may notice the difference in foods like pickles, pasta sauce and iced tea mix. Still, generics are a great way to save as long as you're happy with what you're getting.

Packaging Can Fool the Eye

Companies sometimes reduce the amount of a product in a package while maintaining the same size and price. For example, you might find that the five-ounce bag of potato chips you used to buy now contains only four ounces, although the package looks exactly the same.

Manufacturers can trick you into paying the same price for a smaller amount because most customers do not read food labels closely. When your favorite brands come out with different packaging, particularly packaging marked "new and improved," be sure to check the contents weight on the label.

More Supermarket Savvy

The best deals sometimes mean doing a little more work. Following are several ideas to help you be a more price-conscious shopper.

Eye the Scanner

Most stores have scanners that read universal product codes (UPCs). Let the clerk bag your groceries, and you watch the register display window to make sure that you are charged the correct amount—particularly on sale items or when you're using coupons. (Some stores give you the product free if you are charged the wrong price.)

Prepare Your Own Food

Be aware that the costliest way to feed yourself or your family is buying prepared foods such as instant pasta with sauce mixes, sandwiches from the deli counter, skinned, boned or stuffed meats, poultry and fish, and salads from the salad bar. With these foods, you are paying for the preparation.

Save a bundle by creating your own meals instead. Plan simple menus. Purchase basic, healthy ingredients such as untrimmed meat, whole heads of lettuce, vegetables and fruits, and your own supply of cheeses, eggs, flour, sugar, and herbs and spices.

Food Dates that Help You Save

You can sometimes get as much as 50% off a food product that is close to its expiration or sell-by date on the label. Since most items can be safely consumed for a few days after that date, you will be getting an item that may be just as good for half the price.

DID YOU KNOW

Shopping Smart Means Reading Labels

Ingredients on a food label are listed in the order of their volume. This means that a product contains more of the first ingredient on the list than any other ingredient, and the least of the last ingredient.

To determine the best buy, compare ingredients lists on product labels to determine what's inside a jar, package or carton. You may be surprised at the variations you'll find. Take spaghetti sauce, for instance. If the first ingredient in product A is tomatoes and the first in product B is water, product A could be a better deal even if it costs more.

INSIDE INFORMATION

Skip the Toiletries Aisle

Toiletries, cosmetics and other non-food items frequently cost more at supermarkets than at discount pharmacies. Supermarkets mark the prices up higher, assuming you won't bother to compare prices or make an extra trip to the drugstore.

To Locate (Or Start) a Food Co-Op near You

For information on setting up your own grocery co-op, phone the **National Cooperative Business Association** at 800-636-NCBA, or write them at 1401 New York Ave. N.W., Suite 1100, Washington, D.C. 20005. www.cooperative.org

Watch Prices and Merchandising

Don't assume prices are always lower at a warehouse club. Some items may actually cost more than at a supermarket. Compare prices and use your warehouse club as a supplement to, not a replacement for, your regular supermarket.

Like supermarkets, warehouses use clever merchandising to get shoppers to buy on impulse. Loss leaders in bulk are placed prominently at entrances. Free samples of expensive gourmet foods may be offered throughout the store, and multipacks of books, compact discs, and snack foods are displayed prominently at the ends of aisles. How to deal with this? Buy only what you can use.

Consider Food Co-Ops

Food cooperatives are small, supermarket-like stores managed and staffed by their patrons. Usually community-based (and sometimes organic), every food co-op operates independently. Products are purchased directly from distributors, resulting in considerable savings for members.

Most co-ops require a one-time membership fee and a commitment to help out periodically as a cashier, shelf stocker or administrator. This is a great way to save cash while getting to know more people in your neighborhood.

Bulk Buying at Food Warehouse Clubs

Food warehouse buying clubs have sprung up in many parts of the country. These huge, no-frills establishments charge members an annual fee to buy in bulk at discount prices. That usually means large-sized containers, cases, or a number of cans or jars packaged together. The markup at buying clubs is around 10%, as opposed to 25% at most supermarkets. Warehouse clubs also sell non-food items, such as appliances, clothes, books and music.

Split Bulk Purchases with Others

If you don't have enough storage space to make buying in bulk practical, think about joining forces with neighbors or friends. Cases of soda or canned goods, or large boxes of paper towels, napkins or toilet tissue, purchased at rock-bottom prices, can be easily divided among several families, resulting in substantial savings for everyone.

Locating a Food Warehouse Near You

Here are a few warehouse chains that have stores around the country.

BJ's Wholesale Club BJ's Wholesale Club (800-747-6791) has around 85 clubs on the East Coast and has just opened a new one in Ohio. Many stores have their own bakery, meat, produce and deli departments, but most of the food products offered are frozen. The markup on most items is 8% to 10%.

Membership is open to anyone for $35 a year. Stores offer business memberships at $30 (and half-price memberships for up to 99 of the cardholder's associates) but no special business hours. In addition to cash and checks, they accept Discover,

MasterCard and Visa. Coupons are also accepted. One-day store passes are available, but there is a 10% non-member surcharge.

Costco Wholesale Costco Wholesale, now incorporating Price Club, has more than 280 clubs in 24 states. A typical store sells an assortment of products from tires and audio equipment to fresh and frozen foods. Some clubs have their own delis, bakeries, and produce and meat departments. Costco offers a Double Guarantee—a full refund to any customer not satisfied with membership or any product. Coupons are not accepted.

Costco's membership fee is $40 a year. You can phone 800-774-2678 for an application and directions to the store nearest you. Bring your application and fee to the membership counter at any store or mail them to Costco Wholesale Membership, P.O. Box 34535, Seattle, WA 98124-1088. Cash, checks, debit cards and Discover are accepted.

Business memberships are available to owners, managers and directors (plus associates and spouses) of licensed businesses, non-profit organizations, government agencies, and farmers and ranchers. And there are special shopping hours just for business members.

Sam's Club Sam's Club (800-925-6278), owned by Wal-Mart, has more than 430 clubs nationwide. A typical store has over 3,000 household items in stock. Food sections consist mainly of fresh and frozen meat and produce, but some clubs also have bakery products. The markup on most items is between 8% and 10%, and membership is $35 a year.

Baked Goods: More Bread for Less Dough

The average markup at grocery stores on bread, rolls, cakes and pies ranges from 10% to 50%. At gourmet or private bakeries, the markup can be as high as 75%.

Of course, making your own bread would save you the most money—about 75% off retail prices. But if you don't have the time (or lack the patience) to wait for your bread to rise, here are a few money-saving strategies.

Twilight Bargains

Consider shopping at night when grocery stores are likely to have completed most of their day's business. In an effort to unload what will be tomorrow's day-old baked goods, many

TRY SOMETHING DIFFERENT

Try Making Quickbreads

Given today's busy schedules, most people don't have time to bake their own bread, even if they have the inclination. One alternative is quickbread, so-called because you don't have to wait for yeast to rise. Fruit breads such as banana, cranberry, or raisin, date and nut breads, or even a good, grainy bread that calls for whole wheat flour or wheat germ, are all quickbreads. If you're really pressed for time, you can even buy inexpensive quickbread mixes at the supermarket that merely require a bread pan, shortening and eggs. And you will have impressive results in about an hour.

Even more impressive is making one of these breads from scratch. Actually, this is not a whole lot more difficult or costly. You just need to crack and chop nuts or cut up fresh or dried fruit, and add your own flour, sugar and eggs. And quickbreads may be frozen for future use and make inexpensive, much-appreciated holiday or house gifts.

Ethnic Markets

More and more people are becoming interested in exotic cuisines. In addition to standard Italian, Chinese, French, German and Japanese foods, you can now explore Indian, Greek, Spanish, Thai, Lebanese and Scandinavian products as they come to the fore.

Ethnic markets, most often found in cities where members of ethnic groups tend to congregate and live, are great places to find inexpensive herbs. Asian markets tend to have reasonable prices on all sorts of herbs, from common ginger to the more exotic ginseng. For a market near you, consult your yellow pages under Grocers.

Wash Away Contaminates From Produce

Much of the produce in your supermarket now comes from outside the U.S., where health and sanitation standards are not what they are here. For example, 40% of cucumbers in the marketplace come from South America. These crops and many others, such as berries and lettuce, may be irrigated and washed with untreated water carrying E. Coli bacteria.

Wash all produce thoroughly, or you may be putting yourself and fellow diners at risk.

supermarkets and bakeries offer discounts of up to 50% after 5 p.m. Day-old bread isn't spoiled. When toasted, for instance, it can be just as tasty as bread straight from the oven. If you don't see these bargains advertised, ask for them.

Thrift Bakeries

Many commercial bakeries collect their unsold products from retail stores and then sell them at greatly reduced prices in their own thrift stores.

Pepperidge Farms operates 86 thrift stores in 23 states east of the Mississippi. The baked goods sold at these thrift stores are either manufacturers' seconds (which fail to meet appearance standards) or market returns (which are approaching their expiration date and have been pulled from retailers' shelves). To locate the Pepperidge Farm thrift store nearest you, call 888-737-7374.

Also try Best Foods Baking Company (800-582-3614), which operates a chain of thrift stores selling day-old products, or Entenmann's (973-785-7606), which runs thrift stores around the country selling imperfect returns and dated goods.

Very Best Deals On Produce

Since good health and nutrition require you to eat a lot of fruits and vegetables, it makes sense to find ways to get the best values at the lowest prices.

Seasonal Fruits

Today, thanks to rapid transport and excellent refrigeration, you can get almost any fruit or vegetable at almost any time of the year. But you pay much higher prices when you buy a fruit or vegetable out of season. You're paying for extensive transportation, frequently from outside the U.S., and all the middlemen along the way.

True, grapefruit and melons, zucchini and eggplant are wonderful to have most any time of the year, but such indulgences can cost you.

Roadside Stands

One of the best ways to get fresh, seasonal fruits and vegetables economically is by shopping at a nearby roadside or farm stand. Open during the local growing season, these stands are usually housed in small, open lean-to's where individual farmers or small growers sell their own produce directly.

The fruits and vegetables you buy are very recently picked, carefully brought to the stand, layered singly to limit bruising, and in some cases kept cool to retain flavor or inhibit over-ripening.

Prices may be a little higher than supermarket specials, but the extra quality makes it worth every penny.

Farmers Market Finds

Farmers markets are a good option for city-dwellers and suburbanites to obtain fresh, high-quality fruits and vegetables. Farmers from the surrounding area, as well as some from considerable distances, truck in their produce to one central place, such as a parking lot or a field. They sell their produce right off their trucks or set up portable stands. Because there are usually a large number of farmers involved, shoppers have a wide selection of good, ripened-in-season produce at fair prices.

The best time to shop? If you come early, you get a greater selection. Sweet corn, always popular, may be sold out by mid-afternoon. If you want to get the lowest prices, however, browse through the market during the closing hour. Many vendors are willing to cut their prices and make a smaller profit rather than cart their goods back to the farm. You will sometimes find discounts of up to 50%.

At the Supermarket

The supermarket may have some of the best produce bargains around. Particularly early in the day, there will be a good choice of fruits and vegetables in season. And if you choose to pay the price, there will also be a selection of produce from other parts of the country or the world.

Usually, your supermarket will be well-stocked in produce grown in your region or state. And prices for those items nearly always beat farm stands and farmers markets because supermarkets buy more inventory and sell it more quickly.

In New Jersey, for instance, in early summer when blueberries from down-state are in season, blueberries are marketed everywhere. Supermarkets consistently offer the best prices.

The Right Amount

No matter where you buy your produce, if you buy more than you can use before it spoils, you'll lose money.

Shop more frequently and buy only what you can use in a day or two. You will appreciate less crowding in your refrigerator and know that you've gotten the most for your money by consuming your produce in its best form.

Roadside May Be Retail

Occasionally, you will find a roadside stand that is not owned and stocked by a farmer or grower. The proprietor may be an outside retailer who bought the produce from someone else. Or a farmer may be selling, in addition to his own produce, a number of products brought in from elsewhere. Cider is a good example. Often sold at country stands along with apples and pumpkins, the brand may be the exact same one that your supermarket carries at a much lower price.

IT PAYS TO ASK

Birthday Freebie

Some restaurants give customers a free dinner on their birthday. Ask at your favorite restaurants when you visit.

Gary Foreman on Cutting Your Family's Food Budget 20% Without Feeling It

Gary Foreman is editor of **The Dollar Stretcher** newsletter and website (www.stretcher.com) in Fort Lauderdale, FL. Foreman uses his experience as a certified financial planner and purchasing manager to teach others how to get the most out of their household budgets.

What's the simplest way to save money on your grocery bill?

You can save real dollars, around 15% to 20%, just by buying a little spiral notebook. I call this "the best 79¢ you'll ever spend."

Make a page for every major item you buy frequently, and take the notebook with you whenever you go food shopping. Then, just jot down that day's date and price (using a constant measure, such as per-ounce). Soon you'll have a price history for these items and will be able to tell when you're really getting a good value—so you can stock up.

What's the biggest waste of money at the supermarket?

Convenience. Look at how much of your food dollar is paying for plastic instead of nutrition. A good example is those little drink boxes for kids. Yeah, they're handy, but when you compare them to the price of buying a half gallon of high-quality fruit juice and some cute little reusable cups with built-in straws, they're ridiculously expensive.

Can saving money on food really effect your overall budget?

Absolutely. If a family with $40,000 in income is trying to make a 5% ($2,000) decrease in their budget, food is the least noticeable area to do it in. Most families don't want to give up one car or move to a smaller house to reduce their mortgage. But if a family of four makes their own hamburgers once a week instead of going to a local drive-thru, they've already saved $275—without diminishing their lifestyle at all.

Is there an easy way to save on making dinner for your family?

You can save a tremendous amount of time and money by making freezer meals. You can usually make two or three meals' worth of food in about the same time it takes you to make one, and this saves on the cost of ingredients and preparation time.

For example, try making three lasagnas instead of one. Then eat one that night and put the other two in the freezer for later in the month. Meatloaf and browned ground beef work well too.

Is it possible to eat out and still save money?

There are ways to do it, but you have to think creatively. In most places in the U.S., lunch runs one-half to two-thirds of the price of dinner at the same restaurant. So consider scheduling a date for lunch instead of dinner.

Another trick—and it won't work with all restaurants—is to contact the headquarters of your favorite chain restaurants and let them know you'd be interested in being a mystery shopper. That's someone management hires to go in and eat at their restaurant to give them a customer's-eye-view of their food and service. You have to write a little report afterward, but you get to eat for free (often with friends or family), and might even get a small payment on top of that.

Herbs, Spice And Advice

You don't have to pay high supermarket prices for spices. Try these alternative shopping techniques and create ways to spice up your home-cooked meals for less.

Sources for Seasonings

Many farmers markets carry brand-name, packaged seasonings at prices 25% less than retail stores. To find a farmers market near you, call the U.S. Department of Agriculture's Wholesale and Alternative Markets Program at 202-720-8317 and ask for a copy of *The National Farmers Market Directory*.

Packaged goods and convenience stores, and even drug stores such as the CVS and Drug Fair chains, now sell dried herbs and spices. They offer good selections from lesser known labels, in convenient jars holding at least twice as much as the usual containers—and the prices are significantly better than at supermarkets.

Share Bulk Buys

Buy in bulk and you might save 70% percent off the price of smaller bottles of spices. Warehouse clubs and mail-order companies are good sources for bulk herb and spice buys. The San Francisco Herb Company (800-227-4530) sells herbs to the public at wholesale prices. The minimum order is $30.

Remember, however, that open packages of herbs stay fresh for only six months, so don't buy more than you can use or share. A good plan is to arrange with friends and family to buy in bulk, and then divide the herbs into smaller bottles. This way, each participant receives herbs or spices in appropriate amounts and at excellent prices.

Grow, Dry and Grind Your Own

Many herbs are easy and inexpensive to grow. All you need is water, sunlight and care. Chives, parsley and basil are particularly easy to grow, as are tarragon, dill, thyme and numerous others. They can be grown indoors in pots and planters for convenient cooking use, or outdoors, preferably in a place convenient to the kitchen. (Find out more about growing your own herbs at your local library.)

Pick your growing herbs throughout the season, bundle them together with rubberbands or string, and hang them in a warm, dry place. Store dried herbs in large, airtight containers and label them with the name and date.

FOR YOUR INFORMATION

Baby Food

Commercial baby food is expensive and may not be of the quality you wish for your child. But you can easily make your own inexpensive infant food at home by cooking vegetables and starches, and then pureeing them. That way, you can be certain that the ingredients are high quality and you can omit additives such as sugar. All it takes is a good blender and a little extra time.

Use Your Leftovers
You can save money by feeding your baby leftovers if the food is still fresh and appropriately nutritional. Mashed potatoes and squashes, cooked root vegetables such as carrots and beets, small pieces of chicken breast (with a bit of stock added), and soft fruits such as bananas, canned pears or apricots, and apple sauce can be tossed into a blender and pureed.

Recipe for Success
One reliable source for healthy baby food recipes is *The Healthy Baby Meal Planner: Mom-tested, Child-approved Recipes for Your Baby and Toddler* by Annabel Karmel, (Simon & Schuster, $15). It presents some general guidelines that will help you prepare nutritional baby food in your home.

Another book full of nutritious baby-food recipes is *The Well-fed Baby: Easy Healthful Recipes for the First 12 Months* by O. Robin Sweet and Thomas A. Bloom (Macmillan, $12).

By grinding the herbs you've grown and dried, you'll not only save money but preserve freshness as well. Use a mortar and pestle, coffee grinder, or even a pepper mill to grind herbs (and even some spices) immediately before adding them to a recipe.

Your herbs will be more flavorful and far less costly than those sold pre-packaged at any store.

Chocolate Values

According to the Chocolate Manufacturers Association, Americans spend nearly $13 billion a year on chocolate and cocoa products, and consume on average about eleven pounds per person a year.

Most people don't plan ahead to buy chocolate, but since many of the best chocolate deals are offered on bulk orders, it often pays to buy in advance.

The best chocolate buys come immediately after the holidays.

Holiday Seasons Mean Sales

Good buys on chocolate can be found several weeks before holidays such as Christmas, Easter and Valentine's Day, when chocolate Santas, bunnies, eggs or heart-shaped boxes of chocolates may be as much as 20% off.

However, the best buys of all come immediately after these holidays. Stores must get rid of this specially-wrapped and shaped chocolate, just as they have to unload other holiday merchandise, and reductions become drastic. Sales of 50% to 75% are common. This is the time for lovers of chocolate to do some serious shopping.

Halloween Competition Lowers Prices

There's no bigger candy-buying holiday than Halloween, when merchants and consumers alike stock up. Pre-Halloween candy specials in both supermarkets and convenience stores, such as CVS and Drug Fair, are widespread because stores count on increased volume and want your business. Competition gets fierce, and you can benefit.

Decide on the candy you wish to offer trick-or-treaters. Then search out the best buys nearest you. Price differences will surprise you, and you can save big.

Buy During the Year

If you're willing to give up the holiday trappings, you can purchase bags of mini bars and individual chocolate candies any time of year and freeze them.

Coffee Values

Coffee comes in many different forms and can vary significantly in taste and price. High-quality, gourmet coffee with better beans and extra flavor costs a good deal more than traditional brands like Maxwell House and Folgers.

Freshness Counts

Freshness is as important a consideration as price, since fresh beans make the best coffee. Coffee that has been stored for a long time, although often less expensive, is not necessarily a bargain. Old beans have lost much of their flavor in storage, and the coffee they produce won't taste as good.

Paying for Packaging

Coffee is commonly packaged in one of three ways: cans, pre-packaged or self-service bags, or foil-wrapped bricks. Bricks and cans of coffee tend to sell for the same price, but buying bricks will save you about 10% over cans. That's because most cans contain 11 to 15 ounces of coffee while bricks contain 13 to 16 ounces, costing you less per ounce.

Don't be misled by the rich aroma that comes from self-service coffee grinders at the supermarket. Though the price of this freshly-ground coffee is higher than pre-packaged, the beans are often of the same quality as those in the cans. Bricks are decidedly the best buy.

Mail-order Gourmet

Mail-order coffee companies offer some of the best deals in gourmet coffee.

For savings of up to 30% over Starbucks and low shipping charges, try the Supreme Bean Coffee Company, a small mail-order house in Redwood City, California. It carries gourmet and specialty coffees made with beans from Guatemala, Colombia and Costa Rica. For information and a catalog, call 888-288-5282.

Or check the prices at Northwestern Coffee Mills (800-243-5283).

HERE'S HOW

Tea for You

Here are a few ways to get high-quality tea for less.

Buy in September

Most tea crops grow between May and August and hit the marketplace in September. This means that supermarkets, tea shops and mail-order houses run specials on the preceding year's inventories in September. You should see price reductions of up to 15%.

Create Your Own Flavors

Flavored teas cost more then regular tea. If you can't live without the flavor, consider creating your own by adding a few drops of mint, lemon or orange essence, or experimenting with spices. You can buy bottles of flavor essences in health food stores and specialty markets.

Ban the Bag

Bags add to the cost of tea. Buy loose tea in bulk and invest in a tea strainer for maximum savings.

BUYER BEWARE

Ask Before You Eat

The listing of a dining card's participating restaurants may be out of date. Be especially cautious if the restaurant has opened in the past year. New restaurants sometimes use discount cards to promote themselves. Often, after restaurants have established a client base, they no longer accept the discount cards. Make sure the restaurant still accepts your charge card before you sit down.

HERE'S HOW

Bargain Meals For One

It's hard to save money on food if you're cooking for one person. Here are a few ways to save money and still make yourself some interesting meals.

Salad Savings

Most supermarkets have salad bars. Although salad bars are expensive for more than one person, they provide a variety of foods from many food groups at a reasonably low cost for singles. And best of all, there's no cooking or waste.

Variety

When you have some time, cook one or two main dishes in large quantities. Freeze what you can't consume in single servings and make a label for each saying what's in it and when it was cooked. If you do this week after week, you will end up with a variety of quick meals to choose from each night.

Think Big to Small

Instead of paying for small and expensive portions, buy foods (particularly meats) in multi-serving packages that can be subdivided and frozen in single servings. Packages of chops, cutlets, beef patties, small steaks or chicken parts cost less in packages of three pounds or more.

Good Wine Doesn't Have to Be Expensive

The taste and aroma of a fine wine should be complex and mix well. The blend should be smooth so that no one characteristic overshadows another. Poor wine is raw, with obvious, sharp tastes. While it's true that the price of a wine is often an indication of its quality, you can buy some excellent wines for less than $10 or $12 a bottle, which is considered a bargain by experts and wine lovers alike.

Bear in mind that tastes are very personal. But if you're willing to taste a number of wines, you can find bargains that you'll enjoy again and again. Following is a list of good quality wines, all currently priced at $12 and under.

Bordeaux (red): Chateau de la Cour d'Argent, France; Chateau Ferrande Graves, France; Chateau Tour-Prignac Medoc, France; Chateau Jonqueyres Bordeaux Superieur, France.

Cabernet Sauvignon (red): Hess Select Cabernet Sauvignon, California; Hawk Crest Cabernet Sauvignon, California; Haywood Cabernet Sauvignon, California; Black Opal Cabernet Sauvignon, Australia; Richemont Cabernet Sauvignon, France; Concha y Toro Cabernet Sauvignon, Chile.

Chardonnay (white): Beaulieu Vineyard Chardonnay, California; Napa Ridge Chardonnay, California; Hess Select Chardonnay, California; Oxford Landing Chardonnay, South Eastern Australia; Concha y Toro Chardonnay, Chile; Joseph Drouhin Laforet Chardonnay, France.

Chianti (red): Badia a Coltibuono, Ceta Mura Chianti, Italy; Cecchi Chianti Classico, Italy; Fattoria di Basciano, Italy.

Merlot (red): Forest Glen Merlot, California; Turning Leaf Merlot, California; Heron Merlot Vin de Pays, France; Dulong Merlot Vin de Pays, France; Pravini Merlot Trentino, Italy; Concha y Toro Merlot, Chile.

Pinot Noir (red): Talus Pinot Noir, California; Robert Mondavi Pinot Noir, California; Bridgeview Pinot Noir, Oregon; Joseph Drouhin Laforet Bourgogne Pinot Noir, France.

Sauvignon Blanc (white): Beringer Sauvignon Blanc, California; Canyon Road Sauvignon Blanc, California; Indigo Hills Sauvignon Blanc, California; Martine Sauvignon Blanc, France; Seaview Sauvignon Blanc, Australia.

WE TASTE GREAT

WE COST LESS

Knives: Slicing For a Bargain

Everyone needs a good set of kitchen knives. If you invest in quality, high-carbon stainless steel or forged-carbon knives and take care of them, they should last you a lifetime. Here's a list of buying and maintenance tips that will help you get the most value from your knives.

• **Paring or utility knife**

• **Bread knife**

• **Slicing knife**

• **Chef's knife**

How Many Knives Do You Need?

Don't waste money on a kitchen full of cutlery. Most chefs use only four basic knives: a serrated or bread knife (used for slicing bread and cakes), a paring or utility knife (used for peeling and trimming), a chef's knife (used for chopping vegetables, fruits, nuts and herbs) and a slicing knife (used for carving meat and slicing large fruits and vegetables).

Invest in Quality Names

Quality knives cost more than their cheaper counterparts, but the extra money is well spent. Investing in well-respected brands like Henckels, Wusthof-Trident, Victorinox, Sabatier and Chicago Cutlery will save you money over time because you may never need to buy another knife.

Know Where the Knives Are

Restaurant supply stores don't sell only to restaurants. Individual customers are frequently welcome and discounts can be up to 70% off department store prices on high-quality knives. Find a supplier in your yellow pages under Restaurant Equipment and Supplies. Garage sales, estate sales and auctions are other places to look for low-cost, high-quality knives with names you recognize.

Hold Out for the Holidays

The holidays are a great time to buy knives. Discounts are typically 20% off regular prices.

Maintain Your Knives

Buy a wooden cutting board and use it—just make sure to clean it thoroughly with soapy water after each use. Cutting on countertops and stone or plastic cutting boards can damage knives. Store your knives in a wooden block (cutting edge up) or on a magnetic strip on the wall.

TRY SOMETHING DIFFERENT

Save Money Around the Kitchen

• Instead of buying cooking spray, save your butter wrappers and use them to grease your cooking pans.

• Use oven racks as a cheap alternative to cooling racks. Simply place the racks on bricks, cups or anything that works as a prop, and wait for your cookies to cool.

• Use toothpaste instead of silver polish. It's less expensive, but just as effective.

• Stick your sponges in the dishwasher every time you run it. They will last up to a month longer, and you'll kill germs too.

• Divide batter into smaller or shallower pans to reduce baking time and save money on gas or electricity.

• Dough bakes faster in glass than in metal. When using glass cookware, reduce the oven temperature by 25 degrees.

Eat Out for Less

If you love going out to eat but want to save money, consider these alternatives to going out for a full dinner.

Lunch: Meeting friends for lunch instead of dinner will save you 20% or more on your total bill. This is a great way to try out popular new restaurants, since it's much easier to get a reservation for lunch than dinner, the food costs less, the service may be better and the food will taste the same.

Dessert and Coffee: Going out for coffee and dessert costs about 80% less than going out for an entire meal.

Appetizers and Salads: Appetizers and salads are priced far lower than entrees, and portions are often more than large enough for an entire meal.

Buffets: Many restaurants offer all-you-can-eat lunch or dinner buffets that cost less than individual items on the menu.

Prix Fixe: If you like to order several courses, try to find restaurants that offer prix-fixe (fixed-price) dinners, which usually include a limited selection of soups, appetizers, entrees and desserts for a reduced price.

Early and Late: Eating at off-peak hours (before 6 p.m. or after 9 p.m.) will usually save you about 10% on your meal. In retirement communities, discounts are often even higher.

Bar Food: Restaurants with bars usually have a limited number of appetizers, sandwiches and entrees you can order in that area. Since food on the bar menu is meant to be a complement to your drinks, it often costs less than it does in the dining room.

Discounts with Dining Cards

There are quite a few discount dining cards offering savings of up to 30% on your bill at participating restaurants. If you go out for dinner twice a week and spend approximately $50 a night, you will save about $1,560 a year with a dining card.

To find a card that covers restaurants in your local area, scan the local newspapers for ads placed by regional dining card companies. If you're a frequent traveler, consider plans that offer the best deals at your travel destinations.

To decide which card is the best for you, call the different dining card companies and ask for a list of restaurants that accept the card. But don't kid yourself. If you don't frequent any of the restaurants listed, don't bother paying for the card.

Dining à la Card For an annual fee of $49.95, Dining à la Card offers a 20% cash-back guarantee at participating restaurants when paying with MasterCard, Visa, American Express or Discover. Dining à la Card grants discounts at over 6,500 establishments nationwide. The catch is that this discount plan can only be used once a month at each participating restaurant. For more information call Member Services at 800-253-5379. www.dalc.com

In Good Taste (IGT) The IGT card offers a 25% discount at participating restaurants for an annual fee of $25. Tips and taxes are not discounted. The IGT Card is currently honored at approximately 3,500 establishments in metropolitan areas such as New York, New Jersey, Connecticut, Philadelphia, Atlanta, Chicago, Miami, Los Angeles, San Francisco and Washington, D.C. For more information, contact IGT at 800-444-8872. www.igtcard.com

Le Card Le Card is a perk offered free to members of the Diners' Club. It grants a 20% discount off of the entire bill, including tax and tip, at over 1,700 restaurants nationwide. Membership in the Diners' Club costs $80 a year. For more information, contact the Diners' Club at 800-234-6377. www.dinersclubus.com

Transmedia Transmedia offers three different discount alternatives at participating restaurants. A base membership offers a 25% discount for an annual fee of $49. The discount covers only food and drink. Tax and tip aren't included. The Transmedia card can be used at approximately 7,000 restaurants worldwide and has various U.S. regional directories. For more information, call Transmedia at 800-422-5090. www.transmediacard.com

Sterling Silver Savings

There are several ways to buy sterling silverware that are less expensive than running out to the local department store. And, although sterling is an expensive investment, once you buy it, it can be passed down through generations.

Buy More for Less

If you're planning on buying your new sterling silver at a retail store, consider waiting until May or November for discounts of up to 40%. And ask if there are discounts for buying larger quantities. The cost of a place setting often drops 20% if you buy eight place settings instead of six.

Consider Mail Order

Buying your silverware through the mail may save you 20% to 70% off retail prices. Check prices at your local department store, and then call these catalog companies to find out if you can get the same silver for less through the mail (including the cost of shipping and handling):

- Albert S. Smyth Company (800-638-3333; www.albertsmyth. com)
- Barrons (800-538-6340; www.barronscatalog.com)
- Gearys (800-243-2797; www.gearys.com)
- Michael C. Fina (800-288-3462; www.michaelcfina.com)
- Michael Round Fine China & Crystal (800-752-6622; www.michaelround.com)
- Nat Schwartz & Company (800-526-1440; www.natschwartz.com)
- Ross-Simons (800-556-7376; www.ross-simons.com)
- Thurbers (800-848-7237; www.thurbers.com)
- Windsor Gifts (800-631-9393; www.windsorgifts.com)

Discontinued Patterns

Stores sometimes offer great deals on discontinued patterns. But consider buying a couple extra place settings, since it may be difficult and expensive to replace lost or damaged pieces in the future.

Secondhand Silver

Secondhand silverware is probably the best deal. Look for place settings and serving utensils at estate sales, auctions, flea markets, secondhand shops and garage sales.

It is sometimes hard to find a complete set, however, and loose pieces tend to cost less than matching sets. So, for an inexpensive

---

HERE'S HOW

How Much Will You Use It?

If you're planning to invest in a full set of sterling, ask yourself the following questions before you buy:

- Will you be inheriting the family silver? If your parents don't use their silver much and are planning on leaving it to you, would they be willing to let you use it now? If not, do you want to buy silver that will match their pattern so you will eventually have a larger matching set?

- Will your silver flatware spend most of its life in a drawer in your dining room? Will you use it frequently for formal entertaining such as luncheons or dinner parties? Will you use it to replace your stainless steel for everyday dining?

- Do you mind polishing silver? If you hate the idea of polishing, you probably won't bother to use your silver that often.

- Would you prefer a second set of stainless steel? If you don't like the idea of polishing and worrying about silver, but want a special set of flatware for holidays and entertaining, consider buying a second set of stainless for more formal occasions.

BARGAIN FINDER

Replacements

Finding replacement pieces for sterling silverware can be expensive and tiresome. For affordable replacements, try calling **Replacements Limited** (800-737-5223), which has over 90,000 different patterns in stock.

and artistic tablesetting, consider creating your own unique silverware set out of a variety of mixed-and-matched patterns.

Silverware can also be purchased at antique shows. If your pattern is an old and discontinued one, you may be able to pick up some rare serving pieces. Prices will pretty much be the going rate, however, since dealers know exactly what each piece is worth.

How will you know it's the real thing? All American silverware is marked "sterling." If it doesn't say sterling, it could be imported silver which has different markings. But beware of people trying to pass off silver plate as sterling.

Cookware and Dinnerware

There is no good reason to ever pay full price for cookware, since sales and deals abound. In April and May—pre-wedding season—department stores offer the year's best savings on cookware and dinnerware. You'll find a good selection for as much as 50% off suggested retail prices.

The Experts Know

Restaurant supply stores usually offer prices 30% to 60% lower than department stores. Look in the yellow pages under Restaurant Suppliers and Equipment to find a store near you, or ask your favorite restaurants where they buy their supplies. Then call ahead and make sure the stores sell to individuals as well as restaurants.

Restaurant Closings

Over 50% of restaurants close in their first year of business. Many have going-out-of-business sales at which you can buy cookware and dinnerware at rock-bottom prices. Look for signs in your neighborhood, and keep an eye out for public notices in the newspaper.

Dinnerware Outlets

Many of the most popular dinnerware brands have their own outlet stores that offer overstocked and out-of-date items at significant discounts. Call these companies for their outlet locations, or look for dinnerware stores at an outlet center near you:

- Corning/Corelle (800-999-3436)
- Crate and Barrel (847-272-2888)
- Dansk (914-697-6400)
- Fitz and Floyd (800-243-2058)
- Mikasa (800-489-2200)
- Pfaltzgraff (800-999-2811)
- Vileroy Boch (609-734-7800)

Automotive Discounts

Here's the most up-to-date information on paying the lowest price on a new car, saving on mechanics' bills, haggling with used-car dealers, understanding no-haggle deals and getting the best performance out of your vehicle.

Getting the Best Deal On a New Car

There's more than one reason people like to buy new cars. Buying new usually assures you of a long, reliable vehicle life, and a two- to three-year full factory warranty covering all repairs during that time period. New cars also offer the latest cutting-edge performance technology and the broadest choice of models, colors and options.

In addition, new cars have the most up-to-date safety features, while used cars that are only a few years old may not have passenger-side airbags or anti-lock brakes.

Finally, you'll never worry about how a new car was treated by its former owner. So you'll never end up paying for the way someone else drove your car.

You Can Buy a Car on the Internet

Some websites offer wholesale vehicles at no-haggle prices. Many provide financing, and even deliver the car to your home. **Auto-by-Tel**, for example, offers specifications, reviews and photographs for all new model cars. Here are a few web-sites to check out:

- **Auto-by-Tel** (www.autobytel.com)
- **Auto-Town** (www.autotown.com)
- **Auto Vantage** (www.autovantage.com)
- **Microsoft Carpoint** (carpoint.msn.com)
- **Carsmart** (www.carsmart.com)

Buying over the Internet allows you to choose the exact car you want. That includes color and options. After you choose, the web-sites refer your request to a dealer who calls you up and quotes you a price, which is sometimes negotiable.

You'll usually get a slightly better price if you shop around at many dealerships, but shopping over the Web can save you a lot of time. Just make sure you compare prices at all the sites and never buy a car without inspecting it and driving it first.

Depreciation

But there are some drawbacks to buying a new car as well.

New cars depreciate (lose value) tremendously during their first two years, usually losing around 30% of their original value. Some luxury models can lose up to 40% of their value.

If you plan on selling your car only a few years after you purchase it, look for vehicles that hold on to their value. Your best bets are sports utility vehicles, pick-up trucks or cars manufactured by Saturn. There are also a few models of sedans, small cars and minivans with low depreciation rates. Look for these in the *Complete Car Cost Guide* (Intellichoice, $45.00).

If you plan on keeping your car for a long time, however, depreciation should not be a big concern.

Do Your Homework

When shopping for a new car, it's best to narrow down your choices to a few makes and models. Then thoroughly research these vehicles:

- Look at the Cartalk website (www.cartalk.com) for up-to-date information (and a few laughs).
- Get safety data from the Institute of Highway Safety (10005 N. Glebe Rd., Arlington, VA 22201, 703-247-1500) or the National Highway Traffic Safety Administration (www.nhtsa.gov).
- Talk to friends who already own the type of car you're interested in buying.

Visit dealerships and test drive the vehicles. Inform salespeople that you will be purchasing a car soon, but not that same day. Auto salespeople are very persistent, and you have to be firm to avoid falling into a pressure sales situation where you'll end up overpaying for a car you're not even ready to buy.

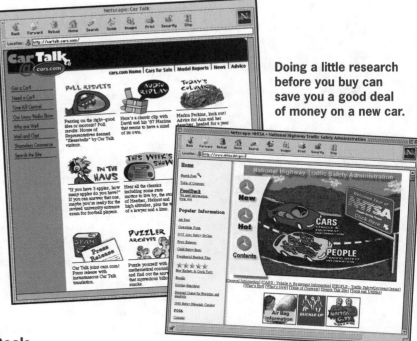

Doing a little research before you buy can save you a good deal of money on a new car.

Stay Flexible

If you don't care exactly what kind of car you drive (as long as it has the features you need), you're bound to get a pretty good deal. But if you have your heart set on one particular model, you'll have a harder time finding a bargain.

No-dicker Deals

Some dealerships, such as Saturn, offer no-haggle or no-dicker deals. This saves you the hassle of negotiating with a salesperson, but you'll pay a higher price for it—often laying out almost twice the usual dealer's profit.

Financing

Financing is a fancy word for car loan. Most people need to finance a new car. You can get your loan either through the dealer or an independent source. The best way to save money on financing is to shop around. Often your local credit union will offer the best deal. If you don't belong to a credit union, try to join one. And investigate your local bank.

If you choose to finance through the dealership, negotiate the rate. But be wary of dealers who offer you a better interest rate—only to then increase the overall price of the vehicle.

The best way to keep your monthly financing payments low is to pay a substantial amount of money up front. Your monthly payment is the amount of money you still owe divided by the number of months your lease lasts (plus interest). Also, make sure you only finance for 24 or 36 months. Any period longer than that will cost you more money in interest and force you to keep making payments even after the vehicle isn't worth much anymore.

BUYER BEWARE

Keep an Eye on Your Credit

Dealership salespeople use a variety of sneaky techniques to figure how much money you have to spend. For example, they may ask you for your driver's license, Social Security or credit card number.

Do not give them any of these. While you're waiting, they may secretly do a thorough credit check on you and even fill out loan applications on your behalf. This allows them to get an upper hand in bargaining because they'll know exactly how much you can spend. If you are pressed by the salespeople for any of these items, show them your license—but don't let them take it. If they pressure you further, walk out.

Grab up the Leftovers

Late in the model year, dealers offer great deals on leftover cars. But as soon as you drive it off the lot, a leftover will automatically lose one year's value. That means that after you've owned the car for only one year, it will have two-years' worth of depreciation. Still, if the price is right and you're planning to keep the car for a long time, leftovers can be great bargains.

INSIDE INFORMATION

Look into Twins

American car manufacturers sometimes produce two of the exact same car, but alter their appearances slightly. The **Ford Taurus** and **Mercury Sable** are common examples of these twins. The only real difference between the two cars is their price tags.

Twins also occur when Japanese car manufacturers assemble a second version of one of their cars in the U.S. and give it an American name. For example, the **Chevy Nova** is essentially the same car as the **Toyota Corolla**. For a bargain, shop for both cars and find out which one will cost you less.

What to Do at the Dealership

Once you've narrowed your search, look up the invoice price or the dealer's price in a book like *Edmund's New Cars* (St. Martin's Press, $8.99). The invoice price is not the Manufacturers Suggested Retail Price (MSRP) or sticker price. The MSRP includes profit for the dealer, while the invoice price does not (and is therefore lower). Start your bargaining at the invoice price and bargain up from there. A good deal is 2% to 5% over the invoice price.

Look at cars that have MSRPs 15% to 20% above your budget, which should put you in the right price range. Remember, if you tell a salesperson that you can afford a $10,000 car, they will show you a car with a $10,000 MSRP and you won't get a bargain. But if you ask to see a $12,000 car, you can probably bargain the dealer down to $10,000.

But be realistic. Dealers need to make a profit, and no dealer is going to sell you a car for $50 over the invoice price.

Supplemental Paks

Many times, dealers post a supplemental pak next to a car's MSRP. The pak includes the price of extras such as paint sealers, rust protection and car alarms. These supplements are hugely overpriced, and sometimes downright undesirable. For example, many auto makers warn against using dealership rust proofing because it can damage electrical equipment. In some cases it will even cancel out your factory corrosion warranty. Dealer-installed car alarms, another common extra, are often overpriced by up to 1000%.

These extras are not automatically included with the car, but dealers do their best to get you to think you need them. If a dealer adds a pak you didn't want to your car, refuse to pay for the supplements or demand to get the same car—without the pak—fresh from the factory.

Options

Options are a way for dealers to increase their profits once they've got you hooked on a specific car. An option can be power steering, power windows, or a sun roof. Don't buy any options that you don't need. If you want a few options, however, ask if the dealership offers an options package. Packages can significantly reduce the price of a group of options, though any package is apt to have some extras you don't want.

Trade in or Sell?

Trading in your old vehicle can help you reduce the cost of your new car. Before you trade, get an idea of how much your old car is worth by looking in the *Kelley Blue Book Used Car Guide* (Kelley Blue Book, $9.95), the *NADA Official Used Car Guide* (NADA Official Used Car Company, $53.50) or *Edmunds Used Cars and Pricings* (St. Martin's Press, $8.99). Then have it evaluated by a few used-car dealers. Quote the highest of these prices as the value of your trade-in when you negotiate with dealers.

Never talk trade-in until you've agreed on a firm price with the dealer. Otherwise, the dealer might give you the full value of your used car while at the same time adding some of that cost to the final price of the car.

For example, say you want $5,000 for your trade in. If you had negotiated price ahead of time, and the final price was $15,000, you might wind up getting $4,500 for your trade in. That means you'd be paying $11,500 total for the new car. But if you do the trade in first, you might get the full $5,000 for your old car, but then pay $17,000 for a final price on the new car. Very tricky. If the dealer tries to give you less than you deserve for your old car, sell it yourself. Selling your old car on your own almost always gets you the most money.

Made-to-Order

Ordering a car from the factory can be a pretty good deal. You'll not only get the exact car you want, but the dealership will be able to give you a better price because it won't have to pay to keep the car on the showroom floor.

Leasing a Car

More than 30% of new cars are leased, not bought. Despite the popularity of leasing, however, it's only really a bargain for a small group of people.

Consider leasing only if you:

1. Don't plan on keeping the car for more than three or four years.
2. Can't afford a down payment of more than 20% of the total value of the car.
3. Are diligent about maintenance and car care.
4. Drive fewer than 15,000 miles a year.

If you fit these four categories, you're a good candidate for leasing.

DID YOU KNOW

Subsidized and Advertised Leases

Subsidized leases are nationally advertised, cut-rate leases, and they offer incredible deals. For a listing of all the subsidized leases available in the U.S., visit **The Car Center** website at www.intellichoice.com.

Leasing Online

If you're still unsure of whether you should lease or buy, **LeaseSource** (www.leasesource.com) can help. You'll find explanations of new leasing laws and other up-to-date information. You can even take an interactive quiz that helps you decide whether to lease or buy.

If you want to calculate the cost of a lease on a particular model, the best places to go are the auto makers' own websites. They'll have online leasing calculators and data on the specific leasing terms of their cars.

Lease Basics

Leasing saves you money by allowing you to pay only for the time you use your car. You also pay sales tax on only a portion of the car's price. But even though you don't own the car, you are responsible for it. You need enough insurance so that if it is stolen or destroyed, you can pay back the car company.

Before shopping for a lease, make sure you understand these basic terms:

Capitalized Cost: The price of the car that the lease is based on.

Money Factor: The interest rate on the lease.

Up-front Charge: The down payment or amount of the capitalized cost you pay upfront, plus other charges. These are usually the first and last months' lease payments, a bank fee and a security deposit.

Mileage Allowance: The yearly amount of mileage you're allowed to put on a car. If you exceed your mileage allowance, you'll pay between 10¢ and 16¢ for each additional mile—and that adds up fast. But if you pay for a higher mileage allowance and come in at a lower rate, you can usually get the extra payment refunded.

End-of-lease Fees: What you have to pay at the end of the lease for any damage to the car beyond normal wear and tear.

Early Bail-out: The cost of terminating your lease early. These penalties are usually quite large, so make sure you can handle the lease throughout its term.

You Better Shop Around

You don't have to get your lease from the dealership. A bank or credit union might offer you a better deal. If it does, choose the car at the dealership but insist on using the financing company you want.

Three Ways to Pay

People choose how to pay for their cars depending on their unique economic and personal circumstances. Any buyer, however, should be able to compare the costs of different payment methods. Here are three ways you might pay for an $18,000 car.

THREE YEAR LOAN	THREE YEAR LEASE	CASH
$4,000 Down payment + $1,260 7% Sales tax + $17,424 Monthly payment at 10% ($484 x 36) **$22,684 Total cost (before resale)**	$500 Leasing fee + $298 Prepayment + $10,728 Monthly payment ($298 x 36) **$11,526 Total cost**	$18,000 Purchase price + $1,260 7% Sales tax **$19,260 Total cost (before resale)**

Figure out the Total Cost

Because leases are complicated and their wording is often confusing, any help can be valuable. A group of consumers headed by Ralph Nader have compiled a *Reality Checklist* that makes it easier to understand and compare leases. Send $1.50 to the Consumer Task Force for Automobile Issues, Box 7648, Atlanta, GA 30357.

You can also simplify the process of lease shopping by using Lease Wise (800-475-7283), a non-profit, national shopping service. For $290, Lease Wise provides you with five competing lease quotes. This can save you time and money—and the hassle of trying to calculate what a lease should cost and whether you could get a better deal by buying.

Negotiate the Lease

Shop around. Leases may offer the biggest rebates and subsidies in the car market. Then negotiate the capitalized cost just like you would the price if you were buying the car: Find out the invoice cost in a new-car price guide and negotiate up from that. But also make sure you get the mileage allowance you want. Some dealers will give you a lower capitalized cost but then lower your mileage allowance.

The money factor (interest) is also negotiable, even though the dealer doesn't have to tell you what it is. Talk only to dealers who will tell you the money factor.

Get It in Writing

When negotiating the lease, make sure you and the dealer discuss exactly what kind of damage exceeds normal wear and tear—and get it in writing. Then, before returning your vehicle, document all car damage and get a repair estimate from your own mechanic. If the dealer's charge for repairs seems too high, take the car to your own mechanic for repairs.

The Length of Your Lease

A two-year lease is a good idea because you'll be covered by the car warranty, and you'll probably have fewer wear-and-tear charges to pay off. But short-term leases are expensive because you're paying for the steepest depreciation on the car. A three-year lease is usually a better deal because there's much less depreciation from the second year to the third.

Buying Out

Leasing gives you the opportunity to test a vehicle's performance for a few years before you decide to buy it. This can be a great source of comfort, especially if you're buying a car model that's only been out for one or two years.

INSIDE INFORMATION

Subsidized Lease Bargains

Cars coming out of a subsidized lease may offer the greatest bargains for buyers interested in higher-end cars. In a subsidized lease, monthly payments are kept low by increasing the cost of buying the car when the lease ends. Because of this, most people don't buy their cars at the end of their lease, but neither will the dealer, who would rather unload it cheaply and quickly.

By shopping for used cars from subsidized leases, you might even find a used sports or luxury car for the same price you would normally pay for a used mid-range car.

DID YOU KNOW

Tax Deductions

If you drive your car for business, leasing can mean a sizable tax deduction. Figure out the percentage of time you use your car for business, and deduct that percentage from your lease payments and your cost of gas, repairs and car insurance.

For instance, if you use your car for business 75% of the time, you can deduct 75% of the cost of the lease. This deduction is greater than what you would receive on a vehicle you own because there are dollar limits on depreciation.

TRY SOMETHING DIFFERENT

It Pays to Be Flexible

The key to getting a really great deal on a used car is flexibility. Remember, every used car is unique because of the way it was driven and maintained. Dealers demand a higher price if they think you're set on one particular car. But if you consider a few cars that have the features you're looking for, you'll be able to get a much better bargain. For example, if you're looking for a family car that gets good mileage and has a good safety record, look at a variety of four-door sedans, station wagons and minivans. Don't just focus on that red Volvo sedan you saw at one used-car lot.

BARGAIN FINDER

Dig up the Dirt

Once you're close to deciding on a specific vehicle, consider checking it out with **Carfax** (www.carfax.com or 888-4-CARFAX). For $14.95 on the Internet or $20 over the phone, Carfax will help you determine if the car you're interested in was ever seriously damaged in a crash. Carfax can tell you if the title is authentic, if the vehicle has been in a flood and if the odometer reading is accurate. Finally, it will determine if the vehicle was ever returned as a lemon. All you need is the VIN (Vehicle Identification Number) listed on the car, and the title.

Info4cars (www.info4cars.com) provides a similar service for $14.95.

If you think you might buy the car at the end of the lease, negotiate with the dealer on a pre-established price for the buy-out option. Otherwise, when the lease expires, the price will be what is called a "fair market price," but is often higher than buying a comparable car secondhand. And remember, everything is negotiable. Unless the car is in incredible demand, it will probably be a good deal for the dealer to cut some money off of the buy-out price in order to unload the vehicle quickly.

Buying out can be costly to you, however. The cost of the lease combined with the buy-out price will probably be higher than if you had chosen to buy the car new in the first place. It is often a better a deal to buy a new model of the car than to buy the one you're currently leasing.

Selling Out

If the dealer wants to let you out of your lease early in order to sell your car to someone else, make the most out of the situation. Consider buying the car at the end of the lease and selling it yourself to make the most cash. Or agree to get out of the lease only if the dealer will sign a new lease for another vehicle—on your terms, which may include waving the up-front charge and reducing your capitalized cost.

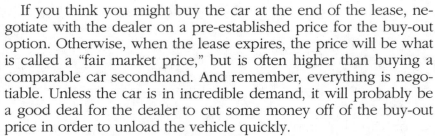

New Ideas on Used Cars

Buying a used car can be a great investment. New cars lose much of their value during the first two years of ownership. For example a $20,000 car will probably be worth about $14,000 after two years—a 30% decrease in value. If you buy this car used, however, you'll save $6,000 you would have lost buying it new and you'll still get a young vehicle with lots of miles left.

The competition to sell used cars is fierce, so there are deals to be had. There are more newer, high-quality, low-mileage cars available than ever before because of the growing popularity of leasing. Finally, the low cost of a used car may be your opportunity to pay cash up front and avoid the extra costs and hassles of financing.

Car Dealers

Some of the best used cars are available through massive superstores like CarMax and Auto Nation. These chains feature no-haggle pricing, meaning that their prices are firmly set and there's no negotiating. They tend to have high-quality vehicles, a huge selection, excellent customer service and on-site financing.

But while you'll most likely get a fair price from a place like this, don't expect a bargain. Average used-car prices have increased $500 or so recently because of no-haggle pricing and these superstores' ability to limit competition. Dealerships that are close to a superstore might beat the superstore price, but not by much.

For a better deal, consider shopping at new- or used-car dealerships in an area that's out of the influence of superstores.

Certified Used Cars

Smaller car dealers are competing with automotive superstores by offering certified used cars. These are low-mileage, late-model vehicles that have newer safety features. They are often referred to as pre-owned cars. Certified cars have a special warranty from the manufacturer and are certified by manufacturers' standards.

If you're comfortable buying a used car and you know how to evaluate a used vehicle, consider shopping for an uncertified car. You might be able to save as much as a few thousand dollars on a higher-end car and as much as a few hundred on a standard or economy car.

But a certified used car sold at a no-haggle price can be a great deal if you don't feel comfortable with mechanical evaluations and negotiating. If you're buying a higher-end certified car, it can be an even better deal because you won't have to pay luxury taxes and gas-guzzler fees. In addition, certified used cars already have a performance record, so they may be a less risky buy than a new and unproven model.

Used-car Dealers

Despite their negative portrayal in the movies, used-car dealerships can be great places to find cars and negotiate good deals. But be warned: These places don't have repair facilities. They sell most cars as-is, which means there is no warranty at all. And the cars that do have warranties are barely covered for repair costs.

Only shop at dealers that have been in business for at least five years. Be sure the car you're considering has a Buyer's Guide sticker with warranty information on it. And compare prices by shopping around and consulting used-car pricing guides. The American Automobile Association (AAA, 800-597-5050) offers a used-car pricing service for members called AutoEase. The cost is $12.99 for members and $6 for each additional car. Consumer Digest (900-884-CARS) has a used-car pricing service that prices cars for $1.95 a minute (average call length is four minutes).

DID YOU KNOW

Buying Used Cars On the Internet

The Internet is the newest source for used-car information. Some free sites like **Auto-by-Tel** (www.autobytel.com), **Auto Town** (www.autotown.com) and **Mr. Car** (www.mrcar.com) offer interactive used-car shopping. They'll find you the exact car you're looking for by searching a dealership database. After that you negotiate with the dealership. Still, never buy a car before you've seen it and test driven it. And don't be surprised if the car you want has already been sold. Many times these sites are not entirely up-to-date.

Unlike ordinary used cars, certified pre-owned cars are certified by manufacturers' standards and have manufacturers' warranties. They also tend to cost a bit more.

Other Places to Buy Used Cars

- **Service Stations.** Although selection is limited, buying a car from a service station can be a good bet. This is especially true if it's the service station where your auto technician works. The station might have worked on the car previously and know its service record.
- **Rental Companies.** Rental companies usually carry a wide selection of used cars. But often they have high mileage and have not been driven with care, so be cautious.
- **Auto Auctions.** Only buy a car at an auction if you're very knowledgeable about automobiles. You're not allowed to drive the vehicles and have only a limited amount of time to look at them. The cars are sold as-is, and there's no telling how they were driven.

Vague classified ads that include non-essential information such as "great family car" indicate an unknowledgeable seller and the possibility of a good deal.

1987 Volvo 740 Wagon
Classic antiqued silver, 114,000 miles, great family car, good body, rides smooth, no air condition, broken antenna, $4,000 or best offer.

Finally, just because a car is sold as-is doesn't mean it won't be safe or reliable. It's illegal for a dealer to sell you a car with faulty safety equipment such as a cracked windshield or broken taillight. Check vehicle reliability records in consumer advocacy publications, evaluate the car you're looking at thoroughly (using the evaluation techniques in our *Buying a Used Car Privately* section) and make sure all the parts are in good working order. If any safety equipment is broken, demand that the dealer repair it before you purchase the car. If the dealer refuses, shop somewhere else.

Buying a Used Car Privately

You'll get the best prices on used cars from friends, co-workers and private owners. That's because they won't be adding operating costs such as rent and advertising to the car's price. And a friend or co-worker might cut you an extra good deal.

Don't Get Lazy

When you buy this way, however, you have to be especially careful. Do the same homework you would do if you were buying from a dealership, and thoroughly examine the car. Also insist on seeing the warranty booklet and all of the car's service records. These records will tell you about the car's repair history. And a car that has all of its records in order has usually been well maintained.

Read Between the Classifieds

You can learn a lot about who is selling a car from the way they write their classified ads. You can also spot potential bargains before even talking to the sellers. The best ads to pursue are usually vague, saying something like "Dodge Minivan, 1994, new tires". This seller probably doesn't know a lot about the car and doesn't want to find out. The seller probably just wants to get rid of the car as quickly and cheaply as possible. Also, "new tires" are not an essential part of a car, indicating that the seller probably isn't a good judge of value and could give you a great bargain.

A heavily-abbreviated ad such as "Ford F150, MT/PS/PB/4WD/AC" usually comes from a knowledgeable seller and hard bargainer. If it's the type of car you're looking for, consider calling up the owner—just don't expect a super deal.

Beware of classified ads that seem like they're posted by private owners but advertise more than one car. This is a sure sign of used-car dealers who are trying to get you down to their lots by posing as private owners. The Cartalk website (www.cartalk.com), periodically weeds out such phonies from their free classifieds.

Evaluating a Seller over the Phone

When talking to a private seller over the phone, ask these questions before you decide whether a trip to see the car is worth your time and money:

- How much does the car cost? This question can rule out a car pretty quickly.
- Are you the original owner? More than one owner is often a sign of poor upkeep.
- How many miles has the car been driven? On the highway or city streets? City miles are much harder on the engine than highway miles. They also strain the brakes and transmission.
- What major repairs have been done? Many repairs can be signs of a lemon or older car.
- May I see the service records? If not, forget about it.
- Who's your mechanic? A good mechanic will usually mean the car's in good shape.
- Why are you selling the car? An answer like "My kid went to college" or "I'm buying a new car" is a good sign. An accident is a bad one. Always ask this question in the middle of the conversation to get a more spontaneous (and more honest) answer.
- Is the car currently registered and insured? It it's not, it probably hasn't been driven in a while. Besides, it's illegal to test drive or have a mechanic work on such a car, so don't bother with it.
- Was it ever vandalized or stolen? These are two sure signs of damage and abuse.
- Do you park it in the garage or on the street? Garaged vehicles have much less weather strain and damage.
- May I have my mechanic inspect the car? If the answer is no, don't go.
- Was the car ever recalled? You can double check this by calling the Department of Transportation Auto Safety Hotline (800-424-9393; www.nhtsa.gov) with the car's make and model.
- Are you the primary driver? The primary driver always knows the car best.

If you're satisfied with the answers to these questions, go take a look at the car.

BUYER BEWARE

Odometer Fraud

Some dishonest sellers will try to roll back the odometer in a car to make you think it has less mileage. Protect yourself by doing the following:

- Check the odometer and its housing for scratches, nicks and other signs of tampering.
- Compare the odometer reading with any oil-change stickers on the windshield, in door jambs or under the hood.
- Examine the title. Previous ownership by a wholesaler or auction company, a P.O. Box as an address, a title from another state or a duplicate title can be a sign of odometer tampering. Ask the seller for identification to confirm that the same name is listed on the title.
- Examine odometer readings on sales and service records, and make sure they increase progressively and consistently. For instance, an odometer that increases 5,000 miles for one six-month period and 500 for the next could mean something fishy is going on. Be polite and tactful, but ask the seller about such inconsistencies.
- Seats, pedals and floor mats that are extremely worn when the mileage is not very high are a sign of tampering. So are brand new replacement seats, pedals and floor mats.

Evaluating a Vehicle on Your Own

If a car still looks good after you've done the following inspections, it's worth hiring a mechanic to check it out.

Tires Place a penny in the tread with the top of Lincoln's head facing down. Move it along the entire tread. If the top of the head is ever visible, the tires are worn out and you'll need new ones.

Irregular or uneven wear can be a sign of an alignment problem, which can mean a $60 repair job plus the price of new tires. It can also mean the car has been in an accident, something you'll probably want to avoid in a used car.

Steering With your foot on the brake, put the car in gear and turn the steering wheel back and forth. Everything should move smoothly. Listen for strange noises such as screeches and howls. While you're turning the wheel, there should be no more than a couple of inches of give before the tires start to move. If there's more, you could have a serious steering problem on your hands.

Brakes If the brakes vibrate, pulsate or screech, the car probably needs brake repair—which could run you a few hundred dollars.

Body The body panels should align properly, fitting together evenly and smoothly. If they don't, it's probably a sign of an accident or previous damage. Also check the entire body for leaks.

Look for rust everywhere, but especially under doors, in the trunk and in the wheel wells. Rust in those places is usually a sign of major body deterioration.

Air Filter Remove the top of the air filter. If there's oil around the bottom and sides, the engine will probably need $300 to $400 worth of repairs.

Take a close look at the major components of a used car before you buy. You might spot hidden rust, blue exhaust fumes or unevenly worn tires, all of which signal potentially serious problems.

Controls and Accessories Check that all the car's controls and accessories are in working condition.

Exhaust Look at the color of the exhaust before and after your test drive. If it's blue, the car could be an oil burner.

Alignment Take the car out on a variety of roads, just as you would a new car. While driving it, check the alignment: On a level road, the car should stay relatively straight, not pulling very much in either direction.

Transmission Make sure that the automatic transmission goes into gear smoothly with no lag time. If the car has a manual transmission, the clutch should always engage. If not, the car could have a major transmission problem.

Auto Insurance

You have to buy auto insurance if you're going to get on the road. And although it can be an expensive prospect, there are a few ways to save a good deal on your premium and make your periodic payments more bearable.

The Basics

Your premium is the base cost of insuring your car (without extras like collision or uninsured motorist coverage). Insurance companies base their premiums on personal information (age, sex, marital status, driving record) and vehicle information (vehicle make, vehicle safety record).

Every company has its own dizzying system of translating this information into how much you have to pay.

Shop Around

Experts agree that the best way to save on insurance is to get quotes from several different insurers. Each insurance company uses it's own complex system to price its policies, so costs for similar policies from different carriers can differ greatly. Although a single male under 25 years old with a couple of speeding tickets and a brand new red sports car is considered a high-risk driver by every company, there is still a range of policy prices available to him.

It's not uncommon for an insurance company to have the cheapest premiums in one market and be completely overpriced in another. For instance, a company may have the worst prices in the state for married drivers over 65 while offering the best prices for single female drivers under 25.

And, once you choose a company, don't plan to stay with it forever. Shop around again every two years to ensure that your company still has the best rates for you.

Ron Pinelli Explains Manufacturers' Promotions

Ron Pinelli is the president of Autodata Corporation in Woodcliff Lake, NJ, a company that helps auto companies keep competitive by analyzing prices. His pricing experience has made him an expert on automobile manufacturers' promotions.

What is a manufacturer's promotion?

Auto manufacturers sometimes need to help dealerships sell their cars, and to do this they sponsor promotions or incentive programs. Promotions sometimes contain rebates, discounts, free equipment and special low-interest financing. In my experience, promotions sell more cars for auto makers, and that's why they're out there.

When is the best time of year to buy a new car?

Promotions may run any time of year, but they heat up during certain times. Keep an eye out for advertised rebates and specials during major holidays. The end of the month or business quarter can be a good time to buy as well, because many dealerships get a bonus for selling a certain number of cars within a specific time period. If they're near their quota, they may unload the last few cars for cheap—and you might get a manufacturer's rebate as well.

What kind of special rebates and discounts are available?

Recent college grads often qualify for a lower rate loan and a $500 rebate.

Many auto makers will give a $1,500 to $2,000 rebate to drivers with physical disabilities, and may even pay for the outfitting of special driving equipment.

Most auto makers offer rebates to members of special organizations such as the Farm Bureau and the Board of Realtors.

Are there any certain cars you're more likely to get a deal on?

Sometimes companies want to have the top-selling car for marketing purposes, and they will spend a fortune at the end of the year trying to sell enough cars to take that number one car spot.

Premium brands like Mercedes and Toyota come at premium prices. Car makers like Nissan and Hyundai have more to prove. Nissan is a good company that's not on a lot of people's shopping lists. So to sell their cars they have to offer big discounts. Hyundai doesn't have a good reputation but has made big improvements. You'll be able to get a better deal from these auto makers, but your resale value will suffer because their products are less desirable in the general marketplace.

Are there promotions for leased cars?

It's not uncommon for a manufacturer to give a lease subsidy of $5,000. That means the lease will be based on a car price that's $5,000 lower than the sticker price—and that's a huge savings. Chances are, if a special lease is being run, you won't be able to find a better deal.

Sometimes, if you're already leasing a car, certain auto makers give you a bonus at the end of the term, called a loyalty bonus. If you sign a new lease with them, they'll waive one monthly payment or the security deposit. They might even waive your termination fee and maintenance fee when you return the car at the end of the lease.

Choosing the Best Coverage

Insurance companies offer different coverage options. Depending on who you are, some coverage may be an unnecessary expense. Here are explanations of some of the different components that make up most policies.

Bodily-injury Liability

In order to figure out your liability, add the value of your house, property, valuables, stocks, bonds and pension funds. This number will tell you how much you have to protect. And buying more than this can't hurt: If you injure or kill another driver and you're not covered, you could be in for a financial nightmare.

This is necessary for everyone. Most experts advise you to buy at least $100,000 of coverage per person and $300,000 per accident.

Uninsured and Underinsured Motorist Coverage

This is important for all drivers. It covers you for damages in a hit-and-run situation or a collision with an uninsured driver. Make sure you have at least $100,000 per person and $300,000 per accident.

Collision and Comprehensive

Collision pays for repairs or replacement of your vehicle due to accident. Comprehensive covers car repairs needed after a theft, fire or flood. Both are necessary for newer cars and cars under lease. But with cars older than four or five years, or worth less than $4,000, you can save yourself a good deal of money by dropping this coverage entirely.

If you choose to get collision coverage, take as high a deductible as you can handle. That way, small claims won't hike up your premiums.

The Deductible

A deductible is the amount of money that you must pay before the insurance company will cover damages. For instance, if you have a $500 collision deductible and you get hit with $600 worth of damage from an accident, you pay $500 and the insurance company pays $100. But if you have $6,000 worth of damage, the insurance company pays $5,500 and you still pay only $500.

Medical Payments

Medical payments coverage pays medical bills for you or your passengers that result from a car accident. If you have good health insurance, don't take medical payments because you'll be

CHECKLIST

Preventing Auto Theft

❏ Always lock the door. With an unlocked door it takes less than 30 seconds for a thief to start and steal your car.

❏ Buy a removable stereo system, and take it with you when you park the car.

❏ Buy an alarm system that disables the ignition when there's a break-in. Many car companies are now installing these kill switches.

❏ Don't leave valuables in plain view.

❏ Don't park where you have to leave your keys with an attendant. Try to find park-it-yourself parking garages.

❏ Install a metal steering wheel collar and use the Club.

❏ Never leave your keys in the car.

❏ Park in busy, well-lit areas.

Putting the Insurance Before The Car

If you're buying a car and want to find out the insurance cost ahead of time, check out the **Intellichoice** (www.intellichoice.com) website. For $4.95, you can price a car and the cost to insure it.

Consumer Reports offers an **Auto Insurance Price Service** at 800-807-8050. The service gives you a personal report showing as many as 25 of the lowest-priced policies available, plus money-saving tips and a guide to auto insurance companies. The service costs $12 for the first vehicle and $8 for each additional one.

paying twice for the same coverage. If you frequently drive passengers without health insurance in your car, however, you'll probably want to buy it.

How to Bring Down Your Premium

Once you've cut out unnecessary coverage, it's time to focus on bringing down your premium. Here are a few factors that affect how much you pay.

Your Choice of Car

Although it might sound a little strange to start shopping for insurance before you even have a car, it's not. Different makes of cars have very different insurance costs, and choosing a car that's less expensive to insure can save you a lot of cash. For example, sports cars and sports utility vehicles cost more to insure, while cars with excellent safety records are cheaper. In addition, safety features such as air bags, automatic seat belts and, in some cases, anti-lock brakes can get you a discount on your premium.

Teenage Drivers

A teenage driver can add a considerable amount to your insurance costs. You can reduce your premium, however, by only insuring your teenager to drive your least expensive car.

Also, encourage your teen to study. Most companies give a discount to teen drivers who maintain over a B average. And if you send your child to a college more than 100 miles away from your home (without a car), you can get an even bigger discount on your premium.

Teenagers cost a lot to insure, but you can cut your costs by letting them drive only your least valuable car.

Good Driving

If you haven't been at fault for an accident in over ten years, you're probably eligible for as much as a 20% discount on medical and collision coverage. You can get a smaller discount for three or more years of clean driving. Also, companies award a 10% discount on the premium to drivers who pass a driver's safety training course. This discount could be void if you're over 65, however.

Anti-theft Devices

Buying a car with an anti-theft device, or installing one yourself, can reduce your premium. In most cases it will save you 10% on your premium, but certain devices, such as the kill switches installed in many Ford and GM cars, may cut your costs up to 25%.

Multiple Cars

Insurance companies provide discounts when you put more than one car on your policy. In such cases, RVs and even trailers count as cars. Also, companies often reduce your premiums if you use them for more than one kind of insurance. So find out what your life insurance or health insurance company charges for car insurance.

Drive Less

A car that is used every day for business costs more to insure than a car used only for pleasure. Consider declaring your car a pleasure vehicle and taking public transportation to work to cut your premium costs. Or, if you have to drive to work, join a carpool. Putting less than 7,500 miles a year on your car can also qualify you for a discount.

If you're planning on not using your car for a month or more, inform your insurance company. They'll deduct your collision coverage for the time your car is not in use.

Garaging It

Drivers who live in certain urban areas are forced to pay a larger premium because of the risk of theft and break-ins. Putting your car in a garage can significantly lower your payment. Even in a suburb, garaging your car reduces wear and tear, and will get you a lower rate.

There's a Price for Value

Just because you're getting the best price for a premium doesn't always mean you're getting the best deal. When shopping for premiums, make sure you talk to other policyholders about collecting claims, customer service and repairs. If they have had any problems, consider trying another company. Also check the state insurance department complaint record on the company.

BUYER BEWARE

Insurance Scam

Some sophisticated crooks have a scam which involves breaking into a car with out-of-state plates and stealing the insurance card. They call up the insurance company taking responsibility for an accident, and then call again posing as the victim. The thief brings a damaged car to the adjuster and gets a check. Your premiums go up. Avoid this by keeping your insurance card with you at all times instead of in the glove compartment.

INSIDE INFORMATION

When to Stay Put

If you've recently received a few traffic violations, consider staying with your old insurance company instead of looking for a new policy. Tickets will immediately affect the pricing of a new policy by a new company—but they often take longer to affect the price of your current one.

How to Drain The Radiator

1. Make sure the engine is cold and the ignition is off. Remove the radiator cap.

2. Open the valve at the bottom of the radiator (called the pet cock). Drain coolant into a bucket. (Make sure you put the bucket under the radiator before you open the valve.)

3. Close the pet cock. Fill the radiator with water.

4. Start the engine. Turn the heat up to full. Add cooling-system cleaner, and then idle the engine for 30 minutes.

5. Stop the engine and let it cool for five minutes. Open the pet cock and drain the system.

6. Close the pet cock. Fill the radiator with water and idle for five minutes. Stop the engine and cool for five minutes. Drain the radiator.

7. Close the pet cock. Install a 50/50 mixture of water and antifreeze.

The Diagnostamatic Database

Cartalk (www.cartalk.com) offers an interactive database to help you figure out what's wrong with your car. Just type in the symptoms you're experiencing and the website will provide you with a good guess at the cause. And if you have to take it to the mechanic anyway, at least you'll sound like you know what you're talking about.

Taking Care of Your Car

One of the best ways to save cash on your car is through careful maintenance. Neglect is the number one cause of car trouble. And the price of car trouble can be enormous. Good car care extends the life of your vehicle. And no matter how many money-saving tips you follow, the best way to save is by taking care of the vehicle you drive now.

Motor Oil

Clean motor oil is the key to keeping your car running smoothly. If your engine is properly lubricated, no moving part should ever come into contact with any other moving part. Oil also cools the engine. But once the oil is older, dirt and sludge build up on engine parts and can cause harmful friction. Since friction will wear your engine down, changing the oil is extremely important.

The 3,000 Mile Myth Experts used to say you should change your oil every three months or 3,000 miles. Today, studies show that changing the oil according to manufacturers recommendations (about every 7,500 miles) is just as effective. So start changing your oil every 7,500 miles, and you'll spend less than half as much a year on oil and oil changes. Even if you drive your car under extreme conditions—in lots of stop-and-go traffic or extreme temperatures—you only need to change your oil about every 6,000 miles. And remember to always change the oil filter when changing the oil.

Check Your Own Oil To check the oil, turn off the car and wait a few minutes so the oil moving through the engine can return to the pan. If you don't wait, your oil level will read lower and you'll end up adding too much oil. A car with too much oil doesn't run efficiently.

Oil Grades and Additives Oil grade is much more important than brand. Most cars run on 5W-30, but always consult your owner's manual to confirm the best grade of oil for your car. Oil brands are fairly similar, so save some cash by buying a less expensive variety. And never use motor oil additives. They won't improve your car's performance, and can sometimes hurt it.

Radiator and Coolant

The radiator is responsible for keeping your engine cool while driving. The coolant or antifreeze also helps cool the engine, protects it from freezing in the winter, and prevents rust and corrosion. Always keep an eye on your coolant level if you want your car to last.

Checking the Coolant Check the radiator overflow area (a plastic container resembling the washer fluid reservoir and connected to the radiator by a plastic pipe or hose). If it's more than halfway below the full-line, open the radiator cap and fill it with a mixture of half water/half antifreeze. If you're driving in extremely cold weather, consider using about 65% percent antifreeze and 35% water.

Never go higher than 65%. Too much antifreeze will actually cause the engine to run hotter. Also, never open the radiator cap when the engine is hot. You can seriously burn yourself.

Flushing Out the Radiator Flush your radiator about once every year. Drain the radiator and wash out all of the particles with a high-powered hose. Then refill with your water/coolant mixture. Or ask your mechanic to do the procedure for you.

Checking the Coolant Hoses It's also important to check the hoses that are connected to your radiator, heater and water pump. If they're damaged or brittle, replace them.

Transmission

Modern transmissions are extremely complicated, and all serious repairs should be handled by a trained mechanic. Still, you can keep your transmission running smoothly by making sure your transmission fluid is always full. Consult your owner's manual for instructions on checking the transmission fluid. And have the transmission fluid and filter changed every two years.

Tires

Keeping your tires filled is not only essential for safety, it also improves your gas mileage, saving you money at the pump. Invest in a high-quality tire gauge to test the pressure, and fill the tires up to the pressure indicated on the sticker inside of the glove compartment or on the door frame. Tires lose air faster in hot weather, so check them more frequently during the summer.

If your tires show signs of bulges or excessive wear, it's time to buy new tires.

What if You Have a Lemon?

A lemon is a car still under warranty that has a problem or defect that damages its value, hinders its use or threatens your safety. For instance, a car with a brake light that continues to malfunction after a few repairs is not a lemon. But a car whose faulty electrical wiring system often bursts into flames, even after a few repairs, certainly is.

If you think you have a lemon, contact the **National Highway Traffic Safety Administration (NHTSA**, 800-424-9393, www.nhtsa.dot.gov) or the **Center for Auto Safety** (202-328-7700, www.autosafety.org).

The NHTSA is a government organization where you can make a complaint. There you can find out if your vehicle was recalled and, if so, where to take it. The Center for Auto Safety is a private, non-profit, consumer organization with similar information that tends to be more up-to-date. The Center can also recommend a lawyer who specializes in lemon laws. And if you have a lemon that's probably what you need. You can try working through the manufacturer, but you may have difficulties. Often a lawyer and the threat of a lawsuit are the only way to get a refund or a replacement vehicle.

And Don't Forget

❏ **Wiper blades.** Change your blades every 6 to 12 months to maintain maximum visibility in the rain.

❏ **Battery.** Check your battery every six months. On a regular battery, pry off the plastic covers and check the water level. If it's low, fill it with distilled water. If you have a low-maintenance battery, check the power gauge or eye. The color yellow means it's time for a new battery.

❏ **Outer surface.** Dirt, debris, salt and chemicals can break down your car's paint and rust protection. Wash your car once or twice a week with a high-powered hose to rinse away salt and dirt that collects under the car. Or take it to a professional car wash.

❏ **Brakes.** Have the brakes inspected by your mechanic once a year.

❏ **Spark plugs.** Replace your spark plugs every 100,000 miles.

❏ **Air Conditioning.** Try out your air conditioning system right before summer. If it's running badly, your car will guzzle gas. And remember to run it once a month in the winter to preserve the seals.

Saving at the Mechanic's

Modern cars have become so complicated that it would be almost impossible to try to fix everything on your own. Besides, there are plenty of good mechanics out there whose expert work will extend the life of your car and save you money in the long run.

Choosing a Mechanic

One of the most important decisions you will make as a car owner is choosing a mechanic. If you can, avoid using someone who works for the dealership. An independent auto repair shop will do repairs more cheaply. In addition, you won't feel like your mechanic has the dealership's best interest in mind when it comes to large repairs and key decisions.

Shop Around

Just like when you're shopping for a car, the key to finding a good mechanic is to do your homework. Get references from friends and co-workers, and try to use the Internet. Cartalk (www.cartalk.com) has a list of viewer-recommended mechanics called the Mechan-X-Files. The American Auto Association (www.aaa.com) has a list of AAA-approved mechanics. Your local Better Business Bureau also keeps a list of approved mechanics.

Once you've chosen someone in your area, bring your car in for an oil change to check the place out. Look around and find out if it's clean, has modern equipment, offers a decent waiting room and has good customer service. Membership in a professional organization, such as the Automotive Service Association or Better Business Bureau, is always a good sign. And avoid the big chains, which usually rate the lowest in service and satisfaction.

Once You've Made Your Choice

Have your new mechanic give your car a thorough tune-up. Then bring your car in for service according to the factory instructions. Don't follow dealer instructions: They often recommend overly frequent service. But it is important to follow your factory service schedule religiously. Failing to maintain your vehicle to factory standards could cause you to lose your warranty entirely. And then you'll receive no free service or parts, and you won't be able to do anything about it if your car turns out to be a lemon. Also, make sure to keep a thorough record of all repairs.

Estimates

Every time you bring your car to the mechanic, make sure you get a written estimate for repair work. An estimate is a list of the repairs that your mechanic plans to do and an educated guess at how much they will cost. It is illegal for a mechanic to charge any more than the estimate without your OK.

If Your Mechanic Screws Up

If you bring in your car for a repair and the problem isn't fixed, don't immediately go shopping for a new mechanic. Modern cars are complicated to repair, and even the best mechanics will have problems with some jobs. Plus, sometimes a repair isn't done properly because you might not have explained the problem clearly. If you stick with your mechanic after a first mistake, you'll probably get VIP treatment the next time.

If there are still problems after the second repair but the shop is willing to try again, give them one more chance. Otherwise look for a new mechanic and ask for a refund. If the repair shop gives you trouble, take all of your receipts and repair records, and make a complaint with a professional organization of which the mechanic is a member. If you can't get help this way either, file a complaint with the local Better Business Bureau and see a lawyer.

If you see another mechanic for repairs and you still have car trouble, you may have a lemon on your hands.

Protect Yourself From Crooked Mechanics

If you've used the above tips on choosing a mechanic, it's unlikely you'll have problems. But you should always be on your guard.

Preventative Maintenance When you go in for an oil change, be wary of preventative maintenance checks. These are a list of seemingly important tasks that turn out to be nothing more complicated than topping off fluids and checking your tire pressure. But they can turn a $20 oil change into a $100 preventative maintenance check.

Shocks Some shops make easy money off of unnecessary shock absorber replacements. Only replace your shocks if your car sways back and forth, if the

HERE'S HOW

Don't Change It Yourself

Your best bet for an oil change is probably your local quick-lube or service station. Although it costs around $10 to $15 less to change your oil yourself, you need to have your own tools and you also have to dispose of the engine oil. Since it's an environmentally hazardous material, you must take old oil to a service station or municipal hazard waste station. That can be a hassle. Besides, many quick-lubes will check all of your fluids, test your tire pressure, and clean your windows and floor mats while changing your oil. Just be sure that they don't try to charge you for any services you don't want.

Another good way to get a deal on an oil change is to have your mechanic handle it when you're dropping off your car for a tune-up. Since you're paying for a bigger repair, the mechanic will likely throw in the oil change for free.

Keep an eye out for mechanics who add surprise charges to your bill. You shouldn't have to pay for anything you didn't approve ahead of time.

front end dips severely when braking or if you experience a very bouncy ride.

Battery If your battery is slow to charge, don't immediately take a mechanic's advice to replace it. First clean the terminals and replace the cables. If this doesn't correct the problem, go ahead and get a new one.

If you want your car to perform well, make sure you know how to operate it properly: Don't strain a cold engine, make sudden starts and stops, or ride the clutch.

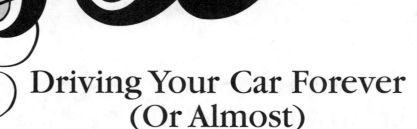

Driving Your Car Forever (Or Almost)

O ne of the best ways to keep your car running longer (and with fewer trips to the repair shop) is to drive it properly. If you follow these tips, you'll put less strain on the engine and other parts, and take less money out of your pocket replacing them.

Warming Up

It may come as a surprise, but not only do cars require very little time to warm up, but letting them warm up for too long puts extra strain on the engine. Idling, or running the car in neutral, for more than 30 seconds is bad for your car. That doesn't mean you should just start your car in the morning and race off, however. Take it easy and drive slowly for the first few miles. Also, never rev the engine during warm up.

Even in the winter, it's not necessary to warm up your car for more than 30 seconds. Just drive cautiously. In cold weather, oil takes longer to reach the cylinders, and hard driving can cause parts to fail, resulting in premature damage to engine bearings. In plain English, this will do some major damage that will cost you

BUYER BEWARE

Don't Be a Victim

Many times, crooked mechanics prey on travelers with out-of-state plates. That's why you should never leave your car unattended at a service station. Some mechanics will steal your gas cap, tamper with your battery or even make it look like your radiator is overheating. Then you end up paying a lot of money for unnecessary services.

big bucks down line. It might even cost you your car. So take it easy and wait about three minutes before turning on the heat or any other power-hungry accessories.

Daily Driving

Avoid quick bursts of acceleration and sudden stops. These strain your engine, shocks, transmission and brakes. Quick acceleration also eats up gas. Also, make sure you don't drive at high speeds for extended periods of time. Besides the fact that speeding is dangerous, cars get their best fuel mileage at 55 miles an hour.

Shift Properly

If you have a manual car, proper shifting can save your transmission and the thousand or so dollars that a replacement costs. Whatever gear you're in, keep the RPM (revolutions per minute) between 2,000 and 3,000. Avoid driving in a low gear at high speeds or in a high gear at low speeds.

Don't Use the Transmission as a Brake Consistently downshifting to slow the car puts a lot of stress on the transmission. And since a worn-out transmission is much more expensive to fix than worn-out brakes, it makes a lot more sense to use the brakes.

Only downshift to slow yourself on long declines. And, if you're making a three-point turn or parking, allow the car to come to a full stop before switching between first and reverse or vice versa.

Don't Ride the Clutch An overused clutch can wear out quickly. When waiting at traffic lights, put the car in neutral. And never use the clutch to hold yourself in place on a hill. That's why you have brakes.

Parking Brakes

Even if you own an automatic car and never park on a hill, you should use your parking brake once in a while. Not only does this keep the cable moving and free from corrosion, but it also works the self adjusters on rear brakes, which helps your drum brakes continue working properly. Remember, if your brakes ever fail, your parking brake is your only back up.

Breaking in a New Car

One of the best ways to get a longer life out of your new car is to break it in properly. For the first 1,000 miles, vary your speed as much as possible and never drive at full throttle. Also change the oil promptly after the first 1,500 miles. This will remove the bits of metal and grit found in every new engine.

Anti-lock Braking Systems

Anti-lock braking systems (ABSs) are superior to traditional brakes. If you use them properly, they'll give you greater control in cornering and on slick surfaces. But they must be used properly. Old braking techniques don't work. Never pump anti-lock brakes. This makes them ineffective. Apply steady pressure and don't let the pedal up. That grinding or pulsing sensation is perfectly normal.

Since many people are used to driving with non-ABS brakes, it's not a bad idea to practice braking in an empty parking lot. If you know how to use your brakes, your car will perform better and be much safer. But don't overestimate them. Anti-lock brakes are not anti-skid brakes.

Dangers of Worn Shocks or Struts

Worn shocks or struts are no bargain. They can lead to decreased braking effectiveness and poorer ride comfort and handling. See your mechanic if you notice that your car:

- Bounces three or more times when crossing an intersection or a dip in the road.
- Rocks back and forth several times when you stop quickly.
- Tends to drift left or right when you apply the brakes firmly at higher speeds.
- Rocks or sways from side to side when changing lanes quickly.
- Leans and sways on a tight curve, such as a freeway ramp.

If You Have a Car Accident...

- Do not rush to have your car towed. If it can stay at the scene for a few hours, use the time to calm down and investigate options for repairs.
- If it must be towed, have it taken to a repair shop—but do not authorize repairs immediately. Call your insurer for its shop recommendations.
- Once the car is repaired, have the insurer send the check for the repairs to you—not directly to the shop—so you can be sure the work is satisfactory. Or have the insurer send an adjuster to inspect the car before a check is issued.

Young Vintage Cars for Fun and Profit

To buy a popular car from the 1950s, 1960s or 1970s that is in good condition, you would have to pay $10,000 or more today. A much better deal is a less well-known model from the same period that hasn't yet fully appreciated. Here are several under-appreciated vintage cars that are likely to grow in value over the next ten years:

Plymouth Barracuda The Barracuda was introduced in 1964—about the same time as the more famous Mustang—and pioneered the idea of putting a sporty, yet affordable, four-seat body on a compact-car chassis. A spectacular car stylistically, with a big, swoopy, wraparound back window, a 1964–1965 V8 Barracuda in good condition now sells for around $5,000.

1957 Fords The 1957 Chevrolets are in hot demand today, yet their body designs were already three years old when they rolled out. By contrast, Fords from the same year were brand-new—from chassis and power train to styling. Today they're a great buy at less than $5,000—a lot less than 1957 Chevys, which go for around $20,000. Buy the sportiest V8 you can afford.

Ford Falcon Sprint If you don't want to pay the high price of a Mustang but want essentially the same car, a 1963 or 1964 Falcon Sprint is ideal. Mechanically, it's a Mustang with a 260-cubic-inch V8 engine—since the Mustang was simply a rebodied Falcon. A V8 in good condition sells for around $5,000.

American Motors AMX The highest-performance car American Motors ever sold, these 1968–1971 models were taut, little fastback coupes with long noses, short rear decks and big backlights. Compared to a Mustang or Camaro of that era, an AMX costs substantially less—from $2,000 to $7,000, depending on its condition.

Cadillac Sevilles The first generation of the Seville—1976 to 1978—was the first of the hard-edge Cadillacs. And the Seville's sharply creased style has held up well. Sevilles have the good old GM 350-cubic-inch V8 engine, and the interiors are luxurious. The body is handsome, and the car goes down the road nicely. It's everything a Cadillac should be. Models in good condition sell for around $8,000.

Cutting Your Personal Finance Costs

Here's how to make the most of your money by cutting down debt, banking for less, investing wisely, maximizing your retirement accounts and lowering your taxes.

Down with Debt

Almost everyone carries some debt at some point in their lives. Whether it's a mortgage you're paying off, a car loan, or a credit card balance left over from the holidays, the way you manage your debt can affect more than your pocketbook. If you have a good credit rating, it can help you get the right job, the right apartment and the right interest rates on your credit cards, loans and mortgages. Here are some tips to help you keep your debt in check:

- Keep track of every penny you spend during the next month. Categorize your spending into the narrowest categories possible: movies, dinners out and concerts instead of a broad category like entertainment. Once you see where the money is going, it is easier to budget a realistic spending amount for the future—and to identify areas where you would be comfortable cutting back.

Sticking to Your Budget

There are some terrific free resources to help you put together a personal finance plan that works.

The **Federal Reserve System** publishes free newsletters on a host of topics relating to money and monetary instruments, banking, investments, international economics and consumer protection. To receive your free copies, contact the Board of Governors of the Federal Reserve System, Publications Service, MS-127, Federal Reserve Board, Washington, D.C. 20551, 202-452-3254. Find consumer information on money topics at www.consumer.gov.

The **Finance Center** (www.financenter.com), a financial website, features dozens of articles and free useful tools, including calculators, which will help you calculate everything from a basic monthly budget to how long it will take you to become a millionaire. Get answers to this and hundreds of other financial questions—for free!

- Cancel overdraft protection for your checking account—it makes it too easy to write checks for more money than you have.
- To get out of credit card debt quickly, pay at least double the minimum payment every month.
- Plan in advance to purchase cars or durable goods with cash. Make a plan for everything your family wants to buy—and prioritize.

Financial Planning—For Free

Planning a realistic budget (one that takes into account your day-to-day priorities, yet enables you to meet your long-term financial goals) is the single most important thing you can do to ensure your financial well-being. If you're having a problem putting together—or sticking to—a budget, or you're trying to make sense of your financial options, free advice may be available. Many County Cooperative Extension offices offer free pamphlets and even free classes to help you make the right decisions.

To find out what kind of help is available in your area, look in your local blue pages for the nearest County Cooperative Extension office, or contact the national office: Cooperative State Research Education and Extension Service, U.S. Department of Agriculture, 800 9th St. S.W., Washington, D.C. 20024, 202-720-3029.

The Bottom Line On Banks

All banks were not created equal. Big commercial banks offer more financial services, but at the price of steep fees and often poor customer care. And new fees at large banks are rising, often outpacing inflation.

While local banks and credit unions usually offer better rates and a more service-oriented environment, the trade-off can be convenience. Smaller banks keep shorter business hours and offer fewer services, sometimes even limiting access to your cash.

The bank and type of account you choose can save you—or cost you—hundreds of dollars a year, so it pays to choose wisely. Also make sure you understand the terms of your account, since many accounts have minimum balance requirements. If your balance dips below the monthly minimum, you may be fined.

Good News about Credit Unions

There are 12,000 credit unions in the nation catering to over 67 million consumers. While most credit unions provide services for the middle class, many are now also targeting moderate and low-income neighborhoods where commercial banks are scarce or their overpriced services are unaffordable for low-income consumers. Not only can you feel good about banking with a credit union, but, because they are not-for-profit, credit unions return surplus funds to their customers in the form of lower rates.

Size Matters Credit unions aren't always a bargain. The smaller organizations are often too small to offer competitive rates. The best deals can be found at the larger credit unions.

Give and Take While credit unions have fewer branch offices and many do not yet have ATMs, these inconveniences are offset by lower and fewer fees and a commitment to customer service.

Keeping Prices Down Credit unions offer comparative bargains on car loans, credit cards and mortgages. Their ATM fees (when they have them) are usually lower and the basic requirements for qualifying for a loan are also generally more relaxed. One thing to watch out for: Most—but not all—credit unions are insured by the FDIC. Make sure yours is.

Call the Credit Union National Association at 800-358-5710 to find out about credit unions in your area.

Checking Accounts:
Getting More and Paying Less

Free checking accounts are becoming harder and harder to find. Banks know that they provide necessary services and most are going to make you pay for them—and pay well. According to the Federal Reserve Board, less than one-tenth of all commercial banks offer free checking. And even if you can find a free checking account, many banks will find ways of slipping in hidden charges, making your account less free than you think. There are ways, however, to beat the banks and lower your checking costs:

- If you're 50 or older, you might be eligible for a low-fee or free checking account for senior citizens.
- Having your canceled checks returned costs the bank—and you—money. If you waive this privilege, you might save on fees.
- Ask your employer if you can have your paycheck deposited directly into your account. You save time, hassle, and you might also save money, since the bank may pass the savings in processing costs on to you in the form of lower fees.

HERE'S HOW

Consumer Credit Counseling Service

Having trouble managing your debts? Confidential counseling is available to you from a trained budget-management counselor, for free or at minimal cost, depending on your financial situation. Under this plan, most creditors will work with you and your counselor to make realistic repayment arrangements. This not-for-profit program is supported mainly with donations. Call the **National Foundation for Consumer Credit** (800-388-2227; www.nfcc.org), at any time, for the office nearest you.

Sneaky Fees

Watch out for these hidden fees on your monthly bank statement:

- Teller fees imposed when you do your banking in person.
- Fees for making deposits without a pre-printed deposit slip.
  - Fees for having your checks returned.
  - Monthly maintenance fees.

HERE'S HOW

Find the Best Bank For You

Nothing beats old-fashioned legwork to help you find the best bank for your needs. Don't be afraid to ask questions. Although banks provide an essential service, banking is a business, and the branch manager may not necessarily have your interests at heart. Don't be lured by special offers that promise perks you'll never take advantage of (like reduced mortgage rates or other negligible savings on loans) in exchange for low or non-existent interest rates.

- The **Federal Deposit Insurance Corporation** (800-934-FDIC) addresses questions and complaints concerning FDIC-regulated institutions. They also publish a free quarterly newsletter.

- **The Bank Rate Monitor** (800-327-7717, www.bankrate.com) has a handy website listing the best deals in 70 cities for mortgages, auto loans, consumer loans, credit lines, credit cards, CDs and money-market accounts. They also publish a newsletter (but it's rather pricey).

- *Your Bank Is Ripping You Off* by Edward Mrkvicka (St. Martin's Press, $12.95) will alert you to some of the underhanded practices your bank may be up to.

- Some banks offer package accounts, allowing you to combine several accounts such as CDs, savings, checking and even your mortgage balance to qualify for free checking and reduced fees on loans and credit cards.

ATM Traps

- Nearly half of all banks now charge you for using ATM machines that are not owned by your bank—often as much as $2 per transaction. If you use ATMs frequently, such charges can quickly erode your balance.
- Reduce electronic banking fees by choosing a bank that doesn't charge for using its ATM (there are still a few out there!) or allows you a reasonable number of free ATM withdrawals per month.
- Avoid ATMs belonging to other banks.
- Withdraw larger amounts that will last you longer.
- Consider banking the old fashioned way—by visiting a teller during bank business hours. Not only will you avoid the hidden costs of electronic banking, but your bank staff will get to know you personally—an important advantage when it comes time to apply for a loan or settle a charge dispute on your monthly statement. But watch out for sneaky teller fees! Some banks now charge you for talking to a teller.

Beware of ATM fees.

Many banks now charge you at least $1 for using ATM machines that are not owned by your bank. These charges can rapidly diminish your account balance.

CDs: High Interest, Low Risk

Certificates of Deposit (CDs) offer security, flexibility and a pretty good yield—if you know where to look. Smaller banks that are aggressively seeking cash to make loans or investments offer the most competitive rates. These can vary considerably from bank to bank—by as much as 2%, depending on the term of the CD. Smart investors shop via phone, mail and the Internet to get the best rates. Use CDs as places to park emergency savings and rainy-day funds rather than as long-term investments. Any CD purchased from an FDIC-affiliated institution is insured for up to $100,000.

To find the CD with the best yield, consult the business pages of your nearest big-city newspaper or your favorite personal finance magazine. *The Wall Street Journal* and the business pages of the Sunday *New York Times* list the best rates across the country.

The ultimate resource for finding the best rates, however, is the Internet. Hundreds of banks offer CDs and money market accounts online—often at rates one percentage point or more above what banks offer at branch offices. Get daily updates from the Bank Rate Monitor's Internet Banking Deals website (www.bankrate.com) or at BanxQuote (www.banxquote.com).

Other Banking Alternatives

Asset Management Accounts Some discount brokerage houses are now offering asset-management accounts: investment accounts that offer the flexibility of a checking account without the hidden expenses. TD Waterhouse (800-934-4448) offers a no-fee Investor Money Management account, with no check minimums and free ATM withdrawals. Although the account requires a $1,000 minimum balance, the money is invested in securities rather than sitting in a low- or no-interest checking account.

Internet Banking If you're already online, you might consider switching to an Internet bank. Although you won't get personal service, you also won't be saddled with teller fees. Several virtual banks are offering no-fee checking accounts with unlimited ATM use and free electronic bill payment. Bank Rate Monitor at www.bankrate.com will alert you to many of the latest online banking deals.

Guaranteed Checks for A Lot Less Money

Postal money orders are a versatile and inexpensive alternative to bank checks, certified checks, and even wire transfers and moneygrams. U.S. postal money orders cost only 85¢ plus the face value of the check up to $700 per money order—making them the cheapest guaranteed check available. At any one time, you can purchase money orders worth up to $3,500.

International money orders are similar bargains, with rates ranging from $3 to $7.50, depending on the country of issue. They can be converted to cash immediately and are fully refundable if lost or stolen, provided you hang on to your receipt.

INSIDE INFORMATION

Free Credit Reports—For Some of Us

Although most credit bureaus won't advertise it, by law they must furnish at least one free credit report annually to residents of Colorado, Georgia, Maryland, Massachusetts, New Jersey and Vermont if requested. Elsewhere, you are entitled to a free copy if you are unemployed, on public assistance, or if you think your credit file contains inaccurate information about you because of fraud. You can also request a free copy if you were denied credit, employment, insurance or housing.

Begin by calling each bureau to request your report—after you've been notified of a credit rejection. Here are the phone numbers of the three national credit bureaus.

- **Equifax** (800-685-1111)
- **Experian** (888-397-3742)
- **Trans Union** (800-888-4213)

BUYER BEWARE

Courtesy Checks

Does your monthly statement arrive with free courtesy checks along with a reminder encouraging you to use them to consolidate your debt, make purchases, or even pay your taxes? Before you start using them, make sure you understand the hidden costs sometimes associated with these checks. Often they are treated as cash advances by your credit card company and carry very high finance charges.

Exchanging Your Travelers Checks

Overseas, banks usually offer better exchange rates on cash than on travelers checks, although they sometimes charge a steep transaction fee. It's best to change as large an amount of money as you're comfortable carrying around if the rates are good but there is a flat fee involved. Legitimate exchange offices will always post two sets of exchange figures in their windows: a buy rate and a sell rate.

When shopping for rates, never ever exchange travelers checks where the rates aren't posted or only the buy rates are posted. You'll invariably get a terrible rate. If the buy and sell rates are very different, it means they're buying low and selling high—and you're getting ripped off either way.

Pay Your Bills Online

If you have a home computer and a modem, you may want to see if your credit card and utility companies offer online payment services. Many companies offer discounts or savings plans to customers who pay online because it saves them the cost of mailing paperwork. **AT&T** (800-222-0300, www.att.com) and **MCI** (800-950-5555, www.mci.com) are among the companies offering substantial discounts to customers who pay online. Other companies have services in the offing.

On Your Next Vacation

You can save a lot by figuring out the best way to carry money on your next trip abroad.

Abroad with Your ATM Card It doesn't make sense to depend exclusively on travelers checks, with their high fees and poor exchange rates, now that the major ATM networks, Cirrus and Plus, have gone international. If you belong to a major ATM network, you can use your bankcard out-of-state—even overseas—just as you would at your neighborhood bank. When using an ATM, you get the bank's higher exchange rate rather than the usually poor retail rate offered to travelers check holders. Most banks charge a nominal fee for each transaction. Ask before you use your card.

All this doesn't mean, however, that you should dispense with travelers checks or cash on your travels altogether. ATM connections can be unreliable, especially in less developed countries. You could wind up in a small town or city and find that your card is not accepted anywhere. Before going on a trip, find out what countries are connected to your ATM network. If you will be traveling widely, it can be useful to take along two ATM cards—one for each major ATM network.

Don't Leave Home without Them Always take along some travelers checks for security. All major brands are more or less equal and will be accepted in most destinations. Whichever brand you pick, don't pay a fee for your checks, which can add up to 1% to 1.5% of the total amount. Free checks are available through the American Automobile Association (AAA), and many savings and loans. Shop around a little, and you will have no difficulty obtaining free checks.

To Charge or Not to Charge

Low-rate no-fee platinum cards, secured cards, affinity cards, rebate cards, Web cards, golfing cards, gas cards, rock 'n roll cards, video rental cards… With literally thousands of credit cards to choose from you can find a card that is tailor-made to fit your lifestyle and spending habits.

Because of intense competition, credit card issuers are trying to lure you with the flashiest and most irresistible introductory teaser APRs, consumer perks and rebates. There are some tremendous deals to be found out there, but don't be had in the process. Credit cards can be a terrific convenience—if you use them responsibly and pay attention to the fine print in your card agreement.

Cheaper Alternatives to Bank Loans

Why owe money to a bank when you can borrow from yourself? You might end up paying a lot less interest. Here are some close-to-home sources for quick cash.

Your IRA

If you only need the money for a short time, consider borrowing from your IRA. There is a 60-day grace period during which you can roll your IRA funds from trustee to trustee. What you do with the money in the interim is your business. Of course, if you are even a day late paying it back, you'll be slapped with a penalty on the total withdrawal plus a 10% penalty if you're under age 59½.

Your Whole Life Insurance Policy

You can usually borrow the equivalent of the cash value of your whole life insurance policy, and the rates are competitive. Remember, of course, that whatever is taken out and not paid back will leave less for your heirs.

Your 401(k)

By law you are allowed to borrow up to 50% of your invested account, up to $50,000. Rates are competitive—often the prime rate plus 1%. And you have up to five years to pay the money back with regular payroll deductions.

Your Brokerage Account

Interest rates when you borrow against your investments are usually lower than the rate your bank would offer.

Banking Cost Cutters

- Analyze your statement to make sure that your bank isn't nibbling away at your balance with sneaky fees and penalties. If you feel that your bank has not been straightforward about charges that are levied on your account, don't hesitate to complain to the manager. If the dispute isn't settled to your satisfaction, contact your **State Banking Commissioner** to help you resolve the problem.

- Pay bills right after a deposit has cleared to reduce the chance of bouncing a check.

- Keep only the minimum required for low fees in your checking account. Put other savings in a higher-interest money market fund or invest them in a short-term CD. Letting your savings languish in low- or no-interest accounts can cost you literally hundreds of dollars a year.

INSIDE INFORMATION

Pay Off Your Credit Card Debt

Don't be fooled by the illusion of security if you have some savings in the bank but almost as much credit card debt. The 15% to 20% you're paying in interest on your card purchases far outweighs the scanty earnings on your savings or money market account. Get ahead now by using your savings to pay off those high-interest credit card bills.

BARGAIN FINDER

The Check's in The Mail

Big commercial banks are currently charging about $15 for 200 basic single checks and up to $32 for designer versions. To save half—even two-thirds—on these steep prices, you are entitled by law to order your checks from a third-party supplier.

Here are some companies offering the best deals in mail-order checks, with prices as low as $4.95 for 200 basic single checks to $9.99 for special editions. And there are often even better deals for first-time customers. Order ahead: Mail-order suppliers have a two- to three-week processing period from the time they receive your order until you receive your new checks.

- **Checks in the Mail** (800-733-4443)
- **Checkstore** (800-424-3257)
- **Current** (800-533-3973)
- **Image Checks** (800-562-8768)

Choose a credit card with terms that best suit your budget.

But they can be damaging to your budget if you forget that carrying a balance is the same as borrowing money—at an unusually high rate of interest.

Different Cards for Different Customers

Shop around for the credit card terms that best suit your budget and repayment style. For instance, if you routinely pay your bills in full each month, focus on the amount of the annual fee and other charges.

If you will be paying your credit card debt off slowly, however, shop for a low APR and consider how your issuer calculates finance charges. In either case, your costs will be affected by whether or not the company offers a grace period.

Here are some key issues to consider:

- Annual Percentage Rate (APR)
- Annual fee
- Grace period
- Cash advance fees
- Late payment charges
- Over-the-limit fees

Elite Cards New elite cards, such as the Visa Signature card and the WorldMasterCard, are giving American Express a run for its money. These cards, aimed at the roughly 3% of American households with annual incomes above $100,000, offer enticing perks, such as guaranteed airport parking, air miles reward programs that can be applied to all airlines, special services at luxury hotels, and VIP access to symphony orchestras and sporting events.

While not quite as comprehensive as the advantages offered to American Express Platinum card holders, Visa and MasterCard issues are also considerably less expensive—with annual fees as much as 80% lower than American Express, depending on the issuer. Visa Signature cards and WorldMasterCards also have no preset spending limits and sometimes low APRs. Terms and fees vary from issuer to issuer.

Rebate Cards A lot of credit card issuers are scaling down or eliminating costly rebate programs. Still, there are some excellent programs out there that provide a way to accumulate air miles or give you a rebate on your next car purchase. But beware of the high APRs more and more frequently associated with rebate cards. These cards can be a great value only if you pay your balance off promptly. A large balance carried month-to-month can easily cancel out any benefits of the rebate.

Mall VIP Visa Offered at more than 400 malls across the nation, the latest incarnation of the rebate card offers cardholders a 2% rebate on card purchases at participating mall outlets such as J.C. Penney and Sears, and a 1% rebate everywhere else. The rebate comes as a coupon redeemable at any of the malls' shops. No annual fee and an introductory interest rate of 6.9% make this card an especially attractive offer for shoppers.

Ask at your local mall about this or similar offers, or call 888-625-5847.

Debt Consolidation If you have a lot of credit card debt spread over different cards, consider consolidating it on one low-rate card. Card issuers supply courtesy- or convenience-checks, or balance transfer forms to pay off your other cards (although sometimes with hefty transfer fees). Make sure that the low interest rate on your new card lasts long enough to pay off your debt. Switching your debt from card to card looks bad on your credit rating.

Plastic Not-so-fantastic

Hard to believe, perhaps, but many card issuers are actually looking for ways to trip you up. Interest rates are swelling and grace periods shrinking. Make one or two late payments and you might be socked with a higher interest rate, not to mention a late charge of $25 or more. Some issuers are levying penalties if a payment is even a day or two late. Also, annual fees associated with cards have started to jump, reaching as high as $35 in some cases.

Even if you pay off your balance within the grace period, banks will sometimes find ways to sneak in extra charges. If you pay your balance off like clockwork, look out for clauses concerning "inactivity" or "account closing fees" in your cardholder agreement. If you keep a zero balance and have a history of good credit, your card issuer may even find ways of penalizing you for your good behavior. Remember, card issuers like customers who keep high balances on their credit cards. This is how they make money. Indeed they may even deny you rewards, cancel your account or deny your application if your credit rating is too high.

Whatever you do, don't forget to read the fine print on credit card applications, cardholder agreements and correspondence from your credit card company. Big traps lie hidden in tiny type.

FOR YOUR INFORMATION

Finding the Right Credit Card

There are some terrific resources for finding the best credit card for your needs. Among the most recent bargains are **NextCard's** 2.9% introductory APR (888-422-6596), and the **GM Card's** 5% earnings on every purchase (800-8GM-CARD).

CardTrak Newsletter If you're not yet among the Web-savvy, **CardTrak**, the country's only consumer credit card newsletter, gives you the latest news on the best credit card deals across the country. The newsletter (updated monthly) costs $5 per issue. Call 800-344-7714, or send $5 to CardTrak, P.O. Box 1700, Frederick, MD 21702.

Federal Reserve System Reports The **Federal Reserve System** (202-452-3254) publishes a bi-annual report on the terms and conditions that apply on credit card plans offered by financial institutions. Consumers are advised to contact the credit card issuer for current rates and to find out about the latest offers.

Virginia Morris on How to Make Smart Financial Decisions and Get The Most out of Your Money

Virginia B. Morris, PhD is the author of several books on money management, and the editor of the *Wall Street Journal Guide to Understanding Personal Finance.*

How do you start making smart financial decisions?

Analyze the way you use money. One way to be smart is to reduce the amount you're paying to banks and credit card companies.

Add up what you're paying your bank for using your own money, and then shop for a bank with lower fees on the services you use. For example, if you use the ATM, look for a bank that doesn't impose a charge for withdrawals. If you write only a few checks each month, look for a basic account. Compare the costs of small local banks to better known large ones that have branches in your community. Find out whether there's a way to get a better deal by consolidating your banking business in one place.

Figure out what using your credit cards is costing you. If you're paying an annual fee, look for a card that doesn't charge one. Compare the interest rates various cards charge, especially if you occasionally have to spread out your payments. Find out what it costs to take a cash advance instead of using an ATM that debits your checking account.

Does having a budget matter?

If you're always out of cash at the end of the month, you have to make changes in the way you're spending. The first step is to know how much is coming in and where it's going. Not everybody has the personality to track every penny. But you do have to have a clear sense of what your fixed costs are and how much you can spend on discretionary items. Creating a budget can help you discipline—and reward—yourself. It can also keep you from slipping into debt.

What are the five biggest financial mistakes people make?

- Not paying your credit card bills in full every month, which means you pay huge amounts of interest.
- Not putting as much as you can into a 401(k), IRA or other retirement plan.
- Withholding too much for income tax, thinking that the money you get back is a gift. It's your money that's been sitting in Uncle Sam's account.
- Sticking with an investment that's producing a poor return just because you're not sure what else to do with your money.
- Letting yourself be persuaded that you can make lots of money risk-free.

What are the five smartest investment decisions that you can make?

- Create a long-term investment plan and stick to it.
- Invest at least 10% of your gross income every year.
- Do your own research before you pay for investment advice.
- Be sure that you thoroughly understand an investment before you put money into it.
- Make sure you don't put all of your eggs into one basket.

Do you have any insider tips for cutting the costs of managing your money?

Financial services are products, the same way clothes or cars are. To get the best deals you have to know what you're looking for. The key to making your money work hardest for you is becoming an educated consumer.

Cut Insurance Costs

Many people don't realize that there's a lot more flexibility in the cost of insurance premiums than your insurance broker may tell you.

Lowering the Cost of Car Insurance

If any of the following apply to you or your car, you may be eligible for a reduction in your premium rates:

- You're a non-smoker.
- You're a non-drinker.
- Your car has airbags, anti-lock breaks or anti-theft devices.
- You've recently taken a driver's education course.
- You drive fewer than 5,000 to 7,000 miles per year.
- You get good grades in high school or college (for young drivers).
- You pay in one annual lump sum (save up to 17% in finance charges).
- You insure more than one car through the same company.

Lowering the Cost of Homeowners Insurance

Here are some ways to get a break on your homeowners insurance that are often overlooked:

- Increase your deductible. By raising your deductible you might be able to save as much as 25% on premiums.
- Take more than one policy out with the same company. For instance, use the same company for your auto or liability insurance as you do for your homeowners policy.
- Buy a new home. Newer homes are generally in better structural condition than old fixer-uppers, so you may get lower premium rates.
- Improve the security of your home with new smoke detectors, alarms and similar devices.
- Be a loyal customer. Some insurers reward customer loyalty with lower rates if you've had a policy with them before.
- Don't smoke. There is a higher incidence of fire in the homes of smokers. Non-smoking families may be able to get lower rates.
- Ask about senior discounts. If you're over 60, the company may offer you a better deal.

BARGAIN FINDER

Group Coverage

Before purchasing an individual policy, see if any clubs, fraternities, alumni groups, or professional associations you belong to offer group insurance plans. Group plans are usually considerably less expensive than individual plans.

FOR YOUR INFORMATION

Choosing and Using a Policy

- If you have complaints, concerns or queries about your insurance policy, call the **National Insurance Consumer Hotline** at 800-942-4242.
- *Best Insurance Reports*, the publication of **A.M. Best Company**, a leading financial rating organization, ranks many insurance products and is a terrific source for consumers. It is available at most public libraries and at the company's website, www.ambest.com.

Tax Refunds

If you'll be getting a large tax refund on your tax return, don't feel too good about it—you just made an interest-free loan to the **IRS**. By filing a new W-4 to eliminate excess wage withholding, you may be able to keep more of each paycheck from the start of the year.

Ways to Save at Tax Time

Tax legislation in recent years has brought with it a dizzying 1000+ changes to the tax code. Some of these changes may save you a good deal of money.

Making the Most of the Tax Law Changes

While the reforms are advantageous to most taxpayers, making sense out of them can be a confusing and time-consuming process. Here are some of the big changes that could benefit you.

Estate Taxes The law makes it possible to leave more money to your heirs tax-free. The amount increased from $600,000 in 1997 to $675,000 in 2000. This figure will increase incrementally to $1 million in 2006. The breaks are even better for heirs of family businesses.

Tax Breaks for Investors The top tax paid on capital gains on stocks, bonds and mutual funds has been reduced from 28% to 20% for investors in the 28% or higher tax bracket. For investors in the 15% tax bracket, taxes have been reduced to 10% on long-term gains.

Things get even better in 2001, when assets held for more than five years are taxed at 18% or 8%, depending on your tax bracket.

Child Tax Credit You can claim a $500 yearly tax credit for each child under 17 years of age. The credit is phased out if your adjusted gross income is higher than $110,000 on a joint return or more than $75,000 on an individual return.

Tax-free Profit on Home Sales You are eligible for $250,000 of tax-free profit on the sale of your home if you file an individual return, and $500,000 if you file jointly. To qualify for the break, you must own and live in the house for two of the five years prior to the sale. This tax break can be used again and again, although only once in any two-year period.

Tax-deductible Gifts Make the most of the federal gift-tax exclusion, which is indexed for inflation starting after 1998 (but has not yet been adjusted). You can give tax-free gifts of up to $10,000 per person per year. These gifts aren't taxable to the person who receives them, either.

The Roth IRA Just because the Roth IRA doesn't offer tax deductions for deposits doesn't mean it's not a bargain. These back-loaded IRAs, which let you take tax-free withdrawals after age 59½, are ideal for higher-income taxpayers who aren't eligible for deductible IRAs.

There are other perks to the Roth IRA. You're still allowed to contribute to one even if you're covered by a retirement plan at work or by a Keogh plan if you're self-employed. And there's no mandatory withdrawal age: Tax-free inheritance can compound for your beneficiaries.

Roth eligibility begins to be phased out at incomes of $150,000 on joint returns and $95,000 on individual returns. The income cutoffs are $160,000 and $110,000 respectively.

Home Office Deductions You can deduct expenses for a home office that you use exclusively and regularly to perform administrative and managerial duties, even if it isn't your primary work place.

Tax-wise Investing

Smart investing isn't only about getting the best return with the least risk, but also about protecting your assets at tax time. Here are a few simple steps you can take to keep more of your money compounding:

- Maximize your retirement account contributions to 401(k)s, 403(b)s and IRAs that allow you to deduct your contribution as well as benefit from tax-deferred compounding on your investment returns.
- Contribute to a non-deductible IRA or Roth IRA if you've maxed out on your 401(k) contributions.
- Consider other investments offering tax-deferred compounding, such as cash-value insurance policies, annuities and Series EE and I savings bonds.
- Favor appreciating assets, such as growth stocks and growth mutual funds that let you make the most of the 20% maximum capital gains tax rate.
- Choose tax-exempt income investments. Municipal bonds issued in your state are exempt from local and state as well as federal taxes. U.S. Treasury bills are free from local and state taxes.

Shrewder Contributions

Make sure your charitable dollars work harder for your favorite cause—and you.

It can be difficult to keep track of small charitable donations made haphazardly throughout the year. Better to plan at the beginning of the year what you're able to give and allot it to just a few of your favorite organizations.

BUYER BEWARE

Giver Beware

Before giving to a charity, find out what percentage of income is spent on programs vs. fund-raising and administration. In most cases, fund-raising and advertising should not exceed 35% of contributions. This figure depends, however, on the type of organization and how long they have been soliciting. For instance, a younger organization will have higher overhead.

As an added precaution, make your check out directly to the charity, and not to the fund-raiser.

TRY SOMETHING DIFFERENT

First-Time Home Buyers

While the tax law lets you withdraw $10,000 penalty-free from your deductible **IRA** to purchase a first home for yourself or your family, that money is still taxable in your highest bracket. If you take the $10,000 from a **Roth IRA** instead, the full withdrawal will be tax-free as long as your account has been open for at least five years.

FOR YOUR INFORMATION

Charity Watchdogs

Before parting with your money, check out your chosen charity with one of the following organizations, which keep an eye on the activities of fund-raising and non-profit groups:

- **The National Charities Information Bureau** (212-929-6300). Visit their website at www.give.org or write to the NCIB, 19 Union Square W., New York, NY 10003 for a free copy of their **Wise Giving Guide**.
- **Philanthropic Advisory Service** rates several hundred charitable organizations. For a free copy of their newsletter **Give but Give Wisely**. Send a self-addressed stamped envelope to PAS, 4200 Wilson Blvd., Suite 800, Arlington, VA 22203.
- **GuideStar** database covers 600,000 organizations recognized as charitable by the IRS at www.guidestar.org.
- **The Internet Nonprofit Center's Nonprofit Locator** at www.nonprofits.org.

Not only will you have a better idea of what you can deduct come tax time, but small donations of $10 or so are often not cost-effective for non-profit organizations to process. Giving larger gifts to fewer organizations will ensure that more of your dollars are working for the causes you care about, and fewer are paying for administrative overhead. If you can't afford to give much, consider pooling it with donations from friends, relatives or co-workers.

Tips for Charitable Givers

- Check to see if your employer offers contribution-matching as part of its benefits package.
- Check the tax status of the organization you're considering giving to. Contributions to tax-exempt groups aren't necessarily tax-deductible. Ask if a charity is designated by the IRS as a 501(c)(3) organization.
- Hang on to receipts for expenses that you have incurred doing charitable work. For example, you may be able to deduct taxi fares, driving costs (including tolls and parking), uniforms, transportation and lodging costs if you travel for charity.
- Protect your charitable deduction by obtaining an acknowledgment letter for any single gift of $250 or more.

Benefit Your Favorite Charities—And Yourself Come Tax Time

- Donate stocks instead of cash. Appreciated securities that you have held for longer than a year are deductible at their current market value. Thus, if you purchased shares of stock for $1,500 five years ago and they are now worth twice that price, you are

Give the Stock vs. Sell the Stock and Give the Cash

Assume you want to donate shares of stock that you bought at $10,000, and are currently worth $40,000.

STOCK	CASH
• Take tax deductions based on current value ($40,000).	• Pay long-term capital gains tax on profit.
• Owe no capital gains tax.	$30,000 x .20 ‾‾‾‾‾‾‾‾ $ 6,000 Tax
• Charity gets full value of your donation.	• Deduct only $34,000 gift.
	• Charity gets only $34,000 instead of $40,000.

entitled to a tax deduction of $3,000, free of capital gains tax, if you make a charitable gift of them.

- Donate your used goods. If you donate used clothing, furniture, appliances, vehicles or other items, you can deduct their fair market value.
- Donate your old car. If you're in the market for a new car, consider donating your old one to your favorite charity, or selling it yourself and donating the proceeds. You can value it for a tax deduction using the *National Automobile Dealer's Association Blue Book*, available in your community library. The Heritage for the Blind (800-2-DONATE) accepts boats, trucks, RVs and more—running or not—and will pay for immediate towing.

DID YOU KNOW

Tax Credits for Older Americans

If you are 65 or older, or under age 65 and retired on permanent or total disability, you might be eligible for up to $1,125 in credit on your tax return. For a copy of the *Older Americans' Tax Guide*, call the **IRS Forms Line** at 800-829-3676 or download it from the IRS's surprisingly snazzy website at www.irs.gov.

Cut Your Investment Costs

Your success as an investor is more important to you than to anyone else. Nobody knows more—or cares more—about your long-term financial needs than you do. Much of the overhead associated with investing comes from paying someone else to make financial decisions for you—someone who may be more interested in selling you products than making you money. Why pay someone to do what you can do yourself? Not only do the following strategies save you money, but they put you in charge of your own financial future.

Golden Rules for Smart Investors

No matter what the market is doing, there a few simple steps you can take to protect your nest egg.

- You're already ahead of the game if you keep your investment costs as low as possible. The better informed you are, the less money you'll have to pay out to investment professionals.
- Choose your investments for the long-term. Market timing is a dangerous game, especially for the amateur investor. Studies consistently show that the people who make money in the market are people who invest for the long haul. Don't be alarmed by short-term market fluctuations.
- Protect your investments from heavy taxation. That means keeping trading to an absolute minimum, whether you're investing independently or with a mutual fund. Choose mutual funds with low portfolio turnovers. And invest for growth, not income.
- Diversifying your portfolio will give you peace of mind. Diversify your investments between stocks and bonds, and between domestic and foreign funds.

HERE'S HOW

Bypassing Broker Commissions

Here are some ways to invest without opening a brokerage account:

- Take part in your company's stock-purchasing plan. Many companies offer their stock to employees at a discount.
- Buy **Dividend Reinvestment Plans (DRIPs)**, which automatically reinvest dividends from stock you already own, so you only need to pay a commission to buy your initial shares.
- Purchase mutual fund shares directly through the company or through a mutual fund network.

The World's Best Financial Websites

Not all financial websites are created equal. Here are some of the best:

- **BigCharts** (www.bigcharts.com). A favorite among serious online traders, this sophisticated, state-of-the-art site will keep you abreast of trends at five-minute intervals. You can graph and compare performance histories of your favorite stocks. BigCharts also posts a daily list of the momentum stocks trading on the **NYSE**, **Amex**, and **Nasdaq**.

- **The Financial Center** (www.tfc.com), lets you get investment advice from the experts.

- **FreeEDGAR** (www.freeedgar.com). Read SEC filings such as annual and quarterly reports.

- **Wall Street Journal Interactive** (www.wsj.com) costs only $29 a year if you already subscribe to any of its publications, such as **The Wall Street Journal** or **Barron's**, and $59 if you don't. It's a great bargain either way for what is considered the best financial site on the Internet.
  WSJ Interactive includes the **Personal Journal** feature that gives you personalized, minute-to-minute information on individual investments and chosen topics.

- **Yahoo! Finance** (quote.yahoo.com). Free, fast, and no-nonsense: This is a favorite of the experts.

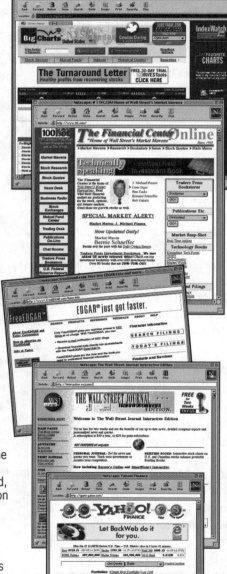

The Virtues of Virtual

Why pay exorbitant brokers' fees when online financial sites provide all the facts (for free) necessary to make informed investment decisions? At last count there were over 250 investment-oriented sites online, and this number is quickly growing. The services and information offered vary from site to site, providing everything from real-time stock quotes and SEC filings such as annual and quarterly reports, to state-of-the-art graphing tools that let you compare the past and present performance—and the future outlook—of your favorite companies.

These sites are giving professional brokers and investment counselors a serious run for their money and offer comprehensive company information. But just because you have Web access doesn't necessarily mean it's time to send your broker packing. The array of information on the Web can be dizzying to the newcomer, and it's important to learn how to evaluate the quality of your sources and information before sinking all your retirement savings into an e-mail stock tip. Start out by choosing a few high-quality sites that offer a diversity of services.

Don't Go Broke with Your Broker

Brokerage houses come in three flavors—full-service, discount and deep-discount. Full-service brokers help clients set investment goals and give advice—in exchange for a 3% commission or more on every purchase or sale.

Many discount brokers are now offering services comparable to their pricier counterparts, such as research and monthly statements—but can save you more than 50% on commissions.

The experienced investor may want to choose among the deep-discount brokerage firms, which cut commissions by as much as 90% but provide no services—and certainly no handholding.

The cheapest way to trade is online. All of these leading discount brokerage houses also offer online trading services:

- Fidelity Broker Services (800-544-7272; www400.fidelity.com)
- Quick and Reilly (800-522-8712; www.quickandreilly.com)
- Rowe Price Discount Brokerage (800-638-5660; www.troweprice.com)
- Charles Schwab (800-648-5300; www.schwab.com)
- TD Waterhouse (800-934-4448; www.tdwaterhouse.com)

Online Brokers

Online trading is revolutionizing Wall Street, and everyone is jumping on the bandwagon. For the knowledgeable investor, trading online keeps overhead to an absolute minimum. Charles Schwab (www.schwab.com), for instance, offers Web trading to its customers for a low $29.95 commission for up to 1,000 shares (and 3¢ for each additional share). Hard to beat is Suretrade (www.suretrade.com), which has a current $7.95 commission for each trade of up to 5,000 shares.

No-load Mutual Funds

No-loads, mutual funds that don't charge commissions when investors open or close accounts or reinvest their dividends, have been outperforming load funds by a full percentage point for the past three years. Here are some tips on how to keep more of your money compounding:

- Even no-load funds sometimes charge 12b-1 fees, which are passed along to investors, to cover advertising and marketing costs. High 12b-1 fees can leave a serious dent in your earnings. Check your prospectus to see whether your mutual fund is assessing 12b-1 fees, and what percentage of your assets they amount to.
- Look for funds that have lower than average expense-to-asset ratios. Management fees can range from as low as .25% to as high as almost 2% of your initial investment.
- Portfolio turnovers (frequency of buying and selling stocks—which means extra fees and sometimes taxes for fund owners) are posted in mutual funds' semi-annual and annual reports. Make sure your fund—or prospective fund—is keeping tax-costly trading down to a minimum.
- Depending on the fund you choose, your investment may also be subject to exit fees (if you leave the fund), redemption fees (if you withdraw some of your investment before a certain period of time has elapsed), or deferred sales charges. Some low-cost funds don't charge these fees. Others waive them after a specified minimum investment period, usually five years.

INSIDE INFORMATION

Real-Time Stock Quotes at Your Fingertips

One serious disadvantage for the virtual trader is that nearly all stock quotes online are delayed by at least 20 minutes. One worthwhile exception is **Thompson Financial Network's** website (www.thomsonrtq.com), which offers up to 100 real-time stock quotes free per day.

BARGAIN FINDER

Picking Bargain Stocks

Much of the information you need to pick out bargain stocks is available free at any of hundreds of financial websites. Many of these sites also offer subscription services and software (at minimal cost) that give you tools to help your detective work.

Microsoft's Investment Finder (investor.msn.com, click on Investment Finder) is one such service. This comprehensive site enables you to create personalized screens that can help you snag future winners.

If you like the idea of bargain stocks but don't feel ready to pick your own, consider investing in a value fund specializing in picking undervalued stocks with temporarily depressed price-to-earnings ratios. They're generally identified for you in articles in financial magazines and the financial pages of big-city newspapers.

Dollar Cost Averaging With Mutual Funds

Most mutual funds will automatically deduct a nominal amount from your checking or money market fund account every month—as low as $25—to buy additional shares, regardless of whether the price of the shares is falling or rising. Not only does this system take some of the hassle out of investing, but studies show that average investors get better returns if they invest regularly regardless of intermittent highs and lows.

Dollar Cost Averaging

	APRIL	MAY	JUNE	JULY
Amount invested	$100	$100	$100	$100
Average share price per month	$22	$17	$14	$18
Number of shares bought	4.55	5.88	7.14	5.56

AVERAGE SHARE PRICE

$$\frac{\text{Average price per month}}{\text{Number of months}} = \text{Average share price}$$

$$\frac{\$22 + 17 + 14 + 18}{4} = \$17.75$$

AVERAGE SHARE COST

$$\frac{\text{Total amount invested}}{\text{Total shares purchased}} = \text{Average share cost}$$

$$\frac{\$400}{4.55 + 5.88 + 7.14 + 556} = \$17.29$$

Mutual Fund Networks

Mutual fund networks make it easier—and cheaper—than ever to diversify your investments among different fund families. This lets you take advantage of strongly performing funds in different families—a growth fund in one and a GMNA fund in another, for example. These top fund networks give access to hundreds of funds in dozens of fund families:

- Fidelity's Funds Network (800-544-6666)
- Charles Schwab's Mutual Fund Marketplace and One-Source (800-435-4000)
- TD Waterhouse (800-934-4448)

Free Investment Advice

How and where you decide to invest is a personal decision, and no investment recipe will be to the taste of every investor. It's important to know where to find reliable data so you can make the right choice.

- The Securities and Exchange Commission (SEC) can provide general information about laws governing securities, including stocks and bonds, as well as tell you whether a particular brokerage house is being investigated. You can also request any of their free publications, including *Invest Wisely: An Introduction to Mutual Funds* and *Get the Facts on Saving & Investing*. SEC, Office of Investor Education and Assistance, 450 5th St. N.W., Washington, D.C. 20549, 202-942-7040.
- Want more facts and less hype? Call a company's investor relations department and ask for a free copy of Form 10-K. It contains no-nonsense information you won't find in annual reports, and can help you make sound investment decisions.
- Weekly top-ten lists of stocks and mutual funds in major newspapers can be excellent information sources if you follow them on a regular basis. A stock or fund new to the list may be a buying opportunity—especially if it is in a sector like technology or drug-company stocks in an under-performing period.
- Morningstar, a Chicago-based firm which tracks the performance of more than 8,000 stocks and mutual funds, is your ultimate resource for finding the best deals and helping you build the portfolio that's right for you.

Morningstar's website provides up-to-date information and lets you generate spreadsheets comparing the performance of funds according to category, risk, volatility and return. The company also publishes two newsletters, *The Morningstar Stock Investor* and *Morningstar Mutual Funds*. Their newsletters may also be available at your local library. Call 800-735-0700 to order the newsletters or check out their free website at www.morningstar.net.

- NETworth (www.networth.galt.com) is an indispensable free database of over 7,000 mutual funds, including their prospectuses.

Keeping in the Green—In More Ways than One

There are at least 25 mutual funds that cater to socially and environmentally conscious investors who want some control over who and what their money finances.

Depending on your concerns, you can select funds that refuse to buy stock in companies that sell tobacco, produce weapons, exploit economically disadvantaged workers or engage in discriminatory practices. Although the performance of some of these funds to date is uneven, there are a few standouts. One such fund is Dreyfus Premier Third Century (800-373-9387), the oldest and one of the best of the socially responsible funds.

Undervalued Stock

Don't be seduced by what some experts call glamour stocks: high-priced growth stocks that often promise more than they deliver. Not only do these stocks carry inflated price tags, but they tend to need a quick turnaround to pay off, so are not well-suited to the average investor. Instead, look for undervalued stocks: those whose prices are temporarily beaten down in relation to their earnings outlook. Although in today's inflated market it's harder than ever to find bargain stocks, there are still some steals out there for the savvy investor.

Undervalued stock presents a golden opportunity for investors with money to invest in the market. Even better, the risk of buying undervalued stock is much less than that of buying stocks that are hitting new highs. Identifying undervalued stock is an investment strategy that can work for you regardless of the economic climate, and their bargain prices will provide insulation from market ups and downs in the years ahead.

Be a Contrarian Consider buying stock in companies that no one else wants to touch. These companies may have delivered recent bad news about earnings or future growth, or they may have suffered adverse legal decisions or damaging litigation—which has sent their stock prices down.

HERE'S HOW

Turning Losses Into Gains

If you lost money in the stock market this year, here's something to make you feel a little better. All capital losses can be applied against capital gains plus $3,000 of personal income. And if you have more losses than you can claim in one year, you can apply the excess to future years.

BUYER BEWARE

When Not to Invest

Find out when the fund you've selected makes its annual capital gains and income distributions—usually in December. Share prices are highest just before they make these payouts. Furthermore, you could end up paying taxes on gains you didn't receive. Wait until after the ex-dividend, or payment, date to make your investment.

FOR YOUR INFORMATION

Background Check

Before you open an account with a broker, put in a call to the **National Association of Security Dealers** (800-289-9999). They will do a complete background check for free on any brokerage house, including its past record.

Look for companies that are in the midst of corporate change. They might be selling off some of their assets, spinning off divisions or subsidiaries, or undergoing top management changes. These stocks can be a steal because they tend to be inefficiently priced, particularly when such developments first become public.

Identifying Undervalued Stock Look for stocks that are currently hitting new lows and are selling at a 40% to 50% discount to the companies' values. To determine a company's value, look at its current and projected cash flows, its assets, and how these compare to the competition.

Compared with cheap stocks, bargain stocks tend to have relatively high price-to-earnings ratios (P/Es), although lower than the average P/E of the S&P 500. P/Es reflect past earnings and are used to project future expectations. If the market believes that a stock has a bright outlook despite poor recent performance, the price will be high in relation to its recent earnings. A stock's P/E can be found in the stock tables of many newspapers.

Writing Your Will—For Free

You needn't spend hundreds of dollars to consult attorneys on how to draw up your will, though most experts advise you to have a lawyer review any will you create. Your **County Cooperative Extension Office** may provide publications—even classes—to help you do it for free. Look in your local blue pages for your county office or contact the Cooperative State Research Education and Extension Service, U.S. Department of Agriculture, 14th & Independence Ave. S.W., Room 3328, South Bldg., Washington, D.C. 20250.

Will

Name: _____
Date: _____
Executor: _____
Beneficiaries:

1) _____
2) _____
3) _____
4) _____

Witnesses: _____
Signature: _____

Fill in the blanks. Please print clearly.

Inexpensive Legal Help

Believe it or not, you needn't pay exorbitant attorneys' fees to answer your legal questions or even settle a dispute. The government will answer many of your questions for free, whether you want to clarify tax issues regarding your retirement and pension plans, create a living will, or file a charge of discrimination. Even if operators can't answer your questions, they can refer you to someone who can.

IRS Legal Hotline If you have tax questions relating to your pension or retirement plan, the IRS operates a legal hotline just for you. Get advice from lawyers specializing in retirement and pension plan issues. The service is offered Monday through Thursday, from 1:30 p.m. to 3:30 p.m. EST at 202-622-6074/6076, Employee Plans Technical and Actuarial Division, Internal Revenue Service, U.S. Department of the Treasury, Room 6550, CP:E:EP, 1111 Constitution Ave. N.W., Washington, D.C. 20224.

Legal Services Corporation The government operates not-for-profit law offices across the country to provide legal services of all kinds to low-income individuals. Staffed by lawyers and paralegals, these offices handle cases directly and for

free. Certain financial criteria apply to determine eligibility. To find out about the program nearest you, look in your local blue pages or contact the Legal Services Corporation, 750 First St. N.E., 11th Floor, Washington, D.C. 20002, 202-336-8800.

Law School Legal Clinics If your case doesn't qualify for the Legal Services Corporation, don't despair. The law school of your local college or university may offer a not-for-profit legal clinic. These on-campus clinics are supervised by legal professors and usually staffed by conscientious law students eager to get practical experience in the field. Contact the law school of your nearest college or university for information.

Personal Finance For Retirees

There are plenty of free and inexpensive resources, government perks and discounts available to help make your retirement years as happy, healthy and comfortable as possible.

Tax Tips Just for You

Did you know that you might be able to deduct all of your home mortgage interest? Or that you might qualify for a 15% tax credit if you're disabled or over 65?

These and other important filing questions are answered in the free newsletter *Protecting Older Americans Against Overpayment of Income Taxes*, published by the United States Senate Special Committee on Aging. Updated every January, this straightforward publication will keep you abreast of the latest changes to the tax laws that affect you, and will let you know in plain English which deductions, exemptions and credits you qualify for. For your free copy, contact the Special Committee on Aging, U.S. Senate SDG 31, Washington, D.C. 20510, 202-224-5364.

Free Tax Counseling

Need help preparing your return? The IRS sponsors a number of programs offering free, individual tax assistance. Volunteers for Tax Counseling for the Elderly (TCE) have been specially trained by the IRS to assist individuals 60 and older with their tax returns. They visit nursing homes and community centers, and will even make a house call if necessary. VITA (Volunteer Income Tax Assistance) is another government program offering individual tax advice to elderly, disabled, low-income and non-English speaking individuals.

DID YOU KNOW

Protecting Your Social Security Benefits

Your Social Security benefits are exempt from your creditors if you're in financial trouble. This means that department stores, credit card issuers and collection agencies can't go after your retirement checks.

BARGAIN FINDER

Seniors Discounts

If you're covered by a homeowners insurance plan or are considering purchasing a policy, ask if the insurer offers a seniors discount. Many companies offer discounts to Americans 60 and up.

FOR YOUR INFORMATION

Free Resources For Seniors

• ***What You Should Know About Your Pension Rights*** is a free booklet published by the Pension and Welfare Benefits Administration. Request this and other publications by phone 800-998-7542. (www.dol.gov/dol/pwba/)

Long-Term Care Insurance

If you're considering buying long-term care insurance to help cover your expenses should you need to enter a nursing home, be sure to do plenty of research before sending off a check.

Many companies offering this type of policy have come under heavy criticism from consumer protection organizations and senior advocate groups.

Not only are premiums steep, but too many purchasers have not been able to collect on their benefits. Some policies do not cover home care or residential facilities, or deny benefits to people afflicted with long-term illnesses such as Alzheimer's. With some policies, the first hundred days at a facility (as long a period as many seniors ever spend in a nursing home) aren't covered. With others, benefits lapse long before a stay at a facility has ended.

Social Security Help by Phone

Call the **Social Security Hotline** if you have any questions about your benefits. A copy of your **Personal Earnings and Benefits** statement, which reflects the income your benefits are based on, is mailed automatically about three months before your birthday. Call the Social Security Hotline at 800-772-1213 or visit www.ssa.gov.

To find out about the VITA or TCE program nearest you, call the IRS Information Line at 800-829-1040.

Legal Services for Seniors

A number of different organizations across the country cater to the specific legal concerns of senior citizens. Some give advice and referrals. Others will handle your case directly. Some work pro bono. Others offer services on a sliding-fee scale based on age and income. Whatever your concerns, these organizations are designed to help you through all aspects of the legal process.

National Offices

National Senior Citizens Law Center
1101 14th St., NW, Suite 400, Washington, DC 20005, 202-289-6976 or 1052 W. Sixth St., Los Angeles, CA 90017, 213-639-0930

California

Senior Legal Hotline, Legal Services of Northern California, 515 12th St., Sacramento, CA 95814
916-551-2140

District of Columbia

Legal Council for the Elderly
601 E St. N.W., Bldg. A, Fourth Floor, Washington, D.C. 20049
202-434-2120

Florida

Legal Hotline for Older Floridians
3000 Biscayne Blvd., Fourth Floor, P.O. Box 370705, Miami, FL 33137, 305-576-5997

Pennsylvania

Legal Council for the Elderly
800-262-5297

Texas

Legal Hotline for Older Texans, State Bar of Texas
P.O. Box 12487, Austin, TX 78711-2487
800-622-2520 or 512-463-1463

Cutting Education Costs

Your child's college education doesn't have to drain your life savings. If you plan ahead and do your research, there are a variety of ways to pay for college and still have money in the bank.

Plan Ahead and Start Saving

Even the least expensive four-year education costs around $10,000, and the most expensive colleges can cost $100,000 or more. By 2015, that number is predicted to be over $250,000. Since most people don't have this kind of cash lying around, it's a good idea to plan ahead to cover the costs of your child's or grandchild's college education. Here are a few of the numbers you'll need to figure out:

1. The estimated cost of a college education for the years your child will be attending school.
2. The future value of your current savings for college.
3. Possible financial aid from outside sources (federal government, private scholarships).

4. The gap between your available financial resources and future need.
5. How much you will need to put aside in a college fund each month to close up the gap between how much you have saved and how much you'll need to have to pay for college.

Look at Your State College or University

State colleges and universities offer some of the best deals in education (for in-state residents). If your child is considering a state college or university in your home state, the tuition will probably be far less than at a comparable private college or university. The University of California, for example, charges California residents as little as $0 in tuition (but almost $3,000 in mandatory fees) to attend state college or university, while annual tuition at Stanford University, a well-known private university in California, is $24,500.

State colleges and universities favor in-state residents for financial aid, giving you the best chance to pay even less for a college education.

Be Wary of State Schools In Other States

The tuition at state colleges and universities is usually relatively expensive for out-of-state students. The University of Colorado at Boulder, for example, charges out-of-state students almost $16,000 (in-state students pay only $3,000). So if your child is looking at a state college or university outside of your home state, be aware that the tuition could be as costly as at private universities and colleges. Consider this example: The 2000–2001 tuition for out-of-state students at the University of Vermont, a state school, is $19,832 a year, while tuition at the private University of Notre Dame is $23,360, less than $4,000 more. And an out-of-state student would probably have more luck getting financial aid from the private school. The myth that a public college education is always inexpensive is just that: a myth.

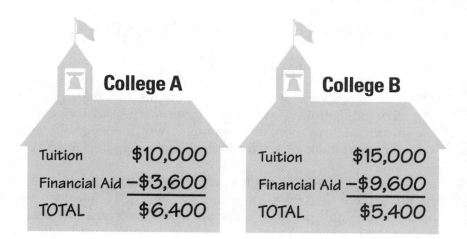

College A

Tuition	$10,000
Financial Aid	−$3,600
TOTAL	$6,400

College B

Tuition	$15,000
Financial Aid	−$9,600
TOTAL	$5,400

What Price Will You Pay?

Don't base your choice of college or university on its listed tuition cost. Wait until you find out what you'll actually have to pay after receiving financial aid. An expensive institution could end up costing you less than a mid-priced one if you get a better financial aid package.

Consider Community College

Community college can be very inexpensive. To save money, your child might want to consider getting a two-year associates degree, or taking the first two years of classes at a community college and then completing a four-year degree elsewhere. Community colleges are partially funded by local and state tax revenues so their classes usually cost far less than those at four-year schools.

Most community colleges provide the same course of study as the first two years of a four-year college or university. If your child begins at a community college and then wants to continue on to complete a bachelor's degree, make sure your child takes courses with credits that will transfer to a four-year school.

Varied Tuition Costs

A local community college might cost you less than one that's further away. In some states, like New Jersey, the tuition costs for a community college are less expensive for students from the county or area of the school than they are for out-of-county students. In other states, like New York, all state residents pay the same tuition.

Savings on Room and Board

Community colleges do not have dorms, so students must be able to live at home or on their own while in school. The cost of commuting to and from school is an issue to consider, but you won't have to pay expensive room and board costs if your child lives at home. And, since there are usually multiple community colleges in a state, there is probably one close to home so that the cost of commuting will be minimal.

INSIDE INFORMATION

Establishing Residency in a New State

The least expensive way to attend a state college or university outside your home state is to become a resident in that state. For example, in the 2000–2001 academic year, tuition at the **State University of New York (SUNY)** is $3,400 for state residents. However, it costs more than twice as much, $8,325, for out-of-state residents.

Each state has its own way of determining who is considered an in-state student, but most require you to have your driver's license in their state for six months to a year or more, register your car, register to vote, establish bank accounts and establish your permanent address in that state.

If it's feasible for your child to move to the new state and work for a year before starting college or graduate school, you could save a bundle in tuition costs. Call the state college or university you are interested in and ask about the quickest way to establish legal residency.

Foreign Student Savings

Many colleges and universities in foreign countries charge lower tuitions than American schools do. Remember, however, that the dollar cost of these schools depends on the current rate of exchange. Here is an example of the 2000 tuition (in United States dollars) for American students at a few foreign universities:

- *Goldsmith's College, University of London* in London, England, 44-20-7919-7171, Tuition: $12,613
- *McGill University*, in Montreal, Quebec, 514-398-4455, Tuition: $5,374 to $5,959
- *University of Edinburgh* in Edinburgh, Scotland, 44-131-650-1000, Tuition: $13,259
- *University of Toronto* in Toronto, Ontario, 416-978-2011, Tuition: $5,200 to $7,150

Not Just for Undergraduates

Vista is the **AmeriCorps** program for college graduates. Like in the regular AmeriCorps, Vista workers receive a living stipend and money to repay their college loans in return for working at one of a variety of service jobs around the country. Call 800-942-2677 for more information.

Working for a Bargain Education

There are several ways college students can help pay for their education. The federal government and the armed forces offer a variety of programs in which college students work or provide military service in exchange for financial aid.

Federal Work-study Programs

Federal work-study (FWS) programs provide part-time jobs for undergraduate and graduate students who demonstrate financial need, allowing them to earn money to help pay for college. These programs encourage community service work and work related to a student's course of study. Each school decides how money earned through FWS programs must be spent.

Most FWS jobs are on-campus, where a student works in one of the school's service departments, such as the cafeteria, financial aid office or research library. FWS payment is dependent upon individual school policy, and is either paid to students or applied directly to their college costs. Call 800-433-3243 for information on how to apply.

AmeriCorps

AmeriCorps is a federal work-study service organization with over 450 different national service programs around the country. AmeriCorps workers earn education vouchers in exchange for one to two years of national service.

A full term of service, one full year, must be completed to receive any education awards. But no more than two education awards (earned for two full terms of service) will be allocated to any individual. If students participate for one year full-time (1,700 hours) they receive an education award of $4,725. If they participate for one year part-time (900 hours) they receive an education award of $2,362.50.

In addition to education awards, AmeriCorps members receive a modest living allowance of approximately $150 a week (varying by location). Members are responsible for covering their own housing and meal expenses using this allowance. Health insurance is also provided, and some members may receive child-care assistance.

When their service is complete, AmeriCorps workers receive their education awards to help pay back student loans or finance college, graduate school or vocational school tuition. Service opportunities are available in the areas of education, public safety, human needs and the environment. Note, however, that your child may be able to make more money for

college working at a regular job. Contact AmeriCorps at 800-942-2677 for more information.

AmeriCorps National Civilian Community Corps

The National Civilian Community Corps is AmeriCorp's residential national service program for 18- to 24-year-olds. The program runs full-time for ten months. Part-time service opportunities are not available for this program. Members receive a modest allowance bi-weekly, and are provided with dormitory-style housing and meals on one of five campuses that participate in this program.

After the full ten months have been completed, members receive a $4,725 education award to help pay off their student loans or pay for future educational expenses. Members of this program receive health insurance as part of their membership. Call 800-942-2677 for an application.

ROTC

The U.S. Armed Forces sponsors the Reserve Officers Training Corps program, (ROTC), a federal, merit-based scholarship program available at many colleges and universities. Students accepted into ROTC receive scholarships that pay up to $16,000 a year of their college tuition, plus money toward textbooks and a small yearly stipend.

In addition to their regular classes, ROTC students must attend special classes sponsored by the U.S. Armed Forces. And upon graduation they are committed to serve as active-duty officers for four years in the branch of the service that sponsored their ROTC program.

Contact your local military recruiter or check college catalogs for more information on the programs available. Or call 800-USA-ROTC (or 800-USA-NAVY for the Navy's ROTC program, which also offers a special two-year program for college juniors and seniors) for more information. ROTC programs are highly competitive and preference is sometimes given to students studying nursing, engineering, science or business.

U.S. Armed Forces Programs

The U.S. Armed Forces also offers other types of financial aid programs that can help reduce the cost of college. Find the phone number for the nearest U.S. Armed Forces recruiting office in the blue pages of your local telephone directory and call for more information.

4 Years College

4 Years Active Duty

Summer School Can Save You Time And Money

Students who want to save money should consider taking summer classes at their local community college.

Taking summer classes at a less expensive school will not only reduce your costs, but may also allow your child to graduate sooner. Summer classes are also a great way to alleviate some of the pressure of an overloaded semester. They tend to be a little more lenient academically and smaller in size, which means that the professor is more accessible for one-on-one discussions and questions.

Students should always make sure that any course credits are transferable to their primary school before they enroll in a summer class.

A Less Expensive Junior Year Abroad

Most people don't realize that it is sometimes far less expensive to enroll in a foreign university directly for a year abroad than to go through an established U.S. university's study-abroad program. You will have to do more research on your own, however, and may have more trouble transferring course credits to U.S. schools.

Many U.S. colleges and universities have affiliations with overseas universities, making the study abroad process quite simple. But most U.S. universities require you to pay full tuition to their school while you're abroad if you go through their programs, which doesn't save you any money.

If your child is already in college and wants to consider studying abroad for a year, contact the center for international studies at your child's school for more information. Also take a look at the annual *Peterson's Study Abroad* (Peterson's, $26.95), which describes over 1,500 semester- and year-abroad programs (mostly through U.S. colleges and universities).

How to Get the Most from Federal Financial Aid

A college education is one of the biggest purchases most families ever make. But don't pay full price until you've exhausted your options. Financial aid comes in many forms—from scholarships to federal grants to private loans and grants.

Scholarships and grants are gifts of money that do not have to be repaid. They are the most desirable forms of financial aid and, consequently, also the most difficult to get. Grants are usually need-based, meaning they are awarded on the basis of financial need, and scholarships are usually merit-based, meaning they are offered on the basis of a student's achievements.

Unlike grants and scholarships, loans have to be repaid.

Federal Financial Aid Requirements

There are government grants and loans, as well as campus-based federal programs, that may be able to assist you in paying for

your child's college education. To be eligible for federal financial aid, a student must:

- Be a citizen of the U.S.
- Have a high school diploma or General Education Development (GED) Certificate.
- Be working toward a degree or certificate in an eligible educational program.
- Have financial need (except for some loan programs).
- Not be in default on a previous federal loan or owe a refund from a previous federal grant.

Defining Financial Aid Eligibility

Not everybody is eligible for financial aid. Most financial aid programs provide funds only to those who are considered dependent by federal law and in need of financial assistance.

What Is Dependency? According to the law, students are considered dependent if they:

- Are 22 years old or younger.
- Are not veterans of the U.S. Armed Forces.
- Are not enrolled in graduate or professional programs.
- Are not married.
- Are not or were not orphans or wards of the court until age 18.
- Do not have legal dependents other than a spouse.

What Is Financial Need? Eligibility for financial aid is not only based on your child's classification as a dependent, but on you and your child's financial situation as well. The federal government determines dependent students' financial need status by looking at their parental income and assets, and the students' own income and assets.

While they consider only 5.6% of parental assets to be available to pay for tuition, they consider 35% of the student's to be available, a much larger chunk of assets. This is one reason why many financial advisors suggest not putting too many assets in your children's names before they graduate from college.

Independents Are Not Ignored Students who are not considered dependents can also receive financial aid. Federal student aid for independent students does not take parental assets into account at all. If your child is no longer considered dependent, talk to your aid administrator to find out what your child's options are.

Applying for Financial Aid

To apply for federal financial aid, your child must file a FAFSA, or Free Application for Federal Student Aid. Get an application from your child's high school or post-secondary school, or contact the Federal Student Aid Information Center, located at P.O. Box 84,

DID YOU KNOW

Free College Is Not Just a Fantasy

Believe it or not, there are several free colleges around the nation. Here are three to consider. Write or call for an application or more information:

- **Berea College**, Admissions Office, Berea, KY 40404, 800-326-5948; www.berea.edu. Offers a wide variety of liberal arts majors, such as agriculture, art, classical languages and mathematics.

- **Cooper Union for the Advancement of Science and Art**, Office of Admissions, 41 Cooper Square, New York, NY 10003, 212-353-4120; www.cooper.edu. Specializes in top-quality architecture, graphic design, engineering and fine arts educations.

- **Williamson Free School of Mechanical Trade**, Office of Admissions, 106 South New Middletown Road, Media, PA 19063, 610-566-1776; www.williamsonschool.org. Offers degrees in horticulture, carpentry, brick masonry, machine shop and other mechanical trades.

BUYER BEWARE

Students Pay More

Since 35% of a student's assets are considered available for tuition (compared with only 5.6% of the parents' assets), students with $48,000 in assets would be required to contribute $18,000 to their education, while their parents could have up to $300,000 in assets before being required to contribute that much.

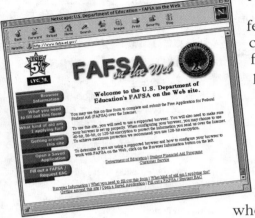

Online Help with Financial Aid

The **U.S. Department of Education's** website (www.ed.gov) is full of information and instructions on how to receive financial aid applications and guidance. If you have access to the Internet, take some time to visit this site, which lays out every step you need to follow when applying for federal financial aid and assistance. You can also access detailed information about the federal government's grants, loans and work-study programs. Plus, get assistance in completing the **FAFSA** or even fill out and submit your application online.

Take a look at the **National Association of Student Financial Aid Administrators'** website **FinAid** (www.finaid.org) to find links to financial aid offices at many colleges and universities, as well as other sources of financial aid.

Washington, D.C. 20044, 800-433-3243. A counselor will assist you and your child in completing the FAFSA, and answer any questions about the application that you may have.

Applying for federal student aid is free. And for most of the federal student aid programs, a FAFSA is the only form your child needs to file. Nonfederal aid, however, such as aid from individual schools, may require additional forms and processing fees. Check with your child's school to see what it requires.

Qualifying for Federal Financial Aid

Within a month of filing a FAFSA, your child will receive a Student Aid Report (SAR) stating your Expected Family Contribution (EFC). This will determine how much you're expected to contribute to your child's college education and whether your family qualifies for federal financial aid. Your child's financial need is determined by subtracting your Expected Family Contribution from the cost of attendance.

If it has been more than four weeks since your child submitted the FAFSA application and you have not heard anything, you can check on the application by contacting the Federal Student Aid Information Center at 319-337-5665.

Watch Out for Deadlines

The FAFSA has a strict deadline for applications, so make sure your child applies on time. Students cannot apply for aid before January 1 of the year they want to attend school, but they should apply as soon after this date as possible.

Each college and university sets its own deadlines for school-administered financial aid. Deadlines are often early in the calendar year, and students must meet these deadlines to receive certain funding like FSEOGs (Federal Supplemental Educational Opportunity Grants) and Federal Work-Study benefits. Get the deadline date from the financial aid administrator at each school.

Getting Four Full Years of Aid

Your child must reapply for federal aid every school year by re-submitting a FAFSA. Theoretically, as long as your child stays in the same college or university, and the school's budget does not change dramatically, you should receive the same amount of aid.

If your child changes schools, however, federal financial aid doesn't automatically follow. So if your child transfers to a new school, check with the new school to find out what steps you must take to continue receiving aid. If your child transfers to a school that is more expensive than the first school, the amount of federal aid you receive may increase.

Money for College from the Federal Government

The federal government has several programs that can save you money on college tuition. To find out more about federal loan requirements, call 800-433-3243 and request *The Student Guide*, a free guide to federal financial aid.

Federal Pell Grants

Students who demonstrate the greatest financial need based on federal standards are eligible for Federal Pell Grants of up to $3,300 a year. The amount of the grant depends on a combination of your Expected Family Contribution and the tuition at the college where your child enrolls. Part-time students are eligible, although the amount of the grant will be less than that for full-time students. Pell Grants are particularly useful for older students who are beginning or returning to college while also managing a profession and a family.

Pell Grants are awarded by the government, but disbursed by individual colleges. Grant funds may be applied directly to your child's school costs, paid to your child directly by check or distributed through a combination of these methods. Make sure that the school tells you in writing how and when your child will be paid, and how much the award will be.

It is important that your child knows how much money to expect and when to expect it. Funds must be paid out at least once per term (semester, trimester or quarter). Schools that don't use the traditional terms must distribute funds at least twice during the academic year.

Federal Supplemental Educational Opportunity Grants

Federal Supplemental Educational Opportunity Grants (FSEOGs) are gift-aid for undergraduates with exceptional financial need. They are federal grants administered directly by the financial aid office at each participating school. FSEOGs are awarded only to undergraduate students who have not yet earned a bachelor's or professional degree.

Federal Pell Grant recipients are given preference for FSEOGs. Unlike Pell Grants, which are administered by the government and guaranteed to all eligible students at a participating school, FSEOGs are only available to recipients selected by each college, and awards are based on the availability of funds at each school.

How much aid students receive depends on their financial need, the amount of other aid they are offered and the availability of funds at their school. Your child could get between $100 and $4,000 a year.

INSIDE INFORMATION

Shop Around for The Best Deal

When you are offered a financial aid package for a particular college or university, don't rush to accept the offer, even if it is from your child's first-choice school.

Often, a comparable school will offer a better package. You can then use any better offers you get from other schools as leverage to receive a larger sum from your child's first-choice school. If you are going to negotiate a better deal, your strongest leverage is a competitive package from a similar school.

There is no advantage to accepting a school's offer before its deadline, and if you rush to accept the deal that one school offers, you lose the opportunity to bargain for a better price.

DID YOU KNOW

Financial Aid Doesn't Have to Be Frightening

If you can't make sense of what a school's tuition will cost, stop worrying. The financial aid administrator at each school you're interested in can tell you what financial aid programs are available and how much your child's total cost of attendance will be. And if you are still confused about procedures, call the federal government's student financial aid center at 800-4-FED-AID.

Navigating Federal Student Aid

Need help navigating the federal student aid process? Call the **Federal Student Aid Information Center** 800-433-3243 (TDD: 800-730-8913) for assistance with:

❏ Completing the **FAFSA**.

❏ Identifying whether a particular school participates in federal student aid programs.

❏ Understanding eligibility requirements.

❏ Understanding the process of determining financial need and awarding aid.

❏ Getting federal student aid publications.

After you have submitted your **FAFSA** application, call 319-337-5665 if you want an information specialist to:

❏ Find out if your child's application has been processed.

❏ Send you a copy of your child's **student aid report (SAR).**

❏ Send your child's application information to a specific school.

❏ Change your child's mailing address.

Like Federal Pell Grant moneys, FSEOG funds may be applied directly to school costs, paid to your child by check or distributed through a combination of these methods. Schools must pay FSEOG money to students at least once per term (semester, trimester or quarter).

Federal Student Loans

Robert T. Stafford Loans provide students with low-interest loans to help them meet the costs of attending colleges, universities, and vocational and technical schools. Loans, unlike grants and scholarships, must eventually be paid back. In cases where there is proven financial need, the government will pay the interest due on these loans so long as students remain in school at least half-time and make satisfactory progress. Once students have graduated, however, they are responsible for paying the interest themselves.

Eligibility for Robert T. Stafford Loans is based on federal financial aid requirements. Students must also sign a statement of educational purpose that says they will only use the loan money for educational expenses. The application deadline for a Federal Stafford Loan is determined by your loan agency and the college your child attends.

Virtually all college students qualify for Stafford Loans. But not every school participates in this program, so check with your school's financial administrator to find out whether you can apply.

Federal Parent Loans

Parent Loans for Undergraduate Students (PLUSs) allow you to borrow the total cost of tuition less the amount of financial aid your child is already eligible to receive.

To be eligible for a PLUS you will be required to pass a credit check. If you fail the credit check, you can still receive a loan for your child if a friend or family member endorses the loan, promising to repay it if you fail to do so.

PLUS eligibility is not determined by financial need, but you must meet some general requirements such as having U.S. citizenship. As with the Stafford Loan, the college or university you are interested in will tell you how to borrow the money. Unlike the Stafford Loan, however, the PLUS has interest payments that cannot be deferred until a later date.

Federal Financial Aid

	1-year Minimum	4-year Maximum
Pell Grant	$400	$10,800
FSEOG	$100	$16,000
Stafford Loan	N/A	$17,125
PLUS	N/A	Cost of Attendance

Profiting from Non-Federal Financial Aid

There are a wide range of scholarships and grants from non-federal sources available for college students. Here are a few you should be sure to consider.

State Scholarships

A state's financial assistance is usually available only for students who are legal residents of that state. That means your child will probably have to attend a college or university in your state to receive this type of aid.

Learn about your state's financial assistance programs by contacting your child's high school guidance counselor, or the college or university your child plans to attend. You may also want to consult your state's higher education agency and check the reference section in your local library under Financial Aid, Student Aid or Scholarships.

Most state scholarships are available exclusively to high school seniors who are going directly to college, but some states have aid available for students already enrolled in college, as well as for graduate students. Requirements differ from state to state, so check with your State Department of Education.

Collegiate Scholarships

Colleges and universities provide some scholarships directly. These scholarships are usually granted to enrolled, or soon-to-be enrolled, students who have a 3.0 grade point average or higher, stand in the upper third of their class and have SAT/ACT scores above the national average.

Students who receive scholarships directly from their college usually have a wide range of interests and are active in school and the community. Some students have above average talent in sports or the arts. Others are doing extremely well at two-year colleges and want to transfer into four-year baccalaureate programs.

Collegiate scholarships are available for both need and merit. Check with each school directly, because offerings vary. Also consider taking a look at *The As and Bs of Academic Scholarships* by Anne Schimke (Octameron Associates, $9.00).

Community-provided Private Scholarships

Mailings from your high school frequently list scholarships available on the local level. Consider checking at your town hall to find out about scholarships from the local PTA, local banks and businesses, and anonymous grants for the "best female athlete" or

FOR YOUR INFORMATION

Finding the Right Scholarship

These directories contain specific information on a wide variety of college scholarships:

- *College Scholarships and Financial Aid* by John Schwartz (ARCO/Macmillan, $27.96).
- *The Complete Scholarship Book* by Student Services, Inc. (Sourcebooks, Inc., $22.95).
- *Directory of Financial Aids for Women* by Gail Ann Schlachter (B. Klein Publications).
- *The Scholarship Book* by Daniel J. Cassidy and Michael J. Alves (Prentice Hall, $32.95).

DID YOU KNOW

Private Scholarships Can Affect Financial Aid

Private scholarships can sometimes reduce the amount of the financial aid package you receive from your child's college or university. If your child receives a private scholarship, make sure to find out how it will affect your financial aid package.

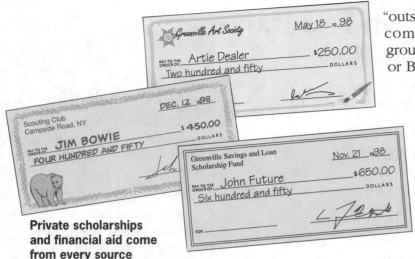

Private scholarships and financial aid come from every source imaginable.

"outstanding art students." Also check with community organizations and civic groups, such as the 4-H Club, and the Girl or Boy Scouts.

Some students receive financial assistance from organizations connected with their primary field of interest, such as science foundations or theater companies. Check in your local newspaper and the *U.S. Department of Labor's Occupational Outlook Handbook* at your local library to find associations that offer money for education.

Private Scholarships

Private scholarships come from a wide range of sources, have separate requirements and vary greatly in amount from very small to quite substantial.

Using a scholarship-search company is often a waste of money, and some are real frauds. Instead, check with these books and websites to find scholarships your child might qualify for at over 3,100 colleges and universities across the country:

- *The College Board College Costs and Financial Aid Handbook* (College Board Publications, $21.95). This book covers all the financial aid bases. In addition, The College Board's website (www.collegeboard.org) provides a free scholarship search service. Click on the scholarship search link and enter your personal information. If you don't have access to the Internet, ask your librarian to help you make the search on a library computer.
- *Peterson's College Money Handbook* (Peterson's, $26.95). Look through this book for step-by-step financial aid information, or visit Peterson's website (www.petersons.com) for access to the Peterson's guides and handbooks and a wealth of information on financial aid for college.
- The FastWEB Scholarship Search site (www.fastweb.com) lets you make a free computer search of more than 500,000 scholarships.

National Merit Scholarships

National Merit Scholarships are probably the best known private scholarships available. More than 7,900 students (Finalists) receive National Merit Scholarships each year, in amounts that range from $500 up to $10,000 to help pay their college tuition.

1. About 2,500 of these Finalists receive a one-time award of $2,000 directly from the National Merit Scholarship Corporation every year.

2. About 1,200 Finalists receive awards provided by corporations, company foundations and other business organizations. These corporate-sponsored awards range from a single payment of $2,000 to $5,000 to a renewable, yearly stipend of between $500 and $10,000.

3. About 4,200 Finalists receive renewable awards from colleges and universities. Every college-sponsored award must be used at the college or university that financed the award. College-sponsored National Merit Scholarship stipends range from $500 to $2,000 per year.

National Merit Scholarship awards are based on a combination of financial need and student scores on a national examination, the Preliminary Scholastic Aptitude Test/National Merit Scholarship Qualifying Test (PSAT/NMSQT), taken by students in their junior year of high school.

Contact your child's high school college advisor for more information. If you still have questions, call the National Merit Scholarship Corporation at 847-866-5100.

Tax Cuts for Education

The 1997 tax law provides new tax credits benefiting adults who want to return to school and parents sending their children to college.

Tax credits reduce the amount of income tax you pay. The amount of a tax credit is subtracted directly from the dollar amount of tax you owe. Each of the new tax credits was developed to reduce the impact of college tuition and required fees after grants, scholarships and other tax-free educational assistance have been applied.

Hope Credit

Hope Credit reduces the amount of income tax you owe. After paying the college or university directly, you get to subtract the amount of the credit from your next tax bill.

A full Hope Credit tax credit allows you to subtract $1,000 for the first $1,000 of tuition and fees for freshman and sophomore year, and $500 for the second $1,000 of tuition and fees for freshman and sophomore year, for a total possible credit of $1,500 per

---

FOR YOUR INFORMATION

Better Ways to Pay For College

Most experts agree that high-interest personal loans are the worst ways to pay for your child's college education. Consider these alternatives that could save you a good deal of money:

Education Loans Taking out a personal loan from a bank is probably the most expensive way to pay for your child's college education. But if you must borrow money, contact the **Student Loan Marketing Association, Sallie Mae** (800-239-4211, www.salliemae.com), and ask about their special low-cost education loans. Or call the Sallie Mae toll-free hotline (800-806-3681) to hear a recording on how to receive their information packet on the best ways to pay for college.

Home-equity Loans Home-equity loans are another alternative to personal loans. The major benefit of a home-equity loan is, in most cases, that the interest on the loan is totally tax deductible. The loan also reduces your equity in your home, which may improve your chances of getting more financial aid in the future.

If you default in the loan payments, however, you could lose your home.

Borrowing against Your Pension You can borrow against the assets in your tax-deferred pension, profit sharing plan or 401(k) plan if you need money for college.

Borrowing will cost you less than withdrawing from your pension because you won't have to pay tax that you would have to pay on a withdrawal. If you are younger than 59½, a withdrawal will also cost you a 10% penalty. With a loan, however, you only have to pay interest on the money you borrow from your account.

Karen Cheney On Getting a High-Quality College Education For a Reasonable Price

Karen Cheney is a staff writer for *Money Magazine* and co-author of *How to Start a Successful Home Business* (Warner Books, $10.99).

Jay Brady Photography

If finances are an issue in deciding where to go to college, is there a certain type of school you should look into first?

I don't think you should immediately eliminate any school, particularly if you are a good student, have done well in high school and have high test scores. There are a lot of schools that can provide you with a good value. Some smaller liberal arts schools, what we call second-tier schools, that are not super-selective offer a lot of very good deals and are doing what they can to lure students to their doors. It's worthwhile to look into many different types of schools.

What are some misconceptions people have about paying for a college education?

I think people instantly believe that it's impossible to pay for, because they hear numbers that are larger than what they paid for their wedding or their first house. But if you start to save when your child is young, putting away a hundred dollars a month, you'd be surprised how much you can save.

Another misconception people have is thinking it's better to invest in their child's name. You probably shouldn't. If you invest in your child's name you're less likely to qualify for financial aid. The way that the financial aid formulas are configured, schools usually expect parents to fork over a small percentage of their assets every year, around 5.6%, but a child is expected to pony up about 35%. That's a big difference.

How do you ensure that you're getting the best deal on your college tuition plan?

The only way you can know that is by comparing it with packages you receive from other similar schools. This is why it's wise to apply to a number of schools. You may pick out one school you want to go to and apply just to it, but then you don't have any negotiating power or ability to compare your package.

So you want to apply to six or eight schools. That way you can ensure that you're getting the best deal. Apply to a couple of schools that you consider a stretch, and some that are sure bets.

How can you get the best deal?

Be wary about applying for early admission. If you do, you're essentially promising a school that you will attend if they let you in early. You're saying that no matter what they give you, even if they give you a lousy aid package, you'll go to their school. So you lose your negotiating power.

Also, apply for financial aid early, or at least on time.

When you get your aid packages back, compare them very closely. You may find that one looks more generous—but when you compare them closely you could find that one is filled with loans while the other is filled with grants.

Are there any money pits in paying for a college education that you can avoid, or be aware of?

You may not realize that your financial aid package can get cut. A lot of schools will lure you in with a very good financial aid package the first year, but there's no guarantee that it will continue after that. So the next year your child is in school you could be faced with a huge bill.

student per year. The Hope Credit applies to freshmen and sophomores who are in school at least half-time. There are no age restrictions for this tax credit.

For example, suppose a married couple with a gross income of $70,000 has two children in college: One child is a freshman at a community college with an annual tuition of $2,000, and the other is a sophomore at a private college with an annual tuition of $11,000. The Hope Credit tax credit would cut this couple's taxes by $3,000, or $1,500 per child.

If you file your taxes jointly, and your combined adjusted gross income (AGI) is under $80,000, you are eligible to take a full Hope tax credit of $1,500. If you are a joint filer whose combined annual income is between $80,000 and $100,000, the Hope tax credit begins to be phased out and you receive less than the full credit amount. The credit does not apply to people with a combined joint income of over $100,000.

If you are a single filer who earns under $40,000 of adjusted gross income, you can take a full Hope tax credit. The tax credit begins to phase out between $40,000 and $50,000 of gross income, and you don't qualify if your AGI is more than $50,000 a year as a single filer.

Lifetime Learning Credits

The Lifetime Learning Credit is a tax credit that directly reduces your income taxes and specifically benefits adults who want to go back to school, change careers or upgrade their skills. This credit also applies to college juniors and seniors, as well as graduate students.

With the Lifetime Learning Credit, you receive a 20% as well as tax credit on the first $5,000 of tuition and fees paid each year through the year 2002, and a 20% tax credit for the first $10,000 of tuition and fees thereafter. For example, suppose a woman whose family income is $65,000 wants to attend a graduate program at college after a 30-year absence from school, and her tuition at a public university is $3,500. Using the Lifetime Learning Credit, her family's income taxes would be cut by $700.

This tax credit is phased out at the same income levels for single and joint filers as the Hope credit.

Education IRAs

You can set up an Education IRA account for any child under 18 years old. The contribution limit is $500 a year per child. The money in an Education IRA account grows tax-deferred and can be withdrawn tax-free to pay for the child's post-secondary education expenses.

You must stop contributing to an Educational IRA when your child reaches 18. And if there is still money in the IRA when your

HERE'S HOW

Safeguard Your Education

If you're going to pay for a quality education, make sure you get it. It is up to you to check out the college or university you or your child is considering attending:

- Ensure through the state's **Department of Education** that the proper accrediting and licensing agencies have evaluated the school and found that it meets their minimum requirements.

- Ask the school's admissions office for its job placement rate and graduation statistics. This information will help you evaluate the school's educational success.

- Ask for a copy of the campus security report, which provides information on the school's campus security policies and crime statistics. Colleges and universities must publish and distribute a security report every year to all current students and employees of the school. The level of security on campus can add to or deter from the quality of education your child receives.

The Sooner You Save, the Easier It Is to Pay

One of the best ways to combat the fear of paying for college is to start saving early. Some experts say that you should start to save money for your children's college education before your first child is even born.

Consider setting aside money for your child's education as early as possible. The amount you can accumulate in 18 years with compound interest will be much more substantial than if you wait until your child is 15 to start saving.

Different Ways To Pay

State-sponsored Tuition Plans Families can use a qualified state-sponsored tuition plan to pay for a state college or university. These programs let you pay your child's tuition now, at today's rates, and guarantee that your costs will be covered when the time comes to enroll, even if it's years away. The programs also guarantee your child's admission to at least one of the institutions covered by the agreement.

Deferred-payment Options Many colleges also offer optional monthly payment plans to help you spread out your expenses. Two plans widely used by universities are offered by **Academic Management Services** (800-635-0120) and **Key Education Resources** (800-KEY-LEND; www.key.com/educate).

child reaches 30, you must transfer it to a younger member of the family or withdraw and pay taxes on the remaining funds.

Joint filers with an adjusted gross income of $160,000 or higher, and single filers with an AGI of $110,000 or more, cannot benefit from this tax break. And note that a student who receives tax-free distributions from an Education IRA may not, in the same year, benefit from the HOPE Scholarship or Lifetime Learning Credits.

Roth IRAs Help You Save

Experts believe that saving for your child's education should come second to saving for your own retirement. But did you know that you may be able to use a retirement account to pay for both?

Roth IRAs were introduced in 1998. Unlike Education IRAs, which were introduced at the same time and have a $500 annual contribution limit, Roth IRAs allow each parent to contribute up to $2,000 a year. Using this account to save money for your child's college expenses will allow you to accumulate quite a large sum, but there are a few catches.

Contributions to Roth IRAs are not tax deductible and the earnings are only tax-free if you withdraw after age 59½. You can withdraw without penalty before you're 59½ to pay for education expenses, but you will owe tax on the earnings. Also, you must have a Roth IRA for at least five years before you can use the money to pay for college. Despite these limitations, many experts believe that the contribution value makes Roth IRAs better investments than Education IRAs.

Cutting the Costs of College Incidentals

The price of tuition is not the only cost involved in going to college. You also need to take into account the cost of school fees, books, room and board (around $4,000 to $6,000 a year), travel expenses and general costs of living. In fact, a four-year college education can easily cost over $100,000 today, and the price continues to rise.

Here are some ways to save money on non-tuition college costs.

Room and Board

Many colleges and universities require that students live on campus during their freshman year, unless they continue to live at home, and some schools require freshman to have a meal plan as well. Most colleges and universities list food and housing costs in their guidebooks, and you can use these figures to compare on-campus and off-campus housing options where your child goes to school.

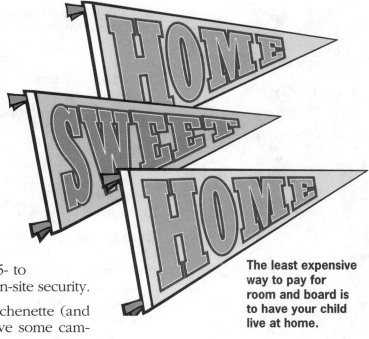

Here are the three primary housing options most college students have to choose among:

1. **Campus dormitories** usually come with a 5- to 21-meal plan (sometimes optional) and on-site security.

2. **Campus apartments** usually include a kitchenette (and don't require a meal plan) and may have some campus security.

The least expensive way to pay for room and board is to have your child live at home.

3. **Off-campus housing or apartments** often have a kitchen and no campus security. Depending on the college or university's location, even a twelve-month lease may be more cost-efficient than the price of on-campus housing for an academic year. Your child may want to stay in the apartment over the summer while working or attending summer school. If not, look into nine-month leases or sublet the apartment over the summer to reduce your boarding expenses even further.

Computers

On-campus computer stores frequently offer students discounts of around 10% on new computers. Compare the price of the same model computer at your child's school computer store, a local computer store and one of the large computer catalog companies, such as CompUSA (800-COMPUSA), Mac Warehouse (800-255-6227) or Micro Warehouse (800-367-7080). Ask about service contracts and what features are included before you buy.

Don't choose a model until you have checked with the college's computer center and asked which system the school uses. Most colleges use a DOS-based system for IBM-compatible units, a Macintosh-based system for Apple models, or both. Students with compatible systems can use the same floppy disk to work in their dorms, at the computer center and at the school library.

Consider spending some extra money to buy your child a laptop computer, because it is useful for transporting to lectures or

TRY SOMETHING DIFFERENT

Housing that Pays For Itself

Save on boarding costs and even make a profit! Look into purchasing an apartment or small house near campus for your child to live in. Then hire your child as the building manager in exchange for free rent, and rent out the extra bedrooms.

Rental income should offset your maintenance costs. Plus, your mortgage payments will give you equity in an asset of value while payments for a dorm or apartment would not. You can then sell the house after your child graduates and get back some or all of your original investment, or possibly even make a profit.

Managing a house is not always an easy thing to do, however, so this option works best with mature, responsible students.

Get Help Paying For Books

Financial aid offices are frequently willing to make adjustments to student budgets if students can document that their books and supplies cost more than average. Save your book receipts and don't be afraid to ask the financial aid department for help if you think your child's book costs are excessive.

the library. Most students will also need a modem for Internet and research purposes.

Books and Textbooks

Consider Used Books Buying used college books and textbooks may be the best book bargain you will find. Most campus bookstores sell the used books of past students at reduced prices.

Students who buy used books should flip through them to make sure the text can be clearly read. Some students highlight and heavily mark their books, and buying a used book you can't read is a waste of money.

Students can save even more money by selling any books they don't need back to the bookstore at the end of the semester.

Shop Around If the option to buy used books is not available, students can still shop around for bargains. Don't depend solely on the campus bookstore. Most college towns have more than one bookstore, so it is not difficult to compare prices.

Textbooks may be difficult to buy at off-campus bookstores unless a professor or department has made its book order there. In recent years, however, some enterprising students have purchased bulk orders of their school's most popular textbooks to sell to fellow students at better prices than what the campus store offers. Check out bulletin boards around the campus or ask upperclassmen to find out what alternatives are available at your school.

Free (and Almost Free) College for Senior Citizens

More than 300 colleges and universities across the country have special programs for seniors who are interested in going back to school.

This usually means free or low-cost tuition. Sometimes there are also discounts on school fees, books and even housing. The tuition and basic fees for seniors are the lowest charged to any student.

Some essentials like books aren't always discounted, and health insurance, parking and fees for degree-seeking candidates may also be full-price or unavailable. Contact the school you wish to attend and ask how to apply for a discount or waiver.

Listen in for Free

At some schools, seniors can audit classes for free. You won't receive academic credit, but you can brush up on your knowledge of history, learn how to use the Internet, or take that poetry course you've always dreamed of without making a dent in your wallet. You usually need to get permission from the professor or the department that schedules the class, but permission is rarely denied.

Most auditors are asked not to engage in class discussions so that they don't reduce the time available for paying students. Auditors are also not required to take any tests or examinations, and they do not receive a class grade.

Finding the Right Program for You

State universities are your best bet for special senior programs.

At least 30 state colleges across the nation have programs and discounts for senior auditors. Most schools require that you be 60 or older to receive free-course privileges. Some schools restrict the privileges to residents of their own state. For example, the University of Colorado at Boulder (303-492-8484) allows Colorado citizens ages 55 or older to audit classes for free.

Some schools, like the University of Arkansas (800-377-8632), allow persons 60 and older from any state to take or audit classes free of charge. They also offer campus housing and meal plans to senior students taking a full course load (usually at least 12 credits or four classes). Boston University (617-353-9852) permits people 60 and older from any state to audit courses for $35 a course year-round, and offers some university housing in the summer.

To find out about senior programs at a college or university near you, call the school's admissions office.

Schools Admitting State Residents

University of Maryland (301-314-8219) has a program called **Golden I.D.** for Maryland seniors 60 and older. You can audit courses year-round for a fee of $175. Auditors have access to the library, pool and fitness center.

University of Utah (801-581-7281) allows residents 62 and older to audit as many classes as they care to for a flat $25 fee per semester. (Some business management classes, art classes and labs are excluded.) With a student ID card, senior auditors have access to the library and computer center, the gymnasium and all other recreational facilities.

Schools Admitting Seniors from Any State

University of California, Los Angeles (310-794-0676) offers the Senior Scholars Program. Seniors pay $150 per course ($125 is tax-deductible).

Pay Less for Graduate School

Many graduate students apply for grants or fellowships to help them pay for school. Look in the library or bookstore for guides on the different types of funding available, or ask the financial office at your school.

One of the most cost-efficient ways to go to graduate school is to become a teaching assistant. Most Ph.D. candidates compete for jobs as teaching assistants to fund their degrees. As a teaching assistant, your course work will be paid for by the university, you will probably receive a living stipend and the work you do is often complementary to your course of study. If you are getting

FOR YOUR INFORMATION

Campus-free Programs

Here are a few colleges and universities that offer campus-free college degree programs:

- **Bemidji State University**, Center for Extended Learning, 1500 Birchmont Drive, NE, Bemidji, MN 56601-2699, 218-755-3924; www.bemidji.msus.edu. Accredited by the **North Central Association of Colleges and Schools**.

- **California College for Health Sciences**, 222 West 24th St., National City, CA 91950, 800-221-7374 or 619-477-4800; www.cchs.edu. Offers BS degrees in Health Services and Business. Accredited by the **National Home Study Council** and **Career College Association**.

- **Central Michigan University Distance and Distributed Learning**, 802 Industrial Ave., Mount Pleasant, MI 48858, 800-688-4268 or 517-774-4461; www.cmich.edu. Offers BS degrees in business. Accredited by the **North Central Association of Colleges and Schools**.

- **Indiana University**, School of Continuing Studies, 101 Owen Hall, Bloomington, IN 47405, 800-334-1011 or 812-855-3693; www.indiana.edu. Offers BA degrees in General Studies. Accredited by the **North Central Association of Colleges and Schools**.

your Ph.D. in psychology, for example, you will probably work as a teaching assistant for undergraduate psychology classes.

Education for the Working World

Your education does not have to stop just because you've graduated and started working, even if money is tight. Many companies and unions have benefit programs that pay for you to continue your education.

Company Benefits

If you're interested in business, you may want to consider working for a company with a benefits program that includes payments for continuing education. Then, if you need an MBA or other graduate degree to move up within your company, they might pay for part or all of your graduate school costs. In exchange, however, you may have to agree to continue working with the company for a specified number of years after receiving your MBA.

Union Education Benefits

If you are a member of a labor union, you may be able to receive money for college or career courses from the union. Ask your union representative. Your union may pay for courses that will make you a more skilled, more valuable employee and union member.

On-the-job Training

In some cases, your boss may require you to take classes on management or new techniques and methods necessary for your job.

But your company may also offer seminars and workshops that are not mandatory. In this instance you can take advantage of the opportunity to increase your knowledge for free. Plus, if your company sees you making the effort to improve your work and abilities, it could lead to a raise or promotion.

Campus-free College Degrees

Did you know that you can get a certified degree from a well-known college without setting foot on campus? Take note, however, that there tend to be a lot of scams in this area. Make sure that the institution is accredited by an association recognized by the U.S. Department of Education or the Council on Postsecondary Accreditation before you apply. Contact the state's Better Business Bureau and Department of Education if you have any doubts about a particular school.

These two books are good sources of reliable information on campus-free college degrees:

- *Campus-Free College Degrees* by Marcie Kisner Thorson (Thorson Guides, $27.95) explains how to get college credit for work and even life experience. This comprehensive guide is filled with facts on colleges offering at-home degrees and information on how to assess them. It lists accredited off-campus degree programs in both the U.S. and Canada. The guide also discusses ways to get your college degree while keeping your present job.
- *How to Earn a College Degree without Going to College* by James P. Duffy (John Wiley and Sons, $15.95) lists descriptions and contact information for programs at well-known, highly esteemed colleges and universities.

IT PAYS TO ASK

Continue Your Education for Free

Many companies like their employees to continue their education after college. Therefore, they may pay for job-related courses, or even unrelated courses if they are being used toward a related degree.

Ask your boss about the policies at your company. If no program exists, explain how a course or two will make you a more valuable employee, and see if the company will help you pay.

Some companies will even pay for part of the cost of unrelated classes as part of their benefits program. Find out what your company's tuition policy is.

Keep Learning at Your Local High School or Middle School

Taking adult classes at your local high school or middle school can add a new spark to your life without costing you a fortune. Most communities have some type of adult classes that can teach you new skills or enrich old ones.

Not Just Remedial Skills

Adult education is not just for those who never completed high school, need to learn English or need help with basic reading and writing skills. In fact, adult education is about enriching your life and adding to your existing skills. And courses are usually available in the day and evening, during the week, and on weekends (to accommodate a wide range of schedules).

Your local public schools aren't just for kids. Many local schools offer a wide variety of night and weekend classes for adults.

All Kinds of Classes

Schools offer a wide variety of classes, usually taught by working members of your community. From personal finance to Southern cooking, adult education courses focus on all aspects of life. You might sign up for a class on quitting smoking or find one on learning to quilt. The types of classes and opportunities to meet new people are endless.

Less than You Would Expect

Community education programs are usually quite inexpensive, ranging around $20 to $70 for an eight-week session, but prices vary according to the duration and type of class. Art, sewing and other classes that require special materials will most likely have an additional materials fee.

Call your local school system to request a brochure on its continuing education program. If your town school does not have a program, or you want a wider variety of classes, contact the school systems in neighboring areas.

In between Public And Private

If you can't find the kind of education you want for your child in traditional public schools, consider some options. Magnet, charter and parochial schools offer low and no-cost alternatives to traditional public and private education.

Magnet Schools

Magnet schools are free public schools that emphasize particular subjects and try to retain economic and cultural diversity. Students from all over the same school district who have a special interest in a particular area of study, such as science, the arts or languages, compete for places at their area magnet schools.

You may find that a magnet school is a less expensive way to provide your child with the courses and instruction you thought you could only find in a private school. For example, some magnet schools use a language immersion program. In these schools, students are taught in both English and a second language, such as Japanese or Spanish. Language immersion schools, which usually teach exclusively in the foreign language until the second grade, have been very popular with parents who want their children to learn a second language.

Find out more about magnet schools in your area by calling Magnet Schools of America at 281-296-9813. Their directory of over 4,000 magnet schools in 43 states around the country costs $69, but they will be happy to give you information on two or three schools in your area over the phone.

Charter Schools

Charter schools are a relatively recent educational development for grades K through 12. In 1991 the first charter school was opened in the U.S. in response to a call for a new type of public school. As of January 1998, over 300 charter schools were up and running in 23 states and Washington, D.C.

Charter schools use certain alternative teaching methods, which you may not find in traditional public school classrooms. Funded by the federal government, charter schools receive the same funding that public elementary and high schools receive, and they do not have enrollment restrictions.

Unlike a public school, however, a charter school will be closed if it does not achieve federally mandated educational results. Almost all states require that charter schools abide by health, safety and civil rights laws. For information, resources and guidance on charter schools in your area, contact the Center for Education Reform at 800-521-2118 or check out their website at www.edreform.com.

The U.S. Charter School website, www.uscharterschools.org, maintains a detailed glossary of charter schools listed by state, as well as links to other charter-school websites. This website was developed by a company called WestEd in collaboration with the California State University Institute for Education Reform and the United States Department of Education.

Parochial Schools

Parochial schools often offer a lower cost alternative to private schools. In addition to a general education, parochial schools teach students the values of the particular religious organization that maintains the school.

Like private schools, parochial schools have discretion over whom they will accept. But tuition costs tend to be lower than at independent private schools. If you don't mind having a religious education included with your child's general education, take a look at your local parochial schools.

Throughout the United States, there are parochial schools maintained by Roman Catholic parishes, a variety of Protestant churches and Jewish organizations. Your child doesn't necessarily have to belong to a particular religion to attend parochial school, although you should consider how comfortable you are with the school's religious practices.

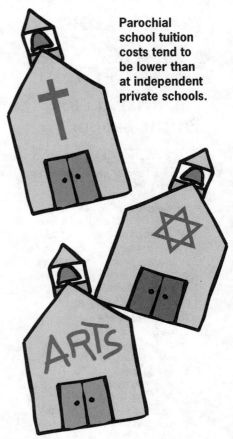

Parochial school tuition costs tend to be lower than at independent private schools.

Although most parochial schools incorporate religion into their daily curriculum, your child may not have to belong to a particular religion to attend.

Financial Aid for Private School

Check out these books or ask your librarian how to find more information on financial aid options for private school:

- **Free Money for Private Schools** by Laurie Blum (Simon and Schuster, out of print—available at the library only) can help you locate private schools in your state. It also includes a comprehensive guide to corporate and employee funding for private school education.

- **The Handbook of Private Schools** (Porter Sargent Publishers, 800-342-7470, $95) is an annual national survey of pre-college independent schools, including military, boarding, single-sex and bilingual options. Use it to locate schools you might be interested in, and then contact them directly for tuition and financial aid information.

- **Peterson's Private Secondary Schools** (Peterson's, $29.95) is an annual guide to secondary private education institutions and the financial aid process.

Bargains on Top-Notch K-12 Educations

A top-notch education is a priceless gift to offer your children, but you shouldn't have to pay for it for the rest of your life. Whether you want to finance a private elementary or high school education, or pay for after-school or weekend activities, there are plenty of ways to save.

Private Doesn't Have to Mean Pricey

Did you know that you can give your child a private school education that doesn't cost an arm and a leg? Here's how.

Look for assistance from corporations or companies, and for financial aid and scholarship programs offered directly by private schools. Each resource has its own qualification requirements, so contact all of your options directly and make sure you speak with the right department. For example, contact the financial assistance office at the school you are interested in to find out if you qualify. Likewise, talk to the Foundation or Programs department of a corporation to see if your child qualifies for any of its scholarship programs.

Corporate Financial Aid

Your own employer may offer financial aid for your child's pre-college education. Many companies offer educational funding to employees and their children, as well as to non-employee applicants who qualify under their giving guidelines. Giving guidelines describe the amount of funding allocated to education grants. Some companies have a large amount of funding, while others have a smaller giving base.

Some corporations offer no-strings-attached cash grants. Others give on a matching basis. When you are funded on a matching basis, you have to match a certain percentage of the amount given to you by the corporation (or find another source to match it). Check with each institution for details.

To find corporate/employee programs that offer educational funding, look in Laurie Blum's *Free Money for Private Schools* (Simon and Schuster, 1992) at your local library. Once you locate a corporation that provides grants for education, get a copy of their *Programs and Guidelines* brochure or annual report. Send your request for more information with a self-addressed, stamped envelope to the Foundation or Fund department.

A few corporations that offer grant assistance both locally and nationally are American Honda Motor Company in California, General Electric Company in Connecticut, and Hitachi Foundation in Washington, D.C.

Private School-sponsored Financial Aid

Private schools offer their own financial aid to students from a variety of income levels. Ask a school's financial assistance office for further information about qualifications, application procedures and deadlines. Schools often give financial awards based on athletic or artistic merit, academic merit and financial need. Most private schools give partial scholarships to assist in paying expensive tuition costs, and partial assistance can really make a difference.

IT PAYS TO ASK

Exhaust Your Options

Some athletic clubs and religious organizations support young people's education by providing grants or academic scholarships for extracurricular achievement to members or members' children. Most of this assistance is regionally-based and restricted to students attending schools in specific locales.

Enhance Your Child's Education

You don't have spend a fortune to send your children to after-school activities. School- and community-based programs offer dance classes, athletic activities and educational workshops for little or no cost.

School-based Programs

Most public schools offer no-cost after-school programs for 5- to 13-year-olds. Programs teach your child a new craft like painting or wood shop, offer homework help and tutoring, or feature instruction in athletics or dance. Your local public school probably has several extracurricular activities running all year long. Check with the guidance office to see what free programs are available in your town.

After-school activities for your children don't have to cost you one cent.

Community-based Programs

When is the last time you visited your local community center, YMCA or JCC? Did you know that they offer many children's programs at low costs? Also stop by your local town hall or community center to find out what free or inexpensive children's programs are available. There are probably many activities, such as nature walks and pottery classes, going on around town that will enhance your child's life and not empty your wallet.

Cutting the Cost of School Supplies

It's easy to spend $50 or more just to supply one child with pens and notebooks for a new school year. Isn't it time to reduce your costs for school supplies?

Shop Early

Consider buying your child's school supplies in August when most retailers drop their prices in an effort to move their merchandise. If you buy your child's school supplies during the four weeks before the post-Labor Day rush, prices are usually 25% to 50% lower than during the rest of the year.

Compare Prices

Believe it or not, an office superstore like Staples may not be the most cost-effective place to buy your child's school supplies. Compare prices with a general merchandise store like Wal-Mart or Kmart before you assume that the office superstore has better prices.

Stick with the Basics

Don't be pressured into buying your child the most fashionable school supplies. Most designer school supplies are more expensive than basic versions, and a fancy design is no guarantee of quality.

Basics don't have to be boring. Buy blank notebooks or make paper-bag book covers and get your children to design their own unique school supplies with colored markers, paints or stickers.

Don't Skimp on Backpacks

A high-quality backpack may be the one item it pays to spend more money on. A well-made backpack can last for years, while a cheap one may not last through the school year. Buying a $5 backpack that falls apart after two months is not a bargain.

Look for a backpack that is large enough to hold a lot of books and has an additional zipped pocket for smaller items like pens, calculators and keys. It should have shoulder straps that are adjustable and padded for comfort. The bottom should be reinforced and the entire backpack waterproofed to protect its contents during wet weather.

Eddie Bauer and L.L. Bean both carry high quality, inexpensive backpacks. Eddie Bauer (800-426-8020) has 50 outlet stores across the country, and L.L. Bean (800-341-4341) has 10 outlet stores. Call to find the location nearest to you or to order a catalog.

Index

T

U

V

W

Y

Z